The Flash™ MX Project

CHERYL BRUMBAUGH-DUNCAN

New Riders

201 W. 103rd Street
Indianapolis, Indiana 46290
An imprint of Pearson Education
Boston • Indianapolis • London • Munich • New York • San Francisco

THE FLASH™ MX PROJECT

Copyright © 2003 by New Riders Publishing

FIRST EDITION: August, 2002

International Standard Book Number: 0-7357-1283-2

Library of Congress Catalog Card Number: 2001099404

06 05 04 03 02   7 6 5 4 3 2 1

Interpretation of the printing code: The rightmost double-digit number is the year of the book's printing; the rightmost single-digit number is the number of the book's printing. For example, the printing code 02-1 shows that the first printing of the book occurred in 2002.

Printed in the United States of America

TRADEMARKS

WARNING AND DISCLAIMER

PUBLISHER
David Dwyer

ASSOCIATE PUBLISHER
Stephanie Wall

PRODUCTION MANAGER
Gina Kanouse

ACQUISITIONS EDITOR
Kate Small

DEVELOPMENT EDITORS
Laura Norman
Lisa Thibault

SENIOR MARKETING MANAGER
Tammy Detrich

PUBLICITY MANAGER
Susan Nixon

TEHNICAL EDITORS
Joseph Mease
Tracy Anne Kelly

PROJECT EDITOR
Tonya Simpson

COPY EDITOR
Megan Wade

INDEXER
Chris Morris

MANUFACTURING COORDINATOR
Jim Conway

BOOK DESIGNER
Ann Jones

COVER DESIGNER
Aren Howell

PROOFREADER
Karen A. Gill

COMPOSITION
Amy Parker

MEDIA DEVELOPER
Jay Payne

PROJECT OVERVIEW

DEDICATION

This book is dedicated to the people who have made it possible: my husband David, my parents Barb and Phil, my in-laws Jack and Doris, my agent Chris Van Buren of Waterside Production, all the people at Macromedia who developed this great product, Joe Mease, and the very talented people at New Riders! I'd also like to add a special dedication of this book to my baby girl, Tasmin Nicole, as she is too sweet not to mention.

TABLE OF CONTENTS

ABOUT THE AUTHOR

 **Cheryl Brumbaugh-Duncan**, founder of Virtually Global Communications, has been developing Web sites for more than five years. Through a combination of Macromedia Flash and HTML, she has created many leading-edge Web sites for her clients, including Qwest, Energy Investments, Inc., and System Services Corporation. Cheryl has a passion for technology, learning, and teaching. She has developed many online education courses and has found Flash to be an ideal medium for the creation and delivery of these courses. With a masters degree in education, she has been teaching individuals and companies through creative techniques, courses, books, and programs for the past 16 years. Recently, she authored *Macromedia Flash 5 from Scratch* (Que Publishing, ©2001) and has been involved in the technical editing process on more than 10 software-related books. To learn more about Cheryl, visit her company's Web site at `www.virtually-global.com`.

ACKNOWLEDGMENTS

Whenever one chooses to write a book, it's an awesome task of many different skills and talents. Writing a book during the holiday season increases the stress and challenges that exist in creating a book. Many people have worked long hours that have cut into their personal lives with this book's development. These people need to be acknowledged. I would like to thank New Riders Publishing and the many talented people who have helped with the development of this book. In particular, Laura Norman and Kate Small for all their support, fantastic insight, and helpful suggestions that have made this book much better than what I had originally submitted. They have truly helped shape the flow and content of this book.

I would also like to thank Joe Mease for his contribution to the book. Joe worked as a technical editor throughout the development of the book. This book's project is a scaled-down version of a Web site, The Honeycomb, which my company developed, and Joe helped create. Joe's knowledge of Flash is as strong as his creativity and ideas. Joe also provided sample files and examples throughout the discussion portions of this book. Visit his site at www.joemease.com.

Thanks also goes to the numerous editors who provided constructive criticism and have checked and double-checked the accuracy of this book's content and information: Tonya Simpson, project editor; Megan Wade, production editor; Chris Morris, indexer; Karen Gill, proofreader; and everyone else who had a hand in this project. Without these talented people, this book would not be half the book it is today.

I also would like to acknowledge the people and programmers at Macromedia. Macromedia Flash is a robust and complex product with much to offer Web developers and graphic designers. It was fun to write this book on such a great product as Flash!

And finally, I would like to thank my husband for his daily support of my efforts to create this book. His love and support have been constant!

TELL US WHAT YOU THINK

As the reader of this book, you are the most important critic and commentator. We value your opinion and want to know what we're doing right, what we could do better, what areas you'd like to see us publish in, and any other words of wisdom you're willing to pass our way.

As the Associate Publisher for New Riders Publishing, I welcome your comments. You can fax, e-mail, or write me directly to let me know what you did or didn't like about this book—as well as what we can do to make our books stronger.

Please note that I cannot help you with technical problems related to the topic of this book, and that due to the high volume of mail I receive, I might not be able to reply to every message.

When you write, please be sure to include this book's title and author as well as your name and phone or fax number. I will carefully review your comments and share them with the author and editors who worked on the book.

Fax: 317-581-4663

Email: stephanie.wall@newriders.com

Mail: Stephanie Wall
            Associate Publisher
            New Riders Publishing
            201 West 103rd Street
            Indianapolis, IN 46290 USA

Introduction

proj•ect, *n.* An extensive task undertaken by a student or group of students to apply, illustrate, or supplement classroom lessons.

About Macromedia Flash MX

Macromedia Flash is one of the leading Web development applications on the market today. It continues to mature with each new release, and the Flash MX version is no different. This book covers many of the new features of Flash MX, while also presenting the fundamental tools and techniques you need to unleash the full power of Flash.

Today, Flash is used to create interactive project interfaces and designs. It can generate low file size animations and sharp, clear graphics and images. This book covers the basics of Flash functionality, the creation and implementation of this functionality, and intermediate-level ActionScript for making a Web site come alive. Although Flash can be used for both online and traditional presentations, this book focuses on using Flash for Web site development.

Because of the added functionality and interactivity Macromedia has gradually added to Flash since its inception, Flash is no longer considered a mere two-dimensional, vector-based animation tool. It goes even further by enabling you to create interactive Web sites and applications. However, the power of animation and movement is still one of the main reasons Flash has come so far so quickly.

Flash combines streaming animation, vector-based graphics, and ActionScript for creating movies. As a beginning user of Flash, you will find the tools similar to other graphic applications, in particular the Macromedia suite of Web development applications. After you master the tools, you can begin to use the power of Flash to create symbols and movie clips. Then, you can combine these symbols with ActionScript to create interactivity and movement. As you become more familiar and experienced with Flash, your only limitation on what you can create is your own imagination.

Who Should Read This Book

This book is for new users of Flash MX who are looking for a complete, informative, and integrated tutorial on the use of Flash MX's basic features and functionality. This book is geared toward people who have worked with HTML or other graphics applications (or previous releases of Flash) and want to learn Flash MX to take their talents further in their fields of expertise. This book quickly progresses to more intermediate skills, such as using ActionScript to control Stage content.

Intermediate and advanced users of Flash can benefit from the book because many practical and time-saving techniques are presented in each seminar. At the completion of this book, you will have a full understanding of the basic principles and practices for using Flash in Web development and computer animation.

How to Use This Book

Each seminar in the book is divided into two parts: a discussion of techniques and concepts of Flash, and a workshop to put those concepts and techniques into practice. Each seminar is built on the foundation of the previous seminar. All seminars have a workshop that provides step-by-step instruction for developing a fully interactive Web site. As you build the Web site, object by object, layer by layer, you'll be learning by doing, which will equip you with a complete understanding of the basics of Flash and Web animation.

Because each seminar is composed of a discussion section and a workshop, you can work through both or just focus on one. The discussion section provides key information on Flash features and functionality accompanied by tips, notes, and warnings. The workshops provide practical, hands-on development of a Web site. Both provide creative solutions for common development issues related to Flash.

This book could be worked through in a week if you were very diligent in your learning. But, to be practical, plan on two to three weeks for completing the book. Allow yourself time to practice and test the new ideas and techniques. Let new information sink in by practicing with the tools and features of Flash, work through the workshops, and explore the sample files in the discussion sections. There are no limitations on creativity when it comes to computer-based animation, so play, experiment, and see just how far you can bend the rules.

The Contents of This Book

Through the workshop sections of this book, you will create a Web site for children. The Web site is called The Honeycomb site. You can see an example of the final site by opening the honeycomb.swf file located in the Seminar16/Samples/ directory on the CD-ROM that accompanies this book.

This site has a login area for the end-user to log in, as well as four buttons. Each button links to an activity, and each activity has its own functionality and interactivity.

The About Me activity is designed to allow the child to keep a journal or diary entry that can be updated daily. The Matching activity uses animals and animal sounds, and the child must match the animal sound with the animal that makes it. The In Quest of Ducks activity is designed as a counting activity—a short video plays and then the child can either count the visible ducks or click on each duck to reach an answer as to the exact number of ducks in a pond. The child must type a number for her answer into a text field; then, she can click the Check button to find out whether the answer is correct or incorrect. The final activity is a slider puzzle. This puzzle is composed of a 3×3 grid with numbered tiles. One empty slot in the puzzle allows the tiles to be rearranged, and the goal of the puzzle is to list the numbers from 1 to 8 in the correct order.

All these activities make up the final Honeycomb site. You will re-create this site by working through each of the workshops. The discussion portion of each seminar covers the skills presented in the workshop.

This book presents information that is at first simple but key to Flash development. It quickly progresses to more intermediate topics. Understanding where you have been is as important as knowing where you are going. Each seminar builds on the previous ones. You need to understand the basics before you can create striking and effective animation and Web sites. This book helps you learn and surpass the basics of Flash.

Seminar 1, "Macromedia Flash MX and Web Site Development"

This seminar covers the features and functionality of Flash. The new features in Flash MX are highlighted and explored. To begin the development of a Web site with Flash, basic Web project management techniques are also covered.

The workshop section of this seminar covers the many project planning documents needed to begin developing The Honeycomb Web site. Although you do not create these documents in this seminar, they are available on the CD-ROM for you to open and review.

Seminar 2, "Setting Up the Macromedia Flash MX Environment"

This seminar introduces you to the Flash Workspace. You explore the Timeline, toolbox, panels, Property Inspector, Stage, and work area. You learn about the

Preferences available in Flash MS, create a guide layer, and import a template image to help guide your movie development. In the workshop section of this seminar, you set your preferences and panel layer for developing The Honeycomb site. You also set your guides and create a guide layer. You then import a graphics template of the site onto the guide layer. This graphics template is used to guide you in the creation of The Honeycomb site.

Seminar 3, "Creating a Movie"

In this seminar, you begin to create your movie using the Flash tools, panels, and tool modifiers. This seminar covers creating and modifying objects and text. You learn how to use the Property Inspector of Flash MX to create and modify Stage objects.

The workshop covers the creation of the basic background images for the design of The Honeycomb site. You create the header and footer objects as well as the login area and menu bar. In this workshop, you create only one button for the menu bar.

Seminar 4, "Using Symbols in a Movie"

In this seminar, you begin to use the power of Flash by creating symbols and using instances of these symbols throughout your movie. You learn how to create a movie clip symbol and use it in animation, and you use your Library and many of the features of the Library for organizing your Stage objects.

The workshop covers the creation of one square symbol, which you will use for the header and footer objects on the Stage. You also use this square symbol for the login area and menu bar. Also, in this workshop, you create all the buttons that link to the activities of The Honeycomb site.

Seminar 5, "Importing Graphics into a Movie"

This seminar covers the Import and Import to Library features of Flash MX in relation to graphics. You import both vector art and bitmap art and learn how to convert bitmap art to vector format and how to optimize it to lower its file size.

In the workshop, you import and optimize graphics that you need for your site. After importing the files, you convert some of the files to vector format and optimize them to be as small in file size as possible.

Seminar 6, "Animation and Special Effects for Flashing Up the Site"

You learn how to work with the Timeline to create animation in this seminar. You also create motion tweens, size and rotation tweens, and color and shape tweens.

The workshop covers the development of the opening animation that introduces the site. You cause the header and footer objects to fly onto the Stage, stopping at their resting position as indicated by the graphics template. You then create a motion guide for generating a motion path for the host character to follow.

Seminar 7, "Site Interactivity and Button Functionality"

Flash is ideal for creating engaging interfaces and interactivity, and that is just what this seminar explains. Button functionality and basic ActionScript actions are covered. You learn how to use the `loadMovie` action and how to create a drop target for positioning a loaded SWF file in the main movie.

In the workshop, you begin to create the ActionScript for the interactivity required to move around in The Honeycomb site. You create all the SWF files that will become the activity movies for loading into The Honeycomb site. You also make all the buttons functional.

Seminar 8, "Using Components in a Macromedia Flash MX Form"

In this seminar, you learn how to use the component feature and preset Flash UI components. You also learn how to customize the appearance of the Flash UI components and how to test them.

In the workshop of this seminar, you create the About Me activity. Through the use of input text fields, static text fields, and a couple of the Flash UI components, you develop a form that can be used to gather information from the end-user.

Seminar 9, "Using Preloaders and Conditional Loops"

This seminar covers how to create a gate page that will prohibit the end-user from advancing into the site until all the features of the site have loaded or streamed down. This requires a conditional loop. You'll also use the Bandwidth Profiler for testing your conditional loop and site functionality.

In this workshop, you create a preloader for The Honeycomb site. You use the `getBytesTotal` and `getBytesLoaded` actions to create a dynamic preloader that updates the end-user on how large the movie is and how much of the movie still needs to be loaded.

Seminar 10, "Using ActionScript to Control Objects"

This seminar covers the fundamentals of controlling Stage objects through ActionScript. You learn how to use the Dot syntax of ActionScript to target and then control other objects on the Stage.

The workshop covers the creation of the Matching activity. Using named instances and an `if` and `else` statement, you create the functionality required for the Matching activity to determine whether the animal sound matches the animal.

Seminar 11, "Communicating with the End-User"

In this seminar, you learn how to create a login. A discussion of database integration with logins is also touched on. In addition, you learn how to use Flash MX's new Accessibility feature, which allows your Flash movies to be accessible and understandable to the visually impaired audience.

Through the workshop, you create a local login for The Honeycomb site and pass this login name to other text fields so that the host character communicates directly with the end-user. You also make The Honeycomb site accessible through the new Flash MX Accessibility feature.

Seminar 12, "Adding Sound to Enhance a Site"

This seminar covers sound, importing it into Flash, and syncing it with your movie. In this seminar, you learn about the various customizations of sound, as well as how to create a music toggle button for turning the sound on or off.

The workshop covers adding sound to The Honeycomb site. You add a buzzy noise that is synced with the appearance of the host character and create a sound toggle button to enable the end-user to turn the buzzing noise off or on. You then modify the compression applied to the Matching activity animal noises so that they are smaller in file size.

Seminar 13, "Enhancing the Site Interface and Interactivity"

This seminar teaches you how to create drop-down menus, transparent buttons, and masks. You will also use the x, y coordinate to control a symbol's location on the Stage.

Through the workshop, you add a drop-down menu for the Puzzles button. This menu will link to the Puzzles activity's SWF file.

Seminar 14, "Dynamic ActionScript for Controlling Stage Content and Movement"

This seminar covers drag-and-drop functionality. You begin to use more advanced ActionScript and troubleshooting techniques throughout this seminar. You learn how to create ActionScript-based movement of Stage objects.

The workshop covers the development of the slider puzzle. You use `if` and `else` statements that compare whether the empty slot in the puzzle is above, below, left, or right of the tile that is being clicked. If the slot is above, below, left, or right of the tile, the tile swaps locations with the empty slot in the puzzle.

Seminar 15, "Adding Digital Video to the Site"

In this seminar, you learn how to use Flash MX's new video feature to embed video clips directly into a movie. Compression settings for video clips are also covered.

In the workshop, you import an AVI file directly into the In Quest of Ducks activity. Then, you create a counting game using ActionScript.

Seminar 16, "Publishing and Testing the Site"

This seminar teaches you how to configure your publishing settings and then how to publish and test your movie.

The workshop provides hands-on practice configuring your Publish settings for The Honeycomb site. You generate a GIF image that can be used as the alternative image in case the end-user does not have the Flash Player 6 plug-in file.

Appendix A, "Setting Up Macromedia Flash"

This Appendix covers the system requirements necessary to run Flash MX as well as how to install the Flash Player 6.0 plug-in either through the Flash MX installation process or through the Macromedia Web site.

Appendix B, "What's on the CD-ROM"

The CD-ROM that accompanies this book is packed with exercise files to help you work with the book and with Flash MX. This appendix contains detailed descriptions of the CD's contents.

How to Use This Book

Each seminar is divided into two sections: a discussion section and a workshop section. The discussion section comes first in each seminar and provides information on the various topics covered and some hands-on practice with sample files. It is used to introduce topics, concepts, techniques, and skills for Flash design and development.

The workshop section is focused on a project Web site, The Honeycomb site. You will create this site from scratch starting with Seminar 1 and finishing it in Seminar 16. Many of the topics, concepts, techniques, and skills in the discussion section of the seminar are covered with hands-on practice in the workshop section. Aside from this information, the workshop also presents design and development tips and techniques that I use on a daily basis for quick and efficient Flash development. The workshop section allows you to learn Flash from actually doing! There is no better way to learn Flash than by hands-on development.

> **Note**
>
> Notes offer comments and asides about the topic at hand, as well as full explanations of certain concepts.

> **Tip**
>
> Tips provide great shortcuts and hints on additional techniques and skills for developing in Flash.

> **Warning**
>
> Warnings help you avoid the pitfalls of development mistakes, thus preventing you from making mistakes that will make your Flash experience much more difficult.

In addition, you'll find various typographic conventions used throughout the book:

- Text you should type appears in `monospaced font`.

- Folders and filenames that are called out appear in `monospaced font`.

- Layer and symbol names that are also called out appear in `monospaced font`.

Relax and have some fun with the book. You will find that Flash is a wonderful tool for Web development as well as for other graphic design and development areas. As with many software applications, after you learn the fundamentals of the program, it is up to you to practice and apply the skills to truly master them. With that all said, let's begin!

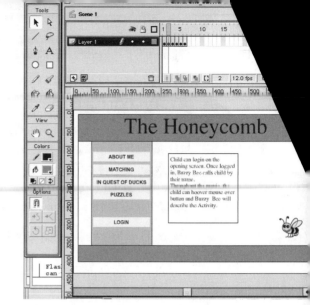

Seminar 1

Macromedia Flash MX and Web Site Development

In this chapter

Workshop: Planning the Movie

Why Macromedia Flash MX?

Macromedia Flash is one of the leading Web development applications on the market today. It continues to mature with each new release, and the Macromedia Flash MX version is no different. This book covers many of the new features of Flash MX while also presenting the fundamental tools and techniques you need to unleash the full power of Flash in your Web site design and development.

Today, Flash is being used to create interactive project interfaces and designs. It can generate low file size animations and sharp, clear graphics and images. Typically a two-dimensional program, depending on your design skills, you can simulate three-dimensional designs. Another advantage of Flash is that it is a vector-based application. This allows your designs to always display in the proportion as you intended, no matter to what size the end-user's browser is set. This book covers the basics of Flash functionality, the creation and implementation of this functionality, and intermediate-level ActionScript for making the project come alive. Although Flash can be used for both online and traditional presentations, this book focuses on using Flash for Web site development. As with many software applications, after you learn the fundamentals of the program, it is up to you to practice and apply the skills to truly master them.

Anatomy of Macromedia Flash MX and Internet Viewing

There are two environments in Flash—the Authoring environment and the Macromedia Flash Player. All Flash movies are created in the Authoring environment and have an FLA extension. When the creating and editing process in Flash is complete, the movie is ready to become an SWF file. You create an SWF file in Flash using the Publish command. SWF stands for small Web format; it's actually just a compressed version of the FLA file and is much lower in file size. An SWF file can be interpreted by the Flash Player. The Flash Player plays the movie with all the functionality and interactivity you developed in the FLA file. The Flash Player is used to test the movie as you develop it. Typical of past releases of Flash, Macromedia includes both the Flash MX application and the Flash Player 6 in the new release.

Note _____

An FLA format movie can be very large in file size because it includes all objects and assets of your Flash movie and the functionality of the movie.

Viewing a Flash Movie on the Internet

To view a Flash movie on the Internet, the compressed SWF file of the movie must be embedded in a server-side language document. A common server-side language is the Hypertext Markup Language (HTML), which most Web browsers can understand. Browsers look at the embedded SWF files as an object and treat them just like a JPEG or GIF image. The embedded object has a location on the page and is a particular width and height.

You do not have to be an HTML programmer to embed the SWF file in an HTML document. Based on the Publish Settings, Flash can generate the HTML document required for viewing the movie in a browser. Therefore, you can design a Web site entirely in Flash using the Flash-generated HTML code to call and display the movie in a browser. If you are accomplished in HTML programming, you can create your own HTML code for embedding a movie as the entire Web site or just a banner ad, button, or cartoon/illustration that appears as any image would in a fully developed HMTL page. More is covered on this in Seminar 16, "Publishing and Testing the Site."

Browsers and Macromedia Flash Player 6

Viewing a Flash movie through a browser is becoming less and less of an issue. Most of the popular browsers from release 4.0 and up have integrated the Flash Player into their products thanks to Macromedia providing the Flash Player code to any party who wants it. This has enabled browser products under development to integrate this code so that the browsers shipped with the Flash Player seamlessly integrate into the browser. Movies created in Flash MX can be viewed on any Flash Player, but if the player is an earlier version, it will not play the Flash MX functionality. Browser compatibility statistics are available from Macromedia on its Web site at `http://www.macro-media.com/software/player_census/flashplayer/version_penetration.html`.

Note

Using Flash for Web site development is a huge advantage in that you do not have to create separate sites that are specifically developed for one browser or the other. You create one movie and embed the movie in a server-side language document. It always displays as you intended because it is not reliant on the browser's interpretation of the movie's code.

Flash MX New Features and Functionality

Flash MX brings a new set of functionality to the already powerful Flash platform. Flash MX is now a dynamic development platform capable of tight integration with server-side applications and the universal language of XML. Macromedia focused on making Flash easier to use, more versatile, and powerful by adding new functionality and ActionScript. Now with Flash MX, you have a redesigned interface, new ActionScripting tools and scripts, international language support, accessibility features, new design tools, and expanded video and import graphic capabilities.

Redesigned Interface

The first new feature you will notice with Flash MX is a redesigned interface of docked panels and a Property Inspector (see Figure 1.1).

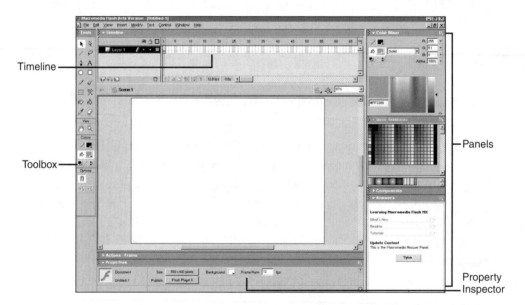

Figure 1.1   The Default Panel Set has the panels and Property Inspector docked for easy access, and they all are collapsible.

Panels, the Timeline, the Property Inspector, and the toolbox are all docked but can be rearranged based on your work habits. All are also collapsible by double-clicking their title bars. This new interface makes developing in Flash easier because you can control what you have displayed on your screen and always know where to find it. You will learn more about this new interface in Seminar 2, "Setting Up the Macromedia Flash MX Environment."

New Property Inspector

Another new feature of Flash MX is the Property Inspector. This inspector combines many of the panels of Flash 5 into a context-sensitive Property Inspector (see Figure 1.2).

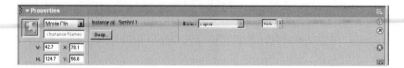

Figure 1.2   Many of the features and attributes of an object are listed in the Property Inspector.

Now when you begin to develop an object on your Stage, you have a one-stop-shop for many of the attributes of the image. You do not have to access three or four panels to design the object as you need. This is a huge time-saving feature, especially when you have many objects in your movie.

Improved Drawing Capabilities

The improved drawing capabilities of Flash include a new Fill Transform tool for adjusting gradient and bitmap fills and the Free Transform tool for manipulating and editing Stage content (see Figure 1.3).

Color management has also been improved in Flash MX. The Color Mixer and Color Swatches now are more versatile than previous releases of Flash in both creating and editing color (see Figure 1.4).

Flash MX now offers pixel-level control that enables precise placement of your Stage objects. If you increase your magnification of the Stage to 400% or above, Flash displays a pixel grid for easily aligning your objects. The Macromedia Flash MX drawing capabilities provide designers with more freedom and control over their designs.

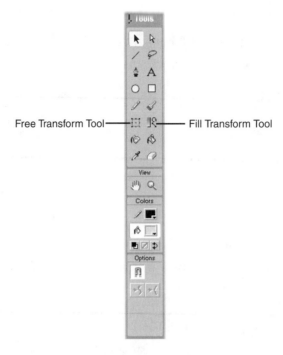

Free Transform Tool———————————Fill Transform Tool

Figure 1.3   Because the Fill Transform tool and the Free Transform tool are located in the toolbox, they are easy to access throughout the design process.

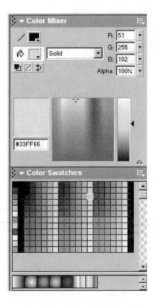

Figure 1.4   As with Flash 5, the Color Mixer and Color Swatches work hand-in-hand for creating and applying color to your movie.

Redesigned Timeline

The Timeline has been redesigned to have better control over movie objects and functionality. Now you can create a Folder layer for grouping other layers together (see Figure 1.5).

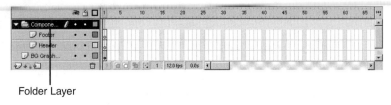

Folder Layer

Figure 1.5   The Timeline is easily collapsed with a single click on the title bar.

Selecting and manipulating frames in the Timeline has also been simplified and improved. Now you can easily recognize keyframes, tweened frames, and other Timeline features. Selection of individual frames or groups of frames is easier, so manipulating and editing the Timeline is now simplified. Information on configuring the Timeline is found in Seminar 2.

New ActionScripting Tools

For the more advanced Flash developer, new ActionScripting and debugging tools have been added. The Actions panel has been redesigned and is now dockable (see Figure 1.6).

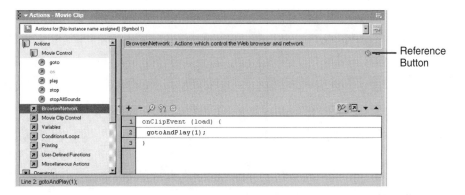

Reference Button

Figure 1.6   The Actions List now categorizes actions based on usage in a movie.

Aside from the redesign of the panel and the new categories for grouping the actions of Flash, Macromedia added code hinting and highlighting. You can also easily access additional help on actions through the Reference button. The Debugger has been enhanced and now allows you to set breakpoints. Through breakpoints, you can step through your code. All these features make the process of scripting and developing ActionScript functionality easier.

Expanded Video, Image, and Sound Capabilities

Flash MX now provides more video support, enabling you to import more video file formats into your movie. Flash MX imports MPG, Digital Video (DV), MOV (QuickTime), and AVI directly into the movie.

Another new feature is the ability to download JPEG and MP3 format files into the Flash Player. Through the use of ActionScript, you can import these file formats into your movie during playback. This really reduces file size of the actual Flash movie because these files are called and downloaded based on the progression through the movie and end-user interaction.

New Flash Components

A neat new feature of Flash MX is the addition of components to the movie development process (see Figure 1.7).

Figure 1.7   Similar to how you use symbols and instances, to use a component in your movie, drag it from the Components panel onto your Stage.

Components are reusable objects similar to Flash 5 Smart Clips. They consist of movie clips with editable parameters that enable you to customize their look and function-ality. You will find them very beneficial for adding objects such as list boxes or check boxes to your movie.

Support for International Languages

Support has been added in Flash MX for languages such as French, German, Korean, and Chinese. The Text tool can now author vertical text and has new formatting options available for applying attributes to Korean and Chinese text.

New Accessibility Features

Macromedia is listening to its users and incorporating the progressing awareness of accessibility for the disabled. You can now develop movies that are accessible to people with disabilities. The Window, Accessibility menu provides access to the Accessibility panel that enables you to set various options for making your movie accessible to all users (see Figure 1.8).

Figure 1.8   By turning on Automatic Labeling, Flash labels buttons, instances, and text boxes with its own text-based labeling system.

> **Note**
>
> This seminar covers only a few of the new features of Flash MX. More is covered on the new features and functionality of Flash MX as you progress through the book.

The Features and Functionality of Flash MX

Before you begin using Flash, you should understand the important characteristics of Flash—mainly its use of vector graphics, streaming animations, and functionality for user interactivity.

Vector-Based Program

Flash is a vector-based program as opposed to a raster- or bitmapped-based program. A *vector graphic* is composed of a mathematical formula or set of instructions. This mathematical formula describes the shape, size, color, and location of an object on the Stage. A vector graphic is composed of endpoints, lines, or curves. Because the image is represented by a mathematical formula, its edges are always clean and smooth. A vector graphic usually is smaller in file size than a raster graphic, but unlike a raster graphic, there are no stray pixels that can cause the image to have a blurry edge or to have the "jaggies" effect. When a vector graphic is enlarged, the mathematical formula simply adjusts and the image is displayed cleanly and in the same proportion as the original image. It maintains its smooth curves and lines. Therefore, any Web browser window, no matter what size, can display a Flash file as it was designed—clean and jaggie free while maintaining the proportion of the design (see Figure 1.9).

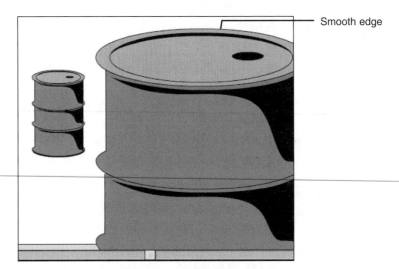

Smooth edge

Figure 1.9   When you enlarge a vector graphic, the edges stay smooth (no jagged edges, or "jaggies") and the image remains clean.

Note ───────────────────────────────────

Although a simple vector graphic is typically smaller in file size than a raster graphic of comparable design, a complex vector graphic can easily exceed the file size of a comparable raster graphic. Complex vector graphics can be very large in file size.

Bitmap or raster is another format for graphics. A *raster graphic* is composed of little dots or pixels. Each pixel tells the computer its RGB color and its location on the screen. Because a raster graphic is composed of pixels, when the image is enlarged, you see jaggies. The edges of the image are not smooth but composed of a staircase effect of dots (see Figure 1.10). The larger you make the image, the worse the jaggies get.

Jaggies

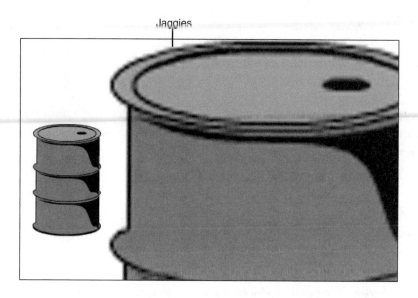

Figure 1.10   When you enlarge a raster graphic, you can see the jaggies and the edges get blurry.

Tip

Raster images can be reduced in size without loss in image quality, but they cannot be enlarged without loss of quality.

Using a mathematical formula to represent graphics images and objects is a big advantage for Flash and its use in Web development and animation. A vector graphic typically is very low in file size. Although broadband width for accessing the Internet is becoming more and more common, the majority of Web users still use a 28.8K–56K modem connection. As a Web developer, you must design a site that allows the majority of Internet users to view it. Therefore, every kilobyte of information matters.

Another advantage of Flash and its roots as a vector-based program is seen in the creation of animation. Flash animation is clean and fluid. Instead of trying to move many pixels from point A to point B, Flash simply adjusts the mathematical formula. The image is therefore moved and redrawn onscreen, smoothly and efficiently.

Flash uses ActionScript for interactivity and functionality. ActionScript is a programming code that is very similar to JavaScript and is native to Flash. When ActionScript is combined with the vector graphics, everything is mathematically and logically controlled, so seamless functionality occurs easily.

Streaming Animation

Flash uses streaming animation for its movies. *Streaming* is a process of downloading information and displaying that information as it is received. When enough of the movie is downloaded to your machine, it begins to play; meanwhile, the rest of the movie is still being downloaded behind the scenes. Visitors are not tempted to leave the site because of a slow download but can begin to explore and enjoy their Internet experience.

Interactivity

From the Flash 4 release to the Flash MX release, ActionScript has grown up. ActionScript is an object-oriented programming language that can be used to create interactivity and animation in Flash. An *object* in Flash is any movie asset, such as a button, a graphic, an image, and even a sequence of animation or script functionality. ActionScript is a set of instructions that cause actions to occur to objects in your movie, such as a button that enables a form to be submitted, a new page to display, or the movie to stop at a certain point in its playback. ActionScript can also cause objects on the Stage to move or animate. It can also be used to allow a user to interact with objects in the movie, such as moving a menu to a new location or displaying mouse trailers as the user moves his mouse. The bottom line is that ActionScript creates interactivity and can be used to control the movie's objects. It is now a fully functioning language, and based on your skill level, you can create almost any type of interactivity or animation you desire.

New with Flash MX are several ActionScripting tools, one of the most helpful being the Reference panel (see Figure 1.11). You access the Reference panel by clicking the Reference button in the Actions panel.

This new panel provides information about the action that is selected in the toolbox list. You can view information about the Flash version in which the action was first introduced and an example of actual script demonstrating how the action should be used. At the bottom of this panel, the required parameters are listed for making the action function. As with other releases of Flash, if you use actions that were introduced in a later release of Flash and your movie is played on an earlier version of the Flash Player, you lose this ActionScript functionality of the movie. Therefore, the movie will not play correctly because the earlier Flash Player does not support the new action of the later release of Flash. The Reference panel can help you identify the actions you need to help meet your audience goals. If you think the majority of your audience will be using older browsers such as Netscape 4.0, you should plan your movie to use only functionality and ActionScript that was introduced in the Flash 4 release or any earlier release.

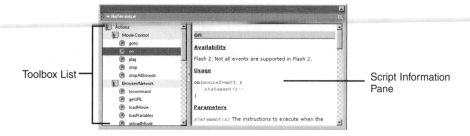

Figure 1.11 The Reference panel displays information on the command that you click in the Toolbox list of the Actions panel.

Integration with Other Applications

Macromedia designed Flash to play well with others. Understanding how Flash integrates with other applications requires knowledge of how Flash works—how it publishes, exports, and imports other file types.

Flash and the Macromedia Suite of Software

As you would expect, Flash works seamlessly with other Macromedia products, in particular with the Macromedia suite of Web development software. This suite comprises Macromedia's FreeHand, Dreamweaver, and Fireworks software. Flash graphics and movies are imported into these packages with a simple menu command, with many of the preset settings intact. For example, you can import Fireworks graphics directly into Flash—a Fireworks graphics file is imported into Flash in vector format with its layers intact.

Note ———

Macromedia plans to use the MX branding across all its applications, therefore integrating many of the features and functionality of the applications to work seamlessly with each other.

Flash with Other HTML Applications

As you've already learned, when a Flash file is published, Flash creates the movie as an SWF file and also can create the HTML file with all the coding necessary to view the SWF file in a browser. The Flash-generated HTML code can be easily used and integrated in any existing HTML code. You can use your favorite HTML editor, such as HomeSite, NotePad, SimpleText, Dreamweaver, and so on, to copy the code from the Flash-generated HTML document into a new or existing page or site.

Flash Import/Export Formats

Flash can import and export many graphics file formats. This enables the sharing of data between many applications. Additionally, if you have QuickTime installed on your machine, Flash can import even more graphics formats. See Table 1.1 for a listing of the importable formats.

Table 1.1   Flash Import File Formats

Without QuickTime	Macintosh	Windows
GIF and Animated GIF	X	X
JPEG	X	X
PNG	X	X
Adobe Illustrator (EPS, AI-version 8.0 or earlier)	X	X
AutoCAD DXF (DXF)	X	X
FreeHand (FH7–FH10)	X	X
FutureSplash Player (SPL)	X	X
Macromedia Flash Player (SWF)	X	X
Bitmap (BMP)		X
Enhanced Metafile (EMF)		X
Windows Metafile (WMF)		X
PICT (PIC, PCT)	X	

Without QuickTime	Macintosh	Windows
MacPaint (PNTG)	X	X
Photoshop (PSD)	X	X
PICT (PIC, PCT)		X
QuickTime Image (QTIF)	X	X
QuickTime Movie (MOV)	X	X
Silicon Graphics (SAI)	X	X
TGA (TGA)	X	X
TIFF (TIFF)	X	X

From Table 1.1, you can see that you can easily create images in other applications and import them into Flash. More is discussed on this topic in Seminar 5, "Importing Graphics into a Movie."

You also can copy and paste images to and from Flash and other applications. Based on the graphics format you are copying—either raster or vector—the image remains in this format when you paste it into Flash. Copy and pasting enables you to copy a chart or graph created in another program, such as Microsoft Excel, and use it in Flash.

Using Flash's very powerful Publish feature, you can quickly convert your Flash artwork to many different file formats. You can set the available formats by using the Formats tab of the Publish Setting dialog box (see Figure 1.12).

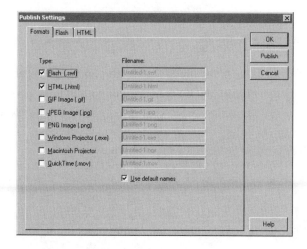

Figure 1.12   You create the HTML code required to display a Flash movie in a browser through the Publish Settings dialog box.

The following is a list of the file formats available in the Publish Settings dialog box:

- **Flash (.swf)**—Flash Player format. The file extension .swf stands for small Web format.

- **HTML (.html)**—Static display language your browser uses to display text, graphics, and other Web content. When this option is selected, Flash automatically publishes the file to both the HTML and Flash formats.

- **GIF Image (.gif)**—Bitmap lossless compression format commonly used in Web pages. Images that have large areas of exact colors convert best in this format.

- **JPEG Image (.jpg)**—Bitmap compression format commonly used in Web pages. Images that are photo quality are commonly converted best in this format. This compression format is lossy.

- **PNG Image (.png)**—New Web graphics format. Files saved in this format use compression similar to JPEGs but also use lossless compression typical of GIF files.

- **Windows Projector (.exe)**—Projector file created to play only on the Windows platform. The Windows Projector includes the Flash Player, so no plug-in is required.

- **Macintosh Projector**—Projector file created to play only on the Macintosh platform. The Macintosh Projector includes the Flash Player, so no plug-in is required.

- **QuickTime (.mov)**—Movie file created to run through Apple's QuickTime player. ActionScript is ignored by the QuickTime player.

Flash also offers a great export feature (found in the File menu) that can be used to export a movie or just an image. If you're proficient with HTML programming, you can export a movie or graphic created in Flash to a specific graphics format and then place the file in your HTML or other markup language document. Figure 1.13 shows the various export formats of Flash for the entire movie.

Converting just an image in Flash is also a breeze. Figure 1.14 shows the various export formats for individual graphics. The Export Image command works by taking the Flash graphic or Stage display and exporting it as a single image.

Figure 1.13   You can use the Export Movie command to convert an entire movie in Flash to many of the common graphics file formats used today.

Figure 1.14   Flash takes the first frame of the movie and exports that image to the specified graphics format.

Web Project Management and Flash

Project management is a must when using Flash to create a Web site. The first thing you must do is understand the project. Gather your initial information: What are the expectations for the Web site? What does the site accomplish? Who is it for? How long will this version of the site need to live? Will the content be dynamic? Who will update it? And how will it be updated? Many clients have no experience with the Web and need to be educated about what can be presented through the Internet. It is your job to help the client understand the process of creation, implementation, and maintenance of the Web site. If you use project management techniques, you and your client will be on the same page and in sync with the development of the site.

Defining Site Goals

All successful solutions begin with a clear definition of the problem. This is also true when planning a Web site. You need to understand what the site accomplishes and set the site's goals. Is the Web site for general marketing of the company information to the public, or is the main function of the site to distribute information in a secure environment to sales representatives across the nation? Each of these examples would have its own set of goals. There usually are many goals for a Web site, and understanding the project will help define them. These goals direct the Web site's development from the beginning to the end.

You should develop a creative brief that describes the Web site. This brief includes a description of the Web site, who it is for, the goals for the Web site, a description of any special interactivity, and a list of server-side issues that need to be addressed. The creative brief outlines the project. Presenting this to the client is a good idea because it can be used as the first checkpoint for beginning the process. This document becomes the overall guide for the development and direction of the Web site.

Defining the Audience

Next in the process of site development is identifying the target audience who will visit your site—will they be more of a corporate audience or home-based users? With what types of connection speeds will the majority of users access your site? Will they have the latest in browsers, or will this vary from user to user? The more you focus your site on these factors and the more precisely defined your target audience is, the more efficiently and effectively you can present the information.

Defining the Site Architecture and Information Layout

After your site goals and audience are defined, you can begin to create your Web site by developing the layout or flow of the site, the interactivity, and the content required for meeting the site goals. This stage of the Web project management process can include many people and departments depending on the type of site you are developing, or it could be just you working in many roles and capacities. When many people are involved in the development of a Web site, usually one person heads up the whole process. This person acts in the role of an *information architect*.

The information architect plans the site, establishes the people required to develop the site, and keeps track of the project as it progresses from stage to stage. She is a big thinker who can see the project from a bird's-eye view. She uses both right- and left-brain thinking and must design the site flow as well as begin to plan for interactivity and the presentation of information.

Creating Site Flow

One of the first processes the information architect must complete is diagramming the flow of the site. This is a must for understanding how site content fits together. The result is a flowchart showing the site layout. By creating a diagram of the flow from area to area or page to page, you begin to logically communicate the information. Logically planning where information exists and how it is accessed is a very left-brain process. Every information architect uses her own diagram for showing the site layout. There is no right or wrong process for this—your goal is to develop a flow that communicates the information to meet the site goals.

Figure 1.15 shows an example of a flowchart for an architecture firm. From the flowchart, you can gather that the site goals are targeting the creation of a site that provides information on the company and showcasing its portfolio. The site allows for client communications in a secure area, so the architecture firm can show the projects' progress privately to each client. Also note that the site has a search function for finding information on various structures or buildings the firm has completed. The Web site promotes the firm's strengths and wide breadth of experience in design.

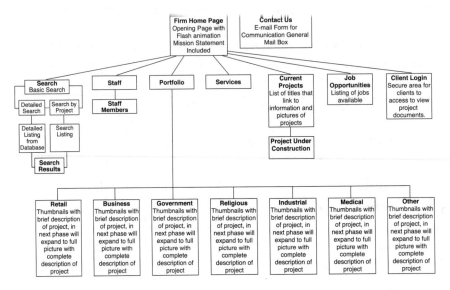

Figure 1.15   This flowchart defines a Web site that showcases a firm's portfolio, enables secure client communication, and has a search feature.

Designing for Usability

When creating the flow of a site, you should keep in mind usability factors. How easy is it for the user to find information he is looking for? Is the navigation of the site consistent from level to level? Is the navigation clearly defined and accessible on each page? Designing for usability is a challenge that every Web developer faces, but if it's done effectively, it ensures a successful experience for all.

> **Tip**
>
> It is a good idea to have a test group available, if possible—people from different technical and non-technical backgrounds. At various points in the development process, have the group test the site. A lot can be learned from this step.

Conceptualizing the Functionality

Many times when using Flash to create a Web site or presentation, you will want to storyboard the functionality and interactivity of the site to help conceptualize the design interface. This requires right-brain thinking and planning. The storyboard of the site helps support the site flow but takes it one step further by describing the interactivity involved or expected. Storyboards are a good way to iron out a lot of potential design and functional issues, before you put forth too much effort in development. Figure 1.16 shows a sample storyboard.

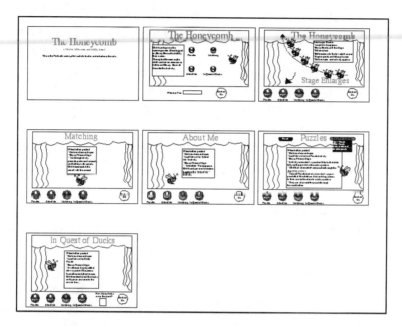

Figure 1.16   You can graphically represent each area of the site and combine that with text for describing the functionality in a storyboard.

Tip
A storyboard is the first graphical representation of the site, and it shows the beginnings of the design interface.

Site Interactivity and Functionality

Mapping out or listing your site functionality is another process in project management. What do you and the client want the site to do? This is an area that is wide open to you as a Flash developer to help the client understand what can be done to support site goals and enhance the site. This list of functionality must be created through Flash ActionScript programming and some special animation effects.

Tip
Don't start building or developing a Web site until the majority of the site has been storyboarded and the majority of the site functionality has been mapped out.

Developing a Creative Composition

The creative brief, site flow diagram, storyboard, and functionality list are all major milestones in planning a site. You can have the client sign off on each of these areas. After this is achieved, you and the client have a good understanding of the site, and you can begin to create a composition of the site design. This can be as simple as just a quick sketch of each area of the site, or how the information is laid out on the screen. You can then take this sketch and fully develop it into a page layout design. The creative composition becomes the actual site design and is referenced as the site is developed. When the client signs off on the creative composition, you are now ready to develop the site.

Other Suggested Readings on Web Project Management

This book covers the bare basics of project management. Many other sources are available for learning more about Web project management and site architecture. It is a very complex and exciting field, and several textbooks, instructional guides, and even classes are available to people interested in learning more about Web project management. Two textbooks that can be recommend based on market success and overall reader reviews are *Secrets of Successful Web Sites: Project Management on the World Wide Web* by David Siegel and *Web Project Management: Delivering Successful Commercial Web Sites* by Ashley Friedlein.

Planning the Movie

Throughout this book, you will be creating a Flash Web site for children. The site is called The Honeycomb, and it uses a host character named Buzzy Bee who guides children through various engaging activities. Flash has been chosen for this site because of how well it handles interactivity and animation. It is also the ideal platform to create a very exciting, informative, and entertaining environment for children.

> **Note**
>
> The following sample files are accessible on the CD-ROM that accompanies this book. Flash could be used to create all the planning documents, but you should use the software you are comfortable with for creating these documents. Although this is a Workshop section, you will not be creating the documents discussed in the following sections. However, you can open the sample files to see how the site was planned. The Honeycomb site is an actual working site and copyrighted by Virtually Global Communications. It has allowed the use of this site as the Workshop for this book. The project Web site in this book is a scaled-down version of the actual Honeycomb site.

Overview of the Site

The Honeycomb site is an interactive site for children and uses an animated bee as the main host character. Four identified areas exist for presenting games and children's activities in the site. One area is for puzzles, another is focused on matching activities, the next covers writing activities, and the fourth is for counting. These activity areas are named Puzzles, About Me, Matching, and In Quest of Ducks.

The site needs to be visually stimulating with sound and animation. Digital video will be used for the "In Quest of Ducks" activity. The animated bee needs to be entertaining and enticing to children, as well as serve as an overall guide throughout the site. He gives instructions and tips for working through the site. The site must allow children the opportunity to log in. The login name will then be used in communication between the animated bee and the child, personalizing the child's experience with the site, Buzzy Bee, and all the activities. This is all the information that has been gathered; now you need to begin the process of planning the site.

Honeycomb Site Goals

As you know, the first step in developing a Web site is defining the site goals. You have gathered your information and now must state the goals of the site. The following list could be the identified goals for The Honeycomb site:

- Create a visually stimulating and very graphically oriented design.

- Develop fun interactivity and consistent transitions from area to area of the site, making it easy to navigate.

- Implement a host character that guides the visitor through the site.

- Develop a host character that is enticing and engaging to children.

- Develop login functionality for all users visiting the site.

- Develop activities to be presented in the site, which are fun and engaging to children.

Honeycomb Site Audience

The audience has already been identified as children and parents of those children. You can assume that their technology will vary greatly. But most likely, they will be using older computers and have slower Internet connections—28.8K or 56K modems. Because you want all children to be able to access the site, you must create the site with a focus on presenting information efficiently and cleanly, while maintaining a low file size. Your graphics and programming for content or interactivity must be simple in design and structure. This is your challenge for beginning the planning process of this site.

Creating a Flowchart

The flowchart for The Honeycomb site will be relatively simple. It incorporates the four areas for the activities and a Contact Us form that is accessible from anywhere in the site. The plan also includes a need for login functionality. Figure 1.17 shows a possible solution for this chart.

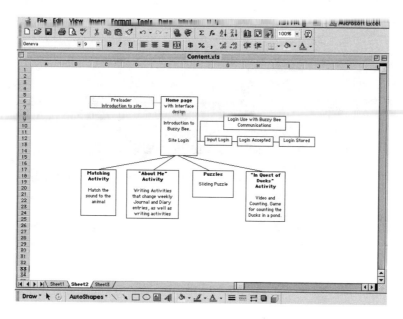

Figure 1.17   The site flowchart illustrates that you will need four buttons for linking to the four areas.

Storyboarding Site Flow

With the flow of the site established, you can now create a storyboard for conceptualizing the site design, functionality, and interactivity.

The storyboard reflects the site flow from activity to activity. Design the storyboard for presenting the activities, as well as the location of the buttons and the site and activity names. The interactivity for each activity is established. Figure 1.18 shows the home page of the site.

Flash is an ideal solution for creating storyboards, although you can use any application with which you are comfortable. The Flash toolbox has many tools that are easy to use for creating quick sketches of each scene in the site. Using the Timeline, you can create the sequence of each board and activity of the site. You will learn more about the Timeline in Seminar 6, "Animation and Special Effects for Flashing Up the Site." On the CD-ROM that accompanies this book is a sample storyboard for the site in Flash format, `Childrens_SB.fla`, located in the `Seminar01\Samples\` directory. To see a hard copy of each storyboard, you must use the Print Margin command. Follow these steps to print the file `Childrens_SB.fla`.

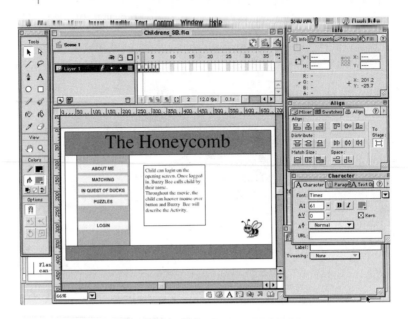

Figure 1.18   By using a storyboard, you begin to create an initial site design.

1. With the Childrens_SB.fla file open, select File, Print Margin to access the Print Margin dialog box.

2. Under Layout, select the Frames option and set this to All Frames. Then select the Layout option and set this to Fit on One Page (see Figure 1.19).

3. Click OK to print.

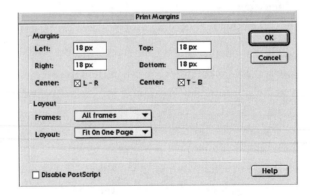

Figure 1.19   You can set your margins and the layout for each page that you print in this dialog box.

4. Click OK to close this dialog box. Now you are ready to print the storyboard.

5. Select File, Print and click OK.

The content of the movie is printed board by board, and the overall storyboard is
conceptualizing the site. Even though this Workshop does not cover how to create
the storyboard in Flash, you'll have the skills to do this by the end of the book.

Planning Site Interactivity

At this point in the site development, you know that the host character will handle
much of the interactivity between the end-user and the site. The character has been
named Buzzy Bee and will be a complex character with wings that flap and eyes that
blink on and off randomly for added realism.

As the storyboard and flowchart reflect, the activity areas of the site are linked
through buttons. To make the site more engaging to children, as well understandable
to a child, some more functionality is planned for the buttons and Buzzy Bee. When
the child hovers her mouse over a button, Buzzy Bee displays a message telling the
child what activity that button triggers and displays.

The site also allows the child to log in, so the next step in the plan is to use locally
controlled login functionality. Keeping the login local ensures that it will exist for
however long the child interacts with the site. As soon as she leaves the site, closes
the browser, or turns off the computer, this login is deleted. The next time the child
accesses the site, she must log in again.

All activities load into the movie because they are created as their own SWF files.
The loadMovie action of ActionScript is used to bring these movies into the site. This
enables a smooth transition from area to area. Also, an opening preloader scene is
used. A *preloader* is the first scene in your movie. It is visually exciting and is the first
introduction to the site. It also lets the user know that something is happening. While
this scene is playing, the rest of the site is *streaming* down or loading in the background as the preloader plays. The preloader does not advance to the main movie
until enough of the site has streamed down to ensure a smooth playing of the site.

Activity Features

Each of the activities will have special functionality that must be created through
ActionScript or other features of Flash. The Puzzle activity consists of one puzzle but
is built so that additional puzzles can be added later to the site. The puzzle is a slider

puzzle where the child must reorder numbers by sliding puzzle pieces left, right, up, or down based on the empty slot in the puzzle. Due to using a drop-down menu to display the puzzle button, the site can be easily updated with addition puzzles listed as buttons in the drop-down menu. The slider puzzle has a reset button to reset it. By using ActionScript and animation, you can create all this functionality.

The "About Me" writing activity uses Flash's powerful form features and components. This activity allows the child to relate information about herself, comparable to a diary or journal. The child can input her information into the About Me form and print the results as a page entry into a diary or journal. Flash MX has very strong database and form connectivity that lends itself well to this activity. You will build the form focusing on the form and its components.

> **Note**
>
> Creating the backend connectivity to a database is outside the scope of this book. To learn more about backend connectivity, check out www.flashkit.com/tutorials/Backend/.

The Matching activity is pretty straightforward—match a sound with an animal. The child clicks a button icon to hear the sound; then she drags the button to the appropriate animal that would make the sound. If the child is correct, the button disappears; if she is not correct, the button returns to its starting point.

The "In Quest of Ducks" activity is a counting activity that uses digital video to show the pond where the ducks live. The child views the video and then can either click each of the ducks to count them, or visually count the ducks and type in her answer. Feedback is communicated indicating whether she is right or wrong. This activity uses dynamic ActionScripting because each child will count the ducks in her own order. The script must dynamically count in numeric sequence as the child finds the ducks in the pond.

Finally, a buzzing noise is added to the movie when Buzzy Bee makes his entrance onto the Stage. The buzzing noise is set to loop so that it is played throughout the movie. A sound toggle button is added to the site so the visitor can toggle the buzzing noise on or off.

Activity Functionality

This is the interactivity that has been identified from the client or has implemented based on experience in the area of Flash design. Table 1.2 illustrates a document that could be created to summarize all the functionality of The Honeycomb site.

Table 1.2 Overview of Honeycomb Site Functionality

Site Object or Area	Functionality
Preloader scene	Limit access to site until enough of the site is streamed to ensure successful playing of the main movie.
Home page	Local login functionality; Buzzy Bee makes his entrance onto the Stage.
Buzzy Bee	Flapping wings; randomly blinking eyes; dialog box displays to explain each button and linking activity.
Puzzles	Slider puzzle uses mouse clicks for moving puzzle pieces to correct locations.
About Me	Data input that can be printed.
Matching	Drag-and-drop interactivity; feedback is provided on right or wrong answers.
In Quest of Ducks	Digital video introducing ducks; hot spots for counting ducks; dynamic ActionScript; feedback is provide on right or wrong answers.
Sound	A buzzing sound is added to accompany Buzzy Bee's entrance onto the Stage. A sound toggle button is present at this point and throughout the remainder of the movie to allow the visitor to turn the buzzing noise off or on.

Honeycomb Creative Composition

From the storyboard, the flowchart of the site, and the required functionality, you can now create the composition of the site design. You must allow for four activity areas, so you need four buttons. You will also need a login area. You know that one of your site goals is to have a fun and enticing site in its design. You must incorporate an area that can be used to consistently present new content. This leads to designing a page that has four activity buttons on the left side of the Stage and most of the right side of the Stage area used to present the activities. Figure 1.20 shows the creative composition for The Honeycomb site.

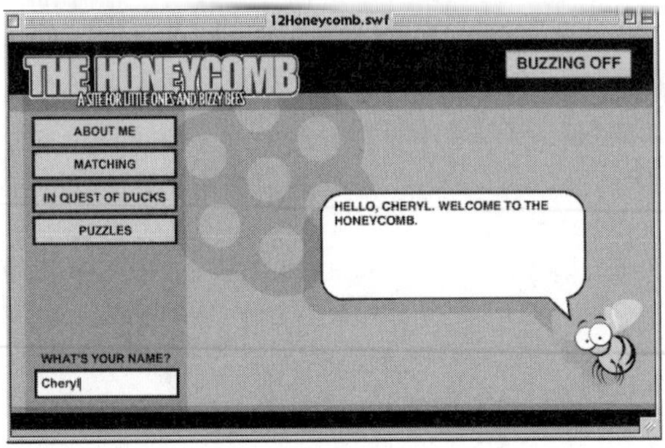

Figure 1.20   By placing the buttons vertically on the left, there is ample room for all activities on the rest of the Stage.

You are now ready to begin the development of your Honeycomb Web site with Flash MX. The project management documents you have on the CD-ROM will guide this development.

Seminar Summary

This seminar covers the basics of Flash functionality and the new features Macromedia Flash MX brings to the table. You should have a good understanding of the characteristics of Flash and how they lend themselves to Web site development for Internet viewing. To summarize these characteristics, Flash is a vector-based design and development application. It uses streaming animation, and it contains its own logical "object-oriented" programming language called ActionScript for creating many types of functionality. This seminar also covered the very basics of the Web project management process—from defining site goals to planning site flow and interactivity. In the Workshop section of this seminar, you applied the project management process to planning the project Web site, The Honeycomb site. Now you are ready to develop the site. The next seminar helps you understand and set up your Flash environment.

Seminar 2

Setting Up the Macromedia Flash MX Environment

In this chapter

Workshop: Customizing the Macromedia Flash
Environment and Setting Up the Movie Design

The Macromedia Flash MX Environment

As with any new application, to successfully use it, you must understand the application environment. Which tools and features do you have at your disposal to begin to develop a movie? Flash MX is no different. This seminar focuses on the various features and tools of Flash MX to get you familiar with the application environment. You will customize the Flash environment to begin to build the workshop project that you will develop throughout this book.

When you first launch Flash MX, it opens into a new blank document or movie. As mentioned in Seminar 1, "Macromedia Flash MX and Web Site Development," this new release of Flash has a redesigned interface composed of new and old features of Flash. Each feature, tool, and panel has its own functionality and use for Flash development. The Flash MX environment is made up of these major areas: the Timeline, the Stage and work area, the Property Inspector, panels, and the toolbox (see Figure 2.1).

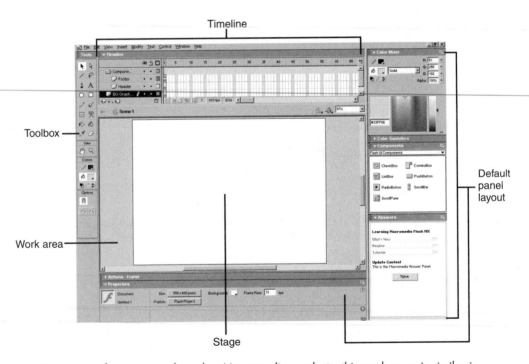

Figure 2.1   If you are used to other Macromedia products, this workspace is similar in its use of panels and the toolbox.

These features comprise the Flash MX environment and are discussed in more detail in this seminar:

- **Stage**—The display area for holding your movie's content. When you publish your movie, it is the area the user sees.

- **Work Area**—Can be compared to your physical desktop. It allows extra space for organizing graphics and images you want to include in a movie but that might not be ready for the Stage.

- **Panels**—Provide you easy access to customization and editing features of the Flash tools and menu commands.

- **Timeline**—Controls your animation and helps organize your Stage content. It is basically the fourth-dimensional view of your project.

- **Toolbox**—Most of the tools you need to create and customize Stage objects are located in the toolbox.

- **Property Inspector**—A new feature of Flash MX. It combines many of the Flash 5 panels into one panel or Inspector and makes it consistent with other Macromedia products. The Property Inspector displays the most commonly used properties or attributes of your Stage content.

The Macromedia Flash MX Interface

The redesigned interface of Macromedia Flash MX is set up to allow easy access and customization of the features, tools, and panels of Macromedia Flash. These features, tools, and panels are now docked in this new interface as a panel set. You can customize a panel set through the various buttons that exist on the title bar of each feature, tool, or panel (see Figure 2.2).

You can rearrange a panel set by clicking and dragging the Move control in the title bar of these docked interface features. If you move a panel to an edge of your screen, it again docks at that location. If you move it to a central location on your screen, it becomes free floating. You can easily collapse any of the panel set features, tools, or panels by clicking the collapse arrow. You can also group panels together by clicking and dragging the Move control in the title bar of a panel into another panel or panel group (see Figure 2.3).

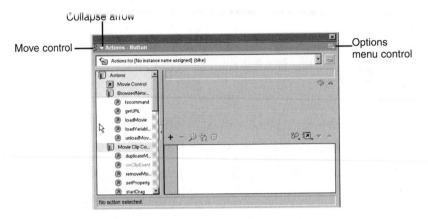

Figure 2.2   All the panels and tools in the new interface have a title bar with common controls.

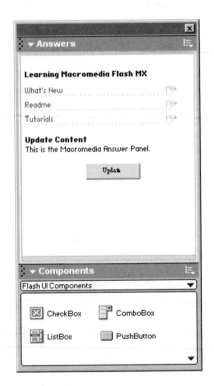

Figure 2.3   You can create as many panel groups as you need for your movie development.

You can save a panel set layout composed of grouped and free-floating panels by selecting Window, Save Panel Layout and typing in the name for your layout (see Figure 2.4). This enables you to customize your Flash environment and the panel set layout to fit your work habits.

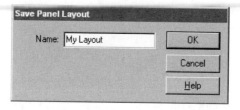

Figure 2.4   You can have as many panel set layouts as you like for developing in Flash.

Tip

If you want to return to the default layout of the Flash interface, select Window, Panel Sets, Default Layout to cause Flash to display the default interface for the commonly used tools and features of Flash.

Tip

When a panel is free floating, you can resize, move, and close it as you would with any window in your computer system interface. You also can collapse it by clicking the collapse arrow or by double-clicking the title bar.

Using the Designer and Developer Panel Set Layout

Macromedia Flash MX also comes with preset interface layout options designed for a Flash designer or developer that displays based on a screen resolution. Again, select Window, Panel Sets to display a submenu listing the various resolutions available on most computer systems used today. You have a choice of the following menu options:

- Designer [1024×768]

- Designer [1280×1024]

- Designer [1600×1200]

- Developer [1024×768]

- Developer [1280×1024]

- Developer [1600×1200]

e Designer options display the commonly used panels that help in the design process. The higher the resolution setting for the Designer options, the more panels that are displayed. The Developer options display the commonly used panels that help in the development of the movie with a focus on ActionScript. Based on the resolution selected, these panels are rearranged and resized. Based on your work habits, you can choose any of these setting for your interface display; you also can customize any of these panel set layouts.

Accessing and Understanding Panels

Flash uses panels for accessing Flash features and settings. When you first launch Flash, you see six panels that display as the default panel set layout (see Figure 2.5). This assumes that you have not changed the default layout of the panel sets. Additional panels exist in Flash, such as the Align panel or Info panel, and all panels can be accessed through the Window menu command.

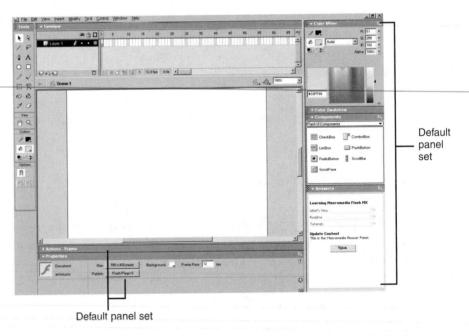

Default panel set

Default panel set

Figure 2.5   You use your panels in conjunction with your toolbox tools or by themselves to customize your Stage content.

Table 2.1 gives a description of all the panels in Flash MX.

Table 2.1 Description of Flash Panels

Panel	Panel Description
Info panel 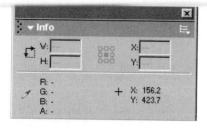	Precisely position and size objects, symbols, and graphics.
Transform panel 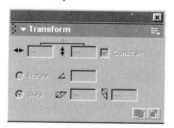	Scale, resize, and rotate objects, symbols, and graphics with precision.
Color Mixer panel 	Select colors in RGB, HSB, or hexadecimal as well as set alpha transparences for shapes. You can set color attributes for both strokes and fills.

continues

Table 2.1   Continued

Panel	Panel Description
Color Swatches panel 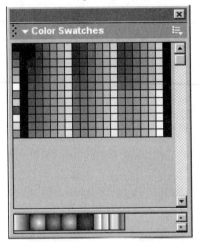	Manage colors and gradient fills for a movie. This panel also enables you to import, save, and sort color sets.
Scene panel 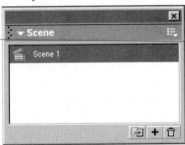	Manage a movie's scenes. This panel enables you to create, rename, delete, reorder, and edit all scenes in a movie.
Align panel 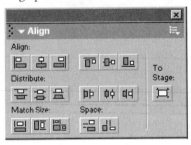	Align, distribute, and match objects relative to each other or the Stage.

Panel	Panel Description
Components panel 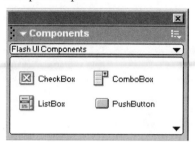	New Feature of Flash MX. Add components with customizable para-meters to a movie.
Answers panel 	Quickly access help and other refer-ences on tools, features, and func-tionality of Flash.
Reference panel 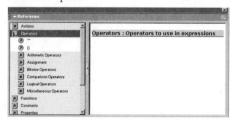	Find answers to questions about fea-tures and tools in Flash.

continues

Table 2.1   Continued

Panel	Panel Description
Actions panel 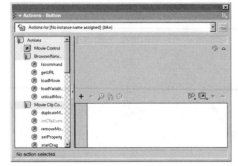	Create ActionScript for interactive functionality and to control movie objects.
Accessibility panel 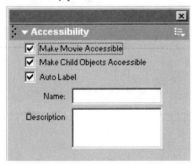	Automatically create names for buttons and objects as well as create text descriptions of movie objects and text fields.
Library panel 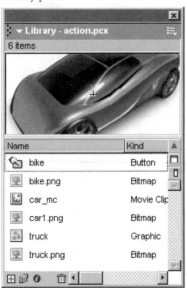	Store movie symbols in a common area for use as instances in a movie.

Tip

You can quickly hide all displayed panels by pressing the Tab key. Press the Tab key again to redisplay the panels.

Tip

You can increase the height and width of any panel by dragging its lower-right corner (Macintosh) or any of the panel's window borders (PC). You can also close a free-floating panel by clicking the close box, and if the panel is docked, you can close it by (Control-clicking)[right-clicking] the title bar and selecting Close from the shortcut menu.

Using the Property Inspector

The Property Inspector is a new feature of Flash MX and one that you will use often throughout your Flash development (see Figure 2.6).

Figure 2.6   The Property Inspector panel combines many of the panel features of Flash 5 into a common panel.

When you select an object on your Stage, the Property Inspector provides information on the object, such as location on the Stage and the type of object. You will use this feature in the next seminar, as well as throughout the remainder of the book.

Working with the Macromedia Flash Toolbox

The toolbox is where you find all the tools you need to create images and graphics, as well as manipulate your Stage view. The toolbox is composed of four areas: Tools, View, Colors, and Options (see Figure 2.7).

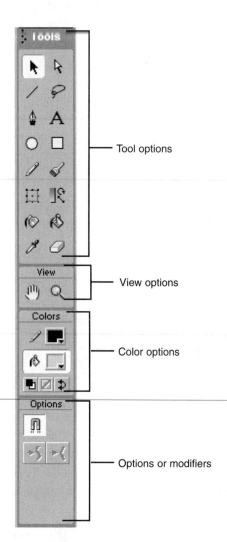

Figure 2.7   You can quickly access any of the tools by clicking them.

The Tools area of the toolbox contains the Flash design tools, which work like many of the tools you have used in other graphics packages. Figure 2.8 shows all the tools available in the toolbox.

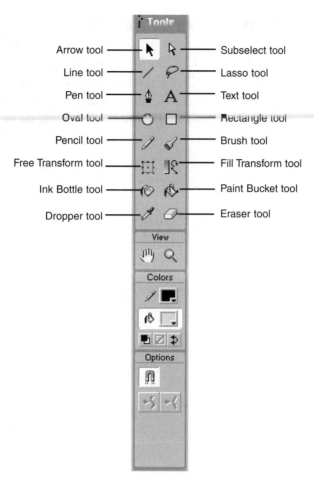

Arrow tool — Subselect tool
Line tool — Lasso tool
Pen tool — Text tool
Oval tool — Rectangle tool
Pencil tool — Brush tool
Free Transform tool — Fill Transform tool
Ink Bottle tool — Paint Bucket tool
Dropper tool — Eraser tool

View

Colors

Options

Figure 2.8 The toolbar contains the tools you need to create your Stage content. You use these tools in conjunction with panels.

Each tool has its own set of option settings that enable you to change or alter a feature of the tool. You can select a tool from the toolbar or view area of the toolbox by clicking it. Click each tool and notice that the Colors and Options area changes to reflect modifier settings that are available for the active tool. You will learn more about the tools in Seminar 3, "Creating a Movie," and throughout the remainder of this book.

Tip

Flash also offers ToolTips for all tools and options of each tool. To display a ToolTip, position your mouse over a tool.

Accessing Tools Through Keyboard Commands

Flash provides a keyboard shortcut for selecting tools from the toolbox. You might have noticed that when you display a ToolTip, at the end of the ToolTip label is a letter in parenthesis. This is the keyboard shortcut, or *hotkey*, for quickly accessing a tool. Press the assigned hotkey to activate the tool in the toolbox. This way your hands do not need to leave the keyboard. Table 2.2 lists all the tools and their assigned hotkeys.

Table 2.2　Hotkeys

Tool	Hotkey
Arrow tool	v
Subselect tool	a
Line tool	n
Lasso tool	l
Pen tool	p
Text tool	t
Oval tool	o
Rectangle tool	r
Pencil tool	y
Brush tool	b
Free Transform tool	q
Fill Transform tool	f
Ink Bottle tool	s
Paint Bucket tool	k
Dropper tool	i
Eraser tool	e
Hand tool	h
Zoom tool	m, z

Tip

You can activate the Hand tool at any time by holding down the spacebar. Your mouse changes to the Hand tool; let go of the spacebar and you'll switch back to the selected tool.

Tip

You can activate the Arrow tool at any time by holding down (Command)[Ctrl]. You'll switch to the Arrow tool no matter what tool is selected. When you let go of (Command)[Ctrl], you switch back to the selected tool.

Using the Stage and Work Area

The Stage is the holding area for all your movie's objects and content. Anything you place on the Stage is part of your movie. If you position something half on the Stage and half in the work area, only the part of the image that is on the Stage appears in your movie. This allows for many special effects with animation. If you want something to appear to fly into a movie from any side of the Stage, position the image in the work area first and then create the animation to carry it onto the Stage. This creates the illusion of the image flying into the movie. You will have hands-on practice creating animation in Seminar 6, "Animation and Special Effects for Flashing Up the Site."

Tip

You can turn the work area on and off through the View, Work Area menu command.

Setting Document Properties

Every document or movie has its own set of properties that determines the size of the Stage, as well as the frames per second (fps) rate for playing the movie and the Stage background color. These properties remain consistent throughout your movie; therefore, you should set your document properties before you begin to develop your movie. You can customize these properties through the Property Inspector (see Figure 2.9).

In the "Workshop" section of this seminar, you will customize the document properties of a movie.

Tip

You can choose between three techniques for opening the Document Properties dialog box:

- Select Modify, Document.
- Double-click the fps field in the Timeline.
- Click the Size button in the Property Inspector when the Stage is active.

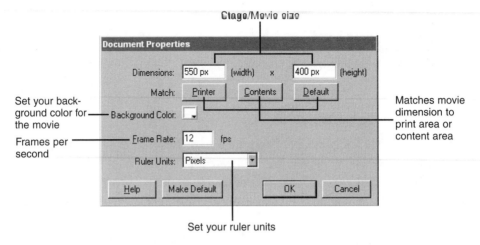

Figure 2.9   You can access the Document Properties dialog box by selecting the Modify, Document menu command.

Understanding X- and Y-Axes and Coordinates

The Stage area of Flash is set to a grid that is composed of x and y coordinates. You use this grid to precisely align objects on the Stage. When you set the dimension of your Stage, you are setting the dimensions of your coordinates. Therefore, if your Stage is 550px by 400px, your x coordinates cover 0–550 and your y coordinates cover 0–400. By default, you align a selected object from the center of the object. The Info panel enables you to set a precise location of an object on the Stage. Open the Info panel by selecting Window, Info. This panel contains options for setting the coordinates for an object (see Figure 2.10).

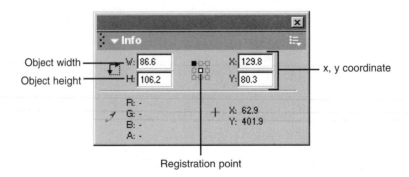

Figure 2.10   You can set the size and location of an object through the Info panel.

> **Tip**
>
> When you start using ActionScript to call and move objects, you program their locations on the Stage with x and y coordinates. Using and understanding the x, y coordinate grid on which the Stage is based is fundamental to working with and maintaining objects in Flash.

Changing Your Stage View

Many times when using Flash, you will want to change your view of the Stage. This enables you to zoom in on an area or object or to zoom out to get a view of your Stage and work area. The most accessible zoom feature of Flash is the Zoom Control in the upper-right corner of the Stage (see Figure 2.11).

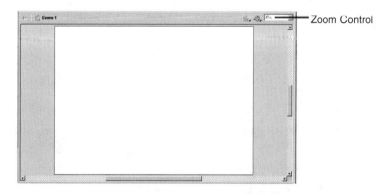
Zoom Control

Figure 2.11   The Zoom Control option enables you to zoom in or out on your Stage.

To view your Stage at different magnifications, you can click the arrow on the Zoom Control and select the magnification from the menu list.

> **Tip**
>
> You also can enter a number in the Zoom Control box to access any magnification you want your Stage to display at.

Most often, you'll want to see your Stage in the largest view that will fit into your Flash window. The Show Frame command sizes the Stage to fit any window. The three techniques for activating this command are as follows:

- Click the arrow on the Zoom Control, and select Show Frame from the menu list.

- Select View, Magnifications, Show Frame.

- Press (Command-2)[Ctrl+2] to quickly display your movie so it fits to your monitor size.

Grids, Guides, and Rulers

As with other graphics programs, Flash offers alignment features for precise placement of objects in your page design, including a grid, guides, and rulers (see Figure 2.12).

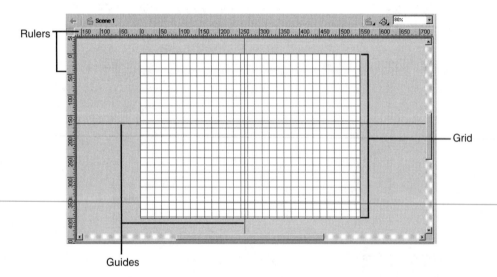

Figure 2.12   These three alignment features can be used alone or in conjunction with each other to attain the design control you need for developing your movie.

Flash has a grid feature that is customizable to however you like to work. You can turn on the grid by selecting View, Grid, Show Grid. Setting your grid before you begin development is a good idea because it aids in creating your design. You can make your grid visible and customize the color of the grid and units of measurement.

If you are used to working with a snap feature, you'll be glad to know that Flash has this feature, too. Snap enables lines and objects to align or *snap* to the grid. You can turn on the snap feature by selecting View, Grid, Snap to Grid. By turning on this command, you cause all new objects on your Stage to snap to the grid. If you change the size of the grid, you have control over how tight or loose your objects are in their alignment to the grid and, therefore, to each other.

Rulers are another alignment feature available to assist you in designing your site layout. Rulers work nicely with the grid option. You can turn on the rulers by selecting View, Rulers.

Flash also offers guides for aligning objects on the Stage. You can pull a guide from your rulers. Make sure your rulers are visible, and then click either ruler and drag out a guide.

Note

Guides take precedence over grid lines. This means an object adheres to the guide even if a grid line is close by.

Using the Align Panel

Using the Align panel, you can align objects to each other and to the Stage. To access this panel, select Window, Align. The Align panel displays (see Figure 2.13). Notice that you have many options for aligning objects. If you hover your mouse over one of the options, a ToolTip appears identifying the type of alignment you can apply.

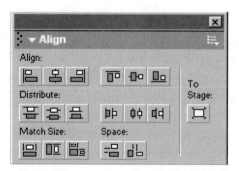

Figure 2.13   If you select the Stage option, objects align to the Stage based on the type of alignment you select. Otherwise, the objects merely align to each other, regardless of Stage position.

Tip

For true precision, many Flash developers use the Info Panel and set the object's x, y coordinate.

Working with the Timeline

The Flash Timeline controls the flow and organization of the movie. The Timeline's major components are folder layers, layers, frames and keyframes, and the playhead (see Figure 2.14).

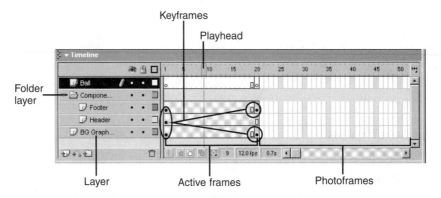

Figure 2.14   A Photoframe is a placeholder for frames and keyframes.

Working with Layers

Layers are a component in the Timeline. They are a fundamental building block for your movie, both for organizing graphics used in a movie and holding animation and special effects. A layer can be compared to a transparency in that a layer enables you to position a graphic on your Stage and still see the background or other layers and their content behind it. You can better organize your movie content by putting objects on their own layers. Because objects are contained in their own layers, you can make changes to parts of your movie more quickly and efficiently. You do not need to re-create entire elements of your movie.

New with Flash MX is the addition of a folder layer. A folder layer is used to bundle layers that contain common movie content in the Timeline. It can be collapsed or expanded to show or hide these bundle layers by clicking the arrow to the left of the layer name. You will learn more about layers and their functionality in Seminar 3, "Creating a Movie."

Layers have special features and buttons that help you work with your Stage content (see Figure 2.15).

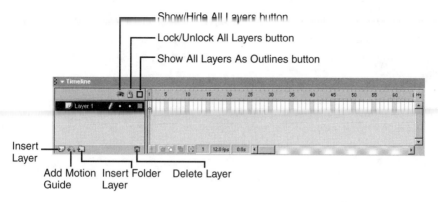

Figure 2.15 Click the Insert Layer button to add a new layer, and click the Delete Layer button to delete a layer.

These features and buttons enable you to create and delete layers, as well as hide and unhide layers. You also can lock and unlock them. Locking a layer ensures that you can't accidentally move its content. You can also view a layer's content in outline form. The ability to lock, hide, and outline individual layers is where the power of layers lies. This enables you to easily focus on a specific object or group of objects without accidentally altering other objects.

> **Tip**
>
> You can drag through any of the columns of dots to apply the layer feature to multiple layers simultaneously.

> **Tip**
>
> If you (Option-click)[Alt+click] the dot in the Eye column to the right of a layer's name, you hide all other layers. This shortcut is a quick way to hide all but the layer you want to work on. This technique works for Hide/Unhide as well as for displaying outlines for a layer.

Frames, Keyframes, and Photoframes

Each layer in a movie contains a series of frames or keyframes that represent Stage content used in the movie. A *frame* holds Stage content, whereas a *keyframe* is a special type of frame in which you designate a change in the animation or to which you attach a frame action for controlling the movie.

The playhead advances through the movie, indicating progression through the Timeline. You can click a certain frame or move the playhead to see the Stage content at that point in the Timeline. You will use frames, photoframes, and keyframes in Seminar 6.

> **Note**
>
> When a new Flash movie is opened, the Timeline displays with one layer composed of one blank keyframe. The Stage is empty, and after the blank keyframe is a series of photoframes, segmented in groups of five. A photoframe is a holding space for frames and keyframes.

Using a Guide Layer

A *guide layer* is a special layer that holds an image you want to use as a guide for creating your site design. The guide layer is used to help in the design process of the movie and is present only in the Flash Authoring environment. When you publish or export your movie, the guide layer and its Stage content are stripped out of the movie and are not actually part of the final Flash SWF file (see Figure 2.16).

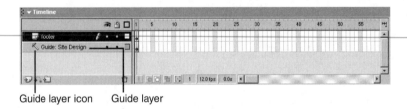

Guide layer icon   Guide layer

Figure 2.16   A guide layer has a new identifying icon to the left of the layer name.

Many designers use a guide layer to help them create a Flash movie: They create a layout for their site designs in a graphics program, such as Photoshop, and then import it into Flash and place it on a guide layer. Be sure to create your design in one of the file formats covered in Seminar 1. In the workshop portion at the end of this seminar, you will add a guide layer and import an image into it for use in creating your workshop project: The Honeycomb Web site.

Resizing the Timeline

You can resize the Timeline to allow for a larger viewing area of your Stage or to view all layers in your Timeline. The default size is spaced to show four layers, but many movies require more than just four layers. So, you need to be able to resize your Timeline to view these features. To do this, just grab the lower Timeline window border and drag up or down to resize the window (see Figure 2.17).

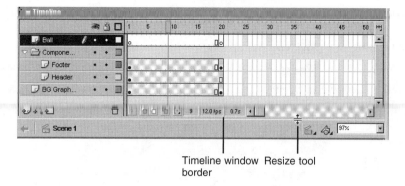

Timeline window   Resize tool
border

Figure 2.17   Your cursor changes to a double arrow resize tool when you position it on the Timeline window's lower border.

You also can change the display of the Timeline. Click the Timeline Display button at the far right of the Timeline (see Figure 2.18). This pops up a menu with display options. Select an option, and the Timeline is displayed in a new format.

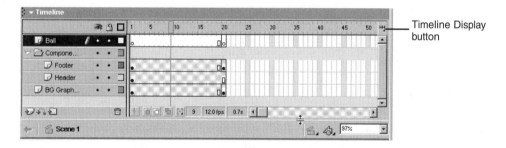

Timeline Display
button

Figure 2.18   You can change your display of the Timeline to show more or less information.

Hiding the Timeline

Sometimes you might want to hide the Timeline to see your Stage in a full view. This can be accomplished by selecting View, Timeline or by collapsing the Timeline by clicking the arrow in the title bar. After you hide the Timeline, you can redisplay it by either selecting the menu command again or clicking the arrow in the title bar. Both techniques toggle the Timeline between hidden and displayed.

Tip

Using more than one monitor when working with Flash can also provide an efficient workspace. You can keep panels and tools on one monitor and use the other strictly for the Stage and Timeline.

Setting Macromedia Flash Preferences

The Macromedia Flash MX Preferences dialog box is accessed by selecting Edit, Preferences (see Figure 2.19). It has five tabs that enable you to set specific preferences for how your Flash environment works.

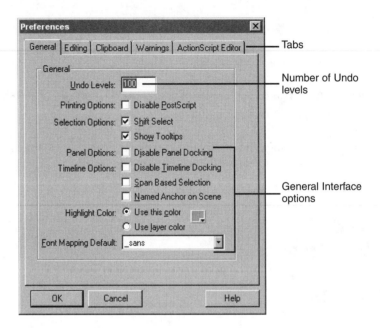

Figure 2.19   The General tab displays by default for the Preferences dialog box. Four other tabs are available for customizing Flash.

General Tab

The General tab enables you to set the number of Undo levels (refer to Figure 2.19).

You have up to 200 levels of Undo when creating any Flash movie. If you make a mistake and want to quickly undo it, you simply select Edit, Undo. You can then back through your process of development, undoing each action or step you perform in the order in which it was initiated until you reach the maximum levels of undo that you set. You also can set different printing and panel settings. If you do not like the docked panel and Timeline interface, you can turn that off by selecting the Disable Panel/Timeline Docking options.

Note

Although the preference setting for the Undo Levels allows you to set the level as high as 200, your computer might not have enough RAM to support it. Generally, sticking with 100 levels is enough for most Flash projects.

Editing Tab

You can set your Editing preferences by clicking the Editing tab (see Figure 2.20). These settings help you draw with the Flash tools. As you begin to work through the workshops in this book, you will learn more about these settings and how to configure this tab to best fit your needs.

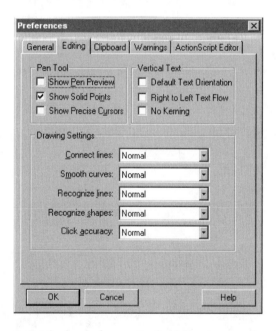

Figure 2.20   You can set the level of accuracy for the tools as well as how they adhere to guides and the grid.

Clipboard Tab

The Clipboard tab of the Preferences dialog box enables you to set your Clipboard settings and how an object is translated when it is copied or cut (see Figure 2.21). The Clipboard is an operating system feature that is used across all applications, not just Flash. Click the Clipboard tab to access these preferences.

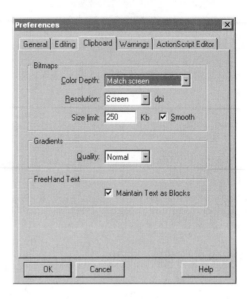

Figure 2.21   You can also set preferences for how Flash imports FreeHand images.

Warnings Tab

The Warnings tab enables you to turn on or off the various warnings that can be displayed when a movie is played by the end-user or as you are developing a movie (see Figure 2.22).

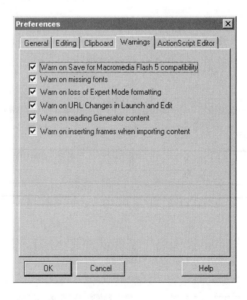

Figure 2.22   Each of these options is a toggle option that can be turned on and off by selecting the option.

ActionScript Editor Tab

The ActionScript Editor tab enables you to set editing, display, and functionality options for your Actions panel (see Figure 2.23).

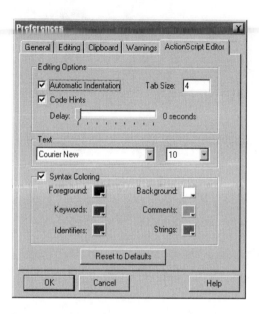

Figure 2.23   You can set the font type you want to display in the Actions panel through the ActionScript Editor preferences.

When you begin to attach ActionScript to your movie, you might want to customize the various syntax coloring for your script. More information on this tab—as well as ActionScript in general—is covered starting in Seminar 7, "Site Interactivity and Button Functionality," and continuing through the remainder of the book.

Customizing the Macromedia Flash Environment and Setting Up the Movie Design

The following Workshop guides you through customizing your Flash environment so that you have the correct settings, grid, and guides for developing The Honeycomb Web site. You will also import an image to be used as a guide for developing the site by creating a guide layer for this image. To start development on the site, you need to open a new document in Flash. Follow these steps to begin developing the site.

1. Launch Flash to open a new document or movie.

2. Save the file by selecting File, Save. Name the file `Honeycomb.fla` and save it in a directory that you will use for creating all files for The Honeycomb site.

Customizing the Grid and Rulers

Before you begin to develop The Honeycomb site, you need to set your grid and display your rulers. To do this, follow these steps:

1. Select File, Grid, Edit Grid to open the Grid dialog box.

2. Set the color of the grid to a red color by selecting the grid color button and clicking a red color chip from the color palette.

3. Click the horizontal and vertical grid spacing boxes and change those to `10 px`.

4. Select the Snap to Grid option to turn on that feature. Your Grid dialog box should look similar to Figure 2.24.

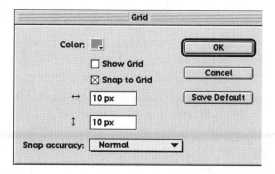

Figure 2.24   Keep the Snap Accuracy at Normal, and click the Snap to Grid option.

5. Click OK to close the Grid dialog box.

6. With the Grid set, you can display your rulers so that you have references for positioning your Stage objects. Select View, Rulers, and the rulers display (see Figure 2.25).

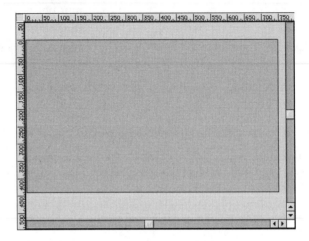

Figure 2.25   The rulers reflect the x- and y-axis and coordinates for your movie.

Setting the Movie Properties

Important settings for your movie's development include the Stage size, background color, and frames per second rate (fps). You set all these settings in the Document Properties dialog box. The Stage size settings determine the size of the viewing area of the movie; the fps rate setting, on the other hand, determines how many frames of the Timeline are viewed in a second. You can set it to any number, but the higher the fps rate, the more computer processing power is required to view the movie and the quicker the movie runs. If you set a low number, your animation is slower and uses less of the end-user's computer processing power. Setting your fps at the beginning of your movie development is a good idea. Your animation runs consistently throughout the movie, so if you change the fps halfway through your development, you must adjust most of the animation you have created in the movie. To set your Stage size and the fps rate, follow these steps:

> **Note**
>
> The setting for the default unit of the Dimensions Width and Height box is px, which is short for pixel. You can type in a number without px; Flash will automatically assume you mean pixel and add this unit to your number entry.

Tip

If you are designing for Web deployment and your audience's suggested settings are for 800×600 or greater, keep in mind that the browser window will consume some of those pixels for scrollbars, menu bars, buttons, and so on. A movie designed for 800×600 should be no larger than 775×440.

1. Select Modify, Document to open the Movie properties dialog box.

2. Click in the Frame Rate box, and set the fps to 12.

3. Click in the Dimensions (width) box; set the Stage width to 750 and the (height) to 440.

4. Your Document Properties dialog box should look similar to Figure 2.26. Leave the Document Properties dialog box open for the next topic of this workshop.

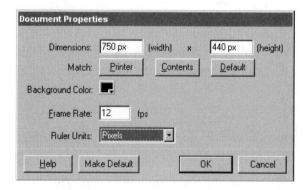

Figure 2.26   If these settings were common settings that you would use for other movies, you could click the Make Default button to save these settings for any new movie you create.

Tip

In Seminar 1, you identified your target audience to have older machines from which they will view the site, so a good setting for the frame per second rate is 12–15fps. You can set this rate higher if you feel your targeted audience will have newer, faster machines. A good rate for this could be 15–50fps.

Tip

You should base your fps setting on other functionality and objects you use in your movie. This could be the number of objects that have an alpha setting or how many shape tweens are used in the movie. Based on these factors, your movie can bog down slower machines. You will learn more about alpha settings in Seminar 3 and more about shape tweens in Seminar 6.

Setting the Stage Background Color

Next, you must set the background color for The Honeycomb Web site. An important consideration when choosing a background color is whether to choose a *Web-safe color*. A Web-safe color is a color that appears the same on any computer platform through any browser. Although Flash allows full use of 16.7 million colors, you should use only the 216 Web-safe colors for objects or backgrounds that come in contact with the outer edge of the movie. The default color palette of Flash is the 216 Web-safe palette, so any color chosen from the default palette is Web safe. As mentioned in Seminar 1, all SWF files are embedded in an HTML file to enable browser viewing. If you want seamless integration between the movie and the HTML page's background, you must use a Web-safe color for your movie's background and any object touching the edge of the Stage. To set the Honeycomb site background color, follow these steps:

1. In the Document Properties dialog box, click the Background Color button to display the color palette.

2. Select the orange color chip that is eight rows down and three columns over from the right edge of the palette (see Figure 2.27).

3. Click OK to set the Stage size, fps rate, and background color for your movie.

Tip

The color palette has an area for inputting a hexadecimal value for a color. Many times in Web development, colors are represented by hexadecimal numbers. You can input any hexadecimal number by clicking in the hexadecimal box and typing the new color number. This enables you to easily match background colors between a Flash movie and the HTML page in which it is embedded.

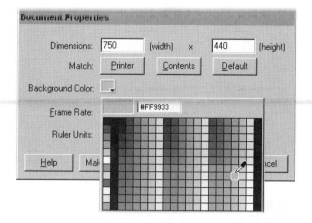

Figure 2.27   The hexadecimal color for this color swatch is FF9933.

Creating a Guide Layer

The next step is to import an image into a guide layer to help guide your creation of The Honeycomb site. You first need to create your guide layer. To do this, follow these steps:

1. (Control-click)(Right-click) Layer 1 in the Timeline and choose Guide from the shortcut menu. This converts Layer1 to a guide layer.

2. Insert a new layer above the guide layer by clicking the Insert Layer button.

3. Click the guide layer to select it.

4. Select File, Import. The Import dialog box appears. In the dialog box, navigate to the CD-ROM directory `Seminar02/Samples` and select the `design_template.jpg` file (see Figure 2.28).

5. To import the image onto the Stage, click Open.

    The file is imported into the Flash movie and resides on the guide layer (see Figure 2.29).

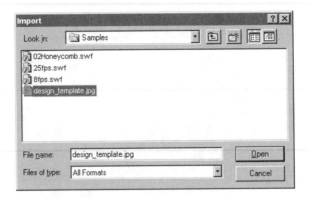

Figure 2.28   New with Flash MX is the capability to import a file directly into the movie or directly into the library. More is covered on the Import features in Seminar 5, "Importing Graphics into a Movie."

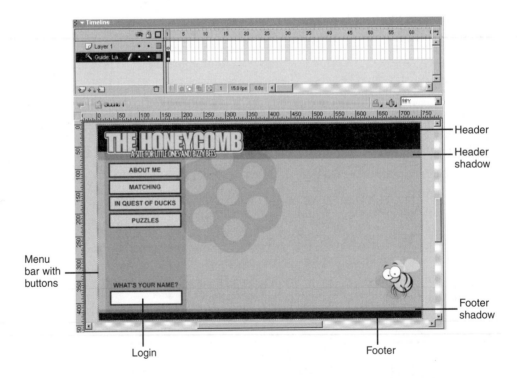

Figure 2.29   The design template shows the various areas of The Honeycomb site.

Now that your guide layer is imported, the last step is to configure Macromedia Flash MX so that the work space is set up as efficiently as possible for your workflow.

Configuring the Macromedia Flash Interface

You will use the Align panel often, so it should be easily accessible. In this part of the workshop, the guide image must be positioned precisely on the Stage. To customize the default panel set layout and include the Align panel, do the following:

1. Select Window, Panel Sets, Default Layout to change the panel set layout to the default layout.

2. Select Window, Align to display the Align panel.

3. Click and drag the Move control on the title bar of the Align panel to the panel group on the right of the Stage. It is added to this panel group (see Figure 2.30).

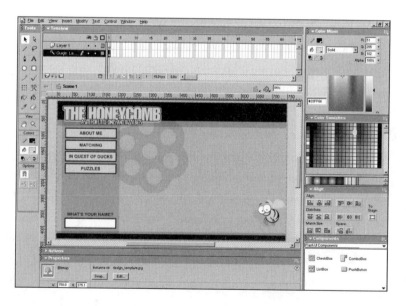

Figure 2.30   You can also rearrange the location of the default panel set if you want to customize your Stage more to your work habits.

4. Select the Arrow tool from the toolbox.

5. Click the image that you imported into the guide layer to make it active.

6. From the Align panel, click the To Stage option; then click the Align Vertical Center and Align Horizontal Center options (see Figure 2.31).

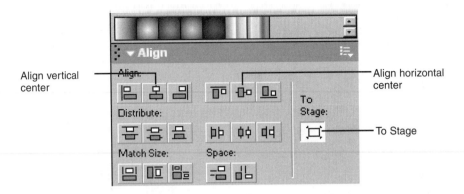

Align vertical center

Align horizontal center

To Stage

Figure 2.31　The guide image aligns itself with the Stage.

Accessing and Setting Guides

To help align the objects that make up the opening scene of the movie, you should set some guides. These guides are used throughout the movie's development. Before you set your guides, you might want to turn off the Snap to Grid feature by selecting View, Grid, Snap to Grid. To set your guides, follow these steps:

1. Click in the horizontal ruler and drag out a horizontal guide.

2. Position the guide at the vertical ruler coordinate of 60 or directly under the header rectangle (see Figure 2.32). You might want to increase your Stage view to a higher magnification to get precision in your guide placement.

3. Pull out three more horizontal guides and position them at vertical ruler coordinates of 80, 415, and 422 (or under the header shadow and above the footer shadow and footer rectangles).

4. To set your vertical guides, click in the vertical ruler and drag out a vertical guide.

5. Position this guide at a horizontal ruler coordinate of 17 to define the left edge of the menu bar.

6. Drag out a second vertical guide and position it at a horizontal ruler coordinate of 206 to define the right edge of the menu bar (see Figure 2.33).

Vertical ruler coordinate of 60

Horizontal guide

Figure 2.32 You might want to increase your view of the Stage to set your guides to the correct coordinate.

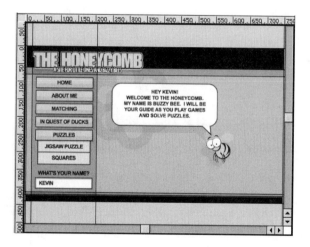

Figure 2.33 These six guides will be used to create your Stage background content.

7. Pull out four more guides, two horizontal and two vertical. Position them around the outer edges of the Stage (see Figure 2.34).

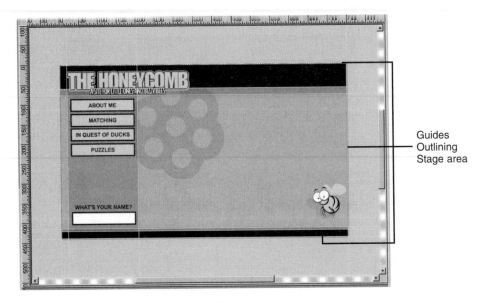

Figure 2.34   These four guides define the Stage area.

8. Lock your guides by selecting View, Guides, Lock Guides. Locking your guides keeps them from being accidentally moved while you develop the movie.

9. Save your file.

Setting Undo Levels in Preferences

The last thing to do before you really get into the hands-on work is to set the number of undo levels you need to have. You must access this setting through your Preference dialog box by following these steps:

1. Select Edit, Preferences to open the Preferences dialog box, and then click the General tab.

2. Click the Undo Levels box and set the number to 50 (see Figure 2.35).

3. Leave the other preferences set at the default settings; then, click OK to save these preference settings and close the Preferences dialog box.

4. Save your file. You are now ready to move on to Seminar 3 and begin creating your Honeycomb site design.

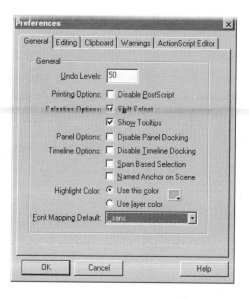

Figure 2.35 You can set your Undo Levels up to 200, but that can be very taxing on your available memory.

Tip

Sometimes in the process of developing your movie, you might need to revert back to the previously saved version of your movie. You can select File, Revert to discard all the work you have done from the point that you last saved. This command opens the last saved version of your movie. This can also be a very beneficial command if you start down a wrong path in your development and need to just get back to your starting point.

Tip

Be sure to save often, and use a good method of movie version control so that you have many copies of your movie as you progress through the development. You never know when a power outage or system crash will occur.

Seminar Summary

This seminar acquainted you with the Macromedia Flash MX environment. You've learned about the Stage and work area, how to set your movie preferences, and how to customize your workspace for your style of working. In this seminar's workshop, you customized your panel sets and set your undo levels. You also started creating The Honeycomb Web site by setting up the Stage size and background color. You created a guide layer and imported an image to use as a guide for the site development; you then set your guides for creating the background images. You are now ready to start creating your Stage content. Seminar 3 covers creating the opening scene of The Honeycomb Web site. You will learn to use the Macromedia Flash MX tools and panels in this seminar.

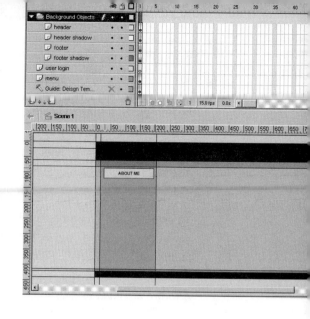

Seminar 3

Creating a Movie

In this chapter

Workshop: Creating the Opening Scene of the Site

Design Principles

Learning to use the Macromedia Flash drawing tools is a must for working with your Stage content and developing your site. Seminar 2, "Setting Up the Macromedia Flash MX Environment," introduced you to the interface, panels, and tools of Flash. This seminar explores the features in more detail.

To begin the design process for a Web site, you need to consider many factors—such as whether the site should be fun, serious, sentimental, or all business. You also need to determine the overall message and feeling you want to communicate. You should explore creating a design that supports that message and is also pleasing to the eye. Another design consideration is usability—how the page is laid out, where the buttons link to, and so on. Colors and layout help in creating a successful design, but most winning Web sites are based on a well thought-out design that is useful to its intended audience.

Developing a design for any Web site requires knowledge of some basic design principles, which include

- Alignment
- Proximity
- Contrast
- Consistency

These four principles apply to any type of communication piece, be that Web, print, or film. They are the fundamental building blocks of a good design. As you begin to develop a site, you need to nail down the site design. Following these four principles will guide you in successful site development.

Alignment

Alignment is a principle of how things line up on your page. You can align to the left, right, or center as your vertical alignment, but you also need to consider how things align horizontally. Horizontal alignment includes top, center, and bottom. When you begin the process of creating a Web site design, you need to consider your alignment for the page and the items on it. The main rule of alignment is that whatever alignment you choose, use it throughout the site.

To help explain this principle further, look at the following two examples, Figure 3.1 and Figure 3.2. Both examples are of the same advertisement, but Figure 3.2 uses the principle of alignment, mainly vertical alignment.

Figure 3.1   Although this advertisement uses center justification on the text blocks, this type of justification does not lend itself to the background of the advertisement.

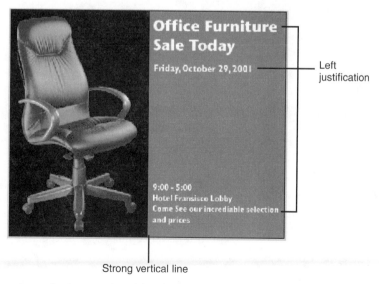

Figure 3.2   This ad uses both vertical and horizontal alignment with a much more effective result.

Figure 3.1 uses a combination of alignments. The chair graphic with its black background creates a very strong vertical line, so the use of center justification on the text blocks does not lend itself to the strong vertical line. The headline is centered on the page, but the other text blocks are centered in the gray area. Your eye wanders around the page, which makes it easy to miss information. The design looks awkward.

Figure 3.2, on the other hand, uses the chair graphic's strong vertical line and aligns all text blocks vertically. All the text blocks have left-justified text, which, coupled with the positioning of the text blocks, creates another strong vertical line. You can also see the use of horizontal alignment—the text blocks on the top and bottom of the page are in alignment with the bottom and top of the chair graphic. This ad is easy on your eye, and information is easy to find.

Proximity

Another principle of design is *proximity*. Proximity refers to how close objects are to each other on a page and creates relationships between items. If the items are close together, they appear to belong with each other. If they are far apart, they appear to not have a relationship. See Figure 3.3 and Figure 3.4 for examples of proximity.

Figure 3.3   The logo and the company name are far apart and appear to have no relationship.

Figure 3.3 is an advertisement for a travel company. Notice that the company name, header, and text blocks do not have any proximity. There appears to be no clearly defined relationships between the items on the page. This makes fully understanding the message of the ad difficult for the viewer.

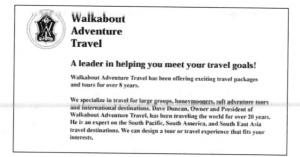

Figure 3.4 Vertical alignment is also used with this advertisement to give it a better design.

Figure 3.4 is the same advertisement, but it uses proximity in creating a relationship between the logo and company name. The header has been moved closer to the text blocks and helps the viewer easily relate that message with the text block information.

Contrast

The principle of contrast is what adds the punch to the page. *Contrast* is created through colors, graphics, type, texture, or a combination of each. It is what draws your eye to the page and how you see the information. Your design must have a focal point, and contrast establishes this focal point (see Figure 3.5).

Figure 3.5 The white circle provides stark contrast with the other elements of the page, drawing your eye to the company name.

Aside from a focal point, your eye must have a logical path to follow for finding information. Contrast that creates prominence is necessary to help the viewer read the most important information first. Figure 3.6 shows a nice progression of information. Contrast with the combination of proximity and alignment is used to create the hierarchy of importance of page elements.

Figure 3.6   This example uses font size for creating contrast. It also uses proximity and alignment to help create a logical flow of information.

Tip

Sometimes you don't want to use contrast. If you want the viewer to read through a page of your site without any interruption, don't use contrast. Putting a graphic or link in the middle of this page is contrast and interrupts the viewer's reading.

Consistency

The principle of consistency is important in Web site design. Repetition of page elements and design establishes consistency throughout a site. Every page in your Web site should look like it belongs to that site. Colors, backgrounds, fonts and font styles, graphics, and page layout are used often throughout the design to achieve consistency.

Consistency is also used in your navigation of the site. If you present your links and buttons in a uniform format and location for all areas of the site, your viewer can easily navigate through the site. All these elements of a Web site create unity of the site.

Understanding How Lines and Shapes Interact

With the concepts of design in mind, it is now time to learn more about Flash and its design tools. Flash has many of the tools and design features that you might be accustomed to in other graphics applications. But Flash behaves a little differently when it comes to objects, fills, and lines. Because Flash is a vector-based program, objects in their basic forms are composed of lines and/or fills. When an object intersects another object, the overlapping fills and lines merge and become one. Anytime a line intersects with another line, it breaks into separate line segments at the point of intersection. You use clicking and double-clicking to select an entire object or part of the object. To understand this better, open the sample file `merge.fla` on the CD-ROM in the `Seminar3/Samples` directory. Then perform the following steps:

1. Open the `merge.fla` file by select File, Open. The file opens with an oval and a rectangle on the Stage. The oval overlaps, as well as displays on top of, the rectangle.

2. Select the Arrow tool from the toolbox and click the fill area of the oval. A marquee appears in the fill area indicating that it is selected (see Figure 3.7). The oval is composed of both a stroke and a fill.

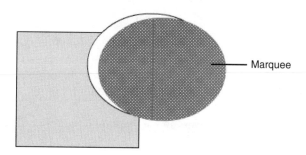

Figure 3.7   If you click and drag the fill, you can move it away from the stroke.

3. Click one of the rectangle's lines. Notice that instead of selecting the entire outline of the rectangle, you select only one line segment of the rectangle (see Figure 3.8).

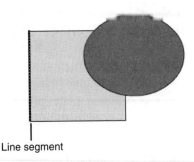

Line segment

Figure 3.8   The lines intersect at each corner, making each side of the rectangle its own line segment.

4. To select the entire oval, including both the fill and the stroke, double-click anywhere in the fill.

5. To select the entire stroke of the oval, click the line segment of the oval.

6. Also note that the oval object has merged with the rectangle shape in the area in which they overlap. With the Arrow tool, select the entire oval by double-clicking, and then move the object. The oval has merged with the rectangle (see Figure 3.9).

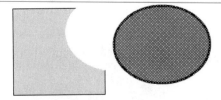

Figure 3.9   The rectangle has a chunk in the shape of the oval missing from its shape.

7. Keep the merge.fla file open for the next topic.

Grouping Your Objects

Having objects merge and lines become segmented at intersections can really cause you headaches if you have to modify the design later. But other features of Flash enable you to work easily with your objects. The first technique is to group the object or multiple objects that you want to keep as one.

You can group any object by selecting it and then selecting Modify, Group. As in other applications, this groups your object or objects as one item. Try this on the oval in the merge.fla file and follow these steps:

1. Using the Arrow tool, double-click the oval on the Stage to select both the fill and the stroke.

2. Select Modify, Group to group the object (see Figure 3.10).

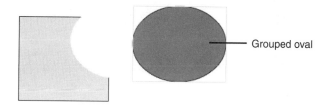

Grouped oval

Figure 3.10 You can now move this grouped object anywhere you want without it separating or merging with other shapes and objects on the Stage.

3. Move the grouped oval on top of the rectangle.

4. Click anywhere on a blank area of the Stage to deselect the oval.

5. Select the oval again and move it off of the rectangle. It does not merge. Grouping makes the oval easy to work with.

6. Leave the merge.fla file open for the next section, and do not save the file.

Note

You can also use symbols to help keep an object or multiple objects as one. Symbols are covered in Seminar 4, "Using Symbols in a Movie."

Tip

When an object is grouped, you can't directly apply new attributes or modify the attributes of that object. This means you can't change the line, fill, or shape of the object as it exists on the Stage. To make changes to the grouped object, you must ungroup it by choosing Modify, Ungroup or edit the object in Group Mode, which is covered next. You also can select Modify, Break Apart to break the grouped image apart.

Working in Group Mode

If you double-click an already grouped shape, you initiate another mode of Flash, the Group Mode. Group Mode can be compared to a bubble. When you initiate the Group Mode, it is like going inside a bubble that contains only the grouped objects. In Group Mode, you can edit grouped objects; they are composed of strokes and fills. While in Group Mode, other Stage objects dim due to looking through the bubble surface. Other objects outside the bubble or Group Mode can't be edited until you exit the mode. To see how Group Mode works, follow these steps:

1. Using the Arrow tool, double-click the oval. This launches Group Mode and your Stage dims. The oval is again represented in its basic form of strokes and fills (see Figure 3.11).

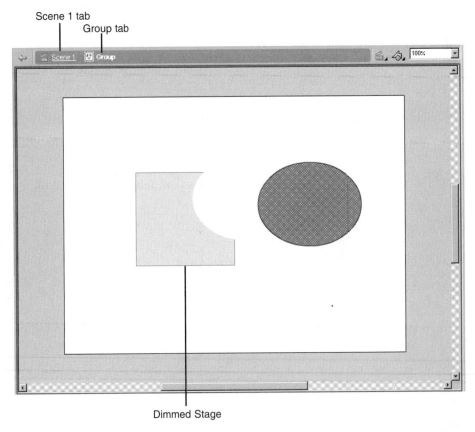

Figure 3.11   The tab that appears in the upper-left corner of your Stage indicates Group Mode.

2. Click the rectangle shape. Notice that you can't access this object. You are in Group Mode for the oval and can edit only the oval.

3. Click the fill of the oval. A marquee displays indicating that it is active. You can now modify or change this fill.

4. To exit Group Mode and return to an active Stage, click the Scene 1 tab next to the Group tab in the upper-left corner. Any changes you made in Group Mode to the oval are now part of the grouped shape.

5. Close the `merge.fla` file, and do not save the changes.

Tip ———————————————————————

Instead of clicking the Scene 1 tab to exit Group Mode, you can also double-click anywhere in a blank area of your Stage.

Warning ———————————————————————

It is a common mistake for new users of Flash to initiate Group Mode without realizing they have. If you are working in Flash and suddenly can't access Stage content, look in the upper-left corner above your Stage area and see whether you have initiated Group Mode. Exit Group Mode, and you will have control over the Stage content again.

Using Tools and Modifiers

The Flash tools in the toolbox work similarly to other graphics application programs you might be used to. Many Flash developers use the Flash drawing tools sparingly for creating their site designs. They prefer to use their favorite graphics applications and import the artwork into Flash. Others use the Flash tools entirely for their designs. It is beneficial to know how the tools work so you can decide which method or combination of methods you want to use to develop your site.

Using the Arrow Tool

One of the most frequently used tools in Flash is the Arrow tool. Regardless of whether you import your artwork or create it in Flash, you need to know how to use this tool. The Arrow tool enables you to select Stage objects to make them active, as you saw while working with `merge.fla` in the previous topic. When the object is active, you can reposition it on the Stage or modify it.

To begin using the Arrow tool, select it from the toolbox (see Figure 3.12).

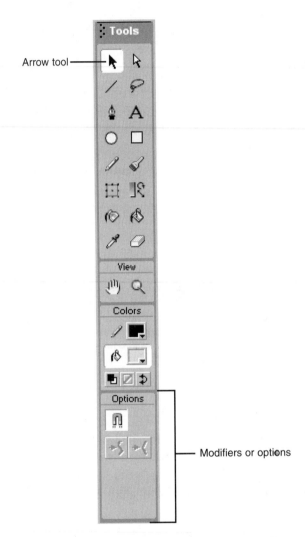

Figure 3.12   All Flash tools have different modifier or option settings. When you select a tool, the Option area of the toolbox reflects these modifiers.

The Arrow tool becomes the active tool, and its modifiers are displayed. After you select an object, you can apply the modifier settings to it by clicking a modifier button. Table 3.1 describes each modifier setting of the Arrow tool.

Table 3.1   Arrow Tool and Options

Tool	Name	Options
🔲	Snap to Objects	Aligns Stage objects to each other.
🔲	Smooth	Smoothes curves and reduces bulges or other variations in a curve's overall path. This modifier can be clicked multiple times to reduce curve variances.
🔲	Straighten	Straightens out existing lines and curves. This modifier can be clicked multiple times to reduce line and curve variances.

Creating Vector Shapes

Basic shapes such as rectangles, ovals, and lines are often used for backgrounds and other Stage content. Vector shapes are composed of either a fill or a stroke or both. The Rectangle, Oval, and Line tools create the vector shapes you might need in your movie. These tools all work basically the same: To create a vector shape, select either the Oval, Rectangle, or Line tool from the toolbox (see Figure 3.13).

Set your color options for the Stroke and the Fill by clicking the associated color palette and selecting a color from the palette. Then click and drag on the Stage to create your object (see Figure 3.14).

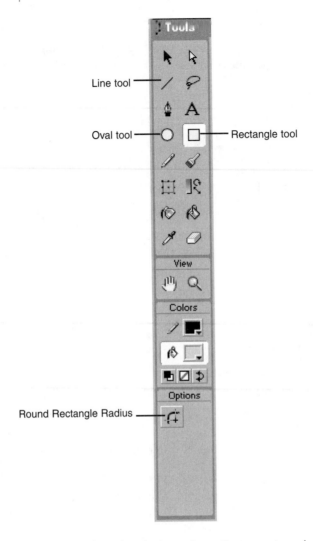

Line tool

Oval tool — Rectangle tool

Round Rectangle Radius

Figure 3.13   The Line and Oval tools do not have Option settings, but the Rectangle tool has the Round Rectangle Radius Option setting.

Figure 3.14   If you hold the Shift key while you draw a basic shape, you constrain the shape to a perfect square, circle, or horizontal/vertical line.

If you want to create a rounded-corner rectangle, click the Round Rectangle Radius modifier before you create the rectangle to display the Rectangle Settings dialog box (see Figure 3.15). To set the degree of the corner radius, click inside the Corner Radius box and enter a numerical value. Now when you draw a rectangle, it will have rounded corners.

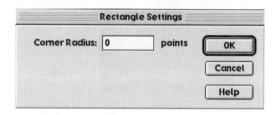

Figure 3.15 A radius numeric value of 90 or above creates a round edge, not just corners.

Editing Vector Shapes with the Arrow Tool

The Arrow tool is also useful for editing and modifying vector shapes. Using the Arrow tool, position it on the edge of the vector shape and, based on whether the Arrow tool is positioned on the vector shape, a different selection tool is available. If you position the Arrow tool on a line or curve of the shape, you get a small curve under the Arrow tool. If you click and drag the vector shape edge, you transform the shape (see Figure 3.16).

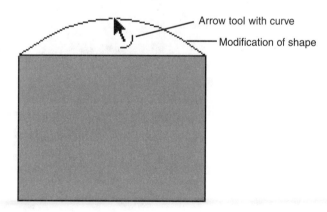

Figure 3.16 You can modify any object that's in its basic form of a stroke or a fill with this technique.

The Arrow tool is also used to modify endpoints or corners of a vector shape. Again, only an object in its basic form can be modified with this technique. Click the Arrow tool and then position it on an endpoint or corner of the vector shape (see Figure 3.17).

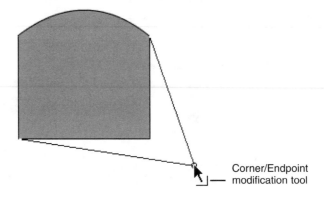

Corner/Endpoint modification tool

Figure 3.17   The mouse displays with a small line in the shape of a corner, indicating that an endpoint is being modified.

Through these two techniques of the Arrow tool, you can edit any vector shape directly on the Stage (see Figure 3.18). Throughout the remainder of this book, you will use the Arrow tool for both positioning and vector shape modification.

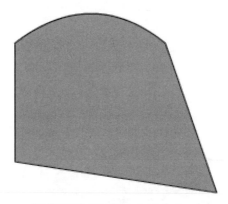

Figure 3.18   This vector shape has both a curve and an endpoint modified.

Tip

To add a new endpoint to an object, press the (Option)[Alt] key while you click and drag an object's line.

Note

You can also use the Subselect tool to modify an object. This tool displays all endpoints. Click and drag the endpoints, or use your Pen tool to access handles for reshaping the object.

Overview of Other Tools

As you work through this book, you will have an opportunity to work with many of the tools and modifiers. This seminar does not go into detail on all the other tools in the toolbox because you will learn how to use most of them as you work through the workshops in each seminar. Table 3.2 provides information on the other Flash tools and their modifier settings. Practice using the tools with various modifier settings.

Table 3.2   Tools and Options

Tool	Tool Name	Options Area Modifier Settings
	Subselect tool	No Option settings.
	Lasso tool	Magic Wand—Selects color areas of broken-apart bitmap graphics based on Magic Wand settings.
		Magic Wand Properties—Settings for selecting colors based on how close the colors are in their color values as well as whether they are next to each other in an image.
		Polygon Mode—Toggle button for selecting either by freehand or by a polygon shape.
	Pen tool	No Option settings.
	Text tool	No Option settings.
	Pencil tool	Pencil Mode—Sets a drawing mode for creating objects. There are three settings: Straighten, Smooth, and Ink.

continues

Table 3.2   Continued

Tool	Tool Name	Options Area Modifier Settings
	Brush tool	Brush Mode—Paints with different effects selecting one of the five menu choices.
		Brush Size—Sets the size of the brush.
		Brush Style—Sets the style of the brush.
		Lock Fill—Locks a gradient fill to flow across multiple objects on the Stage.
	Free Transform Tool	Rotate and Skew—Rotates and skews the selected object.
		Scale—Modifies an object's height and width.
		Distort—Distorts an object's shape.
		Envelope—Warps and distorts an object's shape. This modifier works only on objects that are in their basic forms. This modifier does not work on grouped shapes or symbols, or on bitmaps, sounds, gradients, text, or video objects.
	Fill Transform Tool	No Option settings.
	Ink Bottle tool	No Option settings.
	Paint Bucket tool	Gap Size—Offers three settings for gap size. If a hole or gap exists in the line of a shape, you can still fill the area based on the setting you select from the Gap Size menu.
		Lock Fill—Locks a gradient fill to flow across multiple objects on the Stage.
	Dropper tool	No modifier settings.

Tool	Tool Name	Options Area Modifier Settings
	Eraser tool	Eraser Mode—Erases with different effects selecting one of the five menu choices.
		Faucet—Pulls out fills or line colors with one click in the area.
		Eraser Size—Sets the size of the eraser.
	Hand tool	No modifier settings.
	Zoom tool	Enlarge—Increases magnification of the Stage by twice the current setting.
		Reduce—Decreases magnification of the Stage by one-half the current setting.

Tip

You can quickly change your magnification to 100%, no matter what magnification your are currently at, by double-clicking the Zoom tool in the toolbox.

Tip

After the Zoom tool is selected, you can toggle between zoom in and zoom out by pressing (Option)[Alt].

Using the Property Inspector and Panels

The Property Inspector and panels are used to gain additional functionality. The Property Inspector is a new feature of Flash MX, and it allows you to set attributes for objects on the Stage. The Property Inspector, panels, and tools work hand-in-hand with each other. For example, the Property Inspector can set stroke size, style, and color for both existing shapes or shapes that are to be created (see Figure 3.19).

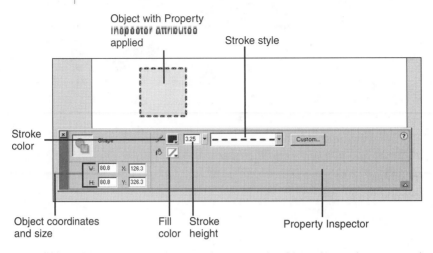

Figure 3.19   The Stroke preview provides a sample of how the attributes you select will look when applied to a stroke.

You will use the Property Inspector frequently in your Flash development. This seminar's workshop, as well as the remainder of the book, provides hands-on practice with this feature of Flash.

Tip

You can select multiple objects on your Stage by Shift-clicking them; you can then apply new attributes to them through the Property Inspector and panels. For instance, you can select both an oval shape and a rectangle shape and apply a common fill or line stroke to both shapes at the same time.

Warning

When using panels to modify an object's stroke or fill or to alter its shape, the object can't be grouped. It must be in the basic form of a stroke and a fill. To ungroup a grouped object, select the object and select Modify, Ungroup or Modify, Break Apart.

Macromedia Flash and Millions of Colors

Typically, Web development has focused on using a Web-safe color palette composed of the 216 Web-safe colors, which are created to appear the same in any browser or on any computer platform. For example, if a design calls for the integration of buttons or images on a background seamlessly, the designer will most likely use a Web-safe color in both elements; otherwise, the design might not appear as intended—depending on the end user's browser or computer platform.

Flash offers functionality for avoiding the Web-safe color issue because it enables you to create a Web site with all the elements contained on the Stage—your design is completely intact. The movie then is compressed as a SWF file. The Stage elements become one, integrated with all the functionality and interactivity in your movie. The need to match colors between images and areas is not an issue, unless you are integrating the SWF file into an HTML page. Then you would use a Web-safe color for the background color of the movie.

Flash has one color palette that is attached to each movie, and all the tools, color panels, and color modifiers use this palette for setting an object's stroke and fill. You can either use the Stroke and Fill modifier settings in the color area of the toolbox to set an object's stroke and fill, or you can use the Color Mixer, Color Swatches, and the Property Inspector (see Figure 3.20). All these features use the movie's color palette.

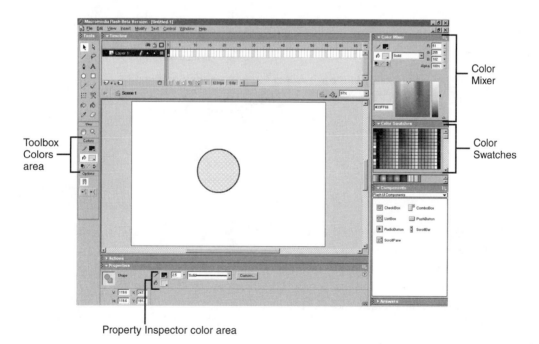

Figure 3.20 Selecting a Fill or Stroke color in a panel also displays the same selected color in the toolbox, and vice versa.

> **Tip**
>
> Flash also enables color swatches and entire color palettes from other applications to be imported into the movie, adding them to or replacing the movie's default color palette. This enables you to consistently use a color scheme no matter where you create the object or design, helping to maintain the design principle of consistency.

Colors can be applied to the stroke and fill of an existing object on your Stage, or set as an attribute for a tool prior to creating any objects. This enables you to easily modify your Stage content—you can create an object with its attributes preset or apply new attributes to existing shapes on the Stage.

Applying Color Through the Toolbox

The toolbox can be used to set color attributes for the tools. The toolbox Colors area contains the Stroke and Fill modifiers as seen in Figure 3.21.

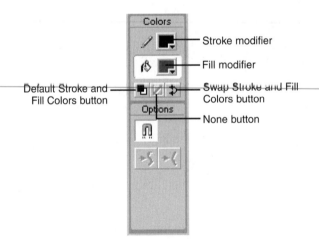

Figure 3.21   Click the Swap Color button to switch the Fill and Stroke colors.

To set a color for all tools that access or create strokes and fills, click the Fill or Stroke modifier on the toolbox and select a color from the palette (see Figure 3.22).

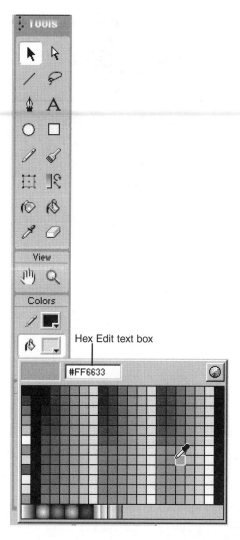

Figure 3.22   You can also type in a hexadecimal number in the Hex Edit text box to set a color.

You can designate a stroke and fill to not have any color by clicking the None button on the Colors area of the toolbox. You must first focus Flash on the Stroke or Fill modifier by clicking the Pencil icon or the Bucket icon to the left of these modifiers on the toolbox. Then click the None button at the bottom of the Colors area. A red line appears in the active modifier's box to indicate that no color is selected for that modifier (see Figure 3.23).

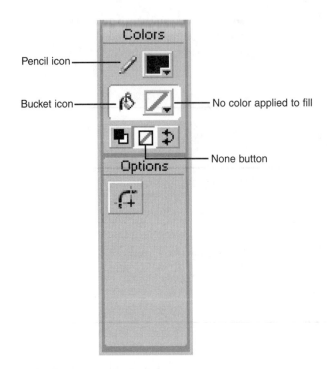

Pencil icon

Bucket icon

No color applied to fill

None button

Figure 3.23   The highlighted modifier is active, and any changes made to the color selection apply to that modifier only.

After these modifier settings are set, you can use a tool to create the object or modify an existing object.

Using Panels to Set Stroke and Fill Attributes

Two panels are used to work with color: the Color Mixer and Color Swatches. Both panels can be used to apply colors to strokes and fills. Each panel has its own special functionality and purpose when working with color in Flash.

The Color Mixer Panel

The Color Mixer uses the movie's color palette and takes these colors one step further: allowing an *alpha effect* to be applied to the color. An alpha effect is a way to apply a transparency value to a color. You can set your Fill or Stroke color by clicking the modifier and selecting a color from the color palette. To apply an alpha effect to a color, click the triangle next to the Alpha box and move the slider to a percentage value (see Figure 3.24).

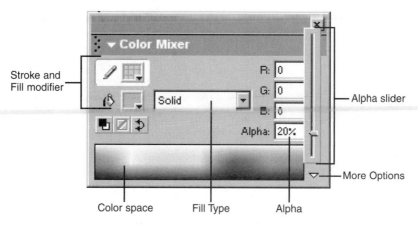

Figure 3.24 Notice that the Stroke modifier setting has a grid in the color, indicating that an alpha setting has been applied.

You also can click the More Options triangle to view a color bar of millions of colors as well as access the Hex Edit text box for setting hexadecimal color values (see Figure 3.25).

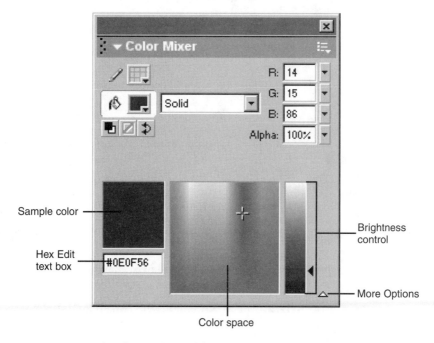

Figure 3.25 Notice that the Stroke modifier setting has a grid in the color, indicating that an alpha setting has been applied.

You will use the Color Mixer in this seminar's workshop as well as throughout the remainder of the book.

The Color Swatches Panel

Another panel for working with color is the Color Swatches. It displays the movie's color palette (see Figure 3.26).

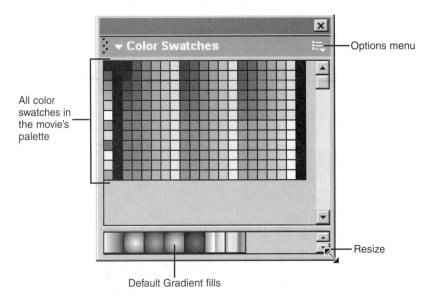

Figure 3.26   Use the scrollbar or resize the panel to view the entire palette.

Color swatches can be used in conjunction with all other color features to set the stroke and fill colors of an object. Click any of the color swatches that appear in this panel and it becomes the new color for either the Fill or Stroke modifier, depending on which one is selected in the other color features. Again, you will use these panels in this seminar's workshop, as well as throughout the remainder of the book.

Modifying the Movie Color Palette

When designing in Flash, you can create your movie working in a palette of your choice, whether that's a palette from another application or a custom palette you create in Flash. If you add a new color palette from another application, the palette is loaded using the Color Swatches panel.

To add or replace the default movie color palette, click the Options menu in the upper-right corner of the Color Swatches to display the Options menu. This menu lists your palette choices. By selecting Add Colors or Replace Colors, you can navigate to the palette you want to use and load it into your movie (see Figure 3.27). Based on your menu choice, the new palette is either added to the movie palette or replaces the default palette for developing your Stage content.

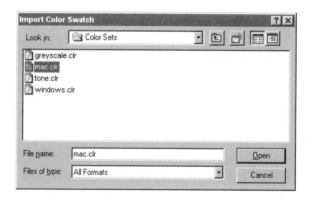

Figure 3.27   Color palettes end with the CLR extension.

To add just a custom color, use the Color Mixer to create a color swatch through the RGB values or the color space. Set your new color by typing in RGB values or by selecting a new color from the color space and setting the brightness of the new color. With a custom color created in the Color Mixer, you can add this color to the Color Swatches by clicking in the blank area below the color swatches. Your mouse becomes a Paint Bucket tool that adds the custom color as a swatch to the movie's palette (see Figure 3.28). These features enable you to use any application to create your movie design and objects, without having to worry about any color issues between applications.

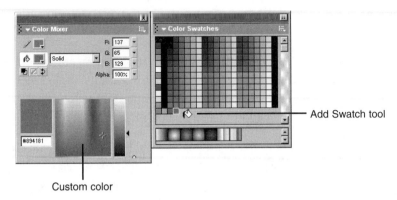

Custom color

Figure 3.28   You can add as many custom colors to the color palette as you need in your movie development.

Adding Gradient Fills

Another very powerful feature of Flash MX is a gradient fill. A *gradient fill* is a color swatch that progresses from one color to another, either in a linear flow or in a radial flow. As already mentioned, in the default movie palette are six preset gradient fills that can be applied to an object by selecting the color swatch.

As with other new colors, a new gradient fill can be created in the Color Mixer. The Fill Style menu provides you with the options of None, Solid, Linear, Radial, and Bitmap. When you select either Linear or Radial, the Gradient definition bar displays with gradient pointers that represent the color flow in the gradient (see Figure 3.29).

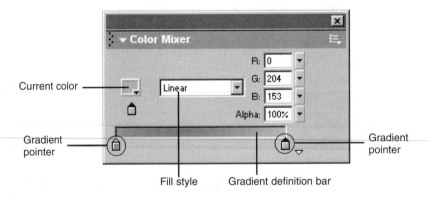

Figure 3.29   When Linear or Radial Gradient is selected, the Color Mixer displays the gradient features of Flash.

The Gradient pointers are used to set the colors to be displayed in the gradient. When you click a Gradient pointer, the Current color button is activated, enabling you to select a new color for that Gradient pointer. You can also add more pointers to the Gradient definition bar by clicking below the bar to add a pointer. Set a color for a new gradient pointer, and your gradient becomes more complex. Each pointer can be adjusted by dragging it left or right to show more or less of a color in the gradient color flow. A total of eight Gradient pointers can be added to define a gradient. In Seminar 5, "Importing Graphics into a Movie," you create and apply a custom gradient to an object.

> **Tip**
>
> To see a sample of a new gradient you are creating, click the More Options button on the Color Mixer to expand it to display the color sample.

> **Warning**
>
> If you are trying to fill an object with a gradient fill and it appears to be just one color, check whether the Lock Fill modifier is selected. The Lock Fill modifier causes Flash to fill the gradient across the Stage for many objects. Because you are working with just one object, the fill appears to be just one color.

Creating a Bitmap Fill

A bitmap fill can be applied to an image in the same way that a solid or gradient fill is applied: through the Color Mixer and the Fill style option. Any time you import a bitmap image into Flash, it is automatically added to the Bitmap menu in the Color Mixer as a selection (see Figure 3.30). You learn more about importing artwork in Seminar 5.

You can apply a bitmap fill to an existing object or set it as an attribute for a Fill modifier. In the Color Mixer, click the Fill Style option and select Bitmap; then select a Bitmap image swatch by clicking it. Next, apply the fill to an existing object or use a tool to create a new object (see Figure 3.31).

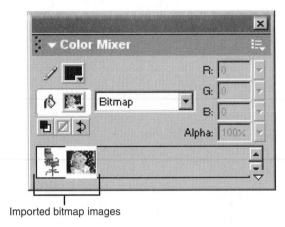

Imported bitmap images

Figure 3.30   This image was imported into Flash and now is a selection for a bitmap fill.

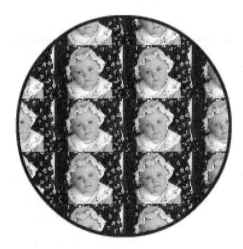

Figure 3.31   The bitmap image tiles the fill area of the object.

The tiling of the bitmap is not very attractive. The fill needs to be just one image. Using a new tool of Flash MX, the Fill Transform tool, this fill can be modified (see Figure 3.32).

Fill Transform tool

Figure 3.32   You can also modify a gradient fill with the Fill Transform tool.

Select the Fill Transform tool and click the object's fill; doing so makes handles appear around one of the tiled images (see Figure 3.33).

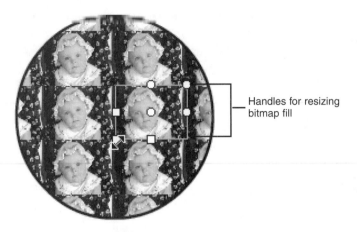

Figure 3.33   Adjust the fill by manipulating the handles.

To cause the bitmap image to display as you want, select the handles and drag to adjust the fill display (see Figure 3.34).

Figure 3.34   The image of the baby is centered in the circle by adjusting the bitmap fill.

The Power of Text

If you browse the Web looking at different sites, you are sure to notice how effective text is for communicating a message. Not only does it state the message, but you can enhance the text by making it larger or skewed. This helps to utilize the design concept of contrast in your Web design. When you begin to animate text, the message can be even more powerful. Many Flash designers use text with special effects to achieve very interesting sites that have a punch.

Three text types are available in Flash: Static Text, Dynamic Text, and Input Text. Each type has its own features for a movie's development. *Static* text is just that—static text on the page. It is used for informational purposes. *Dynamic* text is text that can change based on the ActionScript in a movie or user interaction—for example, an area that displays the name of an object on the Stage when the end-user clicks the object. In other words, it is a text block that displays information based on what is happening in the movie. *Input* text is used to collect data from the user. It is essentially form fields in your movie that allow the user to type in his information.

Features of Text in Macromedia Flash MX

Flash treats text similarly to other applications, such as QuarkXPress and Photoshop. A Text tool creates a text block for typing text, and the text block is editable, meaning at any time you can reaccess the text block and make edits to the text.

> **Tip**
>
> A text block can be rotated, scaled, or skewed. Even though you have altered it, it still retains its text features. Therefore, you can still edit and change the text in the altered text block.

Setting Text Attributes

To create text in Flash, you use a combination of the Text tool and the Property Inspector (see Figure 3.35).

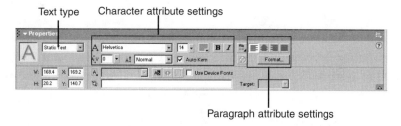

Figure 3.35   The Property Inspector allows you to edit text attributes of entire text blocks or individual words within a text block.

To set font attributes, select the Text tool prior to creating a text block and simply select the attribute setting that you want to apply. You can also apply new attributes to existing text blocks by selecting them to make them the active object on the Stage and then selecting the attribute settings you want. The existing text block reflects the new setting. More is covered on how to create and edit text blocks in the workshop section of this seminar.

> **Note**
>
> Seminar 8, "Using Components in a Macromedia Flash Form," covers in more detail the options for input text fields and how to create a form in your movie. Seminar 9, "Using Preloaders and Conditional Loops," covers in more detail the options for dynamic text fields.

Converting Text to a Vector Shape

Occasionally, when you are using text in Flash, you might need to convert existing text to a vector shape. To convert text to a vector shape, select the text block and select Modify, Break Apart (see Figure 3.36).

Figure 3.36   The text block is broken into individual letters, each in its own text block.

> **Tip**
>
> New to Flash MX is the capability to break a static text block into its individual letters, each in its own text block.

Then select the Modify, Break Apart command again, and each individual letter becomes a vector shape, with each letter being its own object (see Figure 3.37). Text converted to a graphic loses its original text attributes, so you can't edit the text or change the font, font size, and so on. The text is now a graphic with graphics attributes.

By converting text to a vector shape, you can get many special effects that can be applied only to vector shapes. For example, the fill area can be modified with a bitmap fill or gradient color, which you can't attain with typical text editing techniques. You also do not have to worry about what fonts the viewer might have on an end-user's machine. Because the text is a vector shape, it is not reliant on system or installed fonts for displaying.

Figure 3.37   Each letter is now its own object made up of a fill.

Tip

You also can embed a font into any of the three text types: static, dynamic and input. This allows the font to always accurately display in any end-user's browser for that text block or field. See Seminar 8 for more information on embedding fonts.

Warning

When you convert a static text block to a vector shape, you can't edit the text as text. This also increases your file size. Only resort to this technique if you can't attain the end result through text-editing techniques.

Creating and Using Layers

As Seminar 2 pointed out, layers are a feature of Flash that enable you to easily work with many Stage objects simultaneously. Layers can be viewed as a transparency or sheet of acetone. By positioning objects on that layer, the vector shapes do not merge with other vector shapes. Through the various layer features, such as hiding and showing layers or folder layers, you can control exactly which objects you want visible on the Stage, allowing you to focus only on these objects.

Layers are invaluable in Flash development. To use them, you must understand the basic layer features and editing techniques. You can add new layers by clicking the Insert Layer button (see Figure 3.38).

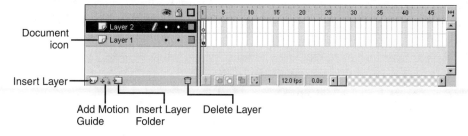

Figure 3.38   You can delete an active layer by clicking the Delete Layer button.

You can easily name a layer to a custom name of your choice by double-clicking the layer name and typing the new name in the editable text box that displays (see Figure 3.39).

Editable text box

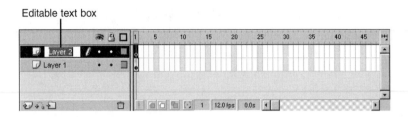

Figure 3.39   You can name a layer any name you want. There are no restrictions on what characters can be used in a layer name.

You also can reorganize the layer stacking order by clicking and dragging an existing layer to a new location in the stacking order (see Figure 3.40).

Horizontal line

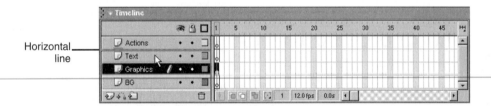

Figure 3.40   The horizontal line indicates the new position of the layer in the stacking order.

Tip ─────────────────────────────────────

If you create a folder layer, you can drag existing layers into the folder layer for grouping and organizing the layers.

You will create layers; rename layers; and use the various layer features of showing or hiding, locking or unlocking, and viewing as an outline in the following workshop and throughout the remainder of the book.

Note ─────────────────────────────────────

Another new feature of Flash MX is the Distribute to Layers feature, accessible by selecting Modify, Distribute to Layers. This new feature is used to distribute multiple objects that exist on one layer, each to its own layer. Flash automatically creates the required layers for holding each object, but generically names each layer—Layer 1, Layer 2, and so on. You will need to rename these new layers to better identify the Stage content that each holds.

Creating the Opening Scene of the Site

Because the project in this book is presented to many people of various skill levels, the book instructs on creating objects that are simple in their shapes and creation processes. Of course, when you develop other movies, you will want to use your skills and talents to the fullest by creating art and illustrations in your own style. The goal of this seminar, as well as the book, is to provide the Flash skills necessary to understand and use the tools and features of Flash MX and to use these skills for your own design purpose.

With your Stage and movie properties set, your guides positioned, and your guide layer set, you are now ready to create the site design of The Honeycomb site. In Seminar 2, you imported a JPG image to use on a guide layer as a template for the site design. You will use this template to begin building The Honeycomb site's design.

As the design template indicates, the background of the site is composed of rectangular headers and footers and a menu bar with buttons. The design principles of alignment, proximity, and consistency are followed to create this design. Center alignment is used for the menu bar and buttons. The buttons are grouped together on the menu bar area, creating proximity that allows the end-users one area for accessing the site buttons. Consistency and contrast are obtained in the site design due to the repetition of the colors used for the various areas of the design (see Figure 3.41).

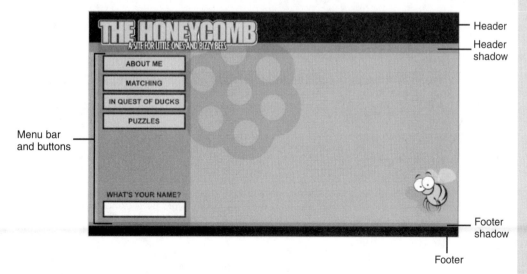

Figure 3.41   To accept the new layer name, click in a blank area of the Stage or press Enter.

Developing the Movie Layers

You must create layers for each of the background images so that each shape exists on its own layer. Display or open the Property Inspector and Color Mixer by choosing them from the Window, Panels menu. Follow these steps to create the background of The Honeycomb site:

1. Use the Honeycomb.fla file you saved at the end of Seminar 2, or open the 02Honeycomb.fla from the Seminar02/Samples directory on the CD-ROM that accompanies this book.

2. Click Layer 1 and rename the layer by double-clicking the layer name and typing menu. This will be the layer for the site menu (see Figure 3.42).

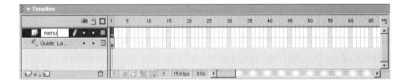

Figure 3.42   To accept the new layer name, click in a blank area of the Stage or press Enter.

3. With the menu layer active, click the Insert Layer button on the Timeline to insert a new layer. Rename this layer user login.

4. Repeat this process to create the layers as shown in Figure 3.43. Create the layers in the same stacking order indicated in Figure 3.43.

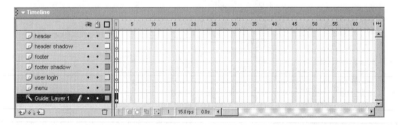

Figure 3.43   You can rearrange the stacking order of these layers by clicking and dragging a layer to a new location.

Tip
To enable viewing of all layers, expand the Timeline by clicking and dragging its bottom border.

Tip

If you create a layer that is in the wrong position in the layer stacking order, either delete the layer and create it in the correct position or reposition the layer by clicking and dragging it to a new location in the stacking order.

5. Rename Guide: Layer 1 to Guide: Design Template.

6. Next, create a folder layer to group the header, header shadow, footer, and footer shadow layers. Click the header layer to make it active, and then click the Insert Folder Layer button to create a folder layer (see Figure 3.44).

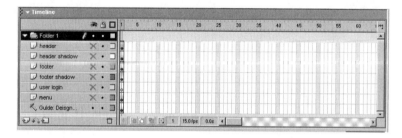

Figure 3.44   The folder layer is inserted above the active header layer.

7. Rename the Folder 1 layer Background Objects.

8. Click the header layer to make it active, and then Shift-click the footer shadow layer to select all the layers from header to footer shadow. Click and drag the highlighted group of layers on top of the Background Objects folder. This causes these four layers to go inside the folder layer (see Figure 3.45).

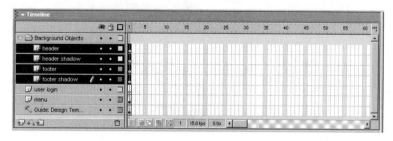

Figure 3.45   You can collapse and expand the folder layer to enable control and access of the four layers that hold the background design elements.

Tip

Throughout the workshop sections of each seminar in this book, you should save your projects often using naming conventions that support the progression of The Honeycomb site.
For instance, you might want to save the site at this point in its development as
03Honeycomb1.fla, indicating that it is the Seminar 3 workshop, first topic. The workshop
instruction does not include this type of saving instruction because most people have their
own conventions and processes for saving their work.

Creating Stage Objects for Site Design

With your layers created for holding the site design, you can now begin to create the
actual Stage content for each of these layers. Always make sure you are on the correct layer before you begin to create your Stage content. To create the site design
using the Design Template as a guide, follow these steps:

1. Select the Rectangle tool from the toolbox and click the footer shadow layer
   to make it active.

2. Access the Color Mixer and click the None button to set the Stroke focus to
   no color.

3. Set the Fill color to black by clicking the Fill modifier and then clicking the
   black color swatch in the upper-left corner of the color palette.

4. Click the Alpha box and type 25. Your Color Mixer settings should look like
   Figure 3.46.

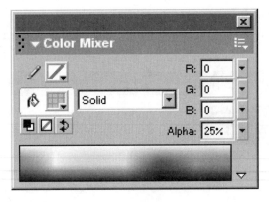

Figure 3.46   The Fill color swatch displays a grid pattern to indicate that an Alpha
Effect has been applied to the Fill color.

5. Using the guide layer image as a template, click and drag a rectangle from the
   left edge of the Stage to the right at the bottom of your Stage at the location
   of the footer shadow (see Figure 3.47).

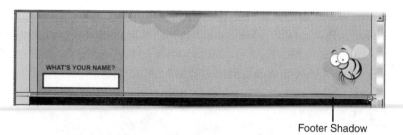

Footer Shadow

Figure 3.47 The horizontal guides cause the mouse to adhere as you drag the rectangle.

6. Click the header shadow layer to make it active.

7. With the Rectangle tool and the same Color Mixer panel settings, click and drag a second rectangle that follows the template design for the rectangle at the top of the Stage.

8. To create the header object, click the toolbox Fill modifier and select the black color swatch from the color palette. Be sure the Stroke modifier is set to None.

9. Click the header layer to make it active, and again drag a rectangle that follows the guide for the black rectangle at the top of the Stage.

10. Click the Arrow tool and select the rectangle you just created for the header layer. Instead of creating a fourth rectangle for the footer, just copy this rectangle by choosing Edit, Copy.

11. Click the footer layer and paste the rectangle by choosing Edit, Paste. Click and drag from the lower-right corner of the rectangle and move it to the bottom of the screen. This causes a circle to display in the lower-right corner as you drag, and it easily adheres to the guides (see Figure 3.48).

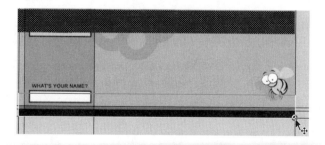

Figure 3.48 When an object is dragged from its edges or corners, a small circle appears when the object adheres to a guide or another object.

12. To resize this footer bar to match the design template, click the Free
Transform tool and then click the footer bar to display handles around the
footer rectangle. Click the top middle handle and resize the rectangle so that
it follows the guide layer image (see Figure 3.49).

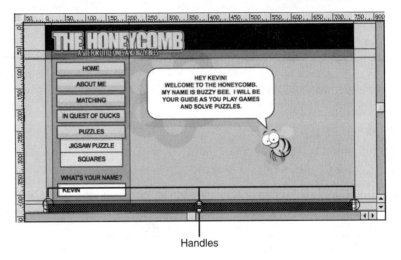

Handles

Figure 3.49   If you adjust a corner handle, you will resize the entire rectangle in both
height and width.

> **Note**
>
> To understand the tools and features of Flash, this seminar covers the creation of the tem-
> plate design objects, but this is not the most efficient way to create this design. In Seminar
> 4, you create a rectangular symbol and use instances of this symbol to replace all these
> objects.

Creating the Menu Bar

This site uses the design principle of alignment. Through a combination of tools, the
Property Inspector, and panels, next you'll create the menu bar for the buttons that
link to the activities of The Honeycomb site:

1. Click the menu layer to make it active.

2. Click the Rectangle tool to select it. Access your Color Mixer and set the
Stroke modifier to None and the Fill modifier to Black with an Alpha Effect
of 20% (see Figure 3.50).

Figure 3.50   You can click the Alpha box and type 20, or you can click the triangle next to Alpha and adjust the slider for 20%.

3. Click and drag a rectangle for the menu bar that extends from the top of the Stage to the bottom and adheres to the vertical guides that designate this area (see Figure 3.51).

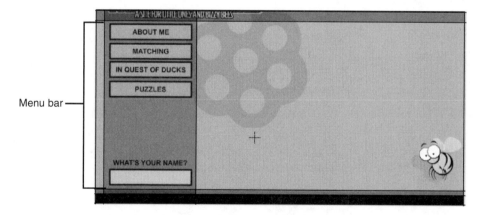

Figure 3.51   You can resize the menu bar by using the Free Transform tool and dragging the menu bar handles.

4. With the Arrow tool, double-click the menu bar to make it active and group it by choosing Modify, Group. Grouping the menu bar keeps other objects from merging with it, such as the buttons that will be placed on it in the next topic.

Tip

You can quickly switch to the Arrow tool from any tool by pressing the (Command)[Ctrl] key. The Arrow tool is activated for however long you hold the (Command)[Ctrl] key.

Creating the About Me Button

With the menu bar area defined, now you will create the About Me button. Instead of creating all five buttons, you will create just one button and create only the key components of the About Me button—its image and the label. To create the About Me button, follow these steps:

1. Using the Zoom tool, increase the Stage view of the About Me button displayed on the design template guide layer image.

Tip

You can quickly change your magnification to 100% no matter what magnification you are at by double-clicking the Zoom tool in the toolbox.

Tip

After the Zoom tool is selected, you can toggle between zoom in and zoom out by pressing (Option)[Alt].

2. Click the Rectangle tool to make it active.

3. In the Property Inspector, click the Stroke Style and select Solid. Click the Stroke Size box and delete its contents; then type 2. Click the Stroke Color modifier and select the black color swatch (see Figure 3.52).

Figure 3.52   The Property Inspector indicates the tool that is active on the left.

4. In the Color Mixer, click the Fill modifier and type FFCE31 in the Hex Edit Text box. This sets your fill to a gold color.

5. With the Rectangle tool, click and drag a rectangle that covers the area for the About Me button as displayed on the design template.

6. Group the button image by double-clicking it with the Arrow tool and selecting Modify, Group. This makes the stroke and fill of the rectangle one object. The background for the button is now created.

Note

Seminar 4 covers another technique for creating and developing the button and the menu bar in full detail. You will use the About Me button you create in this workshop and develop it further in the next workshop.

Creating the Button Labels

Next, you create the About Me label for the button. This requires the Text tool and the Property Inspector. To create the button label, follow these steps:

1. Select the menu layer if it is not active.

2. Select the Text tool in the toolbox.

3. In the Property Inspector, click the triangle to the right of Font and select Arial. Click the Font Size box and type 14. Select Bold and Auto Kern; then click the Font Color option and select the black color swatch from the palette. Select the Center Justification option (see Figure 3.53).

Figure 3.53 For the Font Size, you could also click the triangle next to the Font Size option and adjust the slider to 14.

Tip

You also can type a font name into the Font box of the Property Inspector instead of selecting it from the Font list.

Note

Auto Kern is a feature that controls the space between pairs of letters so that they are spaced evenly apart. Due to many letters such as A or W requiring different spacing, many fonts have built-in kerning space for each letter. If you turn on the Auto Kern option in the Property Inspector, the built-in spacing is applied to the text you create.

4. Click to set a text block on the Stage and type ABOUT ME using uppercase characters (see Figure 3.54).

Figure 3.54 Don't worry about exact placement of the text label; you'll align the two objects next.

Tip ———

You can change individual words in a text block by selecting your Text tool and then clicking inside the text block containing the word or words you want to change. This sets your cursor in the text block. Using traditional word processing techniques, highlight the word or words to be changed and select the new font attribute option settings you want.

Using the Align Panel

The Align panel enables you to get precise alignment for your Stage objects. Follow these steps to align the label with the button shape:

1. Click the Arrow tool and click the text block.
2. Press and hold the Shift key, and click the grouped button object. This selects both the text block and the button objects.
3. Click the Align panel to make it active. Click the Align Vertical Center and Align Horizontal Center options (see Figure 3.55).
4. With the two objects selected, group them. The About Me button becomes easily accessible as one object.
5. Hide the Guide: Design Template layer by clicking the dot in the Show/Hide All Layers icon. This enables you to view the objects you have created for The Honeycomb Site opening scene (see Figure 3.56).

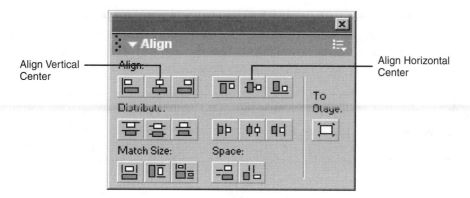

Align Vertical Center

Align Horizontal Center

Figure 3.55   The ABOUT ME label is centered precisely in the grouped button object.

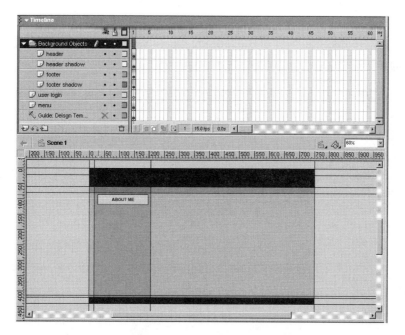

Figure 3.56   You have the basics of your site design developed at this point. All but the user login layer have Stage objects.

6. Single-click the layer name for the header layer (double-clicking the layer name accesses the Edit text box), and notice that the header rectangular object highlights on the Stage. This lets you see which objects are contained on a layer. Repeat this with the other layers to double-check that you have only one object—and the correct object—for each of these layers: header, header shadow, footer, and menu.

7. Save the movie as Honeycomb.fla. If you would like to compare your Honeycomb site with a movie that is completed up to this point in the book, open the `03Honeycomb.fla` file located in the `Seminar03/Samples` directory on the CD-ROM that accompanies this book.

Seminar Summary

This seminar covered a lot of information. You had a short review on the design principles that are important to follow to create a pleasing design. You learned about layers, how to create them and delete them, how to rename them, and how to work with them. Then, the seminar covered creating and working with objects in Flash through the various tools, panels, and features. In the workshop, you used these tools, panels, and features in conjunction with each other to create the basic design of the Honeycomb site. Not all the tools or panels were covered, but the following seminars cover many of these features in detail.

Color and the movie's color palette were also discussed in this seminar. Many of the techniques for applying stroke and fill colors were covered, as well as how to create your own custom colors. You also learned how to import a palette into Flash.

The Text tool was covered, and you applied many of these features to your workshop project by developing a simplified About Me button. You are now ready to begin using the power of Flash in Seminar 4.

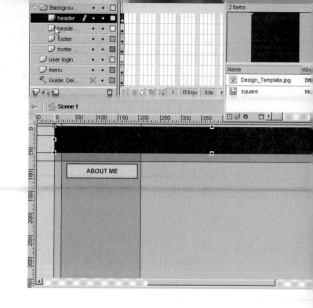

Seminar 4

Using Symbols in a Movie

In this chapter

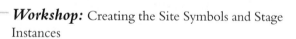

Workshop: Creating the Site Symbols and Stage Instances

What's So Important About Symbols and Instances?

To use Macromedia Flash MX to its fullest extent, you have to use symbols and instances of those symbols in your movie's development. This seminar introduces symbols and how to create instances for your movie's content. Symbols are your first challenge in Flash. If you use them effectively, your movie will be more interactive and rich, ensuring the end-user a very intuitive and fun Internet experience.

Much of the power of Macromedia Flash MX comes from the use of symbols. A *symbol* is a reusable object in Flash MX. It can be any graphic, picture file, sound file, button, video clip, or movie clip that you create or import into your movie. Each symbol is a complete description of the item, which includes its size, shape, color, and behavior. When you place a symbol on the Stage, an instance of the symbol is created. You can use as many instances of a symbol in your movie as you need. When the Flash MX file is viewed in a browser, the symbol is downloaded to the browser just once and is reused many times as the Flash MX movie plays. This reduces the file size of the SWF file when the movie is exported.

When you create the symbols to be used in your movie, they are stored in the movie's library (see Figure 4.1).

Typical of a public library, the Flash MX library can hold many symbols and can have these symbols grouped in folders to create common classifications for easy access. Open a movie's library by selecting Window, Library.

> **Tip** ───
>
> Any time you plan to use a movie object more than one time, you should convert it to a symbol.

You also can open libraries from other Macromedia Flash MX movies and use symbols from them. Just as every movie has one color palette, every movie has just one library. When you use a symbol from another movie's library, that symbol automatically becomes a symbol in your movie's library. Thus, it becomes an *asset* of your movie.

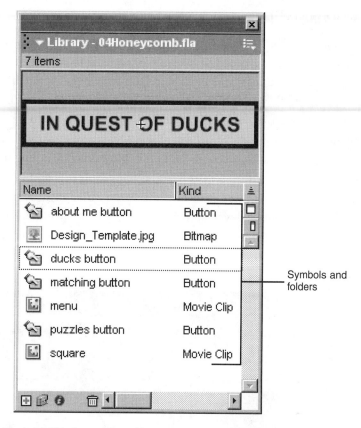

Figure 4.1   Each Flash MX file has its own library, which is basically an area for grouping and storing symbols for use in a movie, accessible at any time.

Recycling Objects: The Power of Macromedia Flash MX

After a symbol is created, it can be used in the movie as an instance. An *instance* is really just a copy of the symbol that points to the original symbol. This causes every instance to be very small in memory because it's a reference or pointer to the symbol that contains all the information on the item's composition. You can use instances as many times as you need to in a movie, which results in very efficient memory usage because the instance is just an occurrence of the original symbol.

Note ────────────────────────────────

You can modify an instance in its size, color, brightness, and alpha setting. These modifications do not change the linked symbol—just the instance.

Symbol and Instance Basics

To understand this concept of symbols and instances, let's look at a basic shape, such as a square. Rectangles and squares are often used in a Web site design for background images, buttons, and menu bars. Relating this to a symbol, if you make a rectangular symbol, you can then reuse this symbol by creating instances of it on your Stage. Every time you place an instance of it on the Stage, you are really just placing a pointer to the symbol. Remember: Flash MX is a vector-based application; therefore, Stage objects are translated into a mathematical formula. The instance is a pointer, which means it's a mathematical translation of x and y coordinates on the Stage that calls the symbol. Instances can be modified in their sizes, locations, and color compositions. So, even though you have a black square symbol, the instance of the symbol can be modified to any color rectangular shape. Figure 4.2 shows an example of using a square symbol in a Web site design.

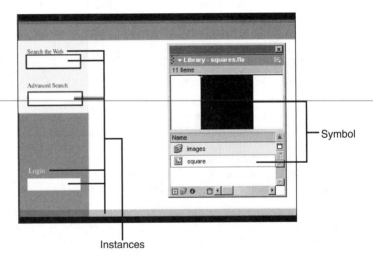

Figure 4.2   Each rectangle seen on the Stage in this figure is simply a modified instance of the square from the movie's library.

To add an instance of a symbol to your Stage, you simply click and drag the symbol from the Library onto the Stage. An instance of the symbol appears, which you can then position in the location that you want on the Stage. By doing so, you create a new instance of this symbol, which is linked to the symbol in the library. Therefore, if you change this library symbol, the linked instance also changes.

Note

If you edit a symbol and change any of its attributes, all instances of the symbol will reflect the new attributes but will maintain any modifications that you might have made to the instance. You will learn more about modifying instances later in this seminar.

Using Symbols in Macromedia Flash MX

As you begin to create a movie, you should think about symbols and how they can be used in your movie. This is your challenge as a Flash developer—what symbols to create and how to use the instances of these symbols most effectively and efficiently in your movie. How you get your artwork into Flash is up to you, but to use the power of Flash, you need to convert these items into symbols.

Converting Existing Artwork into Symbols

Typically, as you develop a Flash movie, you convert existing Stage objects into symbols. You create an object for the movie and immediately convert it to a symbol. Converting existing artwork that you have on your Stage into symbols is easy. Just follow these steps:

1. Select any object by clicking it with the Arrow tool; it becomes the active item on your Stage. Then select Insert, Convert to Symbol.

2. In the Convert to Symbol dialog box that displays, type a name for the symbol in the Name box. Then select a behavior for the symbol (see Figure 4.3).

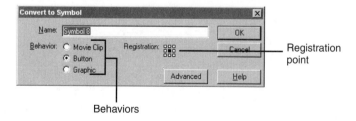

Behaviors

Figure 4.3   Name a symbol something that makes sense and describes the symbol.

3. Click OK to close the dialog box. The object is converted into a symbol, and the Stage displays an instance of this symbol. The symbol also appears in the library window (see Figure 4.4).

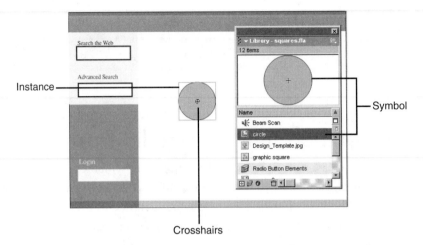

Figure 4.4   You can identify certain instances on the Stage by the crosshairs that appear in the center of the symbol.

<hr />

Note ────────────────────────────────

When you create a symbol, you don't need to group your objects. When you use an instance of this symbol, it is automatically grouped as a symbol.

<hr />

Tip ────────────────────────────────

You can also press the F8 keyboard shortcut to convert a selected object to a symbol.

<hr />

Warning ────────────────────────────────

If you have set your function keys to handle global actions on your computer, the assigned function keys for Flash MX functionality might not work.

Exploring Symbol Behavior

When you create a symbol, you can designate three symbol behaviors: Movie Clip, Button, and Graphic. Each symbol behavior has its own functionality in a Flash movie:

- **Movie Clip**—This symbol behavior is used to create reusable animation that will play independently from the Flash movie Timeline. A *movie clip* symbol can be compared to a mini-movie that is animated according to its own Timeline within the main movie. Movie clip symbols can contain sound, interactivity, and other movie clip instances. Movie clip instances can be part of a button so that the button is animated, too.

- **Button**—This symbol behavior is used for interactive buttons in a movie. A button symbol responds to regular mouse events such as clicking or *rollovers* (when the user moves the mouse cursor over a button instance but does not click it). When you create a button symbol, you can create images of the three button states for the symbol: Up, Over, and Down. You learn more about button symbols and button states in Seminar 7, "Site Interactivity and Button Functionality."

- **Graphic**—This symbol behavior is used for static images or animation that is fixed to the movie Timeline. This means that the animation plays in conjunction with the Timeline progression. This type of symbol can't be controlled by ActionScript.

> **Note**
>
> Imagine the power and low file size of a movie clip symbol that is placed inside another movie clip or a button symbol. Instead of duplicating file size for repeated use of the movie clip, you are pointing to an already defined movie clip within the new movie clip or button symbol. This is referred to as *nesting* symbols inside other symbols.

Creating a Symbol from Scratch

You don't always need to convert existing objects on the Stage into symbols. Flash MX also allows you to create a symbol from scratch.

To create a symbol from scratch, you must activate another mode of Flash MX: the Symbol-Editing Mode. Similar to Group Mode, this mode enables you to create objects using Flash MX tools. To activate the Symbol-Editing Mode to create a new symbol, select Insert, New Symbol. The Symbol Properties dialog box appears. Type a name for the symbol in the Name box and set the behavior. Click OK, and a new window displays (see Figure 4.5).

Now that you've switched to Symbol-Editing Mode, notice that the screen is slightly different from the typical Flash MX screen. Two tabs are present in the upper-left corner—Scene 1 and the new symbol name. The library holds the new symbol, and the library Preview window is blank. Now you can create a new symbol by using the drawing tools or importing existing graphics into the Symbol-Editing Mode.

Based on the behavior you assign to a symbol, the Timeline reflects a different look for creating the functionality you need for that symbol. If the symbol has a Button behavior, the Timeline reflects the button states for the symbol (see Figure 4.6).

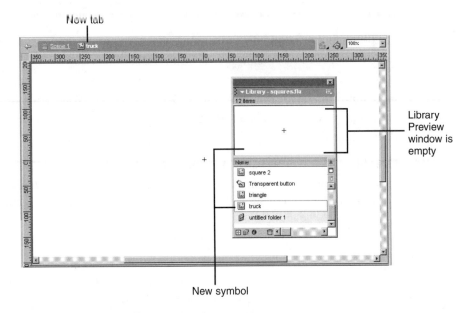

Figure 4.5   In the empty window of this Symbol-Editing Mode, you can create a symbol without having other images or symbols distract your design process.

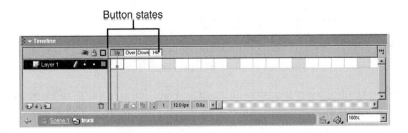

Figure 4.6   You can create as many layers as you need when creating buttons.

When a symbol has a Movie Clip or Graphics behavior, it has its own Timeline in the Symbol-Editing Mode (see Figure 4.7). Both the movie clip or graphics symbol can also be created using as many layers as you need. The difference between the two is their Timelines. The Timeline of a graphics symbol adheres and runs in sync with the movie's Timeline. In contrast, a movie clip symbol's Timeline is independent of the movie's Timeline.

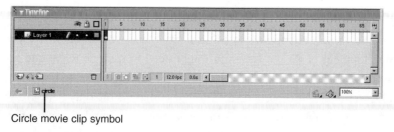

Circle movie clip symbol

Figure 4.7   You can also create folder layers for grouping other layers in a movie clip or graphic symbol.

After you create a symbol in the Symbol-Editing Mode, you must exit this mode and return to your movie window. Select Edit, Edit Document or click the Scene 1 tab in the upper-left corner of the symbol-editing window. Either method returns you to your movie. The library contains your new symbol, and you can now access this symbol to create instances of it in your movie.

> **Tip**
>
> You can also click the Back button that is located above the Stage area on the left. This button is similar in functionality to the Back button on most browsers.

Changing a Symbol's Behavior

You can change the symbol behavior for any existing symbol, such as changing a graphics symbol to a button or movie clip symbol. You can change a symbol's behavior by doing the following:

1. Select the symbol in the library to be modified.

2. (Control-click)[Right-click] the symbol in the library to access the shortcut menu, select Behavior, and select the new behavior from the menu list.

> **Warning**
>
> When you change a symbol's behavior, all instances of the symbol that were previously created from the symbol maintain the first applied behavior. For instance, if you create a symbol with a Graphic behavior and then place three instances of this symbol on the Stage, when you change this symbol's behavior to a Movie Clip behavior, all three instances still maintain the Graphic behavior. You will learn about changing an instance's behavior in the section "Changing the Behavior of an Instance," later in this seminar.

Editing a Symbol

You can use various techniques to edit a symbol, and—based on where you are in your development of the movie—you might need to use one technique instead of another to perform the edit. For instance, if you need to make several changes to a symbol, you might want to isolate the symbol so that it's the only item in a window. Other times, you might want to make a quick change to a symbol and see the change in relation to other objects on your Stage. You would perform this edit to your symbol directly on the Stage. The following techniques activate the Symbol-Editing Mode:

- Double-click the icon next to the symbol in the library.

- Double-click the symbol image in the Preview window.

- Double-click the instance of the symbol on the Stage.

- Select the symbol on the Stage and select Edit, Edit Symbols.

- Select the symbol on the Stage and press (Command-E)[Ctrl+E].

Your symbol displays in the Symbol-Editing Mode, and you can edit the symbol's composition using the Flash MX tools, Property Inspector, or panels. After you edit a symbol, any instances of the symbol that you have used in your movie are updated with the new features or modifications. Remember: An instance is just a pointer or reference to the symbol and, therefore, reflects any new changes that are added to the symbol.

> **Tip**
>
> To exit the Symbol-Editing Mode and return to the movie, click the Scene 1 tab in the upper-left corner of the Stage or press the Back arrow.

Setting a Symbol's Reference Point

The Symbol-Editing Mode has its own Stage and rulers that are relative to the symbol. When you first create a new symbol, by default, the registration point is set for the center of the symbol and is represented by crosshairs on the Stage of the Symbol-Editing Mode (see Figure 4.8).

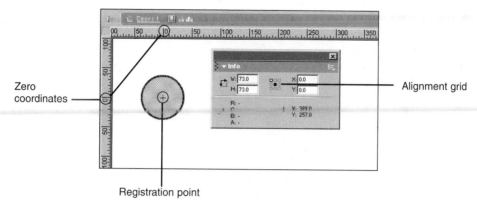

Figure 4.8   In this figure, the Info panel reflects the x, y coordinate of the symbol's registration point.

You have a choice of a center or any of the out-edge locations for the registration point of a symbol. Setting the registration point for your symbol sets a point of control for interactivity. The Info panel is used to work with an object's coordinates. All objects reside within a rectangular bounding box. Many times you will want to set a symbol's registration point to be its upper-left corner and then align the symbol so that its zero coordinates are the upper-left corner (see Figure 4.9).

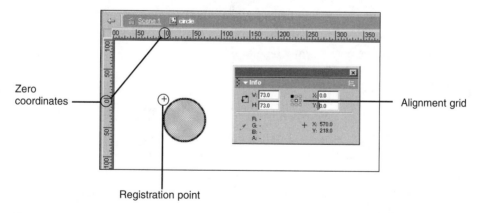

Figure 4.9   Setting your geometric symbols to have an upper-left corner registration point can be useful for attaining precision in your site design.

> **Tip**
>
> If a symbol has a center registration point, when the object is resized, it resizes from all sides. The object expands or contracts from the center point. If an object has an upper-left corner registration point, the object resizes from that corner, which can be easier to work with when designing with precision.

Editing a Symbol on the Stage

Another useful symbol-editing technique is to use the Edit in Place command. This command enables you to edit a symbol on the Stage in relation to all the other items on the Stage. To activate this command, select the instance of the symbol you want to edit on the Stage and (Control-click)[right-click] to access the shortcut menu. Then select the Edit in Place command.

> **Tip**
>
> You can also double-click an instance on the Stage to launch the Edit in Place command.

Using the Edit in Place command takes you to Symbol-Editing Mode for the symbol of this instance. The Stage dims, and only the symbol is accessible. Two tabs appear in the upper-left corner of the Flash window to indicate that you have switched to the Symbol-Editing Mode. Editing a symbol in relation to other objects on your Stage is very helpful for maintaining proportion and relationships with other Stage objects. After you've made the necessary changes to the symbol, select Edit, Edit Document to exit the Symbol-Editing Mode.

Altering Instance Properties

So far, this seminar has focused on symbols, which are only one half of the equation for the power of Flash MX. The other half is the *instances*, which are created by dragging a symbol from the library and positioning it on the Stage. You can have as many instances of a symbol as you want for developing your movie. To allow for variety in your use of instances, certain attributes of each instance can be altered. You can change the color effects applied to it, alter the shape by skewing it, or change the size and rotation of the instance. You can also change the color or tint of an instance. Finally, you can change the assigned symbol linked to an instance. This flexibility gives you the control you need to develop your movie and easily make changes and edits when you need to achieve a certain effect.

Changing the Size and Orientation of an Instance

You can change the size and orientation of any instance. This allows for variety and creativity in your movie objects and design, so your instances won't all be the same size or in the same position. Always select the instance first and then access or open your Transform panel (see Figure 4.10).

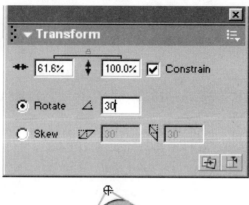

Figure 4.10 The Transform panel enables you to change any instance to a precise size and rotation.

Set your size or the skew percentage, or set the rotation degrees in the panel; the selected instances will then reflect these new modifications.

Tip ———————————————————————————————

You can also precisely rotate any instance by selecting Modify, Transform, Scale and Rotate or Rotate and Skew, and entering exact numbers or degrees in the dialog box. This method also produces a very precise and uniform result when altering any instance or graphic on the Stage.

Note ———————————————————————————————

The Free Transform tool in the toolbox can be used to scale or rotate an instance. But this tool is not as precise because you must eyeball the transform as you scale and rotate the graphic.

Applying Color Effects to an Instance

You can change the color effects of an instance through the Property Inspector. Always select the instance that you want to modify first; the Property Inspector reflects the different attributes that can be applied to the instance (see Figure 4.11).

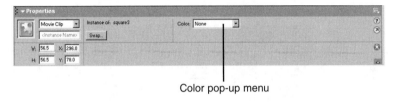

Color pop-up menu

Figure 4.11   By selecting the Color pop-up menu, you can change the brightness, tint, or alpha of an instance.

Select the color effect to apply to the instance. The following list describes each of the menu choices for applying new color effects for an instance:

- **Brightness**—Adjusts the brightness of the instance by adding white or black to the instance. You can type a percentage for brightness, or you can adjust the slider to set the brightness.

- **Tint**—Adjusts the overall color balance of the instance (see Figure 4.12). Click the Tint Color button and select a new color. You can also create a custom color through the Tint amount and RGB settings or by selecting a new color from the color bar.

Tint Color palette

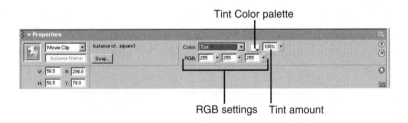

RGB settings   Tint amount

Figure 4.12   You can also use traditional RGB values to create a new tint color.

- **Alpha**—Adjusts the transparency of the image allowing other Stage objects to be viewed behind the instance with the applied alpha effect (see Figure 4.13). You can compare this to a color transparency you overlay on top of an image. In the Alpha box, enter a percentage to change the transparency applied to the instance.

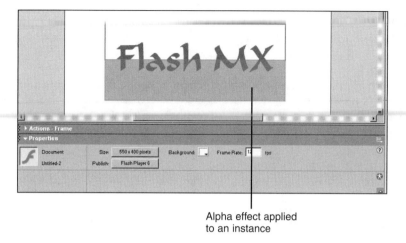

Alpha effect applied
to an instance

Figure 4.13   In this figure, the bottom rectangle instance has a 50% alpha effect applied and allows the lower half of the Flash MX to display even though the instance is positioned on top of the text.

- **Advanced**—Controls the brightness, alpha, and tint of an instance. To access this option, select Advanced from the Color pop-up menu and click the Settings button (see Figure 4.14). This option enables you to access all settings in one panel. The settings on the left reduce the tint and the alpha values by a specified percentage, whereas the settings on the right either reduce or increase the tint and the alpha values by a constant value. The current values are multiplied by the numbers on the left and then added to the values on the right.

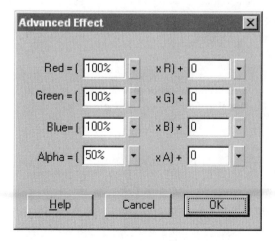

Figure 4.14   You can adjust all three color effects for an instance either by typing the new setting in the input box or by adjusting the associated slider.

Note

When applying a color effect to an instance, you can apply only one effect at a time. For example, if you apply a brightness effect to an instance and then decide to apply an alpha effect, too, the instance returns to its original composition when you select Alpha from the Color pop-up menu. If you want to apply more than one color effect to an instance, you must use the Advanced menu choice. The Advanced option enables you to apply all three effects—Brightness, Tint, and Alpha—to an instance simultaneously.

Tip

If you select multiple instances on the Stage, you can apply the same color effect to all the instances simultaneously.

Changing the Behavior of an Instance

When you create a symbol, you set a behavior for it. Even though all instances are pointers to this symbol, you can change the behavior of an instance by using the Property Inspector (see Figure 4.15). This process is different from changing a symbol's behavior because you are changing the instance's behavior, which does not affect the original symbol's behavior. First, you must select the instance on the Stage for which you want to change the behavior. In the Property Inspector, click the Behavior menu and select the new behavior from the list.

Figure 4.15   You can also name an instance with a Movie Clip or Button behavior in the Property Inspector. Naming an instance is beneficial for calling the instance in ActionScript code.

Breaking the Instance and Symbol Link

Sometimes you need to break the link between an instance and its symbol. For example, you might need to alter one instance's shape to convey a new concept or to make it really stand out. You don't want to change all the instances linked to this symbol by changing the symbol's shape, so you need to break the link between this instance and the symbol. To do so, select the instance on the Stage for which you want to break the link and select Modify, Break Apart to break the instance/symbol link. The instance becomes a vector shape, which enables you to modify it as you would any other vector shape. The file size of the movie is then increased by the vector shape size. After the link is broken, any changes made to the symbol do not affect the vector shape that used to be the instance of the symbol.

The Power of the Movie Clip Symbol

The movie clip symbol is a key component for attaining interactivity and a range of functionality in Flash MX. The movie clip symbol has its own Timeline that is independent of the movie's Timeline. When an instance is created from the movie clip symbol, it has its own functionality that runs regardless of what is happening on the Stage. This allows for special interactivity in the SWF file, such as enabling the end-user to drag and drop a movie clip instance anywhere he wants on the Stage regardless of what is happening as the movie plays through its Timeline. You will use movie clips quite often in your development of a Flash MX movie and throughout the workshop sections of each seminar from this point forward in the book. It is a very powerful feature for gaining additional functionality in your movies.

Identifying the Symbols Used in a Movie

Flash MX offers an easily accessible button on the Stage that lists all the symbols used in a movie. Click the Edit Symbols button in the upper-right corner of the Stage to display the pop-up menu that lists all the symbols used in the current movie (see Figure 4.16).

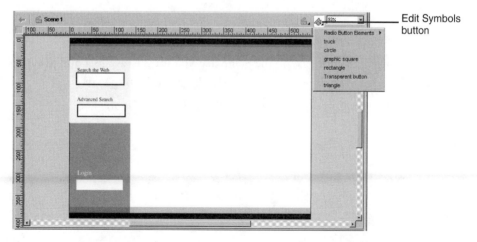

Figure 4.16　The Edit Symbols button displays a list of all symbols used in a movie.

Selecting one of the symbols from the pop-up menu launches the Symbol-Editing Mode, enabling you to edit the symbol.

Nesting a Symbol Inside Other Symbols

A neat trick and memory-saving technique that Flash MX offers is nesting a symbol inside another symbol. You reduce the size of the movie and the new symbol by nesting an existing symbol inside it. You can take this one step further and create a new symbol by using many existing symbols. In essence, you are creating a reference loop from a new symbol to existing symbols and therefore barely adding any new data to the symbol memory size.

To nest a symbol inside of another symbol, place an instance of the symbols you want to use to create your new symbol on the Stage. Make any additions or changes to the instances, and then select all these instances by Shift-clicking to make them active. Now make them into a new symbol by selecting Insert, Convert to Symbol. Your new symbol is composed of all the instances you selected from the Stage.

Warning ───
You can't nest a symbol inside itself.

Swapping a Symbol

Sometimes you might need to replace the symbol to which an instance is linked. This causes that individual instance to change to an instance of the new symbol, but any color effects or transformations you might have applied to that instance are preserved.

To assign a different symbol to an instance, follow these steps:

1. Select the instance on the Stage that you want to assign a different symbol, and then click the Swap button in the Property Inspector (see Figure 4.17).

   This displays the Swap Symbol dialog box (see Figure 4.18).

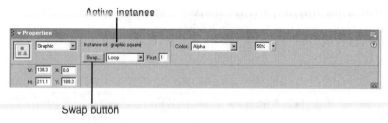

Active instance

Swap button

Figure 4.17   You must have an instance active on the Stage to display all the instance properties in the Property Inspector.

Currently assigned symbol

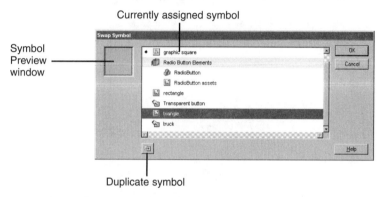

Symbol Preview window

Duplicate symbol

Figure 4.18   The active symbol for the instance on the Stage is shown in the Symbol Preview window.

2. Click a new symbol from the list to be assigned to the instance and click OK. The new instance of the symbol is placed with its center point at the same coordinates as the previous instance's center point. This might require resizing or repositioning the new instance on the Stage.

Using the Macromedia Flash MX Library

The Flash MX library has many features and is very flexible. It stores all the symbols, sounds, video clips, and bitmapped images used in a movie. As stated earlier, you can compare this library to your local public library. The Flash library enables you to group and organize your files just as a public library groups and organizes books. A difference, though, in this analogy, is that the Flash MX library never runs out of copies (or instances) of its symbols.

Identifying Features of the Library

Every movie has one and only one library attached to it. You can open another movie library if you need to access symbols stored in that library, but any symbols you use from that library are copied to the current movie's library. Every library has features, buttons, and menus for organizing and manipulating the library's symbols (see Figure 4.19).

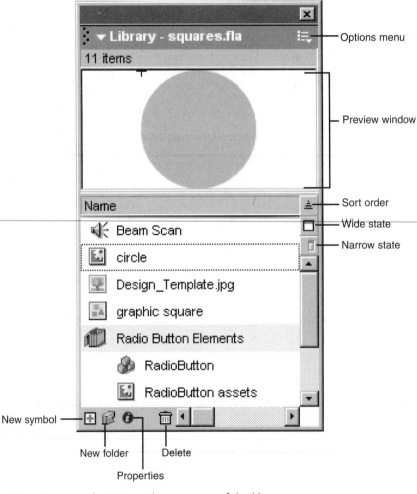

Figure 4.19   Features, buttons, and menu items of the library.

Note

When a library from another movie is opened, this library docks with the Library panel of the current movie, creating a panel group. This is a new feature of Flash MX that helps to keep one panel group for displaying any opened libraries. Typical of panel groups, you can pull a Library panel to separate it from the panel group.

The following list gives more information on each of these library features:

- **Options menu**—Contains many of the menu commands you need to organize symbols and use the library features.

- **Preview window**—Previews the selected symbol.

- **Sort Order**—Sorts the symbol list in descending or ascending order.

- **Wide state**—Maximizes the library window.

- **Narrow state**—Restores the library window to its previous size.

- **Delete**—Deletes the selected symbol.

- **Properties**—Opens the Properties dialog box for the selected symbol. There, you can change any of the properties of the selected symbol as well as the name of the symbol.

- **New Folder**—Creates a new folder.

- **New Symbol**—Creates a new symbol and launches the Symbol-Editing Mode.

Identifying Library Symbols

The library houses all the bitmapped graphics imported into the movie as well as all the graphics symbols, buttons, movie clips, video clips, and sounds created for the movie. Remember that a symbol can have the behavior of a Movie Clip, Button, or Graphic. Each of these symbol types, and even the imported bitmapped images, sounds, and video clips, are represented by a different symbol icon in the library. You can easily identify a symbol's behavior or type by looking at the associated icon next to the object name (see Table 4.1).

Table 4.1   Symbol Icons

Symbol Icon	Symbol Type	Symbol Description
	Bitmap graphic	Anytime a graphic is imported into Flash MX, it automatically appears in the library as an object.
	Graphic symbol	You must create or convert a graphic or an item to a symbol and then assign it the Graphic behavior.
	Button symbol	You must create or convert a graphic or an item to a symbol and then assign it the Button behavior.
	Movie Clip symbol	You must create or convert a graphic or an item to a symbol and then assign it the Movie Clip behavior.
	Component	Components are special, intelligent movie clips that have parameters associated with them. They are a new feature of Flash MX and replace, as well as extend, the Flash 5 feature of Smart Clips. You can create your own components from an existing complex movie clip so that you can use this functionality in any movie. Each component displays with its own symbol icon in your library.
	Sound symbol	You can import any MP3, WAV, or AIFF sound file into Flash MX, and it will appear as a Sound symbol in your library.
	Video Clip symbol	New with Flash MX is the video symbol. Now you can add video to a movie. You learn more about this in Seminar 15, "Adding Digital Video to the Site."

Note

When you select a Movie Clip symbol in the library, the Preview window displays the movie clip with a control panel in the upper-right corner. You can click the Play button to preview the animation of the movie clip.

Using the Library to Organize Symbols

The procedure for organizing your library objects is similar to the way you organize your folders and files at the operating-system level of your computer. First, you need to create a folder in your library. Click the New Folder button in the lower-left corner of the library panel. A new folder displays (see Figure 4.20).

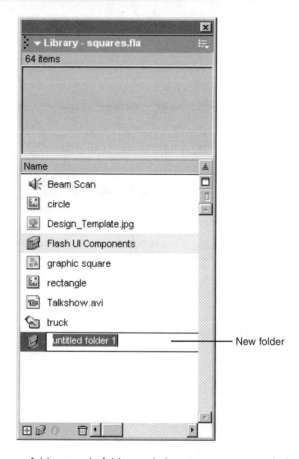

Figure 4.20 You can nest folders inside folders to help organize your symbols.

Type a name for the new folder; use a name that makes identifying the contents of the folder easy. You can create as many folders as necessary for organizing the movie's library.

To put symbols or other folders inside a folder, click and drag them on top of the folder. The folder is highlighted, and they drop inside. To open a folder, double-click the folder icon next to the folder name (see Figure 4.21).

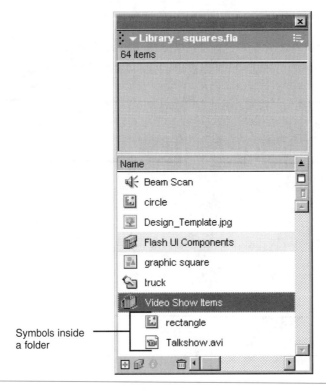

Symbols inside
a folder

Figure 4.21   Double-click the folder icon again to close the folder.

Renaming Library Symbols

The most direct way to rename a symbol in the library is to double-click the text next to the Graphics icon. This opens a text edit box, enabling you to edit the symbol name (see Figure 4.22).

You can also use the Properties button at the bottom of the library window. The Symbol Properties dialog box opens with the symbol name highlighted in the text edit box (see Figure 4.23).

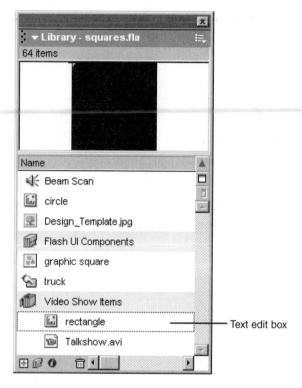

Figure 4.22   If you double-click the icon next to the symbol name, you launch the symbol-editing mode for the symbol.

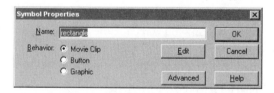

Figure 4.23   You can also change the symbol's behavior through the Symbol Properties dialog box.

Sorting Symbols in the Library Window

Sorting library content is another nice feature of the library. As you develop movies in Flash MX, you will use many symbols, and your library can have quite a few symbols and folders. Just as you need to be able to quickly locate files on your desktop, you also need to locate symbols in your library. Five sort options can be applied to the library for organizing your files. You can sort by Name, Kind, Use Count, Linkage, and Date Modified. As Figure 4.24 displays, if you display the library in Wide format, you can then view all the information about each symbol in the library.

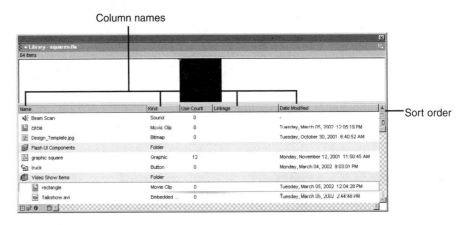

Figure 4.24   Click the Sort Order button to change from descending to ascending order for any of the category headers.

Similar to your operating system, you can click the column names to sort the library contents by that feature.

Identifying Unused Library Symbols

As you develop a movie, at certain times you will want to see what symbols have not been used yet. This can be done through the Options menu in the upper-right corner of the library panel. You can select either Keep Use Counts Updated or Update Use Counts Now from this menu. Each of these commands causes the library to display the number of times a symbol has been used in your movie under the Count column name (see Figure 4.25).

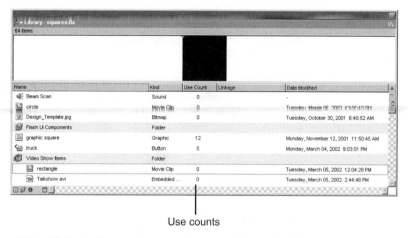

Figure 4.25   Click the Count column name to sort the symbols by use count.

If you select Keep Use Counts Updated, the library automatically updates the symbol usage as you develop the movie. This menu choice is a toggle switch; notice that if you select it to turn on this feature, a check mark appears by the menu choice. Reselect the choice to turn it off. If you want to manually update the usage count, select Update Use Counts Now.

Opening Other Movies' Libraries

You can open libraries from other movies and use any symbols in these libraries in your Flash MX movie. To open another movie's library, select File, Open as Library and select the movie that contains the library you want to use. When the second library opens, it docks itself with the movie library creating a panel group (see Figure 4.26).

You can drag any symbol from this new library onto your Stage or into your movie's library. Any instance of a symbol you use from another movie's library is automatically added as a symbol to your movie's library.

Tip _____

Flash MX ships with other libraries that can be used in a movie. Select Window, Common Libraries to access the submenu listing the other libraries. These common libraries are Buttons, Learning Interactions, and Sounds.

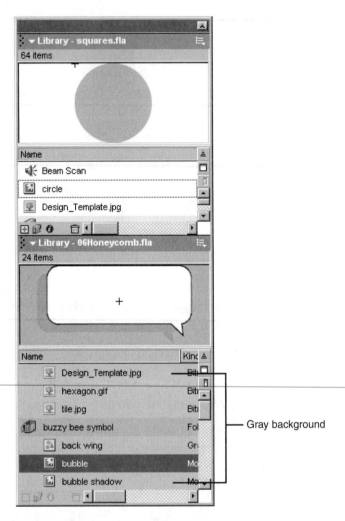

Figure 4.26   The imported library has a gray background, helping to visually distinguish which library is not attached to the movie.

What Is a Shared Library?

A shared library is a special library designed for teams of developers working on multiple projects. It enables multiple people working on a project to access the objects in a common library. Geographic boundaries are not an issue with a shared library because it is stored outside the Flash MX movie file, unlike a movie's library, which is attached to the movie. Any changes made to a symbol in the shared library are reflected in all instances of this symbol in any movie that uses it. The update occurs when the movies are published to SWF format.

To create a shared library, follow these steps:

1. Open a new Flash MX movie and save it as `shared.fla`. You need to create a movie so you can use its library as the shared library.

2. Add any of the symbols you want to share to this library.

3. Now you must set the linkage for each of the symbols in your shared library. Click the first symbol to make it the active symbol in the library.

4. Click the Options menu from the shared library and select Linkage. This opens the Linkage Properties dialog box (see Figure 4.27).

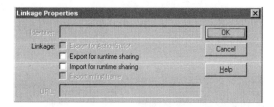

Figure 4.27   The Identifier field enables you to name the symbol so you can later link back to it.

5. Select the Export for Runtime Sharing option, and type the name of the symbol in the Identifier box.

Warning —————————————————————————————

Do not use spaces in the Identifier name for a shared library symbol.

Tip —————————————————————————————

The Linkage Identifier can also be used to identify a button or movie clip that is called in ActionScript.

6. In the URL box, type the URL for the location of the SWF file of the shared library movie. Click OK to close the dialog box.

7. Before you can use this shared library symbol in another destination movie, you need to publish the shared library movie to SWF format by selecting File, Publish. When you publish a movie, it creates the SWF file in the same directory as the `shared.fla`. Close the `shared.fla` movie.

8. With the shared library created, you now can link to the symbols in this library from the destination movie. Open the destination movie.

9. Open the shared library by selecting File, Open as Library. Navigate to the `shared.fla` file.

10. Drag instances of a symbol from the shared library onto the Stage or into the library of the destination movie.

11. Select a symbol in the destination movie library that you've added to the movie and then click the Properties button in the lower-left corner of the library panel.

12. Click the Advanced button to expand the Symbol Properties dialog box (see Figure 4.28).

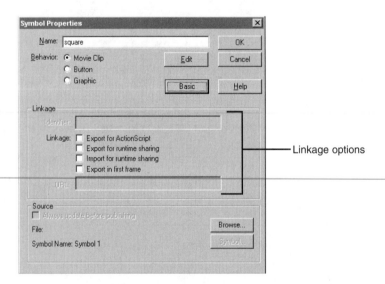

Figure 4.28   You can expand the Symbol Properties dialog box for any symbol, which also enables you to set the linkage.

13. In the Symbol Properties dialog box, select the Import for Runtime Sharing option and set the Identifier to the same name you named the symbol in the shared library (do not use spaces). Then type the URL of the location of the SWF filename in the URL box (see Figure 4.29). Click OK to close the Symbol Properties dialog box.

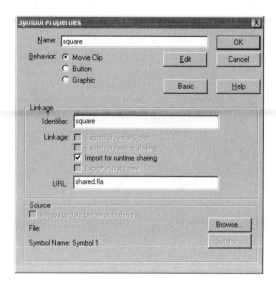

Figure 4.29   If you save the movie in the same directory as the shared.swf file, you just need to use the filename in the URL box.

14. Publish the movie by selecting File, Publish. This sets the link to the shared.swf file.

Now, any time you make changes to the shared library symbols, you can cause all movies that use the symbol to update. You must publish your shared.fla movie to publish the changes of the shared symbol to the SWF file; then publish the movies that have symbols linked to the shared library. All symbols will update with the changes used in the shared library.

Creating the Site Symbols and Stage Instances

Now that you know a little more about Flash MX's functionality and its use of symbols, it is time to convert your Honeycomb Web site objects into symbols. Typically, the process of creating your design and converting objects into symbols occurs simultaneously as you develop your movie. As you plan any movie, you should think about your use of symbols and how can you create and use your symbols most efficiently and effectively in your site. In regard to The Honeycomb site, several rectangular shapes are used in the design and for the buttons. This should be the first symbol you create because it can be used as an instance throughout the design.

Creating a Square Symbol

Looking at the design you have created so far for The Honeycomb site, you realize that all the shapes you've used are rectangular. Creating a square symbol is a smart move at this point in your site development. Instances of the symbol can be used for the footer, footer shadow, header, header shadow, menu bar, and buttons. Now, you will begin to build the site using this symbol. Follow these steps to create the square symbol:

1. Use your `Honeycomb.fla` file from Seminar 3, "Creating a Movie," or open `03Honeycomb.fla` from the `Seminar04/Samples` directory on the CD-ROM that accompanies this book.

2. Select Insert, New Symbol to open the Symbol-Editing Mode for creating your square symbol.

3. In the Symbol Properties dialog box, name the symbol `square` and select the Movie Clip behavior (see Figure 4.30). Click OK to close the dialog box.

4. The Symbol-Editing Mode opens with a blank Stage. Select the Rectangle tool, and set the Fill modifier setting to Black and the Stroke modifier to None. Click and drag a rectangle on the Stage.

5. With the Arrow tool, click the rectangular shape to make it active, and then access or open the Info panel. Set the Width to `50` and the Height to `50`. Set the registration point to the upper-left corner, and then set the x and y coordinates to `0` (see Figure 4.31).

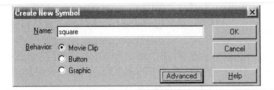

Figure 4.30   This symbol will be used for many objects in The Honeycomb site, so you should make it a movie clip symbol because this behavior is more versatile than just a Graphic behavior.

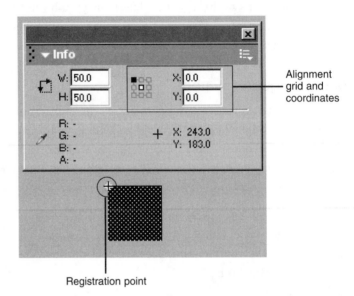

Alignment grid and coordinates

Registration point

Figure 4.31   Setting a registration point with x and y coordinates of 0 in the upper-left corner makes precisely aligning and sizing the symbol instances used in the site easier.

6. Exit Symbol-Editing Mode by clicking the Scene 1 tab or the back arrow in the upper-left corner of the Flash MX Stage.

7. You have created your square symbol. To view it, open your library by selecting Window, Library (see Figure 4.32).

Figure 4.32 Notice that you have the design template as a bitmap symbol also in the library. When you import an image, it automatically is added to your library as a bitmap symbol.

Creating the Background Design

Now that you have the square symbol, you can place instances of this symbol for re-creating the background design. In Seminar 3, you created the basics of the background design to learn the tools, panels, and features of Flash. Now you will re-create each of these objects using the square symbol. This requires deleting the background design that you have created up to this point. Follow these steps to create the background design with the square symbol:

1. If you have turned off the Snap to Guides feature, turn that on by selecting View, Guides, Snap to Guides.

2. With the Arrow tool, select the header object on the Stage. This also makes the header layer active. Delete the header object from the Stage.

3. Drag an instance of the square symbol onto the Stage. Click in the upper-left corner of the instance and drag it to the upper-left corner of your Stage. A circle displays at the drag point and adheres to the guides that outline the Stage.

4. With the instance of the square symbol active, click the Free Transform tool from the toolbox. Handles display around the instance; drag the middle handle on the right side so that it adheres to the guide that outlines the right edge of the Stage. Click and drag the bottom middle handle of the instance, and drag that to the guide that defines the bottom edge of the header rectangle (see Figure 4.33).

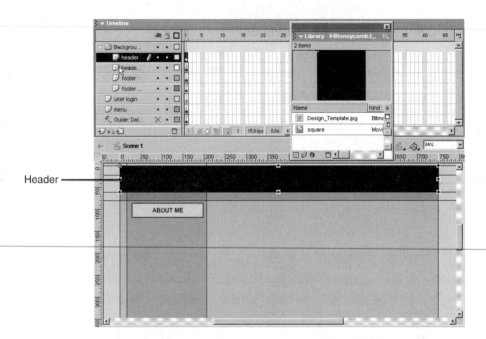

Header

Figure 4.33   You also could have used the Info panel or Align panel to align the instance to the upper-left corner of the Stage.

5. Select the header shadow layer to make it active. The header shadow object on the Stage also becomes active. Delete the header shadow object. Drag another instance of the square rectangle onto the Stage.

6. Again, click and drag the instance by the upper-left corner so that it adheres to the guides that define the upper-left corner of the header shadow.

7. Select the Free Transform tool from the toolbox and adjust the handles so that the instance adheres to the guides that define the header shadow area.

8. In the Property Inspector, click the Color pop-up menu and select Alpha. Then click the Alpha box and type in 25 (see Figure 4.34).

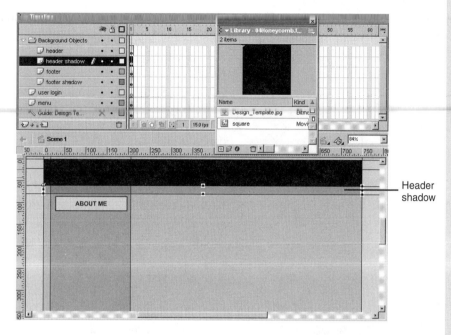

Figure 4.34 This sets the alpha effect for this instance to 25% transparency.

9. Repeat steps 5–8 to re-create the footer and footer shadow on the appropriate layer. Use Table 4.2 to configure the correct Color Effects for these instances.

Table 4.2 Honeycomb Background Design Composition

Object	Effect	Settings
Footer	None	
Footer Shadow	Alpha	25% Alpha Effect

Creating the Menu Bar

The next step is to create the menu bar using symbols. This requires a background object and the buttons. All the rectangular shapes can be created using the square symbol. Therefore, you will nest an instance of a square symbol inside a new symbol to create the button on the menu bar. Follow these steps:

1. Select the menu bar layer to make all that layer's contents active and delete these objects.

2. From the library, click and drag an instance of the square symbol onto the Stage. From the upper-left corner of the instance, click and drag it to the top of the Stage but keep it aligned with the guides that define the left edge of the menu bar area.

3. Click the Free Transform tool from the toolbox and resize the instance so that it adheres to the guides that define the right edge of the menu bar area. Click the middle handle at the bottom of the instance and resize it so that it adheres to the bottom guide that defines the bottom edge of the Stage.

4. In the Property Inspector, set the Color pop-up menu to Alpha and then type 20 in the Alpha box (see Figure 4.35). Press Enter to apply this setting.

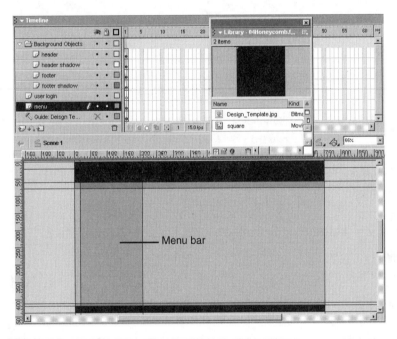

Figure 4.35   This sets the alpha effect for this instance to 20% transparency.

5. The menu bar holds all the site's buttons, so make it its own symbol by selecting it and selecting Insert, Convert to Symbol. You are now nesting the square instance for the menu bar inside of a new symbol.

6. In the Symbol Properties dialog box, name the symbol menu and keep its behavior as Movie Clip.

A new symbol for the menu is now accessible in the library (see Figure 4.36).

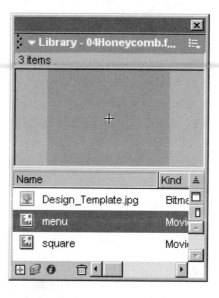

Figure 4.36   The menu symbol nests the square symbol inside it.

The background design has been re-created using just one symbol: the square symbol. An instance of the square symbol was also used to create the menu bar. The menu bar instance has been converted to its own symbol, thereby nesting the square symbol inside the new symbol. Next, you will create a button symbol and use it for the four activity buttons. Instances of the square symbol can also be used for these buttons.

Creating the Activity Button

The buttons for the four activity areas of the site are the next objects to be developed. In the workshop for Seminar 3, you created only one button, not all four. This workshop develops all the buttons using instances of the symbol and text blocks. You can do this by focusing first on the About Me button and making it its own symbol. Then you can duplicate this symbol, rename it, and modify it to reflect the other buttons for the activity areas. Follow these steps to create your buttons:

1. Create a new symbol for the About Me button by selecting Insert, New Symbol. Name the symbol about me button. Select the Button behavior, and then click OK to go to the Symbol-Editing Mode.

2. Rename Layer 1 to `button background`.

3. With the `button background` layer active, access or open the library by selecting Window, Library; then drag an instance of the square symbol onto the Stage.

4. In the Property Inspector, set the Width to 169 and the Height to 33; then press Enter to apply these settings to the instance of the square symbol.

5. From the library, drag another instance of the square symbol onto the Stage. Using the Property Inspector, set this instance to a Width of 163 and a Height of 27.

6. With the second, smaller instance of the square symbol selected, in the Property Inspector, select the Color pop-up menu and select Tint. Click the Tint Color modifier to display the color palette and set the hexadecimal value to FFCE31 (see Figure 4.37).

Figure 4.37   This changes the square instance to a yellow color.

7. Now align both instances to each other so that the yellow instance is centered inside the black instance and they both are centered on the Stage. Using the Arrow tool, select both instances by Shift-clicking each of them. Access or open your Align panel and click the Align to Stage button. Then click the Align Vertical Center button and the Align Horizontal Center button (see Figure 4.38).

8. Next, you'll create the label for this button. Insert a new layer above the `button background` layer. Name this layer `button label`.

9. Click the Text tool from the toolbox and in the Property Inspector, set the font to Arial, the font size to 14, and the font color to black. Then select the Auto Kern option and select the Bold option. With the button label layer active, click anywhere on the Stage to set a text block, and type ABOUT ME (using all uppercase).

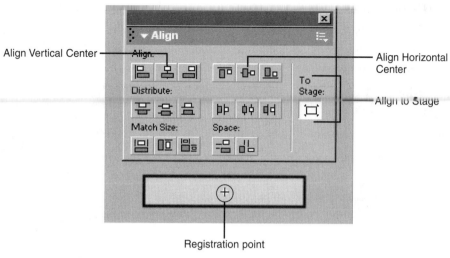

Align Vertical Center

Align Horizontal Center

Align to Stage

Registration point

Figure 4.38   The registration point for the Home button instance is in the center.

10. Click the Arrow tool to make the text block active. From the Align panel, with the Align to Stage button active, again click the Align Vertical Center button and the Align Horizontal Center button (see Figure 4.39).

ABOUT ME

Figure 4.39   The About Me text block is centered in the button background.

11. The button design is now set; exit the Symbol-Editing Mode by clicking the Scene 1 tab in the upper-left corner above the Stage area.

Creating the Other Buttons

With the About Me button created, you can now create your other buttons. To save time and energy, you will just duplicate the About Me button and then change the text block to reflect the activity area of the site. Do the following to create these other buttons:

1. From the library, select the About Me button to make it the active library symbol.

2. Click the Options menu in the upper-right corner of the library and select Duplicate. This opens the Symbol Properties dialog box.

3. Rename the button to matching button. Leave the behavior set to Button and click OK.

4. From the library, double-click the matching button symbol to launch the Symbol-Editing Mode.

5. With the Arrow tool, double-click the ABOUT ME text block so that you can make edits to the text.

6. Change the button label to MATCHING.

7. With the Arrow tool, click the text block to make it the active object on the Stage. Access or open the Align panel and align the text block both vertically and horizontally centered to the Stage.

8. Repeat steps 2–7 to create two more button symbols named puzzles button and ducks button. Label the puzzles button as PUZZLES and the ducks button as IN QUEST OF DUCKS, using all uppercase. Your movie library should resemble Figure 4.40.

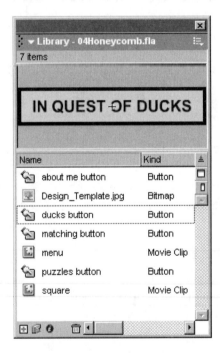

Figure 4.40   Keep the behavior set to Button because you are creating another button.

9. Exit the Symbol-Editing Mode.

Adding the Buttons to the Menu Bar

At this point in the site development, you have all the button symbols created as well as the menu symbol. You have also nested the square symbol as a component of each of these symbols. Now you must finish developing the menu symbol by placing buttons on it. You will also use a new feature of Flash MX: pixel-level control. This feature enables you to precisely create and position objects on the Stage using the movie grid and gives you the ability to place and size objects at the pixel level. Because you are working from the Design Template for button positioning, it is beneficial to edit the menu symbol directly on the Stage. Therefore, you will perform an Edit in Place command on the menu symbol located on the Stage. To do this, follow these steps:

1. If the Guide: Design Template layer is hidden, unhide it and then lock it so that it can't be accessed.

2. Using the Arrow tool, double-click the instance of the menu symbol on the Stage to make it active. This launches the Symbol-Editing Mode using the Edit in Place feature (see Figure 4.41). You know you are in Symbol-Editing Mode by the Menu tab located above the Stage area on the left.

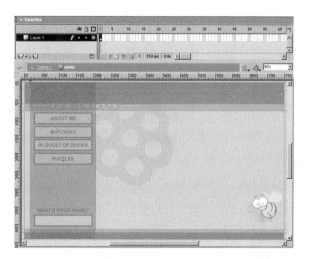

Figure 4.41   The Stage dims so that you can focus on the menu symbol but still see other Stage content to use as a reference.

3. Turn on pixel snapping by selecting View, Snap to Pixels. Increase your view to focus on just the four buttons by clicking the Zoom tool and dragging a marquee around the four buttons. This new feature of Flash MX enables you to adjust the position and size of an object one pixel at a time.

Tip

If you increase your Stage magnification above 400% and have View, Snap to Pixels turned on, the movie grid displays, further enabling you to have precision in your design and object placement.

4. From the library, drag an instance of the `about me button` symbol onto the Stage. Position it on top of the About Me button, as indicated in the Design Template (see Figure 4.42). You are now nesting the `about me button` symbol inside the menu bar symbol.

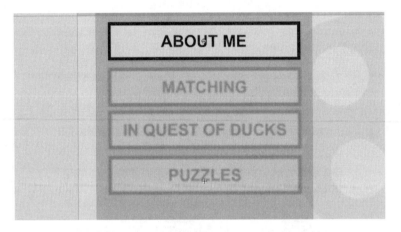

Figure 4.42   By turning on pixel snapping, you are precisely positioning the instance of the `about me button` symbol.

5. From the library, drag instances of the other three buttons and position them on the Stage as the design template indicates.

6. Exit the Symbol-Editing Mode by clicking the Scene 1 tab or the Back button in the area above the Stage on the left.

Creating the Login

Finally, to finish The Honeycomb site design, you need to create the login area of the site. You will again use the square symbol as an instance for creating this area. Follow these steps to create the login area:

1. Select the `user login` layer to make it active.

2. Create a new symbol by selecting Insert, New Symbol.

3. In the Create New Symbol dialog box, name the symbol login and set its behavior to Movie Clip. Click OK to launch the Symbol-Editing Mode.

4. To save time and to ensure you have the same dimension for the login area as the activity buttons, you can open a button symbol and copy the Stage objects that make up these buttons. From the library, double-click the About Me button symbol to access this button in the Symbol-Editing Mode. Select Edit, Select All to select all the components of the About Me button. Then copy these components by pressing (Command-C)[Ctrl+C].

5. Now switch back to the login symbol by double-clicking it from the library.

6. Paste the copied button by selecting Edit, Paste in Place. The Paste in Place command pastes the copied object in the same location in which it existed in the original object (see Figure 4.43).

Figure 4.43 The copied components of the Home button are now centered on the Stage.

7. Click just the ABOUT ME text block to make it active and delete it.

8. Click the yellow instance of the square symbol, and in the Property Inspector, click the Color pop-up menu and select Tint. Click the Tint Color modifier and select the white color swatch.

9. Rename Layer 1 to login background. Insert a new layer above this layer and name this layer login label.

10. On the new login label layer, create a text block by clicking the Text tool, and in the Property Inspector, set the font to Arial, the font size to 14, and the font color to black. Also, select the Auto Kern and Bold options.

11. Click above the login box to set a text block, and type WHAT'S YOUR NAME?. Using the Arrow tool, click the text block and position it above the login box.

12. To center the text block vertically to the Stage, access the Align panel. Click the Align to Stage button and the Align Vertical Center button.

13. Exit the Symbol-Editing Mode by clicking the Scene 1 tab.

14. Click the login layer and place an instance of the login symbol on the Stage. Position it based on the design template (see Figure 4.44).

Figure 4.44   The login area enables the end-user to log in to the site.

Tip ———————————————————————————————

If you need to adjust the **login** instance to match the Design Template exactly, double-click the **login** instance on the Stage. This launches the Edit in Place feature of the Symbol-Editing Mode, dimming your Stage and focusing on just the login symbol. Reposition the objects of the login area based on the design template. Exit the Symbol-Editing Mode to return to the movie.

Tip ———————————————————————————————

You can use the left and right arrow keys to position the **login** instance on the Stage. Each arrow key moves the active object 1 pixel per keypress. If you hold down the Shift key while pressing the arrow keys, you will move the active object 10 pixels per keypress.

Organizing the Movie Library

Now that you have many of the symbols created for the movie, you should organize your library. A common practice is to make a folder you can use for grouping your movie buttons. This movie has four buttons and a menu bar that will be the main navigation for the site. Follow these steps to organize your movie's library:

1. Open or access The Honeycomb movie library.

2. Click the New Folder icon in the lower-left corner of the library panel. A new folder displays in the library; rename the folder menu bar.

3. Click and drag the menu symbol on top of the menu bar folder. It is dropped inside the library as you release the mouse button.

Note

When you create a new folder, it displays with a folder icon that is thin, indicating that it contains nothing. When you add a symbol to the folder, the folder icon gets wider, indicating that it now contains a symbol or symbols.

4. Repeat step 3 for the `about me` button, `ducks` button, `matching` button, and `puzzles` button to drop each of these symbols into the `menu bar` folder (see Figure 4.45).

Figure 4.45   Double-click the menu bar folder to open or close it.

Viewing the Site

You should always check your work as you develop in Flash MX. The design template is nice for helping to create the site, but it limits you from seeing what you have designed. You must hide the `Guide: Design Template` layer. To do this, follow these steps:

1. Click the dot in the Show/Hide column of the layers area of the Timeline (see Figure 4.46).

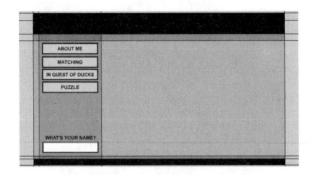

Figure 4.46   Hiding the Guide layer enables you to see your design of the movie. Your movie should match this figure.

2. Save the movie as Honeycomb.fla.

If you want to compare your Honeycomb site with a movie that is completed up to this point in the book, open the `04Honeycomb.fla` file located in the `Seminar04/Samples` directory on the CD-ROM that accompanies this book.

Seminar Summary

This seminar covered a great deal of ground concerning the principles and powerful features of Flash MX. You learned how to create and edit symbols and should now feel comfortable using the library as well as organizing your symbols through the library's features. You will use symbols and instances of your symbols in the other Flash movies you develop. Remember your challenge for using your symbols and instances as effectively and as efficiently in all your other Flash development.

The seminar also covered how to create and alter instances, as well as how to swap a symbol for an instance. In the next seminar, you learn how to import graphics and artwork created in other applications into your movie. You also learn how to optimize and manipulate imported objects.

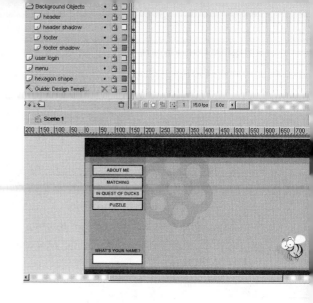

Seminar 5

Importing Graphics into a Movie

In this chapter

Working with Imported Objects

Macromedia Flash MX does many things very well—most people find the drawing tools of Flash MX good for creating Stage objects and shapes. But because it is a vector-based application, some effects that you can attain in raster applications can't be created in Flash MX. Good examples are soft edges for an object and a filter effect of PhotoShop. Whether to create your movie objects and design in Macromedia Flash MX or to use another graphics application is decided by the design of the site. You know from Seminar 1, "Macromedia Flash MX and Web Site Development," that many file types can be imported into Flash. When you import an object, it becomes an asset of your movie. Knowing how to work with imported objects is the next step.

This seminar focuses on the import features of Flash MX in regard to graphics files and provides information on how to optimize and work with the imported graphics images. Seminar 12, "Adding Sound to Enhance a Site," covers importing sound files, and Seminar 15, "Adding Digital Video to the Site," covers importing video clips.

Using the Import Commands of Macromedia Flash MX

Flash MX can import many different objects into any movie. This includes many of the popular bitmap, vector, sound, SWF, and video formatted files. No matter which file type you are importing, the process for importing is the same: You use either the File, Import menu command or the new Flash MX command, File, Import to Library (see Figure 5.1).

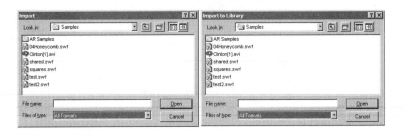

Figure 5.1   In either of the Import dialog boxes, to import an object or image, you must navigate to the file, select it, and then click Open.

Note

When importing into Flash from a Macintosh running OS 9.x or earlier, the Import dialog box looks different from Figure 5.1. You must click Add to add the selected file to the Import list and then click Import. This enables you to select multiple files to import at one time.

Importing Raster and Vector Images in Macromedia Flash MX

This seminar covers the importing feature of Flash with a focus on importing graphics, either raster or vector. Seminar 1 discussed the many file formats that can be imported into Flash MX. The most most common graphics formats are

- GIF
- JPEG
- PNG
- Bitmap
- EPS
- Vector—SWF

Importing GIF and JPG Graphics

Common graphics formats in Web development are GIF and JPEG. Flash MX can import these file types through either of the import commands. One difference between the Import command and the Import to Library command is seen when you import a bitmap file. As you know from Seminar 4, "Using Symbols in a Movie," when a bitmap file is imported using the File, Import command, it is placed on the Stage in the active layer and automatically becomes a Bitmap symbol in the movie library. If the File, Import to Library command is used, the raster image is placed only in the Library as a Bitmap symbol. You will use both Import commands in the workshop of this seminar as well as throughout the remainder of this book.

Importing SWF Files

Flash MX can import a vector file that is saved in SWF format. SWF objects import beautifully into Flash MX because this file type retains all aspects of its shape, including layers. Macromedia FreeHand 9 exports files in SWF format, as does Adobe Illustrator 9.0 and 10.

Another application that can create SWF files is Swift 3-D. This application is used for creating three-dimensional objects and animated scenes that can be exported for use in Flash MX movies or other applications. This program uses frames and other features that are similar to Flash MX. Using the Swift 3-D tools and effects, you can virtually render any type of three-dimensional object and create animated scenes of the object.

Importing and Working with Vector Graphics

Vector graphics are created through a mathematical formula for representing the strokes and fills of an object. Illustration programs such as Adobe Illustrator and Macromedia FreeHand create vector graphics, as opposed to photo-editing programs such as Adobe PhotoShop, which create bitmap images. Flash MX imports artwork generated from either application.

> **Tip**
>
> You can cut, copy, and paste from Illustrator 9.0 and 10, as well as from FreeHand 8 and 9, directly into Flash MX.

When you import a FreeHand file through either the File, Import or File, Import to Library command, the FreeHand Import dialog box displays (see Figure 5.2).

Through this dialog box, Flash MX supports the mapping of a multipage FreeHand document into Flash MX scenes or individual keyframes. FreeHand layers are also imported into Flash MX layers. There is no loss in precise color mapping that might have been used in a FreeHand graphic. Lens fills, such as magnify or transparency, are converted to a Flash MX equivalent, and any symbols that might have been used in a FreeHand Library are automatically imported into the Flash MX Library.

When an Illustrator file is imported into Flash, you get another dialog box that also maintains many of the features of an Illustrator image (see Figure 5.3).

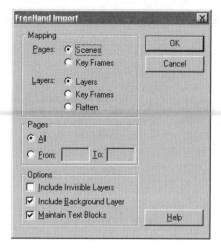

Figure 5.2   You can maintain many of the features of a FreeHand image through the FreeHand Import dialog box.

Figure 5.3   You can maintain many of the features of a Illustrator image through the Illustrator Import dialog box.

Importing PNG Images

PNG files can also be imported into Flash. PNG files have special features of both a raster image and a vector image. Flash MX enables PNG files to be imported as flattened images or editable objects. If you import a file as a flattened image, the entire file is rasterized, including any of the vector shapes that might be comprised in the image's composition. It imports into a rectangular area. If, on the other hand, you import the file as an editable object, some of the vector formatting is maintained in the PNG file. It imports without a rectangular area, enabling you to place it tightly behind a raster image. This includes any placed bitmaps, text blocks, and the guides used in the original PNG file.

Tip

When you import a PNG file as a flattened image, it can be edited by launching Fireworks in the external editor while in Flash.

Tip

When a PNG image is imported in either a flattened or an editable image, it can be broken apart, giving you access to individual areas that then can be manipulated or erased. You will learn more about the Modify, Break Apart command later in this seminar.

Working with Raster Images

Flash MX can import raster or bitmap graphics. When these images are imported into Flash MX, they display as one image, with all the areas that comprise the image becoming one (see Figure 5.4).

Figure 5.4   Because the image is one large object on the Stage, you might need to optimize or convert it to a vector format to use it in your movie.

After a raster image is imported into Flash MX, you can take one of three approaches to working with it:

- **It can be left as is**—It maintains the clarity of the original file and can be used for a background or as an object in the movie.

- **It can be broken apart**—This enables you to work with individual areas, colors, or shapes that make up the image. It also reduces the image in file size. This file type maintains the original clarity of the original file but has some features of a vector. When you break a raster image apart, the image exists in a state somewhere between vector and raster and can be comparable to a fill in Flash MX.

- **It can be converted to a vector image**—Upon conversion to vector art, it is then composed entirely of fill areas. When you convert a raster image to vector, the image displays with a watercolor effect. This conversion can really reduce file size from the original raster image. But if the raster is complex, the resulting vector image can be very large in file size—much larger than the original raster image.

> **Tip**
>
> Always import raster images without any compression applied. You then can set a compression for the file in Flash, which typically results in a very clear image and a much lower file size graphic.

> **Tip**
>
> Another rule of thumb when working with raster images in Flash is to always size the image in the physical dimensions that you need for the Flash movie, before importing it. If you try to resize the graphic to a larger size in the Flash movie, it will give the image the jaggies and distort the image quality.

Each approach to file optimization offers advantages and disadvantages for Flash MX development. The next section of this seminar discusses each of these three options for working with raster images in Flash; in addition, the workshop provides hands-on practice using many of these optimization techniques.

Setting Compression for Raster Images

Once imported into a movie, a raster image can be used throughout the movie without making any changes to it. A bitmap symbol of the image is automatically added to the library. Generally, it is better to import a raster image without any compression to maintain the original clarity in image quality. But this can cause the image to be quite large in file size. You can set compression for a raster image using the Bitmap Properties dialog box of the Library panel (see Figure 5.5). To access this dialog box, select the bitmap symbol in the Library and click the Properties button.

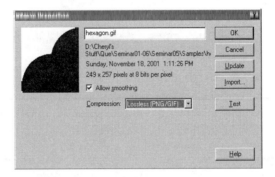

Figure 5.5   If you select the Allow Smoothing option, you can smooth the edges of the image through antialiasing.

You should select a compression of Lossless for images composed of simple shapes or few colors, as is the case with most GIF images. Lossless compression doesn't discard any information about the image.

If you are applying compression to a photograph image or an image that uses gradients, you should select Photo (JPEG) from the Compression pop-up menu. When this option is selected, you have two more compression options you can set. The Use Document Default Quality option maintains the original image composition, or you can set a Quality setting that enables you to set the amount of compression applied to the image (see Figure 5.6).

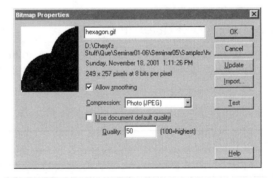

Figure 5.6   You can also update and reimport an image using the buttons on the right of this dialog box.

Tip

You can edit bitmap images in an external editor while working in Flash MX. You must have a photo-editing application on your system. If you use Fireworks, you need the 3.0 version or later to use this for your external editor. To launch the photo-editing application, simply right-click a bitmap symbol in the movie library and select Edit With.

Breaking Apart a Raster Image

Another way to work with a raster image is to break it apart. By breaking apart a raster image, you convert the entire image into a fill similar to a Bitmap fill. The advantage of this is that you significantly reduce the file size of the image. To do this, select the imported raster image on the Stage and then select Modify, Break Apart (see Figure 5.7).

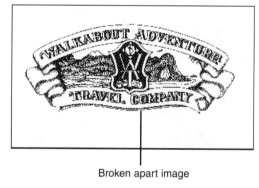

Broken apart image

Figure 5.7   The Break Apart command enables you to select individual areas of a raster image based on colors.

With the image broken apart, you can then use the Lasso tool's Magic Wand modifiers to edit and modify the image. You will work with a broken-apart image in the workshop of this seminar.

Tip

When a raster image is broken apart, the image is greatly reduced in file size.

Warning

The broken-apart graphic is reliant on the Library's Bitmap symbol for the composition and form of its shape. If you delete the Bitmap symbol from the Library, you will also delete the image detail for the broken-apart instance of this image on your Stage.

Converting Raster Images to Vector Images

Many times in Flash MX development, you might want to convert a raster image to a vector shape. One advantage to this is that the resulting vector shape can often be much lower in file size than the original raster image. You can also work with or modify the image as you would any vector shape. Therefore, all the tools and techniques of Flash MX can be applied to create the effects and interactivity that you need for your movie. The downside of this conversion, though, is image quality. You can never maintain the original quality of a raster image because the resulting vector image is now comprised of individual color fills (see Figure 5.8).

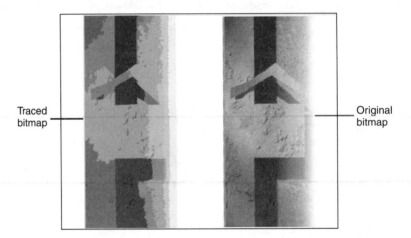

Traced bitmap — ⟷ — Original bitmap

Figure 5.8   The traced bitmap image is now composed of color fills, so the image displays with a watercolor effect.

> **Warning**
>
> Be aware that converting a complex raster image to a vector shape can also produce a very large file size—sometimes significantly increasing the file's size when compared to the original raster image file size.

To convert a raster image into a vector shape, you use the Modify, Trace Bitmap command. This command enables you to set the Trace settings for converting the image (see Figure 5.9).

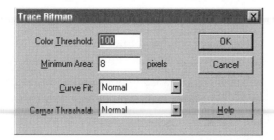

Figure 5.9   The Trace Bitmap dialog box converts a bitmapped image into a vector image by tracing the image's color areas based on the setting you input.

Be aware that you can easily create an image much larger than the original file by being precise with your settings for tracing the bitmapped image. The settings in the Trace Bitmap dialog box control how closely the traced image matches the bitmap image. The following list explains these settings:

- **Color Threshold**—Can be set to any number from 1 to 500. The Threshold setting can be compared to the Tolerance setting of Photoshop, in that it identifies colors based on how close they are to each other in color value. For example, if you have four shades of blue in an area of an image and set a low Threshold setting, Flash identifies each color of blue as its own color. If you set a high setting, on the other hand, Flash identifies the four variances of the color as one.

- **Minimum Area**—Determines how many of the adjacent pixels will be included in the color area. A large number includes more pixels in each color area, whereas a small number includes a smaller number of pixels in a color area—assuming that the surrounding pixels are similar in color. The smaller the number, the tighter the pixel-by-pixel color match becomes. Conversely, the larger the number, the more inclusive Flash MX is in its color identification.

- **Curve Fit**—Controls how smooth the edges of each area will be.

- **Corner Threshold**—Determines how sharp or smooth the corners are for each area.

Tip

A traced bitmap graphic is its own graphic. The link between the bitmap symbol in the library is broken. If you delete the bitmap symbol from the library, you will not delete the traced bitmap graphic on the Stage.

Optimizing a Traced Bitmap Image

After you trace a bitmap image, you might need to optimize it to help lower its file size. Flash MX has an optimization command that automatically optimizes the image by reducing the number of curves and endpoints in the image. To optimize a traced image, select the image and select Modify, Optimize. The Optimize Curves dialog box displays (see Figure 5.10).

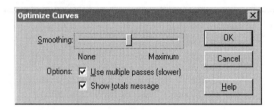

Figure 5.10   Drag the slider to set the level of optimization.

If you select the Show Totals Message box in the Optimize Curves dialog box, a summary Flash MX dialog box displays. This dialog box indicates the amount of reduction that has been applied to your image (see Figure 5.11).

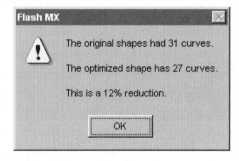

Figure 5.11   The file is reduced in file size by the percentage indicated in the message.

Tip

When you optimize a traced raster image, you alter the image's composition slightly. To determine whether the optimization was effective, you must weigh the effect this optimization has on the image with the quality of the image you want to achieve.

Importing Images for Site Activities and the Background

So far in The Honeycomb Site development, you have created the background design using the Design Template as a guide. You might notice that some features are missing from your site when compared to the design template—the Honeycomb logo and Buzzy Bee. There is also a hexagon shape that is used as part of the background. These objects will now be imported and optimized in the movie.

Importing the Hexagon Shape

Part of the background design of The Honeycomb site is a hexagon shape. You'll find this image in GIF format on the CD-ROM that accompanies this book. Follow these steps to import this object into your movie:

1. Use your `Honeycomb.fla` file that you saved from Seminar 4, or open `04Honeycomb.fla` from the `Seminar04/Samples` directory on the CD-ROM that accompanies this book.

2. Click the Guide: Design Template layer to make it active, and create a new layer above it. Name the layer `hexagon shape`. Hide and lock all but the hexagon shape layer so you can more easily work with the Stage content for this layer. Unhide the guide layer.

3. Select File, Import and navigate to `Seminar05/Samples/hexagon.gif`. Import this image into your movie (see Figure 5.12).

Figure 5.12   This image will be converted into an object that resembles the honeycomb shape shown in the design template.

1. Select the hexagon shape and convert it to a symbol named hexagon. Set the registration point to the center of the symbol and assign it a Graphic behavior. Click OK to close the dialog box.

Working with the Hexagon Shape

Because the hexagon shape is in raster format, you need to reduce the file size by breaking it apart using the Modify, Break apart command. This optimization also enables you to work with and modify the image. To make the hexagon image match the Design Template, it needs seven circular holes created. To modify this raster image, follow these steps:

1. From the Library, open the new hexagon symbol in the symbol-editing mode by double-clicking the symbol.

2. To modify this object, you now must break it apart by selecting Modify, Break Apart (see Figure 5.13).

Figure 5.13   Breaking apart the image causes the image to appear as if it were one large square, but you are seeing the transparent area around the hexagon as well as the hexagon shape.

3. Select Edit, Deselect to deselect the hexagon image. Click the Lasso tool to access the Magic Wand modifiers, and set the Threshold to 2 and the Smoothing to Smooth. Click OK to set these properties.

4. Click the Magic Wand modifier and position the tool on a corner area outside the hexagon shape. Click to select this area, and then delete the selection (see Figure 5.14).

Figure 5.14   You are selecting the transparent area of the GIF file.

Tip ————————————————————————————————

Use your Magnifier tool to zoom in on the edges of the image to view the effects of various Smoothing settings.

5. Repeat step 4 to delete the other areas that surround the hexagon shape (see Figure 5.15).

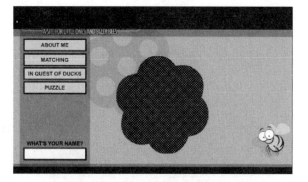

Figure 5.15   Your hexagon shape should resemble this figure.

6. Next, create the six circular holes that the Design Template shows for this object. Click the Oval tool and set the modifier settings to a Stroke of bright green and a Fill of None. Draw a circle on your Stage.

7. With the Arrow tool, select the stroke of the circle you just drew. Then, using the Property Inspector, set the Width and Height of the circle to 50.

8. With the Arrow tool, position the circle inside one of the six hexagon curves that compose the image. Copy the circle and paste it six more times; then, position these circles as indicated by Figure 5.16.

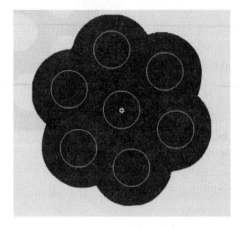

Figure 5.16   You can manipulate and edit the hexagon image because it has been broken apart.

9. Click inside one of the circles to select this area and delete it (see Figure 5.17). Delete the center of each of the other six circles.

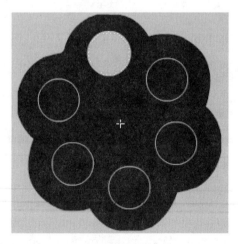

Figure 5.17   Because of how Flash MX represents shapes, the stroke of the circle merges with the image, creating a fill area inside the circle. This enables the fill area of the circle to be selected.

10. Now delete the green stroke for each of the circles (see Figure 5.18)

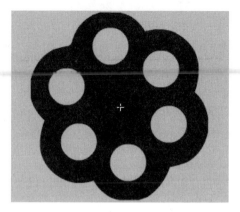

Figure 5.18   The hexagon symbol should resemble this figure.

> **Note**
>
> If you do not like the way your hexagon turned out, you can import a final version of the hexagon image called `final_hex.ai` at this point in the book from the CD-ROM located in the `Semanar05/Samples` directory.

11. Exit the symbol–editing mode to return to the movie. Unhide the `Guide: Design Template` layer, and position the instance of the hexagon symbol as indicated on the template.

12. The hexagon instance needs to have an alpha effect applied to it. Select the instance on the Stage, and from the Property Inspector, set a Color effect of Alpha and a setting of 15% (see Figure 5.19).

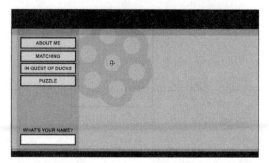

Figure 5.19   The hexagon shape resembles the shape in the design template. Don't worry if it is not exactly the same image.

Applying and Adjusting a Gradient Fill in the Hexagon Shape

To add a little more variety to the hexagon shape, a gradient fill can be applied. Because this shape is modifiable due to being broken apart, you can apply whatever fill you want to it. Follow these steps to add a gradient fill to the hexagon shape:

1. Open the hexagon shape symbol in the symbol-editing mode so that you can edit the symbol again. Select the fill area of the shape so that it is active.

2. Now you will create and apply a custom radial gradient fill for the hexagon shape. Open the Color Mixer and set the Fill Type to Radial.

3. Click the left color pointer to select it, and then click the color modifier. Type the hexadecimal value of **CC3300** into the Hex Edit text box.

4. Click the right color pointer and set its color modifier to black (see Figure 5.20).

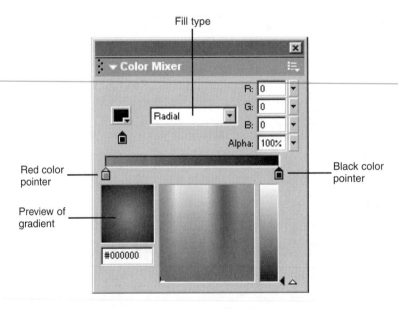

Figure 5.20   You can adjust the color pointers on the Gradient Definition Bar by dragging them left or right, respectively.

5. Close or collapse the Color Mixer. Notice that the new gradient is applied to the hexagon shape (see Figure 5.21).

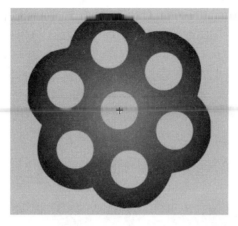

Figure 5.21   The hexagon shape resembles the shape in the design template. Don't worry if it is not exactly the same image.

6. Now adjust the gradient fill to show more of the black color and less of the red in the radial gradient fill. Click the Fill Transform tool in the toolbox. This is a new feature of Flash MX that enables you to adjust gradient fills applied to a Stage object.

7. With the Fill Transform tool active, click the hexagon shape to display handles around the shape (see Figure 5.22).

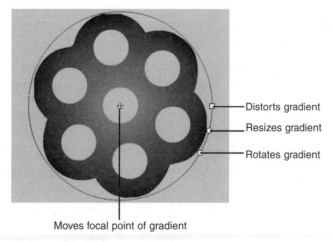

Figure 5.22   This is a radial gradient fill. A linear gradient fill has the same handles but represented in a different fashion.

8. Each handle has a function in transforming the gradient. The gradient would be nicer if it were a little larger in its flow of red to black. Click the Resize handle and make the gradient flow larger (see Figure 5.23).

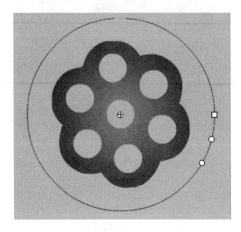

Figure 5.23   This is a radial gradient fill; a linear gradient fill has the same handles but represented in a different fashion.

9. Click the Arrow tool and exit the symbol-editing mode. The hexagon shape now appears with a slight red glow created by the radial gradient.

Importing Buzzy Bee and The Honeycomb Logo

Next, you'll import the Buzzy Bee character and The Honeycomb logo. One file is a FreeHand file, and the other is an Adobe Illustrator file. Each command has an Import dialog box that displays and enables you to preserve the vector elements that make up these images. Follow these steps to import the objects:

1. To import The Honeycomb logo, select File, Import; then navigate to the CD-ROM and the `Seminar05/Samples/Honeycomb_logo.fh9` file. Click the Open button. If you are using a Macintosh, click the Add button to add the image, and then click the Import button. This displays the FreeHand Import dialog box (see Figure 5.24).

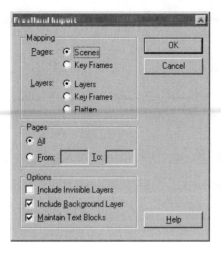

Figure 5.24   Flash MX maintains many of the features used to create the FreeHand image through the FreeHand Import dialog box.

2. Keep the default settings for this dialog box and import the image. It appears on its own layer at the bottom of the layer stacking order. Hide all other layers but the new Layer 1.

3. Select this layer and unlock it. Rename the imported Layer 1 **honeycomb logo** and move this layer in the stacking order above the header layer.

4. Hide all other layers but the honeycomb logo and the Guide: Design Template layers. This enables you to focus on the template and the positioning of The Honeycomb logo.

5. Select all the elements of The Honeycomb logo and convert it to a symbol. Name the symbol **honeycomb logo**, and give it a Graphic behavior. Keep the registration point set to the center.

6. Reposition the honeycomb logo layer above the header layer (see Figure 5.25).

Tip ───

The Arrow keys can be used to precisely move an object one pixel at a time. If you hold down the Shift key and press and Arrow key, the object moves multiple pixels relative to the zoom setting.

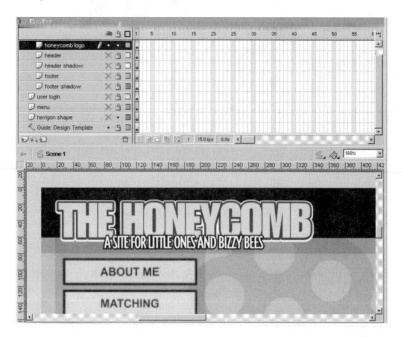

Figure 5.25   To align The Honeycomb logo instance with the design template, you might need to use your arrow keys to move the instance one pixel at a time.

7. To import the Buzzy Bee character, first insert a new layer above the Background Objects folder layer. Name this layer **buzzy bee**.

8. With the buzzy bee layer active, select File, Import and navigate to the buzzy.ai file that is located on the CD-ROM in the Seminar05/Samples directory. Click Open to import the image; this displays the Illustrator Import dialog box (see Figure 5.26).

Figure 5.26   By selecting Layers in the Layers area of the dialog box, all the vector shapes used to create the bee character are preserved.

9. Leave the Illustrator Import settings at the default settings, as Figure 5.26 shows, and click OK. Buzzy Bee is imported into its own layer at the bottom of the layer stacking order (see Figure 5.27).

Figure 5.27   Buzzy Bee displays on the Stage with all the individual vector elements that compose his shape in tact.

10. Hide all layers but the new Layer 1 and the buzzy bee layer.

11. Select all the elements of Buzzy Bee on Layer 1, and convert them to a symbol. Name the symbol **buzzy bee**, and give it a Movie Clip behavior. Set the registration point in the upper-left corner. Click OK to close the Convert to Symbol dialog box.

12. Cut the instance of the buzzy bee symbol from the new layer, and then delete both the Layer 1 and Guides layers that were created with the imported file.

13. Click the buzzy bee layer and paste the instance of the buzzy bee symbol onto this layer. Position the instance of the buzzy bee symbol on the Stage as the design template indicates.

Importing and Working with the Communication Bubble

Next, you'll import the bubble that appears above Buzzy Bee to enable communication with the end-user. This bubble does not need to be positioned on the Stage for the opening scene of the movie, but it is used later. Therefore, you will import this symbol into the movie library. To work with this image, it must be converted to a vector shape. Follow these steps to import and convert this image:

1. To import the bubble GIF image, select File, Import to Library. In the Import to Library dialog box, navigate to the `Seminar05/Samples/bubble.gif` file on the CD-ROM; import this image. The GIF image is added to the library as a Bitmap symbol.

2. Next, create a new symbol for this imported image. Name the new symbol **bubble** and give it a Movie Clip behavior. Set the registration point to the center. Click OK to close the dialog box, and symbol-editing mode is launched.

3. Drag an instance of the bubble bitmap symbol onto the Stage of the symbol-editing mode.

4. To convert the raster image to vector format, select the bubble image and select Modify, Trace Bitmap. In the Trace Bitmap dialog box that displays, configure your settings as Figure 5.28 indicates.

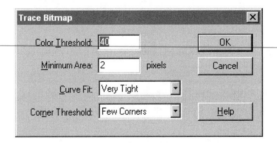

Figure 5.28   You want the vector image to be composed of two colors: white and black. Therefore, you set your Color Threshold to 40 so that any slight variance in color value will be viewed as black or white.

5. Click OK to begin the tracing process for converting this image to a vector. The bubble displays as a vector image. If you select the white fill of the bubble, it can be moved out of the black outline of the bubble. To prevent this from happening, group the bubble by selecting it and selecting Modify, Group. The bubble symbol is now a vector art shape. You will use this symbol later in the book for communicating information to the end-user.

Creating the Shadow for Buzzy Bee and the Communication Bubble

With the character Buzzy Bee and the communication bubble created as symbols into the movie, you can now use both symbols to create the shadow that appears behind these two objects. To create the shadow, you use the symbols you have in your Library and covert an instance of each object into its own symbol. These new symbols will have a black fill applied. Then you place an instance of these shadows with the original symbol, nesting the shadow symbol inside the original symbol. Follow these steps to create these shadows:

1. To add the shadow of Buzzy Bee, you first must create a new symbol. Select Insert, New Symbol and name the symbol **buzzy shadow**. Click OK to close the dialog box. This launches the symbol-editing mode.

2. While in the symbol-editing mode, open the Library and drag an instance of the buzzy bee symbol onto the Stage. Align it centered both vertically and horizontally to the Stage.

3. You will use this instance of the buzzy bee symbol to create the shadow. This requires changing all the individual vector shapes of the buzzy bee symbol to a fill of black. You do not want to change the original buzzy bee symbol; therefore, you need to break the link between the symbol and the Stage instance. Select Modify, Break Apart. The instance is now broken into the originally imported vector made up of individual vector shapes.

4. With the link broken between the symbol and the instance, now you can change all the fill areas of Buzzy to black. To do this, you must break the buzzy bee vector shape into its basic form of strokes and fills. Again, select Modify, Break Apart (see Figure 5.29).

Figure 5.29   Each individual object that makes up the buzzy bee symbol is broken into its fill and stroke areas.

5. Because the image uses a black stroke already, a black fill is all that is necessary for converting this image to black. Access the Color Mixer and select a black color for the Fill modifier (see Figure 5.30).

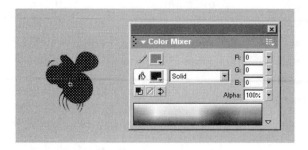

Figure 5.30   If you have a Fill area active in an object on the Stage, as soon as you apply a new fill through a Fill modifier, the active shape reflects this new fill.

6. Open the buzzy bee symbol in the symbol-editing mode by double-clicking it from the Library.

7. Rename Layer 1 to **buzzy** and then insert a new layer. Name this new layer **shadow**, and move it to the bottom of the layer stacking order.

8. From the Library, drag an instance of the buzzy shadow onto the Stage. You are nesting the buzzy shadow instance in the buzzy bee symbol. Position the instance of the buzzy shadow symbol to the lower left of the buzzy bee instance (see Figure 5.31).

Figure 5.31   This new shadow displays in the instance of the buzzy bee symbol on the Stage of the main movie.

9. From the Effects panel, set an Alpha Effect of 100% for the shadow instance to apply a transparency to the instance.

10. Exit the symbol-editing mode to return to the movie. Notice that the instance of the `buzzy bee` symbol now has a shadow.

Tip ───────────────────────────────────

If you need to align the shadow so that it matches the Design Template, (Control-click)[right-click] the `buzzy bee` instance and select Edit in Place. Then position the instance of the `buzzy shadow` as needed.

11. To create the communication bubble shadow, repeat steps 1–10. Name the new symbol **bubble shadow** with the same settings in the Symbol Properties dialog box as the `buzzy bee shadow`. Nest the `bubble shadow` on its own layer in the `bubble` symbol and position it to the lower left of the bubble vector shape (see Figure 5.32).

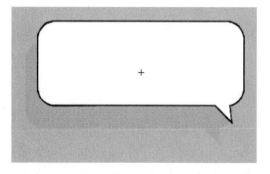

Figure 5.32   Keep the shadow to the lower left of the bubble so that it is consistent with the shadow light effect used with Buzzy Bee.

Tip ───────────────────────────────────

If you have trouble with step 11, you can use the **05Honeycomb.fla** file found on the CD-ROM in `Seminar05/Samples` directory.

Note ───────────────────────────────────

You should keep up with the organization of your library as your movie develops. Quite a few bitmap symbols could be grouped together in a folder. Create a new folder named **Bitmap Symbols** in the library, and place the three Bitmap symbols in the Bitmap Symbols folder (see Figure 5.33).

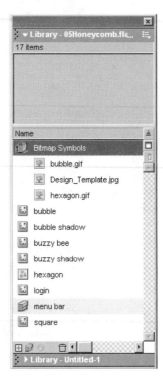

Figure 5.33   The bitmap symbols are easily found and accessible in the new folder.

12. Save the movie as Honeycomb.fla. Your movie should be similar to Figure 5.34. If you want to compare your Honeycomb site with a movie that is completed up to this point in the book, open the 05Honeycomb.fla file located in the Seminar05/Samples directory on the CD-ROM that accompanies this book.

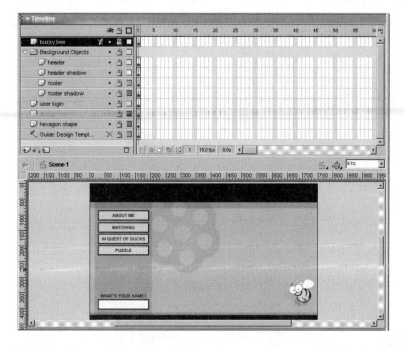

Figure 5.34 The Honeycomb site has the opening scene intact at this point in the development of the movie.

Seminar Summary

This seminar covered the skills necessary to import and work with artwork created in other software applications. You also learned skills for optimizing an imported graphic to bring down its file size. You should now have an idea of which applications can work with Flash MX when you create your graphics for a Flash MX movie. The next seminar covers creating the animation and special effects for bringing some life to The Honeycomb site.

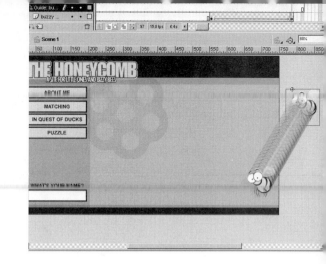

Seminar 6

Animation and Special Effects for Flashing Up the Site

In this chapter

Workshop: Creating the Opening Stage Animation

Overview of Web-Based Animation

Macromedia Flash MX is no longer considered a mere two-dimensional, vector-based animation tool due to the extra functionality and interactivity Macromedia has gradually added to Flash since its inception. However, the power of animation and movement is still one of the main reasons Macromedia Flash MX has come so far so quickly.

Most people are under the false impression that animation means cartoon animation, when actually *animation* means movement in general, plain and simple. Animation can be a menu bar that opens slowly, a graceful figure skater who glides across the ice, or a flag blowing in the wind. This seminar introduces you to how to create animation in Flash MX.

Web-based animation depends on many factors—primarily, physical memory (RAM), bandwidth, and most importantly, the processing power of the end-user's computer system. Unfortunately, these factors vary—sometimes greatly—from system to system.

When a computer downloads any file from the Internet, that file is stored as data in binary format, a computer's native language of 1s and 0s. When called on, this data is then compiled by the processor and displayed to the end-user via the monitor. Depending on a user's processor speed, this "process" can take place very quickly or quite slowly. All these factors play a part in the creation of animation with Flash MX.

> **Note**
>
> It's best to always create a Flash MX movie focused on what we in the industry call the *lowest common denominator*. This means building your movie and animations to play well on a majority of users' machines, not just users with a 1.5GHz Pentium 4 and 500MB of RAM.

Working with the Timeline

In Flash MX, when you create animation, you are working between the Timeline and the Stage. The Timeline is the holding area for all the layers in the movie; it enables you to sequence the frames so that you develop a progression of time. Animation is really a trick of the eye. As the playhead moves from one frame to the next, your Stage changes in its content, creating the illusion of motion. Three types of frames exist in Flash MX: *keyframes*, *frames*, and *photoframes* (see Figure 6.1).

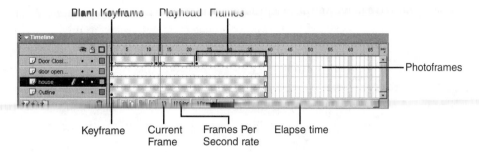

Figure 6.1 The hollow circle in a frame designates a blank keyframe.

A frame holds static Stage content, content that is not moving on the Stage. A keyframe is used to hold any content on the Stage where there is a change in Stage content or to hold frame labels or ActionScript. A photoframe is strictly a container space in the Timeline used to hold either a frame or keyframe. By working with layers, frames, and keyframes, you begin to build your movie. You will have hands-on practice in the workshop section of this seminar working with frames and keyframes in The Honeycomb site.

Selecting Frames and Keyframes in the Timeline

To begin to create animation, you first must know how to work with the Timeline, how to select frames, and how to create and manipulate the location of frames and keyframes. In Flash MX, Macromedia changed the functionality of the Timeline by incorporating features of the Timeline from previous releases of Flash with new features of Flash MX. This has made the Timeline easier to use and frames easier to manipulate.

To select a frame, keyframe, or photoframe from the Timeline, simply click it. The frame, keyframe, or photoframe becomes highlighted, indicating that it is the active element in the Timeline.

Creating a Keyframe

If you want to add a keyframe to the Timeline, you must first select a frame, keyframe, or photoframe. Then, you can either insert a blank keyframe by selecting Insert, Blank Keyframe or insert a keyframe by selecting Insert, Keyframe. The difference between a keyframe and a blank keyframe is in the Stage content. A *blank keyframe* is automatically created when you create a new layer because the Stage for that layer is blank. If you insert a blank keyframe into a layer that has Stage content, the Stage is cleared for that location of the Timeline. When you insert a keyframe into the Timeline, Flash MX copies the Stage content exactly as it exists in the previous keyframe into that new keyframe. This is very beneficial for making changes that you want when you apply a *motion tween* to the two keyframes. You do not have to re-create the Stage content you will animate in the second keyframe because Flash MX duplicates the previous keyframe Stage content automatically and creates frames in between the two keyframes. You just need to alter the position, size, or color of the object on the Stage to set your keyframe content.

Note

The keyboard equivalent for the Insert, Keyframe command is F6. The keyboard equivalent for the Insert, Blank Keyframe command is F7.

Tip

You can (Control-click)[right-click] a photoframe, frame, or keyframe that will hold a new keyframe and select Insert Keyframe to insert a new keyframe into the photoframe.

Creating a Frame

A *frame* is different from a keyframe. A frame is used to show static content on the Stage or objects that are stationary in a layer. You can create a frame by selecting Insert, Frame or pressing F5. For example, many times in a movie's development, you will want to extend a layer's content farther out on the Timeline but do not plan to create any animation with this content—you want it to remain the same through the end of the movie. To create this static Stage content, you insert a frame at the end of this layer (see Figure 6.2).

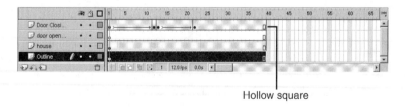

Hollow square

Figure 6.2   The small, hollow square at the end of the layer represents static Stage content.

Tip

You can (Control-click)[right-click] the photoframe that will hold the new frame and select Insert Frame to insert the new frame into the photoframe.

Manipulating Frames and Keyframes

Frames and keyframes in the Timeline can be manipulated or moved from one location to another. For example, if you had a character that appeared in a movie at a keyframe in Frame 10 but decided later that the character needed to appear later in the Timeline, you would need to move the corresponding keyframe to a position later in the Timeline for that layer. If you wanted to move a keyframe to a new location in the Timeline, you would simply click the keyframe and drag it to a new location (see Figure 6.3).

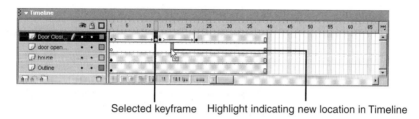

Selected keyframe   Highlight indicating new location in Timeline

Figure 6.3   You can drag a keyframe to a new location in the Timeline for that layer or to another layer.

You can also replace multiple frames and keyframes in your Timeline to move them to a new location. You can use two techniques, depending on which group of frames of keyframes you want to move. If you are moving a group of frames between two keyframes, double-click any of the frames between the two keyframes to select them all. If, on the other hand, you are moving a group of frames that are not between two keyframes, use the Shift-click technique. With an active selection, now you can drag the series of frames and keyframes to a new location in the Timeline (see Figure 6.4).

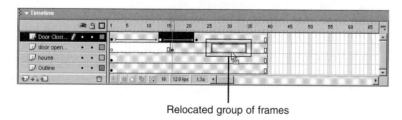

Relocated group of frames

Figure 6.4   You can drag the series of frames and keyframes to a new location in the same layer or to any other layer.

Tip ————————————————————————

You can also use menu commands to cut or copy frames and keyframes to a new location in the Timeline. Select the frames first, and then select Edit, Cut Frames or Copy Frames (Command-Option-X) [Ctrl+Alt+X]; then you can select Edit, Paste Frames (Command-Option-V) [Ctrl+Alt+V] to relocate the frame(s) to a new location in the Timeline. By cutting or copying the keyframe, you also cut or copy the Stage content that exists for that keyframe.

Testing Your Movie

As you develop the Timeline for a movie, you will need to test or check your work. Three techniques are available for testing your movie. You can test a movie in the Flash Authoring environment with two of the techniques—scrubbing through the movie and playing the movie. You can also test your movie in the Flash Player Testing Mode. The Flash Player Testing Mode is more powerful because it can play all the ActionScript and movie clips you include in your movie. The Flash Authoring environment can play only the main movie's Timeline, has limited playback on ActionScript and buttons, and will not play a movie clip Timeline. More is covered on each of these techniques next.

Scrubbing Through the Movie

Flash MX offers a feature called *scrubbing* that allows you to check your Timeline progression one frame at a time. To scrub through your Timeline, click and drag the playhead left or right through the Timeline. This causes the Stage content to reflect the progression of the Timeline, simulating movement one frame at a time.

Playing the Movie

You can also play back a movie in the Flash Authoring environment by selecting Control, Play or by pressing (Return)[Enter].

To play back with the Controller panel, select Window, Toolbars, Controller and use the Controller buttons to control your playback (see Figure 6.5).

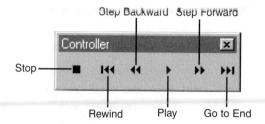

Figure 6.5   You can position the Controller anywhere you want by clicking and dragging it by the title bar to the new location on your screen.

Testing the Movie

Another nice feature Flash MX offers is a quick way to preview the Flash MX SWF file of the movie. Select Control, Test Movie to convert the movie from FLA format to the compressed SWF format. This launches the Flash Player Testing Mode; your movie then displays and begins to play. Previewing a movie in this testing mode enables you to see all the elements of a movie functioning. When you use movie clips and more advanced interactivity via ActionScript, you must convert the movie to SWF format to view all the movie's functionality.

Tip
The keyboard shortcut for the Test Movie command is (Command-Return)[Ctrl+Enter].

What Is Tweening?

Tweening is a term applied to keyframe animation and the creation of the frames to show the change of an object from point A to point B. The following discussion covers both types of tweening—motion and shape—as well as frame-by-frame animation.

Using Motion Tweening

A key component of animation in Flash MX is motion tweening. It's used often in Flash development for creating many of the animation effects that make a movie come alive. Motion tweens create smooth movement or change of objects on the Stage through the use of size, color, and Stage positioning.

To create a motion tween, you start with an instance of a symbol in a keyframe, which is your starting point, or point A. By adding another keyframe in the same layer as the first, but farther down the Timeline, you copy the instance on the Stage of the first keyframe and have your ending point, or point B. Using the modifiable attributes of an instance—its position or size, brightness, tint, or alpha—you can change the instance for its ending state. In other words, you set a starting position for the instance and an ending position. Through the Insert, Create Motion Tween command, Flash creates all the in-between frames from point A to B (see Figure 6.6). You create many motion tweens in the workshop section of this seminar.

Figure 6.6   When a motion tween is applied, the fill area between the two keyframes becomes blue, and an arrow appears indicating that a motion tween has been applied to these frames.

> **Note**
>
> Figure 6.6 has the feature of onion-skinning turned on so that the Stage content for all frames in the motion tween are visible. You will learn more about onion-skinning later in this seminar as well as in the workshop.

To see an example of a motion tween, open tween1.fla from the Seminar06/ Samples directory on the CD-ROM that accompanies this book. To see the animation play, scrub through Frames 1–10 by dragging the playhead. This sample file shows a motion tween applied to a text block. The text block is smaller when the animation starts and then moves slowly to the bottom of the Stage as it gets larger.

Tip

The more frames between the keyframes of a motion tween, the slower and smoother the animation. If only a few frames are between keyframes, the animation is faster and choppier. You should experiment with the number of frames to create the animation effect you want.

Note

Motion tweens can be applied only to instances in the movie. If you apply a motion tween to an object that is not an instance, Flash MX automatically converts the object to a symbol in your library. Flash MX generically names the symbol Tween1 or, depending on how many times you forget to convert an object into a symbol, Tween2, Tween3, and so on. If you forget to use symbols for your motion tweens, your library will be full of "Tween" symbols, making it very hard to identify the symbols and even knowing where they are used on the Stage.

Using Tweening to Create Other Animation Effects

Motion tweening becomes more interesting when you begin to modify multiple attributes of the tweened instance for each of the keyframes. Seminar 4, "Using Symbols in a Movie," covered the four attributes you can change for an instance: size/orientation, color, brightness, and alpha effect. As long as you use the same instance for each of the keyframes in your motion tween, you can change one or multiple attributes of each instance. When a motion tween is applied, Flash MX automatically creates the change in the object for all the frames up to the second keyframe to show this new attribute(s) of the instance as it changes. To see an example of a motion tween by changing multiple attributes of an instance, look at `tween2.fla` located in the `Seminar06/Samples` directory. This sample file uses size, alpha, and tint color effects to create the animation.

The following list provides information on some of the effects that can be achieved by applying different attributes to an instance:

- **Fade in/Fade Out**—Changes the instance attribute of Alpha for one or both of the instances in a motion tween

- **Perspective/Distance**—Changes the instance attribute of size and orientation for one or both of the instances in a motion tween

- **Fade to Black/Fade to White**—Changes the instance attribute of brightness for one or both of the instances in a motion tween

- **Color Cycle**—Changes the instance attribute of tint for one or both of the instances

> **Note** ───────────────────────────────
>
> Fade in/fade out transitions between different areas of your movie are nice for helping to distinguish the end of one scene in your movie and the beginning of another. For instance, if you want your Stage content or even just a layer's content to slowly fade to black, you can create this effect with a motion tween and an alpha effect or a Brightness effect. You could apply an alpha effect to all the Stage content to cause it to slowly fade to black or to just one image.

> **Warning** ────────────────────────────
>
> An alpha effect used in a motion tween can tap the processor on a slower machine depending on the instance size and composition that it is being applied, too. Use alpha effects wisely in your movie.

Using Shape Tweening

A shape tween in Flash MX is similar to the morphing effect you probably have seen in movies and commercials. This is where you take an object and then transition or "morph" it into another object. Shape tweens consume a lot of file space because they convert all the elements that make up one shape into another shape. It is recommended that you use very few shape tweens when you are creating a movie that will be accessed via the Internet.

Motion Tweening Versus Shape Tweening

When compared to a motion tween that transitions the same instance from point A to point B focusing on its attributes, shape tweens are applied to two different objects. This presents some issues that are different from a motion tween. Because you are converting one shape into another, Flash MX needs to have both objects broken into their basic vector forms of strokes and fills. This enables the mathematical formula that represents these shapes to be manipulated to create the effect of morphing. For example, if you wanted to cause a black bar that extends across the Stage to morph into a word, such as a company name, you would use a shape tween to create this animation effect (see Figure 6.7). To see an example of a shape tween, open `tween3.fla` located in the `Seminar06/Samples` directory on the CD-ROM that accompanies this book.

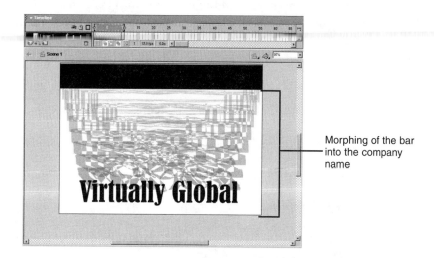

Morphing of the bar into the company name

Figure 6.7   When a shape tween is applied, a green highlight appears between the two keyframes that set both point A and point B of the animation.

A shape tween is created similarly to a motion tween by setting beginning and ending keyframes and Stage content. But unlike a motion tween, which requires one instance of a symbol to be the tweened object, shape tweens requires two objects and each object must be broken down to its basic vector form of strokes and fills. They can't be grouped or be an instance of a symbol.

Creating Shape Tweening

No menu command exists for applying a shape tween, so it must be applied using the Property Inspector. Follow these steps to apply a shape tween:

1. Click the frame you want to begin the shape tween, and select Insert, Keyframe.

2. Create the image you want to start with for the morph, and leave this image in its basic vector form of strokes and fills. Do not group or make this image into a symbol.

3. Click the frame you want to end the shape tween, and select Insert, Blank Keyframe. By inserting a blank keyframe, you clear your Stage at the point in the Timeline.

4. Create the image you want to use as the final image that the first image morphs into. Again, leave this image in its basic vector form of strokes and fills.

5. Click any frame between the starting and ending keyframes and, in the Property Inspector, set the Tween option to Shape (see Figure 6.8). With the shape tween applied, the Stage content shows the morphing of the shape.

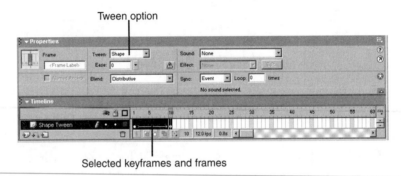

Figure 6.8   A green fill displays between the keyframes indicating that a shape tween has been applied.

Tip

When you have a shape tween created, open your Frame panel. The Ease setting in the Frame panel causes a shape tween to start slowly and end quickly if you set the Ease to a negative number. Conversely, you can make the shape tween start quickly and end slowly if you set the Ease to a positive number.

Using Onion-Skinning

The Timeline also offers a feature of Onion Skin for working with animation. *Onion-skinning* allows you to see multiple consecutive frames in the Timeline and their Stage content by dimming or outlining the Stage content. The onion-skinning feature is composed of four buttons located on the bottom of the Timeline (see Figure 6.9).

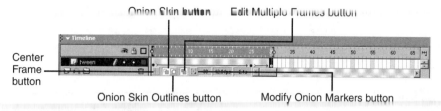

Onion Skin button   Edit Multiple Frames button

Center Frame button

Onion Skin Outlines button   Modify Onion Markers button

Figure 6.9   Additional buttons are available on the Timeline that can help you design and troubleshoot your images and animations.

Normally, Flash shows Stage content one frame at a time. But if you turn on the Onion Skin feature, you can view multiple frames and Stage content. The Onion Skin feature can be compared to a sheet of acetate with an image on it. Each frame in an animation is its own sheet with Stage content, and all sheets are stacked one on top of another. Therefore, the animation displays showing multiple frames of Stage content in either a dimmed view or an outline view depending on the onion-skin button you have selected (see Figure 6.10). Onion-skinning allows you to view a progression of the Timeline and Stage content for an animation.

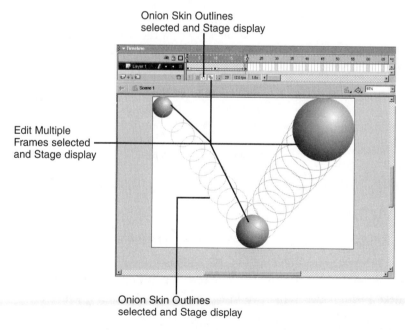

Onion Skin Outlines selected and Stage display

Edit Multiple Frames selected and Stage display

Onion Skin Outlines selected and Stage display

Figure 6.10   You can view the entire motion tween by adjusting your Onion Markers above the Timeline. To adjust a marker, click and drag it.

Table 6.1 explains each button and gives examples of possible uses in Flash MX

Table 6.1   Description of Onion Skin Features

Feature	Description
Onion Skin	Click this button to turn on the onion-skinning. Your Stage shows an outline of the Timeline content for three frames. You use this feature to view the flow of your animation with other Stage content to get the exact placement of your objects.
Onion Skin Outlines	Click this button to turn on the outline view of your Stage content. Objects appear in their assigned layer outline colors and fade out as the frames get further back. This feature makes viewing animation for edits and manipulations easier.
Edit Multiple Frames	Click this button to turn on an onion-skinning view that allows the object on the Stage of each keyframe to be accessible. You can adjust both the starting and the ending Stage object of each of the keyframes by simply clicking the object and editing its location or size.
Modify Onion Markers	Click this button to display a shortcut menu that enables you to select menu commands for controlling your Onion Markers. To manually adjust your Onion Markers, click and drag them to a new location in the Timeline.

Using a Motion Guide

Another popular animation technique that allows for modification of the path of a motion tween is a *motion guide*. A motion guide sets a path for an object's motion. A motion tween causes an instance to appear to move from point A to point B in the simplest and quickest path between the two instances—a straight path. If you want to vary this path, you can do so through a motion guide (see Figure 6.11).

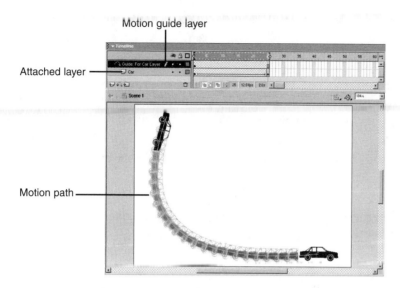

Motion guide layer

Attached layer

Motion path

Figure 6.11   The layer below the motion guide layer indents to the right indicating that it is attached to the motion guide layer.

Creating a Motion Path

The key to a motion path is to first create your motion tween, setting your point A and point B for Stage content. Then, you can create a motion guide layer by clicking the Add Motion Guide button in the layer's area of the Timeline. The motion path is created with a stroke. You can use any of the Flash MX tools that have a stroke, and the stroke can be any color or stroke size. The motion path causes the tweened instance to adhere and follow the stroke or path. In the workshop section of this seminar, you will create a motion guide and adhere a tweened object to that motion path. To view an example of a car that follows a motion path, open `motion_guide.fla` located in `Seminar06/Samples/` directory on the CD-ROM that accompanies this book.

> **Tip**
>
> The motion guide layer is only part of the movie in the Flash MX Authoring environment. When you publish your movie, guide layers, whether they are guide layers or motion guide layers, are not included in the SWF file.

Orienting the Motion Tween to the Motion Path

After you apply a motion guide to a motion-tweened animation, you can apply some techniques to cause the animation to adhere more tightly and with better orientation to the path. For example, in the motion_guide.fla file, a car travels down a curved path. For this to be realistic motion for the car, it would need to follow the path head first. When you apply a motion guide to a tweened animation, you do not necessarily get the realistic motion you might want for your animation. In the example of the car, when a motion guide is first applied, the car travels down the path with unnatural orientation (see Figure 6.12).

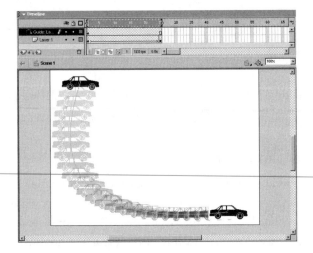

Figure 6.12   The car is oriented horizontally when the path is a curve. This does not create realistic motion for the car's movement.

Through the Property Inspector, you can modify or customize the motion tween to cause it to adhere more tightly and naturally in its progression along the motion path, from point A to point B. By selecting a frame between the first and last keyframes of the motion tween, the Property Inspector displays other settings for customizing tween objects to the motion path. The Orient to Path option causes an object to follow the motion path tightly (see Figure 6.13).

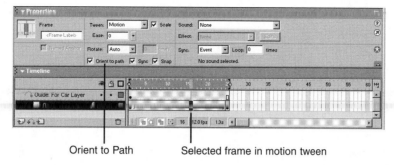

Orient to Path   Selected frame in motion tween

Figure 6.13   If you click the Rotate option and set it to either CW (clockwise) or CCW (counter clockwise) and then set a number in the Times box, you can cause a tweened animation to twirl as it follows the motion path.

Tip

You might need to adjust the orientation by sizing or rotating the tweened instance on the Stage to get a more realistic motion of the instance following the path.

To view an example of a motion tweened object that is oriented to a motion path, look at the `motion_guide.fla` file located in the `Seminar06/Samples` directory on the CD-ROM that accompanies this book.

Frame-by-Frame Animation

You can also create frame-by-frame animation in Flash MX. Motion and shape tweens are great animation techniques, but they do not always create the effect you want. Remember that animation is really a trick of the eye, relying on the progression of the Timeline moving from frame to frame more quickly than the eye can process the information. Therefore, frame-by-frame animation can also be used for any type of animation that switches quickly between two images on the Stage. This could be the flapping of wings going up and down, legs walking, eyes blinking, and so on. Again, the key to this type of animation is keyframes—inserting either a keyframe or a blank keyframe in the Timeline next to the starting keyframe and positioning an object or instance on the Stage to show the transition between two objects. Because the Timeline moves more quickly than the eye can see, the two objects appear to move.

Next, you'll apply what you've learned in the discussion portion of this seminar to The Honeycomb Web site. To prepare for this, close all other movies that you might have opened while working through the discussion portion of this seminar.

Creating the Opening Stage Animation

As you are probably realizing by now, symbols and instances are where much of the power of Flash MX is, but animation is where the fun is. Next, you'll learn how to create and use animation to add some excitement to the Honeycomb Web site project. To see an example of the animation that you will create for this site, open `06honeycomb.swf`, which is on the CD-ROM in the `Seminar06/Samples` directory.

The Honeycomb Web site uses some simple animation that creates a fun and interesting effect for the Web site. The header and footer bars will slowly fly onto the Stage from the top and the bottom of the Stage, and then the shadows for both the header and the footer follow, but they appear transparent at first and slowly display to a 25% transparency. Then, the logo appears—first in white—and slowly changes to its normal appearance. Next, the menu bar drops into the movie from the top, followed by the login box moving into the movie from the bottom. The background design is set at this point but is missing one character, Buzzy Bee. Buzzy Bee appears by flying onto the Stage. His wings flap, and his path simulates the motion of flying. The site suddenly comes alive by the use of this animation and has more appeal.

These animations are created using Flash MX's tween function for motion, size, and various color effects. Each animation must appear on its own layer because you can't apply motion tweens to more than one object per layer at the same time. In Seminar 3, "Creating a Movie," you created the layers necessary for creating these animations.

Creating the Opening Scene Header and Footer Animation

When the header and footer first display, they quickly enter the Stage but then slow to gradually move to their final resting positions. A motion tween is applied to create each of these animation effects. By applying a motion tween to two keyframes that are located very close to each other, you can cause your animation to appear to move very quickly. The more frames between your keyframes in a motion tween, the slower and smoother the animation. Follow these steps to create the animations:

1. Use your `Honeycomb.fla` file that you saved at the end of Seminar 5, "Importing Graphics into a Movie," or open `05Honeycomb.fla` from the `Seminar06/Samples` directory on the CD-ROM that accompanies this book.

2. Click the `header` layer to make it active. This also makes the header instance on the Stage active. Lock and hide all other layers but this layer by (Control-clicking)[right-clicking] the layer and choosing Lock Others and Hide Others form the shortcut menu. This makes focusing on the animation you are creating for the `header` layer easier.

3. The header instance flies onto the Stage from the top. When it first displays, it quickly enters the Stage but then slows to gradually move to its final resting point. To create this animation, you first need to set your Stage content for the animation. Move the header instance so that the bottom edge aligns with the guide that defines the top of the Stage (see Figure 6.14).

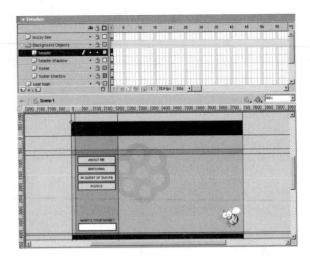

Figure 6.14   By positioning the instance in the work area, the object appears to fly onto the Stage. Only content directly on the Stage is part of the SWF file.

4. Click Photoframe 5 of the header layer and insert a keyframe by selecting Insert, Keyframe (F6). This copies the header instance from the keyframe in Frame 1 into the keyframe in Frame 5 in the same position and size. Move the header instance in the keyframe in Frame 5 so that it aligns with its ending position as defined by the guides. Move the instance three pixels up using the arrow key (see Figure 6.15).

5. Click Photoframe 15 of the header layer and insert a keyframe. This copies the keyframe in Frame 5 Stage content into the keyframe for Frame 15. Position the header instance so that it adheres to the guides that define its ending position (see Figure 6.16).

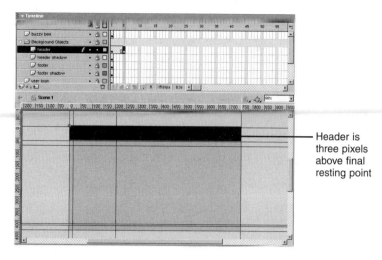

Header is three pixels above final resting point

Figure 6.15   Because of the need to cover the distance from point A to this location in five frames, the header instance appears to move very quickly.

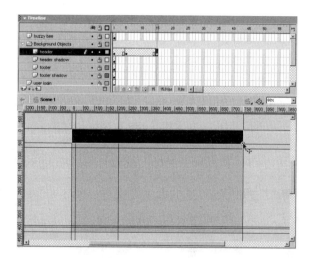

Figure 6.16   You are using 10 frames to cover three pixels of distance. The header will very slowly move to its resting position.

6. Next, create the motion tween for each movement of this instance. (Control-click)[Right-click] any frame between the keyframe in Frame 1 and the keyframe in Frame 5, and select Create Motion Tween from the shortcut menu. A motion tween is applied as indicated by the arrow and blue shading in the Timeline. Repeat this step and apply a motion tween between the keyframes in Frames 5 and 15 (see Figure 6.17). Lock the header layer.

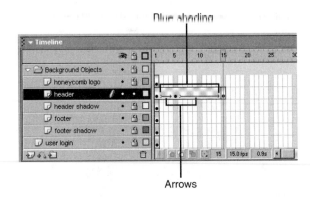

Figure 6.17   Blue shading and the arrow are visual reminders that you have a motion tween applied at that location in the Timeline.

7. Play the movie by pressing (Return)[Enter]. The header instance should move very quickly onto the Stage but then slow down and gradually move to a resting position.

8. Move your playhead back to the beginning of the Timeline. The footer needs to appear at the same time as the header, so click the footer layer. Show and unlock this layer; the footer instance on the Stage becomes active.

9. Again, position the footer instance so that it is in the work area but aligns its top edge to the guide that defines the bottom of the Stage (see Figure 6.18).

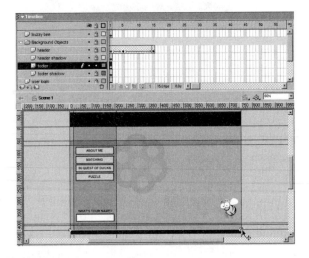

Figure 6.18   Click and drag the instance from its upper-right corner to cause it to adhere to the guides that define the bottom and right edges of the Stage.

10. Click Photoframe 5 of the `footer` layer and insert a keyframe to copy the instance for the keyframe in Frame 1 to the keyframe for Frame 5. Position the footer instance so that it aligns with its ending position as defined by the guides. Move the instance two pixels down by pressing the Down arrow key two times (see Figure 6.19).

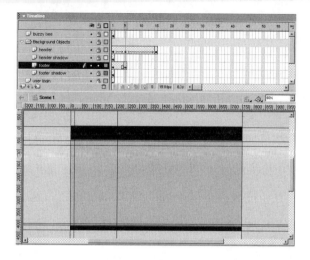

Figure 6.19 The footer instance appears to move very quickly because only five frames are tweened.

11. Click Photoframe 15 of the `footer` layer and insert a keyframe by pressing F6. This copies the instance in the keyframe in Frame 5 to the keyframe in Frame 15. Now position the `footer` instance on the Stage so that it adheres to the guides that define its resting position (see Figure 6.20).

12. Next, create the motion tween for each movement of this instance. (Control-click)[Right-click] any frame between the keyframe in Frame 1 and the keyframe in Frame 5, and select Create Motion Tween from the shortcut menu. A motion tween is applied as indicated by the arrow and blue shading in the Timeline. Repeat this step and apply a motion tween between the keyframes in Frame 5 and 15.

13. Play your movie by pressing (Return)[Enter]. The header and the footer quickly fly onto the Stage and then slowly move to their resting positions. Lock the `footer` layer.

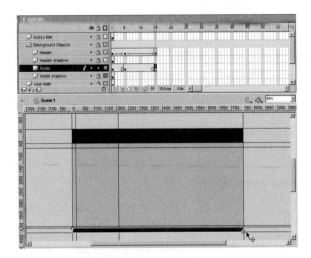

Figure 6.20   You could also use your Align panel and align the instance to the bottom of the Stage.

Creating Opening Scene Header Shadow and Footer Shadow Animation

Both the header shadow and footer shadow instances slowly appear on the Stage in a larger size and then shrink to their resting positions. You will apply both a size and a color effect tween to these instances to make each shadow slowly appear and shrink in size. Follow these steps to create the shadow animation:

1. The header shadow appears shortly after the header and footer appear. Move your playhead back to the beginning of the Timeline. Click the header shadow layer to make it active; then, show and unlock this layer. The header shadow on the Stage becomes active. Click the keyframe in Frame 1 of the header shadow layer and drag this keyframe to Photoframe 8 (see Figure 6.21).

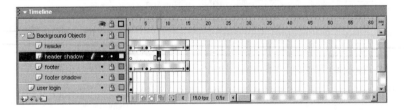

Figure 6.21   This is your starting point or point A for this animation.

2. Insert a keyframe in Photoframe 21 of the header shadow layer to copy the instance of the header shadow to this location in the Timeline. Notice that the header and footer disappear from the Stage. This is because their Stage content is visible only through Frame 15. Don't worry about this—you will fix this later in the workshop.

3. Click the keyframe in Frame 8, and click the header shadow instance to make it the active Stage object. Through the Property Inspector, resize the height of this instance to 154 and apply an Alpha effect of 0%.

4. Create the motion tween for this instance by (Control-clicking)[right-clicking] any frame between the keyframe in Frame 8 and the keyframe in Frame 21. Then, select Create Motion Tween from the shortcut menu. The header shadow slowly appears while shrinking from a larger size to its resting position. Lock the header shadow layer.

5. The footer shadow appears at the same time as the header shadow. Move your playhead back to the beginning of the Timeline. Click the footer shadow layer to make it active; then, show and unlock this layer. The footer instance on the Stage becomes active. Click the keyframe in Frame 1 of the Timeline and drag this keyframe to Photoframe 8.

6. Insert a keyframe in Photoframe 21 of the footer shadow layer to copy the instance of the footer shadow to this location in the Timeline.

7. Click the keyframe in Frame 8 of the footer shadow layer to make the footer shadow active. Through the Property Inspector, resize the height of this instance to 54.

8. Drag the instance from its bottom-right corner so that it adheres to the guides that define the bottom edge of the footer shadow (see Figure 6.22).

9. With the instance of the footer shadow active for the keyframe in Frame 8 of the footer shadow layer, apply an Alpha effect of 0% using the Property Inspector.

10. (Control-click)[right-click] any frame between the keyframe in Frame 8 and the keyframe in Frame 21 of the footer shadow layer; then, select Create Motion Tween from the shortcut menu. The footer shadow slowly appears while shrinking from a larger size to its resting position and size.

11. Move the playhead to the beginning of the Timeline and play the movie.

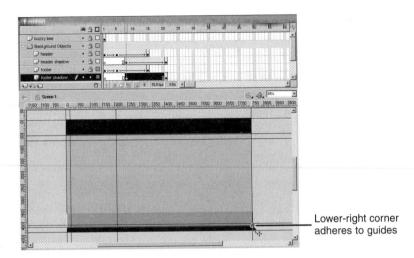

Lower-right corner
adheres to guides

Figure 6.22   The footer shadow will appear above its resting position and slowly shrink to its resting position.

As you can see from playing your movie, there is a problem of the header and footer disappearing from the Stage before the header and footer shadows finish their animations. In the next section of this workshop, you will fix the problem by extending the Timeline for these layers.

Extending the Header and Footer Layers

Because you want the header, footer, and two shadows to remain on the Stage throughout the movie, you must extend the Timeline for the header, footer, header shadow, and footer shadow layers to Frame 100. To do this, follow these steps:

1. Click Photoframe 100 for the header layer. Shift-click Photoframe 100 for the footer shadow layer so that all four header/footer layers are selected (see Figure 6.23).

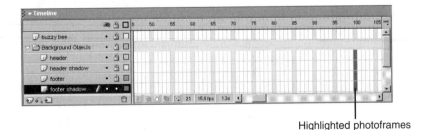

Highlighted photoframes

Figure 6.23   You can select multiple frames in multiple layers by Shift-clicking.

2. Select Insert, Frame to insert a frame in each of these four layers, extending the Timeline for the layers to Frame 100 (see Figure 6.24). You could also use the keyboard shortcut of F5 to insert these frames.

Gray shading

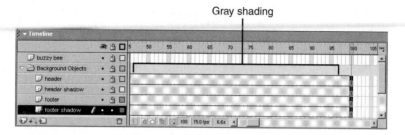

Figure 6.24 By extending the Timeline out to Frame 100, the header and footer objects remain on the Stage throughout the movie.

3. Play your movie and notice that it now shows all four layers and their animation, as well as plays through Frame 100.

Tip ─────

If you need to extend the Timeline further, simply select the frame in the layers to be extended and select Insert, Frame (F5). If you need to shorten the Timeline, you can do so by selecting the frames to be removed and selecting Insert, Remove Frames (or Shift+F5).

Tip ─────

You also can extend the Timeline by positioning the playhead at the point in the Timeline that you want to begin inserting frames, and then clicking the playhead to deselect everything on the Stage. Press F5 to insert a new frame for all layers. Press F5 repeatedly to insert many frames, extending the Timeline.

Creating the Menu Bar and Login Animation

The next step is to have the menu bar and login animation fly onto the screen. The menu bar animation begins very quickly and ends slowly. The login animation just flies onto the Stage. Again, you will use a motion tween and vary the number of frames between the keyframes for the starting and ending positions of the animations. Follow these steps to create this animation:

1. Move the playhead to the beginning of the Timeline. Click the menu layer to make it active; then, show and unlock this layer. Click the keyframe in Frame 1 of the menu and drag this keyframe to Photoframe 35.

Tip

You can also use Edit, Cut Frames and Edit, Paste Frames to cut the keyframe from Frame 1 to Frame 35 in step 1.

2. The menu needs to fly quickly onto the Stage and then slow as it finds its resting position. Just as you created this effect with the `header` and `footer` layers, you must create two more keyframes—one that is close to keyframe 35 and another that extends farther out on the Timeline. Click Photoframe 41 of the `menu` layer and insert a keyframe. Click Photoframe 52 and again insert a keyframe.

3. Click keyframe 35 and reposition the `menu` instance so that its bottom edge aligns with the guide that defines the top of the Stage (see Figure 6.25).

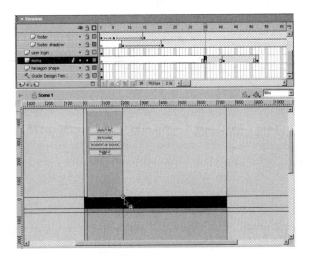

Figure 6.25   The menu instance is located entirely in the work area.

4. Click the keyframe in Frame 41 in the `menu` layer and position the menu instance slightly above the footer shadow (see Figure 6.26).

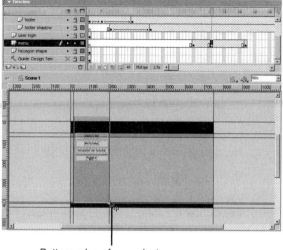

Bottom edge of menu instance

Figure 6.26   The bottom edge of the menu should be about 5 pixels above the top edge of the footer shadow.

5. Create the motion tween for this animation by (Control-clicking)[right-clicking] any frame between the keyframe in Frames 35 and 41, and select Create Motion Tween from the shortcut menu.

6. The keyframe in Frame 52 has the menu instance in its resting position so you do not need to position this instance on the Stage—just create another motion tween between the keyframes in Frames 41 and 52.

7. Rewind and play the movie to test your work. The menu bar flies into the movie and then slowly moves to its resting position. Lock the menu layer.

8. Now create the animation for the login box flying onto the Stage. Move the playhead to the beginning of the Timeline, and click the user login layer to make it active. Show and unlock this layer; then, click and drag the keyframe in Frame 1 to Photoframe 52.

9. Click Photoframe 63 and insert another keyframe.

10. Click the keyframe in Frame 52 to access the start position for this motion tween, and reposition the login instance so that its top edge adheres to the guide that defines the bottom edge of the Stage (see Figure 6.27).

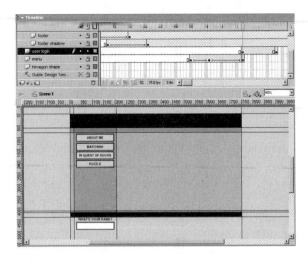

Figure 6.27   Position this instance so that it is vertically centered between the two guides that define the edges of the menu.

11. Create the motion tween for this animation by (Control-clicking)[right-clicking] any frame between the keyframes in Frames 35 and 41 and select Create Motion Tween from the shortcut menu.

12. Rewind and play the movie.

13. Notice that the Timeline needs to be extended for the menu layer, user login layer, and Guide: Design Template layer to Photoframe 100. Click Photoframe 100 of the user login layer, and then Shift-click Photoframe 100 of the Guide: Design Template layer to select Photoframe 100 for all four layers. Insert a frame by selecting Insert, Frame; the Timeline extends to Frame 100 for these four layers.

14. Rewind and play the movie to test your work again. The login box flies onto the Stage to its resting position. Lock the login layer.

Your opening scene is getting more interesting as the various objects that make up the design fly onto the Stage. One more item needs to be added to the opening scene—the Honeycomb Logo. You will add this object next.

Creating the Honeycomb Logo Animation

The Honeycomb Logo displays shortly after the header and footer animations finish. This logo appears on the Stage in all white and slowly transitions to display as it was designed. This effect can be created using a motion tween and the color effect of brightness. Follow these steps to create this animation:

1. Move the playhead to the beginning of the Timeline, and select the `honeycomb logo` layer. Click the keyframe in Frame 1 of the Timeline and drag this keyframe to Photoframe 24.

2. Click Photoframe 38 of this layer and insert a keyframe.

3. Click the keyframe in Frame 24 of the honeycomb logo, and click the instance of the Honeycomb logo on the Stage. In the Property Inspector, apply a Brightness color effect of 100% to this instance. The instance displays all in white.

4. (Control-click)[right-click] any frame between the keyframes in Frames 24 and 38, and select Create Motion Tween from the shortcut menu. The logo tweens from a display of all white to its original design.

5. Extend the Timeline for this layer to Frame 100 by inserting a frame in Photoframe 100 for the `honeycomb logo` layer.

6. Because you have all the site design objects created and animated, lock all the movie's layers so you do not accidentally move any of the objects. Save the file.

Creating Buzzy Bee's Flapping Wings

Next, you'll make Buzzy Bee flap his wings. The buzzy bee symbol is a movie clip symbol; therefore, it has its own Timeline. The flapping movement of the wings is created through frame-by-frame animation. You do not need to apply a motion tween to get the animation effect of the wings flapping back and forth. You can achieve this by first creating symbols of each wing and then nesting these two symbols in a new movie clip symbol named flapping wings. Using frame-by-frame animation, position two keyframes next to each other in the Timeline, and then position the Stage content of each wing moving forward and backward by simply nesting each wing. Finally, the flapping wings symbol needs to be nested inside the buzzy bee symbol. Therefore, you are nesting each wing symbol inside the flapping wings symbol, which is nested inside the buzzy bee symbol. It might sound confusing, but if you follow these steps, you'll find it's a fairly straightforward process:

1. Open or access the library and create a new folder. Name the folder buzzy bee symbol. Drag the bubble, bubble shadow, buzzy bee, and buzzy shadow symbols inside the new folder (see Figure 6.28).

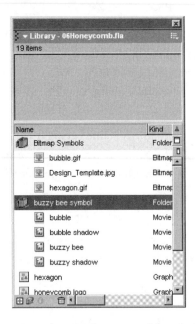

Figure 6.28   All these symbols and a couple more will be used in a movie clip symbol of buzzy bee to enable communication between Buzzy Bee and the end-user.

2. From the library, open the buzzy bee symbol in the Symbol-Editing Mode by double-clicking the symbol. This launches the Symbol-Editing Mode for the buzzy bee symbol.

3. Click the front wing to select it, and choose Insert, Convert to Symbol. Name the symbol front wing, and give it a Graphic behavior. Set the registration point to the lower-left corner.

Note

By setting the registration point to the lower-left corner, any rotation of the wing is controlled from this point. Because the wings attach to the bee's back at this point, a natural rotation or flapping of the wing can be achieved just as it does in the real world.

4. Click the back wing to select it, and convert it to a symbol. Name this symbol `back wing`, and give it a Graphic behavior. Again, set the registration point to the lower-left corner.

5. Select both the `front wing` and `back wing` instances in the buzzy bee symbol by Shift-clicking each instance, and convert them to a symbol. Name this symbol `flapping wings`, and give it a Movie Clip behavior. Again, set the registration point to the lower-left corner. Click OK to close the dialog box. The Stage dims because you are now editing the `flapping wings` symbol through the Edit in Place feature of the Symbol-Editing Mode (see Figure 6.29).

Tabs representing a nested symbol inside another symbol

Bee symbol dims

Active symbol

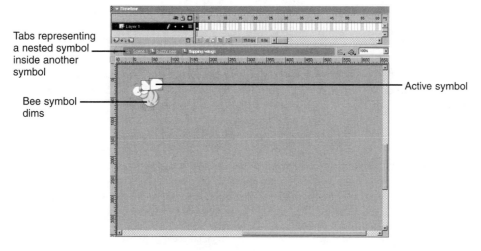

Figure 6.29 The tabs indicate the nesting order of the symbols starting with the parent symbol and drilling down, symbol by symbol, in the nesting order of other symbols.

Note

One goal in Flash development is to always use your symbols and instances wisely. By nesting symbols inside other symbols to create your Stage objects, you are reducing the overall size of your SWF file.

Tip

If you double-click a nested symbol inside a symbol that is already being edited in Symbol-Editing Mode, you activate this symbol for edits. The tabs in the upper-left corner of the Stage reflect the nesting order. If you click the parent symbol tab in the upper-left corner of the symbol-editing Stage, you access this symbol in Symbol-Editing Mode. Therefore, you can drill up or down as you work with a symbol that is comprised of many nested symbols without exiting Symbol-Editing Mode.

6. Rename Layer 1 `flapping wings`. Click Photoframe 2 in the `flapping wings` layer and insert a keyframe.

7. With the keyframe in Frame 2 selected, use the Free Transform tool and the rotate modifier to rotate both wings slightly so that they both appear to fly up (see Figure 6.30).

Figure 6.30   After you rotate the wing, you must position it closer to the other wing, keeping the instances above and centered with the center point for the Stage in Symbol-Editing Mode.

Tip

When using the Free Transform tool, you do not need to select a modifier. You can just move the pointer of the Free Transform tool over and around a handle in the active object and the point changes to either the rotate or scale modifier, depending on its position in relation to the handle. Try this because you will use this often throughout this book and your Flash development.

8. To view the flapping wings, drag the playhead from Frame 1 to Frame 2 and back again. The wings appear to flap due to the frame-by-frame animation of the two keyframes.

9. Return to editing the `buzzy bee` symbol by clicking the buzzy bee tab in the upper-left corner of the Stage.

10. There is one small problem with the wings: They are on top of the bee's body instead of behind it. This is an easy fix. Click the `flapping wings` symbol and cut it from the Stage. Insert a new layer above the `shadow` layer and name it `wings`. Now copy the `flapping wings` symbol using the Edit, Paste in Place command.

> **Tip**
>
> The Paste in Place command pastes any cut or copied object in exactly the same location that it resided prior to cutting or copying it. This is a great command to move objects from one layer to another without having to reposition them on the Stage.

11. To make the wings more realistic, apply an Alpha effect of `50%` to the `flapping wings` instance using the Property Inspector and the Color option.

12. Exit the Symbol-Editing Mode. Organize your library by placing the `flapping wings`, `front wing`, and `back wing` symbols inside the `buzzy bee` symbol folder.

13. Test the movie by selecting Control, Test Movie.

> **Note**
>
> You will not see the frame-by-frame animation of the wings flapping in the Flash Authoring environment. The flapping wings symbol is a movie clip, and movie clips have their own Timelines independent of the movie Timeline. Only the first frame of a movie clip symbol is displayed in the movie in the Flash Authoring environment. To view a movie clip symbol, you must test the movie in the Flash Player Testing Mode to see it play.

> **Tip**
>
> Movie clip symbols automatically loop through their Timelines, repeating the animation for as long as the movie plays. To have a movie clip play only once through the Timeline, you must apply the Stop action using ActionScript. You learn more about ActionScript in Seminar 7, "Site Interactivity and Button Functionality."

Controlling Buzzy Bee's Movement on the Stage

Buzzy Bee exists only in keyframe 1 of the `buzzy bee` layer. He needs to appear in the movie toward the end, after the header and footers, honeycomb logo, menu, and login appear on the Stage. You also want Buzzy Bee to fly onto the Stage but to have a more irregular flight pattern than what a motion tween can provide. You need to apply a motion guide for creating Buzzy Bee's flight pattern onto the Stage. Follow these steps to create this flight pattern:

1. Click the `buzzy bee` layer to make it active; then show and unlock this layer.

2. Because Buzzy Bee makes his entrance into the movie after all the background design animation occurs, click and drag the keyframe in Frame 1 of this layer to Photoframe 74. Then, reposition the instance of the `buzzy bee` symbol in the work area off the right top edge of the Stage (see Figure 6.31).

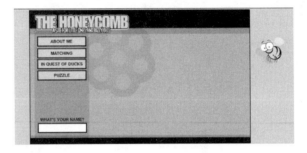

Figure 6.31   To create the animation effect of Buzzy Bee flying onto the Stage, position this instance in the work area

3. Unhide the `Guide: Design Template` layer so you can reposition Buzzy Bee on the Stage in his resting position. Insert a keyframe in Photoframe 97 of the `buzzy bee` layer. Reposition the instance of the buzzy bee symbol as indicated in the design template. Hide the `Guide: Design Template` layer.

4. Create a motion tween for the `buzzy bee` layer by (Control-clicking)[right-clicking] any frame between the keyframes in Frames 74 and 97 and selecting Insert Motion Tween from the shortcut menu.

5. With the motion tween set for Buzzy Bee's entrance on the Stage, you can now create a motion guide for controlling his flight pattern. First create the Motion Guide layer by (Control-clicking)[right-clicking] the `buzzy bee` layer and selecting Add Motion Guide from the shortcut menu (see Figure 6.32).

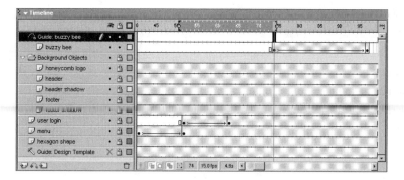

Figure 6.32   The Motion Guide layer appears above the buzzy bee layer and indents the buzzy bee layer, indicating that this layer will adhere to the guide path.

6. To set up Flash for applying a path as a motion guide, you should turn on the Onion Skin features. Click the Onion Skin button and the Edit Multiple Frames button on the Timeline. Adjust the Onion Markers so that they show the full flight of Buzzy Bee (see Figure 6.33).

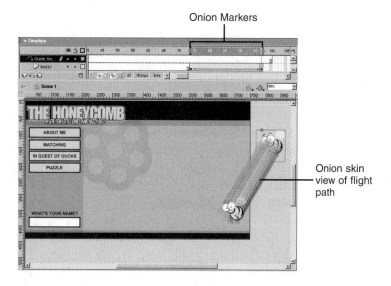

Figure 6.33   The Onion Markers need to be set on or before Frame 74 and on or after Frame 97 above the Timeline.

7. Lock the buzzy bee layer so that you cannot modify it. With the first and last instance of the motion tween for the buzzy bee layer visible, click Photoframe 74 in the Guide: buzzy bee layer; then, click the Pencil tool. Set the Stroke color to a bright red stroke. This color makes identifying the path that you will create easy.

8. Insert a keyframe in Photoframe 74 of the Guide: buzzy bee layer.

9. The key to creating a motion path for guiding a tween object is to set both the beginning and the end of the path at the registration point of the tweened symbol. Because you want Buzzy Bee to follow a motion path, you need to start your path at the registration point of the buzzy bee symbol. Open the library and notice that the registration point is in the upper-left corner of the symbol. The first instance to follow the motion path is positioned off the Stage. With the Pencil tool, create a stroke that starts at the registration point of this instance and ends at the registration point of the instance that is in the lower-right corner of the Stage. If you hit the registration points for both instances, you will see Buzzy Bee adhere to the motion path (see Figure 6.34).

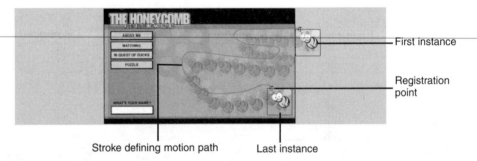

First instance

Registration point

Stroke defining motion path   Last instance

Figure 6.34   The stroke will not appear in the SWF movie. Flash MX removes all guide layers in the conversion from FLA to SWF.

Warning
If you create a motion path that crosses over itself, Flash might get confused and not follow the correct flow of the path as you drew it.

10. If you do not see the motion tween adhere to the guide path, click the keyframe in Frame 74 to activate the first instance of Buzzy Bee and locate the center registration point. Using the Arrow tool, drag the stroke to adhere to this instance reference point (see Figure 6.35). Click the keyframe in

Frame 97 to activate the last instance of Buzzy Bee, and again reposition the stroke endpoint so that it adheres to the registration point of this instance.

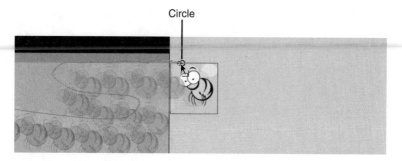

Circle

Figure 6.35 If you hit the center point of the instance with the end of the stroke, you will see a small circle display, indicating that the end of the path adheres to the instance center reference point.

11. Extend the `buzzy bee` layer to Frame 100 by inserting a frame in Photoframe 100. Turn off the Onion Skin features by clicking them again. Lock the `buzzy bee` layer.

12. Finally, test your movie by selecting Control, Test Movie to launch the Flash Player testing mode.

Pat yourself on the back, and save the movie as `Honeycomb.fla`. If you want to compare your Honeycomb site with a movie that is completed up to this point in the book, open the `06Honeycomb.fla` file located in the `Seminar06/Samples` directory on the CD-ROM that accompanies this book.

Seminar Summary

This seminar covered many of the animation techniques you can use to create your movie. You learned how to create a motion tween and a shape tween. Color tweening and size tweening were also covered. You will benefit if you practice these skills to gain a strong comfort level with animation. The Honeycomb movie is progressing; you now have an interesting opening scene for the site that visually entertains the end-user as the movie begins to play. You should now see how symbols and instances further fit into the picture of Flash MX functionality. Without them, animation would be extremely complicated and would create movies that are very large in file size.

In the next seminar, you will learn about buttons and button states. You will begin to use ActionScripting by creating the interactivity for these buttons that enable the end-user to navigate through the site.

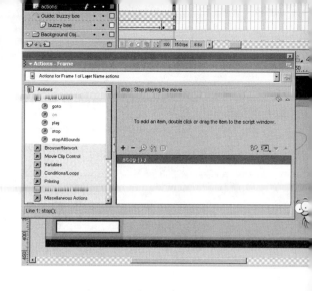

Seminar 7

Site Interactivity and Button Functionality

In this chapter

Workshop: Creating the Site Interactivity

Getting Interactive with the Click of a Button

Buttons symbols are a major component in Macromedia Flash for creating interactivity. Now with Flash MX, button symbols and dynamic and input text blocks are treated as objects, just as a movie clip is treated as an object in Flash 5. This opens a new door for the Flash development. Because it's an object, you can control and manipulate a button symbol with ActionScript. This new functionality enables buttons to be even more powerful with Flash MX.

> **Note**
>
> In previous releases of Flash, Movie Clip symbols were the only objects that could be controlled by ActionScript. Because of this limitation, if you wanted to control a button with ActionScript, you had to nest an instance of a button inside a Movie Clip symbol—not so with Macromedia Flash MX.

Developing a Multistate Button

Buttons in Flash MX can be compared to a four-framed interactive movie clip. The first three frames compose the possible button states: Up, Over, and Down. The fourth frame represents the button's hit area or hot spot area and is referred to as the *Hit state*. When you open a button symbol in the Symbol-Editing Mode, you see these four button states (see Figure 7.1).

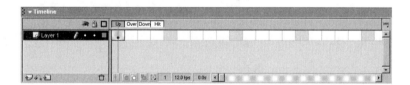

Figure 7.1 By creating different objects for each of the button states, you create the button appearance.

The following list defines each of these button states:

- **Up**—This state holds the image of the button as it resides on the Stage without user interaction.

- **Over**—This state is the image or animation triggered by the end-user rolling over the button with the mouse or when the mouse is physically over the button.

- **Down**—This state is the image triggered when the button is clicked.

- **Hit**—This state defines the area of the button that is active; in other words, it's the area that is the hot spot for triggering an action. The mouse must touch this hot spot area to trigger either the Over or Down state.

Multistate buttons have an image in all three states of the button. For instance, you can create a button that enlarges when the end-user rolls her mouse over the button by placing a larger instance of the image in the Over state for that button. To further add to the design element of your buttons, you can insert as many layers as needed to create a complex design for each button state. That's a lot of functionality for each and every button that exists in your movie.

The key to using the different states for a button is to first create a keyframe for holding the content that resides in that button state. Then you can create the various images for each button state. You will develop The Honeycomb site buttons for each of the activities in the workshop section of this seminar.

> **Tip**
>
> If you insert frames or keyframes after the first four frames that represent the button states, any Stage content for these additional frames will not display.

Defining the Hit Area of a Button

As mentioned, the Hit state of a button is basically used to define the hot spot or hit area for the button. This area is defined by inserting a keyframe or blank keyframe into the photoframe for the Hit state. Then, using any of the Flash tools, create a shape to define the Hit area of the button. You don't need to set the fill or stroke of the shape because this image doesn't appear on the Stage; the shape is simply used to define the area that triggers the button.

Testing a Button

After you have developed the button states, you should test your button. You can test your button in one of two ways. You can test a button in the Flash Authoring environment by selecting Control, Enable Simple Buttons. Then, when you move your pointer over the button, the mouse turns to the pointing hand tool, enabling you to trigger the button. If you have developed the Down and Over states with new button images, you will see these images display in relation to your interaction with the button. But if you used a movie clip instance for any of the button states, typical of any movie clip instance, you will need to test the movie in the Flash Player testing mode to see the movie clip. You do this by selecting Control, Test Movie. Testing the buttons in the Flash Player testing mode is the second technique.

> **Note** ————————————————————————————————————
>
> The Control, Enable Simple Buttons Is a toggle menu. You must turn off this feature to work with your button further in the Flash Authoring environment.

Combining Movie Clips with Buttons

A fun effect to add to a button is using animation in the Over state. Buttons can morph from one shape to another, or they can show a progression of movement or color effects through the animation. This is accomplished using a movie clip instance in the Over state of a button. A movie clip has its own Timeline that exists outside the movie Timeline. Because the movie clip Timeline is independent of the movie Timeline, the movie clip animation can be played regardless of the movie Timeline. Any type of movie clip that you can create can be added to a button state. To look at a sample movie of a button that has a movie clip in the Over state, open file `button_final.fla`, which you'll find in the `Seminar07/Samples` directory on the CD-ROM that accompanies this book.

The `button_final.fla` movie has one button on the Stage. To see this button in action, test it in the Flash Player Testing Mode by selecting Control, Test Movie. Notice that the button has a simple design of a gray rectangle background and a text label. This is the button's Up state image. When you roll your mouse over the button, it plays a movie clip displaying the button background morphing to three rectangles. This is the button's Over state. Close the Flash Player Testing Mode to return to the movie.

Because this button has a movie clip in the Over state, you can view this movie clip through the library. In the library, select the `button movie` symbol so that it displays in the library Preview Window. Play the movie clip by clicking the Play button; the button morphs from a rectangle to three red rectangles.

To see how this button symbol is developed, it must be opened in the Symbol-Editing Mode. When you launch the Symbol-Editing Mode for the button symbol, the four-framed movie clip composed of the three buttons states and the hit area is displayed (see Figure 7.2).

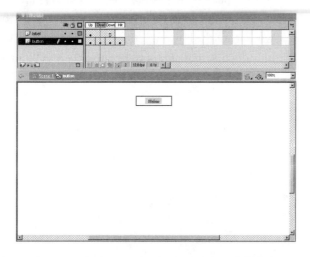

Figure 7.2   The text layer holds the text for the button for all the button states.

The button layer holds all the background images for the Up, Over, and Down states of the button. If you click these keyframes, you'll see the button images used for each state. The label layer has one keyframe in the Up state but extends this image over both the Over and Down states through a frame that was inserted in the Down state. This is how the button is composed.

> **Warning**
>
> There are some limitations to using a movie clip in a button state. Unfortunately, the movie clip is instantly stopped in its animation if the end-user causes another button state to occur or if he changes his mind and moves to another button. Test the `button_final.fla` file again; notice that if you click the button during the movie clip, it is cut off immediately in its animation. This could be a problem if you want the movie clip to play through this animation without interruption. The secret to avoiding this is to nest a simple button symbol inside a movie clip symbol and simulate the button functionality with layers and keyframes in the movie clip. The workshop of this seminar teaches you how to create multistate buttons. In Seminar 13, "Enhancing the Site Interface and Interactivity," you'll learn how to create a drop-down menu that requires the use of a movie clip symbol that nests a button.

Transparent Buttons and Their Use in Macromedia Flash

Another nice feature of buttons and their use in Flash is the transparent button. This type of button is the equivalent of an image map that is used in HTML development. It basically is a button with all button functionality, but it does not have an image in the Up, Over, or Down state of the button. It does, however, have a shape in the Hit state. This shape defines the hot spot area, and because there isn't another image in the other states, it appears transparent, allowing the Stage content behind it to show through (see Figure 7.3). You will create transparent buttons in the workshops throughout this book.

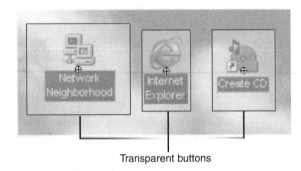

Transparent buttons

Figure 7.3   This figure shows an example of using transparent buttons that define hot spots on a bitmap image of desktop icons.

Up to this point, you have learned about buttons and button states, but until you attach an action to a button, the button is not functional. To create a trigger (or mouse event) for a button, it needs to have the on action attached. This seminar covers basic ActionScript and the on action next.

Actions and ActionScript

ActionScript first made its appearance in the Macromedia Flash 4 version. It grew up in Flash 5, and now in Flash MX, ActionScript has gained additional functionality to make it truly an object-oriented programming language. Macromedia not only added many new actions and functionality to ActionScript in the Flash 5 and Flash MX releases, but it also gave ActionScript a face lift by reworking the syntax to be similar to JavaScript. If you are familiar with JavaScript, I hope you are smiling. If you are not familiar with programming of any kind, fear not—new users can easily create script to add the interactivity they need to their movies.

Features of the Actions Panel

ActionScript can be attached to a keyframe in the Timeline or to an object on the Stage through the Actions panel (see Figure 7.4).

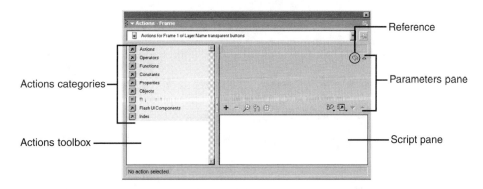

Figure 7.4   By working between the major areas of the Actions panel, Actions toolbox, Parameters pane, and Script pane, you can create the ActionScript necessary for your movie.

Understanding how to use the Actions panel requires knowledge of the various features of the panel. Figure 7.4 identifies the major areas and features the Actions panel when viewed in Normal Mode, and Table 7.1 describes the functionality of these features.

Table 7.1   Descriptions of Action Panel Features

Feature	Description
Actions toolbox	Click any of the category icons to expand a list of actions that compose the action category. Double-click these actions to add a line of code to the Actions list.
Script pane	Displays the ActionScript actions and syntax.
Parameters pane	Displays the parameters associated with an action.
Action Categories	Listing of all actions in ActionScript divided into categories based on functionality.

continues

Table 7.1   Continued

Feature	Description
Reference	This panel not only provides a description of the selected action as well as the version of Flash the action was introduced, but it also provides a sample script for how to use the action correctly. All this information is just a click away while you are in the Actions panel. If you have a question about a particular action, you can select the action from the Actions toolbox and click the Reference button (see Figure 7.5).

Figure 7.5   A new feature of Flash MX that is very useful when programming with ActionScript is the Reference panel. You can learn how to use different actions through this panel while you are creating your script.

Tip ──

Because the Actions panel is dockable or undockable as well as collapsible, you can arrange your Flash workspace as necessary.

Using the Two Modes of the Actions Panel

Depending on your knowledge of ActionScript, two modes are available for creating your script: Normal Mode and Expert Mode (see Figure 7.6).

If you are new to ActionScript, you should use Normal Mode to create your code because it has many click-and-drag features to make coding easier. If, on the other hand, you have a strong knowledge of programming and are comfortable with ActionScript and its syntax, you can switch to Expert Mode and type the code directly into the Script panel. You can switch between both modes by clicking the Actions pop-up menu in the upper-right corner of the Actions panel and selecting either Normal Mode or Expert Mode (see Figure 7.7).

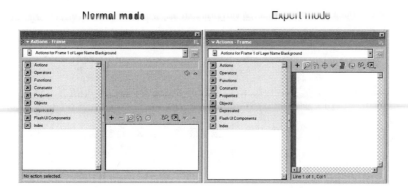

Figure 7.6   By default, when Flash is first launched, it is set to display the Actions panel in Normal mode.

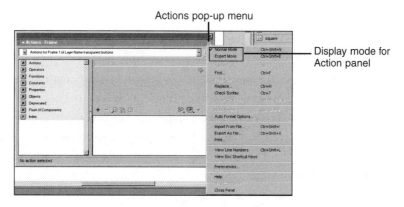

Figure 7.7   You can switch between modes by clicking the Actions menu in the upper-right corner of the Actions panel and selecting either Normal Mode or Expert Mode.

Identifying an Active Object with the Actions Panel

Based on the active object—either a keyframe or an object on the Stage—the title bar of the Actions panel displays a different title in its title bar (see Figure 7.8).

> **Warning**
>
> You should always reconfirm what is the active object by looking at the title bar of the Actions panel before attaching an action. Many times as a new user to Flash, you might have a frame selected when you really want to have an object selected on the Stage. Before creating your ActionScript, double-check the title bar to ensure you have the correct object selected.

Title bar displaying active object

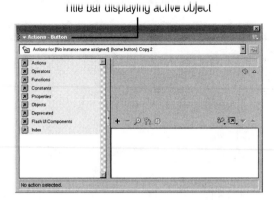

Figure 7.8   If you have a movie clip object active on the Stage, the Actions panel displays Actions - Movie Clip. If you have a frame selected, the Actions panel displays Actions - Frame in the title bar.

Attaching Actions

Working between either the Timeline or objects on the Stage and the Actions panel, you can attach actions that cause your movie to function interactively with the end-user. For example, you can cause a different area of a movie to display when the end-user clicks a button. Or, you can have events triggered when the movie reaches a certain frame in the Timeline. You can attach an action to either an object in the movie or to the Timeline.

Controlling Objects with Actions

Actions can be attached to an object such as a movie clip or a button on the Stage. To attach an Action to an object, the object must be active. Then, through the Actions toolbox, you can select an action. You must first click an action category and, if necessary, drill down to the action you need by clicking the appropriate sub-category. When you see the action you want to use, double-click it. The script for the action displays in the Script pane (see Figure 7.9).

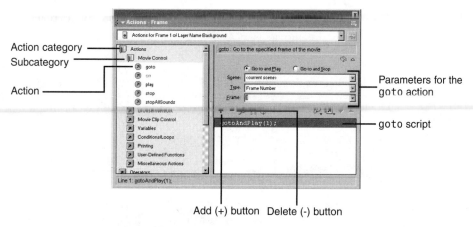

Figure 7.9   You can also add actions through the Add (+) button and delete existing lines of script from the Script pane with the Delete (-) button.

You can add more than one action to an object. Depending on the interactivity you are trying to achieve, you might need many lines of script. In Normal Mode, if you want to add more than one line of script, select an existing line of code in the Script pane and then select another action from the Actions toolbox. The new action is added below the active line of script. In Expert Mode, you can just create a new line and type the next line of script. You will get plenty of practice creating ActionScript in the workshop section of this seminar as well as throughout the rest of the book.

Tip
You can also attach actions by clicking the Add (+) button and again selecting the appropriate action category and drilling down to the action you need. You can delete a line of script by selecting it in the Script pane and clicking the Delete (-) button or pressing the Delete key.

Controlling the Timeline with Actions

To attach an action to the Timeline, the action must be attached to a keyframe. Keyframes are essential for any new information you want the movie to process, whether that is a change in objects on the Stage or any actions attached to the Timeline. After you have a keyframe inserted and selected in the movie Timeline, open the Actions panel to attach the frame actions you want for that frame. For example, this could be the stop action requesting that Flash stop at this keyframe or the goto action directing Flash to another location in the Timeline. The attached action is initiated when the movie is played and reaches that keyframe in the Timeline.

When an action is attached to the Timeline, the keyframe where that action resides displays a small *a* (see Figure 7.10).

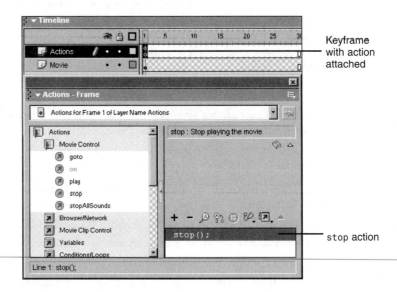

Figure 7.10   A common action applied to the Timeline is the stop action. This action stops the movie at the keyframe to which it is attached.

Testing Your Script

Just as you have two techniques for testing a button, you also have two techniques for testing ActionScript. You can test some of the frame actions you attach to the Timeline while in the Flash Authoring environment by selecting Control, Enable Simple Frame Actions. This is a toggle menu command, so if you want to turn off this feature, select Control, Enable Simple Frame Actions again. But to see the full interactivity of your movie, you must test the movie in the Flash Player.

Making a Button Functional

When working with buttons, the on action must be attached to set the trigger for activating the button. The on action is found in the Actions category under the Movie Control subcategory (see Figure 7.11).

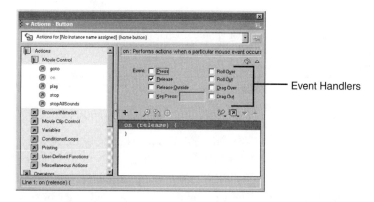

Figure 7.11   The default event for the on action is release.

The on action sets the event that must be performed by the end-user to trigger the button. In the world of ActionScript, this trigger is called an *event handler*. When the on action is double-clicked from the Category list, its code displays in the Script pane and the parameters area of the Actions panel becomes active and displays the event handlers for the on action. The on action has eight event handlers, or triggers, that can be performed by the end-user and added to the action (see Figure 7.12). To set an event handler, select it from the Parameters pane; the Script pane reflects the script for the on action.

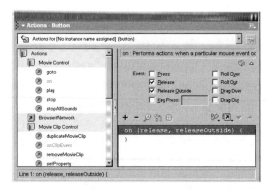

Figure 7.12   You can select one or multiple mouse event handlers to attach to the button.

Warning

Never use the events of Press and Release together. Each of these will trigger the button. Any ActionScript attached to the button will be triggered twice.

Table 7.2 describes each of the event handlers for the on action.

Table 7.2   On Action Event Handlers

Feature	Description
Press	The action of the mouse button being pressed down.
Release	The action of the mouse button being pressed and released. This is the default event handler because it is the standard clicking behavior.
Release Outside	The action of the mouse button being pressed while the pointer is on the button but released outside the button's hot spot or hit state area.
Key Press	Assigns a keyboard shortcut for activating the button.
Roll Over	The action of the mouse pointer rolling over the button's hot spot or hit state area.
Roll Out	The action of the mouse pointer rolling outside the button's hot spot or hit state area.
Drag Over	The action of pressing the mouse button with the mouse pointer on the button's hot spot or hit state area and then dragging off and then back over the button with the mouse pointer.
Drag Out	The action of pressing the mouse button with the mouse pointer on the button and then dragging the pointer outside the button's hot spot or hit state area.

Note

You do not always need to start the script for a button with the **on** action. Anytime an action is attached to a button, Flash knows that the object is a button and automatically creates the **on** action script. For instance, if you wanted to cause a button to go to a frame farther down the Timeline, you could just select the **goto** action; the **on** action would automatically display in the Script pane above the **goto** action script.

Other Common Actions for Buttons

After you set the event handler, you then must attach another action to tell Flash what to do next if the button is activated. This could be the goto action telling Flash to go to a certain frame in the Timeline or the getURL action telling Flash to get a certain URL that you designate. To attach another action, simply select the action from the Actions toolbox. The ActionScript for this action then displays under the highlighted line of script in the Scripting pane (see Figure 7.13).

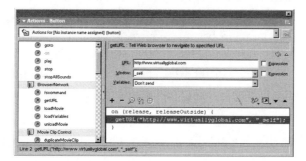

Figure 7.13   The ActionScript in this figure tells Flash to open a URL when the Release event hander is triggered.

The following list describes the more frequently used actions that can be used for button interactivity and how they control navigation and user interaction in the movie:

- Go To—Jumps to a frame or scene in the movie

- Play, Stop—Control whether a movie is played or stopped

- Stop All Sounds—Stops all sounds in the movie

- Get URL—Opens a URL in the user's default browser

- FSCommand—Controls the Flash Player that's playing the movie

- `Load Movie, Unload Movie`—Loads or unloads other movies, SWF files, and JPEGs into the active movie

You will use many of these commands in the workshop section of this seminar, as well as throughout the remainder of this book.

Labeling Keyframes for More Dynamic Scripting

Another nice feature of Flash that lends itself well to ActionScript is labels. Labels can be attached to a keyframe in the Timeline to name a specific location. After it's named, you can then call that frame of the Timeline through the label name. By using a label for a location in the Timeline, you do not have to worry about any changes or edits that you might make to the Timeline. For instance, if you attach the `goto` action, call Frame 45 in the action, and then delete four frames before Frame 45 from the Timeline, Frame 45 becomes Frame 41. The `goto` action is still calling Frame 45, though, so your movie is now off. However, if you attached a label to Frame 45, it does not matter whether you add or delete frames because the label stays with the keyframe no matter where it is relocated in the Timeline. Labels make a movie more dynamic!

To create a label for a frame in the Timeline, you again must have a keyframe inserted at that location in the Timeline. Select the keyframe, and in the Property Inspector, type in the label name (see Figure 7.14).

Frame Label

Figure 7.14   The Property Inspector also lists the other frame attributes, such as what type of tweening might be applied to a frame.

After a frame label is created, the actual keyframe in the Timeline displays the label name to the left of a red flag (see Figure 7.15).

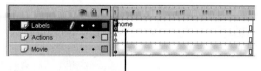

Home label attached to a keyframe

Figure 7.15 If no adjacent frames are to the right of a keyframe with an attached label, only the red flag displays in the keyframe.

Any time you create a label, it can be called in another action, such as the `goto` action. You could create a button that is triggered by the `release` event handler and set the action for the button to always go to the frame labeled Home—in other words, the first frame of the movie (see Figure 7.16).

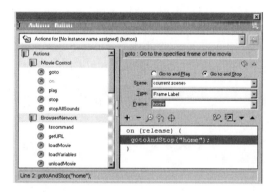

Figure 7.16 This figure displays a sample script of a button that causes the movie to go to the frame labeled Home and then stop at that frame.

Tip

Just as you should create a layer for frame actions in a movie, you should also create a layer for holding all the labels in the movie or movie clip. Both layers are best used if they are located at the top of the layer stacking order. Some Flash developers use one layer to hold both actions and labels; others use a layer dedicated to just that feature. This is a personal preference.

Loading Other Movies into the Main Movie

Both HTML code and Flash movies are viewed in a browser. But unlike HTML code—which must be refreshed to show new content—a Flash movie can stay loaded in the browser and be continuously updated without having to be refreshed. This enables the switching of content on the Stage as the movie plays.

A very useful command for switching Stage content or loading new movies into the main movie is the loadMovie action. The loadMovie action enables you to play or switch out other SWF files or JPEG images without having to close the Flash Player. For instance, if you wanted to show a news clip movie when a button is pressed, you could use the loadMovie action to load the news clip SWF file into the main movie. Because the news clip movie really isn't part of the main movie Timeline, you would have cut down the movie file size because the news clip movie is loaded only when called and exists as its own file. Figure 7.17 shows a sample script for loading a movie into a movie.

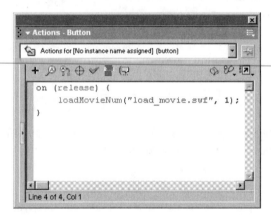

Figure 7.17   You can set the location for loading a SWF file either into the movie on a level or to a target movie clip.

To understand the parameters of the loadMovie action, you must understand how Flash loads a SWF file into the main movie. Flash creates levels for loading a SWF file. The main movie, or the *root movie*, always is level 0. SWF files can be loaded into level 1 on up to 16,000. To load a SWF file in any existing movie, enter a level number that is not occupied by another loaded SWF file. To replace an existing SWF file with the loading SWF file, enter the same level number as the existing SWF file for the loading SWF file. You can also replace the root movie with a SWF file by using the level number 0. That's a lot of levels and depth in each and every Flash movie. You will get hands-on practice using the `loadMovie` action to load SWF files for all the activity buttons into The Honeycomb site.

After you load a SWF file, you can use the `unloadMovie` action to unload it. Using the previous example of the loaded news clip movie, if you wanted to have a different news clip movie display when the end-user clicks another button, you could use the `loadMovie` and `unloadMovie` actions to switch the movies on the Stage.

> **Note**
>
> A characteristic of the **loadMovie** action is that the main movie properties override any properties of the SWF file. So, if you have a movie with a 15fps and a black background color, any SWF file loaded into the root or main movie will have the same properties, no matter how that incoming SWF file was created.

Creating and Using a Load Target

Typically, a SWF file is loaded into the root movie upon the end-user's request. Therefore, the root movie loads much more quickly because many of the other movies that make up the site content are loaded in based on when the end-user wants to see them. There is one small issue with the loaded SWF file: It appears on top of the main movie. So, if you have other Stage content that might animate or appear in the same position on the Stage as the loaded movie content, this content appears on top of the main movie content. This can be a problem if you are integrating existing content of the root movie with a loaded SWF file. For instance, you might want to have a text message that is part of the main movie scroll across the loaded SWF file. If the loaded SWF file is on top of the main movie and all its content, the scrolling text message will be behind the loaded SWF file and will not be visible.

There is a way around this—setting up a load target. You can create a load target using a movie clip symbol. Through ActionScript, movie clips can talk to and control each other. By setting a target path for the load movie, you can replace an instance of an empty movie clip with the loaded movie. The key to this is to create a movie clip that doesn't contain any objects—just a registration point that is set to the upper-left corner by the alignment grid in the Info panel. Then you position this movie clip on its own layer on the Stage. The position of the layer in the movie determines which existing Stage content displays behind or in front of the loaded movie.

Another important feature of a load target is to name the target. For ActionScript to call a target, the load target movie clip instance must be identified by naming the instance. The Property Inspector is again used to name an instance (see Figure 7.18).

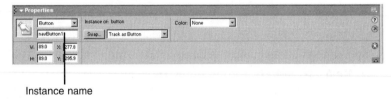

Instance name

Figure 7.18   When you start working with movie clips that target each other or talk to each other, you must name the movie clip instance.

Tip ———

You can name an instance anything you want, but you cannot have spaces between words for the instance name. For example, you would use **myInstance** as an instance name that is composed of two words.

After the instance is named, it can be called in the ActionScript as the target for the target path. Figure 7.19 shows an example of a movie loaded into a target movie clip.

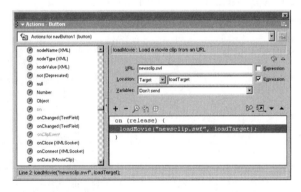

Figure 7.19   The Absolute setting is the default setting that enables you to see all the named instances in the main movie.

When you test the movie, you'll notice that the loaded SWF file replaces the movie clip instance in the load target layer, enabling Stage content to appear in front of or behind it based on the layer stacking order of the main movie. Because you are targeting the movie clip, if you load another SWF file into the target movie clip, Flash simply switches the previously loaded SWF file with the new SWT file—no need for the `unloadMovie` action. The workshop section of this seminar provides hands-on practice for targeting a movie clip with a loaded SWF file.

Note

Any SWF file loaded into an empty movie clip assumes any of the attributes of the movie clip. This means that if the movie clip has been scaled or rotated or has an alpha effect applied to it, the loaded SWF file will have these attributes applied, too.

Creating the Site Interactivity

The Honeycomb site has been built with most of the symbols and instances necessary for creating the site functionality. At this point, though, the buttons do not trigger any events, nor are they developed to completion with four button states. You do not have any of the activities created for the site. You will use the `loadMovie` action with a load target to load the activity movies into the root Honeycomb movie. Throughout the remainder of the book, the activity movies will be developed. You will make the Honeycomb buttons active and functional in this workshop so that they load the activity movies.

Developing the Menu Symbol

The menu symbol needs further development. Presently, it holds all the buttons of the site in one layer. In this workshop, you will add additional layers to hold each button. Follow these steps to develop this symbol:

1. Use your `Honeycomb.fla` file from Seminar 6, "Animation and Special Effects for Flashing Up the Site," or open `Honeycomb06.fla` from the `Seminar07/Samples` directory on the CD-ROM that accompanies this book. Save it as `Honeycomb.fla`.

2. Open or access the library, and open the `menu` symbol in the Symbol-Editing Mode by double-clicking it from the library.

3. The `menu` symbol holds all four buttons presently on one layer. Select all four activity buttons on the Stage and choose Modify, Distribute to Layers. This is a new feature of Flash MX, and it automatically places each selected object on its own layer and names the layer based on any identifying text applied to the object.

4. Rename Layer 1 to `menu BG` and move it to the bottom of the stacking order. This causes the menu background image to appear behind all the buttons. The menu movie clip Timeline should resemble Figure 7.20.

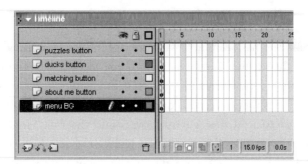

Figure 7.20   Each button resides on its own layer for the menu movie clip symbol.

Creating Button States for the Activity Buttons

Presently, all the buttons for the Honeycomb site are simple Up state buttons. Now, you will develop these buttons to have the other three states: Over, Down, and Hit. The menu symbol nests each of the buttons, and you can edit these buttons by drilling down in the nesting order while in the Symbol-Editing Mode. Follow these steps to create the buttons:

1. While in the Symbol-Editing Mode for the menu symbol, select the About Me button on the about me button layer to make it active. Double-click this symbol. This causes the instance of the About Me button, which is nested in the menu symbol, to display and the rest of the Stage to dim (see Figure 7.21).

2. Add one layer above the button background layer, and name this new layer button.

3. Click the button background layer to select it. This button is composed of two square instances; one instance is tinted black and the other is tinted gold. Click the gold tinted instance to make it active and cut it from the layer. Now click the button layer to make it active. Paste the gold tinted rectangular instance in place by selecting Edit, Paste in Place (see Figure 7.22).

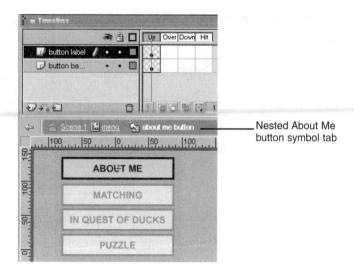

Nested About Me button symbol tab

Figure 7.21   Notice the new tab in the upper-left corner indicating that you are now editing a symbol that is nested inside another symbol.

Figure 7.22   Each layer now holds its respective Stage content as indicated by the layer name.

4. Now develop the button states. The button background layer contains the black rectangle. Because it's slightly larger than the yellow rectangle, it appears to be an outline around the button, when in reality it is an entire rectangle shape with the yellow rectangle centered inside it. This shape will be the Hit area or hot spot area. Because you want the outline to be visible throughout all the button states, click the Hit frame in the button background layer and insert a frame by selecting Insert, Frame (F5) (see Figure 7.23).

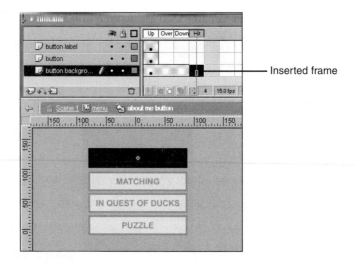

Figure 7.23   The black rectangle is now visible in all the button states due to inserting the frame in the Hit state for that layer; all other layers have Stage content only in the Up state.

5. Click the Over state frame for the `button` layer and insert a keyframe. This copies the Up state keyframe and Stage content. Click the yellow rectangle, which is an instance of the square symbol; through the Property Inspector, apply a Tint effect of color value `#FFFF99`. The instance changes to a light yellow color that will display when the end-user rolls over the button with her pointer.

6. Click the Down state frame for the `button` layer and again insert a keyframe. This copies the Over state keyframe and Stage content. Click the light yellow rectangle and apply a Tint effect of white.

7. Because your Hit area is defined with the black rectangle, you do not need to create a Hit state for this layer. But, you do need to make the text label visible throughout each button state. Click the Down state frame in the `text` layer and insert a frame (see Figure 7.24).

8. To return to the menu symbol while still in the Symbol-Editing Mode, click the Menu tab in the upper-left corner of the Flash screen. Now you can access the other four buttons and develop their button states.

9. Click a button that needs to be developed and repeat steps 1–10 to develop each button and its button states. Repeating these steps makes all the activity buttons look and act the same except for the button labels.

Figure 7.24 The text block is visible in the Over and Down states of the text layer by inserting a frame in the Down state.

Return to the menu symbol in the Symbol-Editing Mode by clicking the menu tab. Even though you are in the Symbol-Editing Mode, you can still test your buttons by selecting Control, Enable Simple Buttons. Move your pointer over each button and click. You should see each button reflect the four states you developed. Exit the Symbol-Editing Mode, returning to The Honeycomb movie. Turn off the Enable Simple Buttons feature by selecting it again.

Tip

While in the Symbol-Editing Mode, you can also copy the button background and button layers and frames for one button by selecting Edit, Copy Frames. Then you can paste these layers and frames into another button symbol through Edit, Paste Frames. This saves time and reduces the chance of error because you don't have to repeat each individual step to create each button state.

Note

If you try to test your button in the main movie while you're in the Flash Authoring environment, it will not work. Remember: The menu instance is a movie clip, and movie clips play only in Macromedia Flash Player. Therefore, you must test your movie in Flash Player Testing Mode by selecting Control, Test Movie.

Creating the Activity Movies

Before you can make the button functional, you need to do a little housekeeping. You will use the `loadMovie` action to load in a new SWF file that holds the activity for each button. Therefore, these activity SWF files must be created. Flash MX offers a new feature called Templates that allows you to create a template movie and then create other movies based on the template. You will use this feature for creating each of the activity movies because all the activity movies need to be the same size to ensure precise positioning of them in the main movie. To create these activity movies, follow these steps:

1. Create a new Flash movie by selecting File, New. A new movie displays.

2. Set the Stage dimension through the movie Properties dialog box to 750×440 pixels for this new movie so that it matches the Honeycomb movie's Stage dimensions. Aligning your Stage content is easier if the two movies match in Stage size.

3. Change Layer 1 to a guide layer by (Control-clicking)(right-clicking) the layer and selecting Guide from the shortcut menu. Rename this layer `Guide: Design Template`.

4. Import the `design template.jpg` file from the `Seminar07/Samples` directory on the CD-ROM that accompanies this book. Align it centered both vertically and horizontally to the Stage through the Align panel.

5. Add a new layer above the `Guide` layer and name it `movie`. Create a text block on the Stage using the following font attributes: Arial font, 14-point font size, black font color, Auto Kern selected, and left justified.

6. Create a text block on the Stage and type `Movie Name` into the text block. Center the text block both vertically and horizontally to the Stage.

7. Convert this to a Flash MX template by selecting File, Save As Template. This displays the Save As Template dialog box.

8. Set the Name field to `activities`. Click the arrow to the right of the category field and select Presentation. Type `Activity movies for loading in to the Honeycomb movie` into the Description field (see Figure 7.25).

9. Click the Save button to save the movie as a template document. You can now use this movie to create the activity movies for The Honeycomb site.

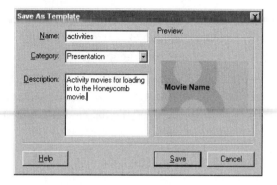

Figure 7.25   You must fill out all fields in this dialog box to save a movie as a template.

10. From the File menu, select New from Template to create the first activity movie. Select the Presentation category list, and then select Activities from the Category Items list (see Figure 7.26). Click Create, and you will create a new movie from this Activities template.

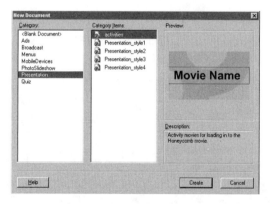

Figure 7.26   You must fill out all fields in this dialog box to save a movie as a template.

11. On the new movie, change the text in the text block to About Me. Save the movie as aboutme.fla in the same directory as your Honeycomb.fla movie.

12. Test the movie by selecting Control, Test Movie. This creates the SWF file of the movie and launches the Flash Player Testing Mode. Close the Flash Player Testing Mode to return to the movie.

13. Repeat steps 10-12 to create the other three activity movies. Change the text block to reflect the activity movies of Matching, In Quest of Ducks, and Puzzles; then save each movie with the following names: ducks.fla, puzzle.fla, and matching.fla. Save each movie in the same directory as the Honeycomb.fla movie. Be sure to test each movie in the Flash Player Testing Mode so that you generate the SWF file for each of these movies.

Attaching the Stop Action to the Movie

You probably have noticed that when you test The Honeycomb site in the Flash Player, it continuously loops. You can handle this looping through ActionScript by putting a stop action at the end of the Timeline. To add a stop action to the Timeline, follow these steps:

1. From the Honeycomb.fla movie or the main movie, click the Guide:buzzy bee layer to make it active. Insert a new layer above it and name the layer actions.

2. Click Photoframe 100 in the actions layer and insert a keyframe. This is the last frame of the movie, so to stop the movie at the end of the Timeline, you need to add the stop action to this frame.

3. Open the Actions panel and click the Actions category to expand the list of actions. Then click the Movie Control subcategory to open this list of actions. Locate and double-click the stop action (see Figure 7.27).

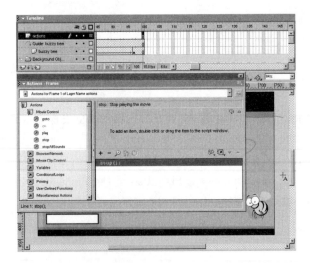

Figure 7.27   The Actions layer will contain all the actions in the movie.

4. Test the movie again in Flash Player Testing Mode. It now will stop when it reaches the end of the Timeline.

Making the Buttons Functional

You want the site to display each activity when the end-user clicks the activity's button. This requires the `loadMovie` action. Using levels for loading the activity movie SWF file into The Honeycomb site will not work because Buzzy Bee needs to be visible at all times. If you load an activity into a movie level, the loaded movie will cover him. Therefore, you need to create a load target with a movie clip that exists on its own layer and target this movie clip instance with the `loadMovie` action.

Setting the Movie Target

Before you can assign the `loadMovie` action to a button, you must create the movie clip instance to be used as the load target. To do this, follow these steps:

1. In the `Honeycomb.fla` movie, click the `menu` layer and insert a new layer above it. Name the layer `load target`. Click Photoframe 73 and insert a keyframe (see Figure 7.28). You select Frame 73 because the site design at this point in the Timeline is visible on all layers.

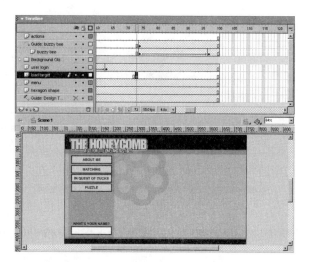

Figure 7.28   The `load target` layer is near the bottom of the layer stacking order. All the layers above this layer will display on top of the loaded movie.

2. Create a new symbol and name it load target. Give it a Movie Clip behavior. Click OK, and the new symbol opens in the Symbol-Editing Mode. By default, the registration point is set to the upper-left corner for a new symbol with x and y coordinate values of 0. The load target symbol is just a target, so do not put any objects on the Stage. Exit the Symbol-Editing Mode.

3. Select the load target layer to make it active and click keyframe 73. Open or access the library and drag an instance of the load target symbol from the library onto the Stage. Position it anywhere—you will use the Info panel to precisely locate it in the upper-left corner of the Stage.

4. With the load target instance active, open or access your Info panel. Set the x coordinate and y coordinate each to 0 (see Figure 7.29). This movie clip will be targeted by the loaded SWF file. Because its reference point is the upper-left corner and it is positioned at 0 for the x, y coordinate, all loaded SWF files will align precisely with the main movie.

Note

The loaded SWF file inherits the position, rotation, and scale attributes of the targeted movie clip. In The Honeycomb Web site, the loaded SWF file's upper-left corner will be placed at the reference point of the load target movie clip instance.

load target instance

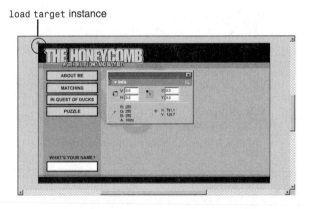

Figure 7.29   The load target instance moves to the upper-left corner of the Stage.

Naming the load target Instance

To be able to call the load target instance in the loadMovie action, the instance needs to be named. You can name any instance on the Stage or in the work area. To name this instance, follow these steps:

1. Click the load target layer to make it active. Click or marquee the load target instance on the Stage to make it the active object.

2. In the Property Inspector, type loadTarget in the Instance Name box (see Figure 7.30). Press the Enter key to set this instance name, ensuring the name is assigned to the load target instance.

Figure 7.30   The Property Inspector reflects that this symbol is a movie clip and that both the height and width settings are 0, indicating that it is an empty movie clip.

> **Tip**
>
> Always press the Enter key after you set a setting in any of the panels and the Property Inspector. If you don't press the Enter key after changing a setting option, sometimes Flash will not acknowledge the new setting, reverting back to the previous setting.

Using the loadMovie Action

With the load target movie clip positioned on the Stage and named, you can now attach the loadMovie action to The Honeycomb activity buttons and target this movie clip to be replaced by the loaded SWF file. Each of the buttons is nested in the menu symbol, so to attach any actions to these buttons, you must first open the menu symbol in the Symbol-Editing Mode. Follow these steps to attach the loadMovie action to each button:

1. In the library, double-click the menu symbol to launch the Symbol-Editing Mode.

2. Click the About Me button on the Stage to make it active.

3. Open the Actions panel and click the Browser/Network category, and then double-click the loadMovie action (see Figure 7.31).

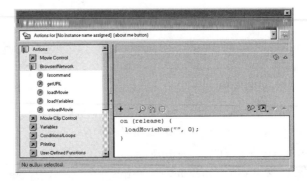

Figure 7.31   The on action automatically displays above the `loadMovie` action because the object is a button.

4. Keep the on action line of script set to the event handler of `release`. Click the `loadMovie` action line of code, click the URL box, and type `aboutme.swf`. When you tested this movie, you created the SWF file of the `aboutme.fla` file in the same directory as the FLA file. You will load the SWF file when the About Me button is clicked. Click the Location option and select Target. Click the Location box and delete its contents (see Figure 7.32).

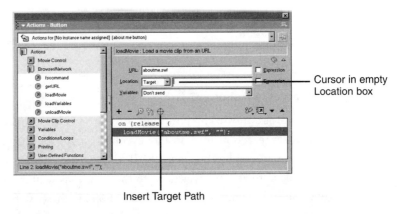

Cursor in empty Location box

Insert Target Path

Figure 7.32   If you do not have a cursor in the Location box, the Insert Target Path button is not accessible.

5. With the cursor in the Location box, click the Insert Target Path button in the bottom-right corner of the Action panel. The Insert Target Path dialog box displays.

6. If the Absolute option is not selected, click it to select it. The Absolute option looks at all objects in a movie. The Relative option focuses only on the selected movie clip. In this case, that would be the menu symbol in which the About Me button is nested. Click the loadTarget instance (see Figure 7.33). Click OK to close the dialog box.

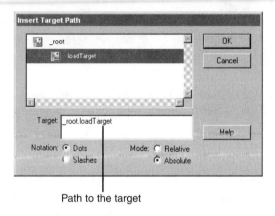

Path to the target

Figure 7.33   The path to the target is displayed in the Target box.

7. The load target path is set, but, by default, it is set as a *string*. A string appears in quotation marks, and Flash looks at it as if it were text. You must select the Expression option to turn it on (see Figure 7.34). You will learn more about strings and expressions in Seminar 8, "Using Components in a Macromedia Flash Form."

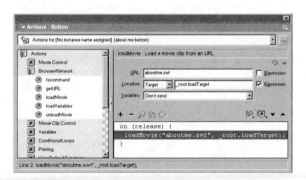

Figure 7.34   The quotation marks are removed, and the load target path is now set as a *statement* that will return a value. In this case, it sets the target path to the loadTarget instance.

Note

Expressions are a combination of operators and values. They also can call a function. An *operator* is a character that specifies how to combine, compare, or modify the values of an expression. Expressions are discussed more throughout the rest of this book.

Note

A *string* is a series of characters. This could be letters, numbers, and punctuation marks. Strings have either single or double quotation marks encompassing them. Flash looks at strings as characters or text, not as a value.

8. Test your movie in the Flash Player. Wait until Buzzy Bee appears on the Stage, and then test the About Me button by clicking it. You should see the text block with the words `About Me` appear on the Stage, indicating that the `aboutme.swf` movie is now loaded.

Tip

If you try to click any of the activity buttons before the movie plays past Frame 73 (which contains the load target movie clip instance), the `loadMovie` action loads the activity movie into the parent movie clip, which is the menu movie clip symbol. It doesn't work correctly because the load target is not present on the Stage yet. You will fix this small detail in Seminar 13.

9. Repeat steps 2–8 and target the appropriate load movie for the matching, puzzle, and ducks button instances.

Tip

Instead of repeating steps 2–8, you can also copy the ActionScript from the About Me button by selecting the About Me button, and then opening the Actions panel. Highlight all three lines of script in the Scripting pane for the About Me button and copy the code by (Control-Clicking)[right-clicking] the highlighted script and choosing Copy from the shortcut menu. Then click another button and in the Actions panel for this object, paste the script into the Scripting pane by (Control-Clicking)[right-clicking] and choosing Copy from the shortcut menu. Click the `loadMovie` action script and change the loaded SWF file URL to match the button. Always double-check your script to ensure that you have the correct code if you copy and paste it into the Action panel.

10. Exit the Symbol-Editing Mode and test The Honeycomb movie in the Flash Player Testing Mode. Try all the buttons. You should see each activity movie loaded into the main movie replacing the `loadTarget` movie clip instance on the Stage. Because the activity movies are loaded into the empty `loadTarget` movie clip instance, they replace each other as the appropriate button is clicked.

11. Save the movie as `Honeycomb.fla`. If you want to compare your Honeycomb site with a movie that is completed up to this point in the book, open the `07Honeycomb.fla` file located in the `Seminar07/Samples` directory on the CD-ROM that accompanies this book.

Seminar Summary

Making a site interactive requires the use of keyframes, buttons, movie clips, and ActionScript. This seminar covered these features. You learned how to make a three-state button and how to set the hit area for the button. You also attached ActionScript to both a button and a frame to give your movie interactivity. You named an instance on the Stage so that it could be called in the ActionScript. You created a `load target` movie clip instance and targeted movies to this movie clip with the `loadMovie` action. Things are getting more exciting on The Honeycomb site, and it is beginning to come alive.

In the next seminar, you will create a form for collecting end-user data. This form is designed to collect the data needed for the About Me activity. You will use input text fields and a new feature of Flash MX: components to create the form features. A component is a special type of movie clip that is customizable. You will learn more about this feature in the next seminar as well as throughout different areas of the book.

WORKSHOP ▼ Creating the Site Interactivity

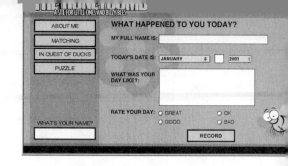

Seminar 8

Using Components in a Macromedia Flash Form

In this chapter

Workshop: Creating a Form for the About Me Activity

Overview of Components and Their Use in Macromedia Flash

A *component* is a movie clip with defined clip parameters that can be edited. Components provide a way to isolate and encapsulate complex interactivity into a special movie clip symbol just as the smart clip did in Flash 5.0. But unlike smart clips, components are intelligent and now can be modified through ActionScript. To understand this new intelligence that has been added to a component, a comparison with smart clips is necessary. For instance, if you were to resize a smart clip, it would be distorted, but the new intelligence of a component enables the component to be resized, keeping the original proportions intact.

Seven preset Flash UI (user interface) components ship with Flash. These components are stored in the Components panel (see Figure 8.1). You can access the Components panel through the Window, Component menu command.

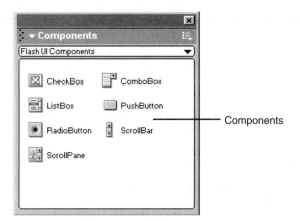

Figure 8.1   Each Flash UI component has its own representing icon and functionality for a Flash movie.

Prior to the addition of the Flash UI components in Flash MX, achieving certain functionality, such as a scrollbar, in a movie required strong ActionScript knowledge. But now with the Flash UI components, you can easily add advanced functionality to your movies. Table 8.1 provides a brief description of each of the seven preset components and their uses in Flash development.

Table 8.1 Descriptions of the Flash UI Components

Component Name	Description of Functionality
CheckBox	Creates check boxes.
ListBox	Creates a list box of many options or choices. The end-user can use arrow keys, the page up or down keys, and the End and Home keys to scroll through the choices in a list box.
RadioButton	Creates radio buttons. Typical of other radio buttons used in HTML code, only one radio button can be selected at a time.
ScrollPane	Creates vertical and horizontal scrollbars for Windows. This is useful if you need to display a movie clip or JPG image in another window for your movie. Scrollbars can be added to a window so that scrolling is enabled in the new window.
ComboBox	Creates scrollable, single-selection drop-down menus. The end-user can type in a search word and find the match in the drop-down menu of the ComboBox.
PushButton	Creates a simple push button that responds to mouse and keyboard interactions. You can also attach a handler for executing actions when the button is triggered.
ScrollBar	Creates vertical and horizontal scrollbars for input and dynamic text blocks. This component must be added to an existing input or dynamic text block. You will learn more about input and dynamic text blocks later in this seminar.

Components are very beneficial for beginning and advanced Flash users alike. Even with limited ActionScript skills, beginning Flash users can add interactive components to their movies. Advanced Flash developers can create their own components to encapsulate complex movie clips that are used through a movie or to share with others. You will add three of the Flash UI components to the About Me activity in this seminar's workshop.

Tip

Because Components are a Flash MX feature, you must have your Publish settings set to a version setting of Flash MX to use them correctly in the Macromedia Flash 6 Player. The Flash 5 Player will not recognize a component. See Seminar 16, "Publishing and Testing the Site," for information on how to set the version setting to Flash MX.

Adding Components to a Movie

Similar to any symbol in the Flash library, to add a component to a movie, simply drag it from the Components panel onto the Stage. It is added to the movie and now appears in the movie library (see Figure 8.2). The movie library displays one folder that contains the Flash UI component. Inside that folder are two other folders: Component Skins and Core Assets – Developer Only. The Component Skins folder contains all the objects that make up the component. These objects or skins can be edited to customize the appearance of the component, which is discussed later in this seminar.

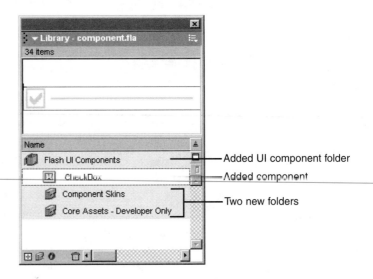

Figure 8.2   Each Flash UI component is composed of additional symbols that make up its composition.

Customizing a Component

After you add a component to your movie, you can customize the parameters for the component as well as the component appearance. When you set the parameters, you are actually setting the values that can be customized in the encapsulated movie clip. When you customize the appearance of the component, you change the actual image of the component through the component skins.

Setting Component Parameters

To access the parameters of a component, make the component instance on the Stage active, and then click the Parameters tab in the upper-right corner of the Property Inspector (see Figure 8.3). A parameter is really a value for the component instance. You can customize the parameter values to fit your movie. You will have hands-on practice in the workshop customizing component parameters.

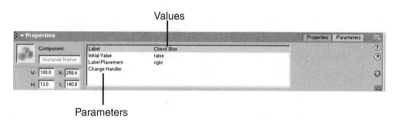

Figure 8.3   You can also change the height and width of the component through the Width and Height box of the Property Inspector.

> **Tip**
>
> You can also (Control-click)[right-click] the component instance on the Stage and select Panels, Component Parameters from the shortcut menu to open the Component Parameters panel. This panel also enables you to customize the values for the component.

Table 8.2 provides information on each of the Flash UI components and their customizable parameters.

Table 8.2   Descriptions of the Parameter Values for Flash UI Components

Component Name	Variable Parameters
CheckBox	`Label`: The name that displays next to the check box.
	`Initial Value`: Uses a Boolean value of either `true` or `false` to set whether the check box is checked.
	`Label Placement`: Specifies where the label displays, either to the left or right of the check box.
	`Change Handler`: A text string that specifies the function to call when the variable value in the check box changes.
ListBox	`Labels`: Creates the label names or menu names for the items in the list box. This is actually an array of text strings.
	`Data`: An array of text strings that makes up the items or menu choices in the list box.
	`Select Multiple`: Enables the end-user to select more than one item in a list box. This is a Boolean value of `true` for allowing multiple selections or `false` for allowing only one selection.
	`Change Handlers`: Specifies the function that is called when the end-user selects an item from the list box.
RadioButton	`Label`: The name of the radio button.
	`Initial State`: Sets the radio button initial display to be selected or deselected. This is a Boolean value of `true` for selected or `false` for deselected.
	`Group Name`: Specifies whether the radio button is part of a group of radio buttons.
	`Label Placement`: Specifies where the label displays, either to the left or right of the radio button.
	`Data`: Specifies the data that is associated with the radio button label.
ScrollPane	`Scroll Content`: String text that specifies the Symbol ID of the movie clip to be displayed in the Scroll pane.
	`Horizontal Scroll`: A Boolean value that determines whether the horizontal scrollbar is visible (`true`) or not visible (`false`).

Component Name	Variable Parameters
	Vertical Scroll: A Boolean value that determines whether the vertical scrollbar is visible (**true**) or not visible (**false**).
	Drag Content: Enables the end-user to change the view by either dragging the content in the Scroll pane (**true**) or using the scrollbars (**false**).
ComboBox	**Editable**: Specifies whether the combo box is editable or static. If the combo box is editable (**true**), the end-user can enter text in a field to search for a matching item from the list. If the end-user is only to select an item, the **false** value needs to be selected.
	Labels: Specifies the items to appear in the combo box. These items are set in the Values dialog box.
	Data: Text strings that specify the values to associate with each label. The Value dialog box is used to create the data values.
	Row Count: Sets the number of values to display in the combo box before the scrollbar is activated. The default value for this parameter is **8**.
	Change Handler: Specifies the function that is called when the end-user selects an item from the combo box or inputs text into the combo box input field.
PushButton	**Label**: The label that displays next to the push button.
	Click Handler: Specifies the function that is called when the end-user presses and releases the push button.
ScrollBar	**Target TextField**: A string that determines the instance name of the text field for the scrollbar. This field is automatically assigned the instance name of the field into which the component is dragged.
	Horizontal: Determines whether the scrollbar is horizontal (**true**) or vertical (**false**).

Customizing Component Skins

Aside from being able to customize component parameters, new with the component feature of Flash MX are component skins. Component skins are the individual images that make up the actual appearance of the component—for example, the color of check boxes, the font type used in menus and labels, the color and fill of scrollbars, and so on.

When you drag an instance of one of the Flash UI components into a movie, the library holds not only the component but two other folders: the Component Skins and the Core Assets - Developer Only folders. Each of these folders contains the individual symbols composed of the various images required to display the component. You can change the appearance of the component by opening a symbol from the skins folder in the Symbol-Editing Mode and making your changes to each graphical element that needs to be modified for the movie. When you make a change to a skin symbol, this change reflects in any other Flash UI instance you have added to your movie. You will customize a component skin in the workshop of this seminar.

Tip

You can't edit the component instance on the Stage by double-clicking it. The component skin must be edited by launching the Symbol-Editing Mode for the skin by double-clicking the skin symbol in the library.

Note

The Global Skins folder contains all the skins for all Flash UI components. If you change a skin from this folder, this affects all Flash UI components that use that skin. For instance, scrollbars are used in both the **ScrollPane** and the **ScrollBar** components. If you change the appearance of the graphical scrollbar element, it is reflected in both the **ScrollPane** and **ScrollBar** components, as well as any other component that uses a scrollbar.

If you edit a component skin and then add another Flash UI component from the Component panel that uses the same skin, you will get a warning message (see Figure 8.4).

Select Use Existing Component if you want to preserve the edits you have made to a skin and apply these edited skins to the new component you are adding. Select Replace Existing Component (Not Undoable) to replace all the skins with the defaults.

As you can see, there's a lot of flexibility in modifying the appearance for a component through the skins feature, and you can modify a component's parameters to customize the component to function as necessary in your movie.

Figure 8.4 This message also displays whenever you have edited skins for an instance of the same component you are adding to a movie.

> **Note**
>
> New with Flash MX is the capability to customize a component through ActionScript. You can set or change a specific property value for a component instance through the `setStyleProperty` method that is available to all components. To learn more about this feature, see `setStyleProperty` in the ActionScript Dictionary accessible in the Flash MX Help.

Viewing the Component

New with Flash MX is a Live Preview setting that, by default, is active when Flash is launched. Live Preview enables all components to display the initial menu choice or label while in the Flash Authoring environment. This is an advantage because it enables you to see the customization to a component in relation to other Stage content. This setting is accessible by selecting Control, Enable Live Preview.

If you want to see the component work and visually see any changes that you might have made to a component skin, you need to view the component in the Flash Player Testing Mode. Remember: A component is still a movie clip with its own Timeline and functionality outside the main movie Timeline. Select Control, Test Movie to view the movie and the component functionality.

Exploring Component Functionality

To understand components better, open the file `components.fla` located in the `Seminar08/Samples` directory. This file contains four instances of a square component on the Stage (see Figure 8.5).

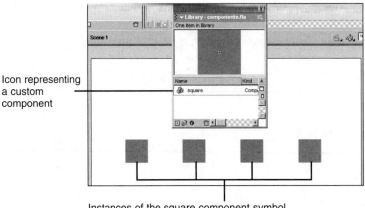

Icon representing
a custom
component

Instances of the square component symbol

Figure 8.5   All instances of the square component symbol appear the same in the Flash Authoring environment.

To see the actual parameter values that have been set for these square instances, test the movie in Flash Player Testing Mode (see Figure 8.6).

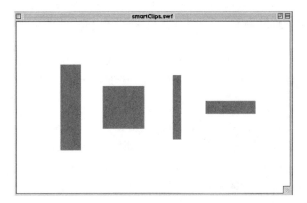

Figure 8.6   The actual movie in Flash Player testing mode displays each of the four squares as variously sized rectangles.

Each square instance in the movie displays as a rectangle of a set height and width. These different dimensions are caused by the parameter values that are set for each of the component instances on the Stage (see Figure 8.7).

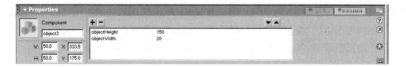

Figure 8.7   This instance is set to display at a width of 200 and a height of 50.

The Property Inspector displays the parameter values that are customizable in this component—objectHeight and objectWidth. To customize the values of these parameters, double-click the value to access the editable value fields and type the new value. Explore the values set for the other three instances of the square component symbol. You'll see that they each reflect different height and width values for that instance.

To view the ActionScript that creates the component functionality, you must open the component in Symbol-Editing Mode by double-clicking the component symbol from the Library panel. In Symbol-Editing Mode, you can see that the symbol is composed of two layers—one for holding the object shape and the other for actions. The keyframe in Frame 1 of the actions layer contains the script for the component. Open the Actions panel to view the script attached to Frame 1 (see Figure 8.8).

Figure 8.8   The setProperty line of code sets the value of a property for a targeted object.

This ActionScript creates the functionality of the component symbol. Although you have not created much in the way of ActionScript at this point in the book, you will in Seminar 10, "Using ActionScript to Control Objects," where you will use ActionScript to control objects as you create the matching activity for The Honeycomb site.

Note

Many third-party sites on the Internet, such as www.flashkit.com and www.praystation.com, distribute examples for creating navigation systems, preloaders, and other techniques for complex interactivity in Flash. You can use the component to begin to develop a library of this type of interactivity so that you can use the component in many of your movies.

Creating Your Own Component

As mentioned already, components are good for beginning Flash users and advanced users alike. Beginning users can add functionality that they might not be able to script themselves. Advanced users can capture ActionScript functionality that allows quick customization of variable values, and the components can then be used by a less skilled Flash developer. The components can also be used to create interface elements, such as radio buttons or pull-down menus. An added benefit of creating a component is the ability to customize the definition and interface of the component.

To create a component, you must first create a movie clip. In the Symbol-Editing Mode, create the ActionScript functionality you want attached to either an object or a frame of the movie clip symbol. With the symbol created, (Control-click)[right-click] the movie clip symbol in the library and select Component Definition from the shortcut menu to open the Component Definition dialog box (see Figure 8.9). Through this dialog box, you can create your component interface and functionality.

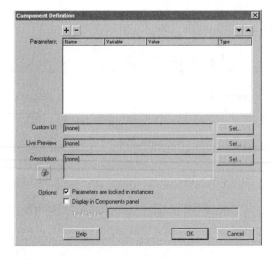

Figure 8.9   Use the buttons on the Component Definition dialog box to create the variable name and value.

Forms and Editable Text Fields

Now, we'll discuss features that greatly extend the power of Flash editable text fields. There are two types of editable text fields—input and dynamic. Seminar 3, "Creating a Movie," introduced the three text types in Flash: static, input, and dynamic text. Up to this point in the book, you have used static text for communicating information or instructions, button labels, and basically any stationary text that is used throughout a movie.

Flash MX offers new functionality for input and dynamic text fields because they are now treated as objects, just as movie clip symbols in previous releases of Flash were treated as objects. Editable text fields can now be assigned an instance name, enabling them to be called and controlled in ActionScript. This is a big area of improvement for further functionality in Flash MX.

Configuring Input Text Fields

Many of the option settings for the input text field are similar to that of HTML form fields. You can control the number of lines that make up the input text field, as well as its appearance. When you create an input text field in a form, you are essentially creating a field in which the end-user can type a response back to you.

The Property Inspector is used to set the Text option settings you want for that editable text field (see Figure 8.10).

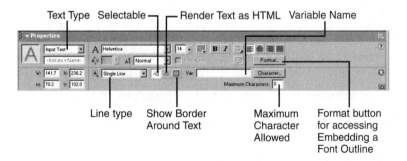

Figure 8.10   This input text field does not have a border or background, so the Stage background and design show through.

The following list describes the option settings of the Input Text Type:

- **Line Type**—Through this option, you can set the input text field to Single Line, Multiline, Multiline No Wrap, or Password. If you select Multiline, the text in the field displays in multiple lines with word wrap automatically applied, enabling the end-user's response to wrap inside the text field. Select Multiline No Wrap if you do not want the word wrap feature. If you want the field to be password-protected, select Password.

- **Selectable**—By default, this is active. This option enables the end-user to select the text in the input field.

- **Show Border Around Text**—If you select this option, your input text field will have a white background and a 1-point, black stroke around it.

- **Render Text As HMTL**—This option allows you to preserve rich text formatting in an input text field. This means you can set HTML formatting options for the input text field. You can use basic text formatting, which includes font name, style, color, and size. Any hyperlinks are preserved by automatically applying the corresponding HTML tags to the editable text fields. You can use these HMTL tags: `<a>`, `<b>`, `<font color>`, `<font face>`, `<font size>`, `<i>`, `<p>`, and `<u>`. The following HTML attributes are supported in text fields: LEFTMARGIN, RIGHTMARGIN, ALIGN, INDENT, and LEADING.

- **Maximum Number of Characters**—You can set this for each field. You always should set a maximum number of characters for any form field you create for use on the Internet. This helps prevent spamming or overloading of a server.

- **Var box**—This enables a variable name to be applied to an input text field and the field and its contents to be called in ActionScript. You can further manipulate end-user information if it is assigned to a variable.

- **Character button**—This opens a dialog box that enables the embedding of a font outline. Font outlines can be embedded in any movie to ensure that the selected font will always display on the end-user's machine, no matter which fonts she might have loaded on her computer system. This increases the movie file size by 20KB when embedding the entire font outline for a font.

Tip

If you enter text into an input text field as you create it, this text can be used as additional instructions or an example of how data can be input into the text block. For example, you could have used `Enter Your Full Name Here` in the input text field you created. The end-users would need to click in the text box and delete the instruction text; however, they would know exactly what you wanted them to type into the box—their full names.

Warning

If you enter text into an input text field as you create it, this text becomes a predefined value of the variable for that field. Be careful because this can cause problems with data integrity if the temporary value is not replaced by the end-user.

Naming Editable Text Fields

As mentioned earlier in this seminar, instance names can be assigned to an editable text field. You can assign a variable name to the editable text field as well. To assign an instance name, type a name in the Instance Name box of the Property Inspector. To assign a variable name, type that name into the Var box of the Property Inspector.

You can think of an editable text field as a container for storing the inputted or dynamic text. Anytime you need to manipulate this text through ActionScript or post this text so that it can be retrieved by the CGI script and used in a data field or document on the Web server, you need to assign an instance or a variable name to the field.

Assigning an instance name to an editable text field allows you to control all the property settings of the text field through ActionScript. For example, you can control the height, width, or alpha setting of an editable text field through its instance name. The variable name is used to control the displayed text in the field. You will learn more about controlling editable text fields with ActionScript in Seminar 10.

Testing Editable Text Fields

To test your editable text fields, you must test your movie in Flash Player testing mode. When the movie exports into the Flash Player testing mode, you can select the editable text fields and type a response. The inputted response becomes the value that can be controlled through either the instance name or the variable name.

Communicating with a Text File or Server-Side Scripts

Connectivity between the front-end Flash form and a back-end application or database is accomplished through a script or *middleware* application. Middleware, such as XML, ASP, CGI, PHP, Tango, and ColdFusion, allows for queries and data relays back and forth from the Flash movie and a database. The middleware composes the data into the correct format that the database requires. By using the `loadVariables` or `GetURL` action, you can send the data (`GET` or `POST`) to the script, or middleware application. The data from each variable used in the form is transferred directly to the database, with information from each variable plugging into a database field coded with the same name. After the data is transferred, you can further manipulate it.

> **Note**
>
> Text files are often used to store the Flash form data. This allows the data to be easily accessible to other applications.

A database can also communicate with a Flash movie. Based on events that occur while an end-user navigates through a site, a Flash movie can receive database information that the end-user provides. One method is to pass parameters in a URL as a query string or from form data. The server script can pass parameters or query stings in a URL as values to the Flash movie. This enables the movie to display contents that are based on what the user has done or where he has been in the site. Popular uses include shopping carts, electronic greeting cards, and personalized pages where it is key to keep track of a user's activities.

Creating a Form for the About Me Activity

The About Me activity is essentially a form that allows the end-user to record information about himself in The Honeycomb site. It is made up of data objects and input text fields. You will use both static text blocks and input text fields to create this activity. You also will need to use components for creating drop-down menus and four radio buttons for this form. Due to the many connectivity technologies that various Internet service providers (ISPs) use, this workshop focuses on building the front-end interface for gathering this information.

> **Note**
>
> Although this workshop covers creating input text fields to capture end-user responses, the input text fields can be used in a greater capacity for other forms of interactivity in Seminar 10.

Setting Up Form Structure

To begin creating this form, you need to add some static text blocks that provide the instructions and field labels for each end-user response. Alignment of form objects becomes important for creating a clear and aesthetically pleasing form. Guides are again used to help the design process of this form. You can also use the Align panel to align objects. Follow these steps to set up the form structure:

1. Open the `aboutme.fla` movie in the `Seminar08/Samples/07Honeycomb/` directory. Save this file in the directory where you've saved your `Honeycomb.fla` file. For the `loadMovie` action to work, the `aboutme.swf` file must be in the same directory as the `Honeycomb.fla` file.

2. Lock the `Guide:Design Template` layer. This makes working with the form objects easier.

3. Delete the `About Me` static text block that is centered on the Stage.

4. Show the rulers by selecting View, Rulers. Drag a guide from the vertical ruler onto the Stage and position it at the horizontal ruler setting of 240. Drag another vertical guide and position it at the setting of 380. Lock the guides by selecting View, Guides, Lock Guides.

5. Click the keyframe in Frame 1 of the `movie` layer and create a static text block by first selecting the Text tool and then setting the Property Inspector options to the following: Static Text, Arial, font size of 18 points, font color of black, Bold, Auto Kern selected, Character Spacing of 0, Character Position of Normal, and Left Justify selected.

6. With your static text options not on the movie layer, click to set an extendable text block on the Stage; then type WHAT HAPPENED TO YOU TODAY?.

7. Position the static text block so that it aligns with the left vertical guide under the header shadow object, as Figure 8.11 indicates.

Figure 8.11   The left guide is used to align all text field labels.

8. With the keyframe in Frame 1 of the movie layer active, create another static text block with the following settings in the Property Inspector: Static text, Arial, font size of 14 points, font color of black, Bold, Auto Kern selected, Character Spacing of 0, Character Position of Normal, and Left Justify. Type, in uppercase, MY FULL NAME IS:.

9. Position this text block under the first text block aligned with the left guide.

10. Repeat steps 8 and 9 to create the following static text blocks:

   • TODAY'S DATE IS:

   • WHAT WAS YOUR DAY LIKE?: (Create a paragraph break to break this text block into two lines, as Figure 8.12 indicates.)

   • RATE YOUR DAY:

11. Align each of the static text blocks created in step 10 to the left guide and position them as Figure 8.12 indicates. You have created the form instructions and field labels.

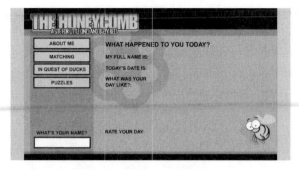

Figure 8.12   The left guide is used to align the static text blocks. The right guide will be used to align all the input text fields and other data objects.

Creating the Form Fields and Assigning Instance Names

Now you will use the right guide to align the input text fields for the About Me activity. You will create a line type of a single-line input text field for capturing the end-user's full name and a multiline input text field for the end-user's response for describing his day. To do this, follow these steps:

1. Select the keyframe in Frame 1 of the movie layer and create an input text field by setting your Property Inspector options to the following: Input Text, Arial, font size of 14 points, font color of black, a Character Position of Normal, Left Justify, a Line Type of Single Line, Show Border Around Text, and Maximum Characters Allowed to 50.

2. Next, embed the Arial font outline—but just the uppercase letters for the text input field. This enables the end-user's response to be displayed in the same font as is used throughout the site. In the Property Inspector, click the Character button to display the Character Options dialog box. Select Only, and then select the Uppercase Letters option (see Figure 8.13). Click Done to close the dialog box.

Warning

If you embed an entire font outline into a movie, you will increase the movie file size by 20KB.

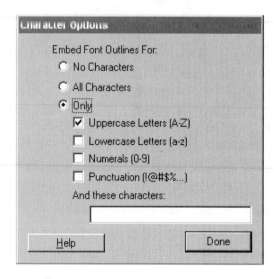

Figure 8.13   You can embed the entire font outline for the active text type by selecting All Characters.

3. With the Text tool, click and drag a text block about 300 pixels wide. Position it so that it aligns with the right guide, as indicated in Figure 8.14.

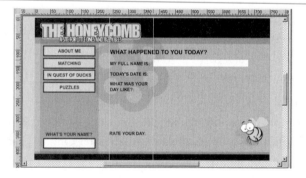

Figure 8.14   By setting the Max Chars option to 50, you limit the end-user response to 50 characters for this input text field.

Tip

Always size editable text fields using the handle of the text field. Double-click the text field to access the handle, and click and drag the handle to resize the text field. Do not use the Free Transform tool because this feature scales the box and distorts individual letter size, instead of resizing the text field.

4 With the Arrow tool, click the input text field you just created to make it active. Then, in the Property Inspector, assign an instance name of `fullName` to this box.

5. On the `movie` layer, create another input text field by setting your Property Inspector options to the following: Input Text, Arial, a font size of 14 points, font color of black, Character Position of Normal, Left Justify, Multiline, Show Border Around Text selected, and Maximum Characters Allowed to `500`.

6. Click the Character button to display the Character Options dialog box, and again embed the font outline for just Uppercase (see step 2 in the previous set of steps). Click Done to close the dialog box.

7. With the Text tool, click and drag an input text field about `260` pixels wide and `130` pixels high. Position it so that it aligns with the right guide, as indicated in Figure 8.15.

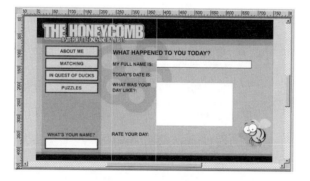

Figure 8.15   By selecting the Multiline option and setting the Maximum Characters Allowed option to 500, the text field is capable of containing multiple lines of text but is limited to 500 characters.

8. With the Arrow tool, click this input text field to make it active; in the Text Option panel, assign an instance name of `today` to this box.

9. Test the movie, and when the movie displays in the Flash Player, test the input text fields by typing in information.

Tip

You can use the Align panel to align your input text fields with the static text blocks by either the top or bottom edge for each section of the form. This creates a cleaner-looking form.

Capturing Today's Date Information

You have the basic input text fields created, and now you want to create the Today's Date fields. A drop-down menu that displays all the months of the year is used so that the end-user can select the current month from the list. Another input text field needs to be created for capturing the actual date; then another drop-down menu is used to capture the present year. Through the component features of Flash MX, you will use the Flash UI ComboBox component to create these drop-down menus. To create the data objects and input text fields to capture the Today's Date information, follow these steps:

1. Click the movie layer to make it active and insert a new layer above this layer. Name the new layer date.

2. Open the Components panel if it is not accessible by selecting Window, Components (see Figure 8.16).

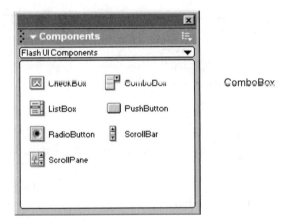

Figure 8.16   You can also create check box and radio button functionality with the other component symbols in the Components panel.

3. Click the keyframe in Frame 1 of the date layer and drag an instance of the ComboBox symbol onto the Stage. Position it so it aligns with the right guide across from the TODAY'S DATE IS: text (see Figure 8.17).

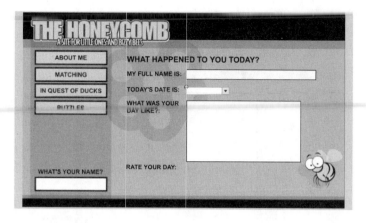

Figure 8.17   You will customize the values of the ComboBox instance so that it lists the 12 months of the year.

4. To set the list of months for the instance of the ComboBox, first make it active by clicking it on the Stage; then click the Parameters tab in the Property Inspector (see Figure 8.18).

Parameters tab

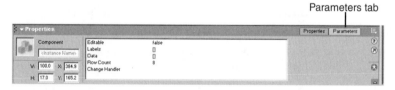

Figure 8.18   The parameters for the ComboBox instance are displayed in the Property Inspector.

5. Double-click the Labels [] value to access the Values panel. Click the plus (+) button to add a new value. Click the defaultValue item in the Values dialog box and type January (see Figure 8.19).

6. Repeat step 5 to create the other 11 months in a year. Click OK to close the Values dialog box.

Figure 8.19   You can add or delete a value by clicking the plus (+) or minus (-) buttons at the top of this dialog box.

7. Double-click the Data [] value to again access the Values panel. Click the plus button to add a new value. Click the defaultValue item in the Values dialog box, and type January. Add the other 11 months as Data values. This assigns a text string value for each of the Label values for the ComboBox instance. Click OK to close the Values dialog box.

8. Click the Row Count value and set it to 5. Leave the Change Handler unassigned.

9. Click the ComboBox instance on the Stage to make it active. Then click the Properties tab in the Property Inspector and assign an instance name of month.

10. On the date layer with the keyframe in Frame 1 selected, create another input text field by setting your Property Inspector to the following: Input Text, Arial, 14 points, black, Character Position of Normal, Left Justify, a Line Type of Single Line, Show Border Around Text option, and the Maximum Characters Allowed of 2. Click the Character button and embed a font outline for Numbers (0–9) because this input text field will hold only numbers. Click Done to close the Value dialog box.

11. With the Text tool, click and drag a small input text field on the Stage. Position it to the right of the month ComboBox component instance, as Figure 8.20 indicates.

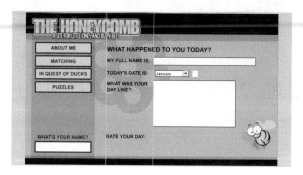

Figure 8.20   Make the input text field large enough to hold just two characters.

12. Click the input text field you just created, and in the Property Inspector, assign the instance name of `date`.

Tip

If you want to get the day input text field instance to be the exact height of the ComboBox instance, set the Height attribute for this instance to **17**.

13. On the `date` layer, add another `ComboBox` component to the Stage. Position it to the right of the date input text field (see Figure 8.21).

14. Repeat step 5 to add the years 2001–2005 as both Label values and Data values in the Values dialog box. Set the Row Count to 5.

15. Click the second `ComboBox` instance on the Stage. Then, in the Property Inspector, click the Properties tab and assign an instance name of `year`.

16. To test the form and see the component instances work, test the movie in Flash Player 6. Try each of the menus and the input text field of the movie. The About Me activity is shaping up because of the use of the Flash form and component features. Exit the Flash Player.

Tip

You can use the Align panel to align your input text fields and the `ComboBox` instances by their top or bottom edges to create a cleaner look for the form.

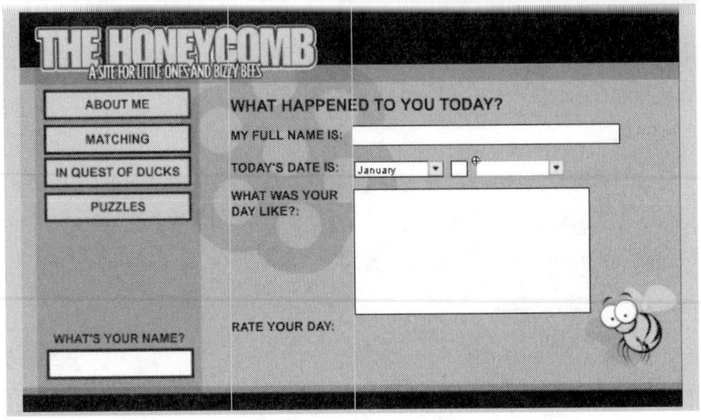

Figure 8.21   This second ComboBox instance displays the years 2001–2005 in its menu list.

Adding a Scrollbar to the Multiline Input Text Field

In the previous topic, you created a multilined input text field for capturing the end-user's description of her day. This text field was given the variable name today. Now you will add a scrollbar to the field so that the end-user can type as much of a description as she wants for describing her day. To add a scrollbar, follow these steps:

1. Click the today input text field to make it active.

2. From the Component panel, drag an instance of the ScrollBar component on top of the today input text field. The component attaches to the today input text field (see Figure 8.22).

3. To have the scrollbar display vertically in the input text field, click the ScrollBar instance to make it active. Then, in the Property Inspector, click the Parameters tab. Keep the Horizontal value set to False.

4. Test the movie in Flash Player Testing Mode to see the new vertical scrollbar in the input text field. Type text into the field and test the vertical scrollbar. Exit the Flash Player Testing Mode.

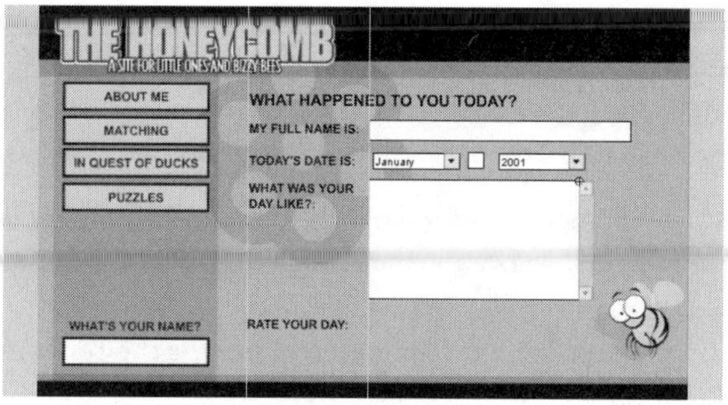

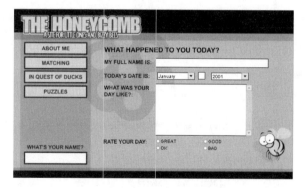

Figure 8.22   You can add either a horizontal scrollbar or a vertical scrollbar, but not both.

Adding Radio Buttons to the Form

Next, you will develop the section of the form for rating the day. This section will include radio button functionality, so you will use the RadioButton component. To create this section of the form, follow these steps:

1. Click the keyframe in Frame 1 of the movie layer and drag four instances of the RadioButton symbol from the Component panel onto the Stage. Position them to the right of the RATE YOUR DAY static text block (see Figure 8.23).

Figure 8.23   The end-user can rate her day by clicking the appropriate radio button.

2. Set the Parameters for each of the RadioButton component instances on the Stage through the Parameters tab of the Property Inspector. Set the component Parameters as Figure 8.24 indicates.

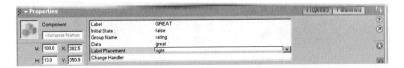

Figure 8.24   By using all uppercase for the label Value GREAT, the text will display in uppercase on the Stage when viewed in the Flash Player.

3. Set the following component Parameter values for the remaining three RadioButton instances on the Stage:

   - GOOD, false, rating, good, right

   - OK, false, rating, ok, right

   - BAD, false, rating, bad, right

4. Next, assign an instance name to each of these radio button instances. Click the GREAT radio button instance to make it the active object on the Stage. Then, in the Property Inspector, assign an instance name of great.

5. Repeat step 4 to assign instance names of good, ok, and bad to the appropriate instance of the component RadioButton symbol on the Stage.

6. To test the radio buttons, export the movie to the Flash Player Testing Mode and click each button. Notice that you can select only one of the buttons at a time. This is a common feature of a radio button in a form. Exit the Flash Player Testing Mode.

Tip ──

When components are added to a movie, the file size for that movie is greatly increased in the Flash Authoring mode. But when the movie is exported into SWF format, the file size decreases significantly when compared to the FLA file.

Customizing the Component Skins for the Scrollbar

To better integrate the ScrollBar component instance into the site design, you need to make the scrollbar in the today text field the same light yellow color as the rollover state of the activity buttons. To customize this ScrollBar component instance, follow these steps:

1. Open the movie library, and then open the Component Skins folder by double-clicking it. Open the FScrollBar Skins folder.

2. Locate the fob_ScrollTrack symbol and double-click it to launch the Symbol-Editing Mode. The ScrollBar skin element for the scroll track displays. Double-click this scroll track symbol to access the nested symbol named scrollTrack (see Figure 8.25).

Tabs

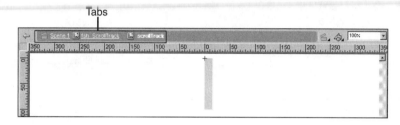

Figure 8.25 The Symbol-Editing Mode tabs reflect the nesting order of all the symbols that make up the skin for the ScrollBar component.

3. Click the image of the scrollTrack symbol on the Stage and change the color of the fill to a hexadecimal value of #FFFF99.

4. Exit the Symbol-Editing Mode and test your movie to see the new scroll track. If you like it, change other skins for the other components you have added to your movie to integrate them better with the site design. Exit the Flash Player Testing Mode.

Adding the Submit Button to the Form

As discussed earlier in this seminar, because of the various connectivity issues for communicating with a database or other middleware application, you need to add a Record button to the form and set up a fictitious URL for transmitting the form data. You have assigned variables to all input text fields and to all form objects to enable these end-users' responses to each of these objects to be transmitted to a database field with the same variable name. To add a Record button to this form, follow these steps:

1. Click the movie layer and insert a new layer above it. Name this layer record.

2. Open as a library the movie input.fla file located on the CD-ROM in the directory Seminar08/Samples.

3. With the record layer active and the keyframe in Frame 1 selected, drag an instance of the record symbol onto the Stage and position it at the bottom of the Stage, as Figure 8.26 indicates.

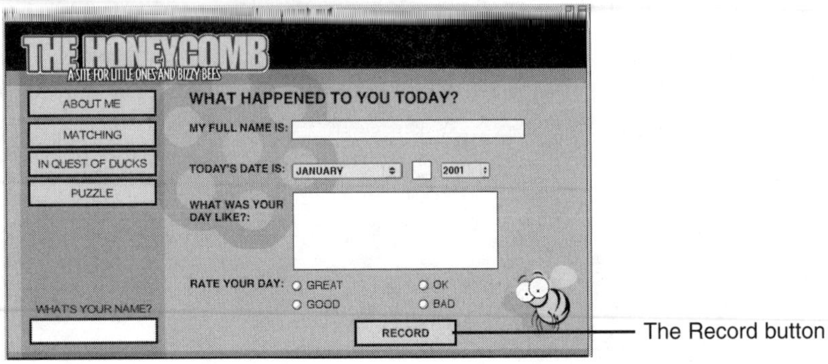

— The Record button

Figure 8.26   The Record button is used to pass the variables to a server-side script.

4. To attach a sample of ActionScript that transfers the data of the form to a database on the Hosting server, click the Record button on the Stage to make it active. Open the Actions panel and click the Action category; then click the Browser/Network subcategory to display the actions for browser or network control. Double-click the getURL action.

5. In the Parameter panel of the Actions panel, click the URL box and type http://www.mywebserver.com/. Make sure that the Expressions option to the right of the URL box is not selected. Flash looks at the URL as a string when this option is not enabled.

Note ──

This fictitious URL is an example of what one would look like. You need to check with your ISP for instructions on submitting form data to its Web server.

6. Click the arrow on the Variables drop-down menu and select Send Using POST from the list (see Figure 8.27).

7. Using the Flash Player Testing Mode, test all the input text fields and component objects. If you click the Record button, you will launch your browser and it will try to find the fictitious URL you attached to this button. When you are done testing your movie, close the Flash Player Testing Mode to return to the Flash Authoring mode.

8. Open the Honeycomb.fla file and test the movie. In the Flash Player, click the About Me button. You should see the newly developed form for this activity load into The Honeycomb movie.

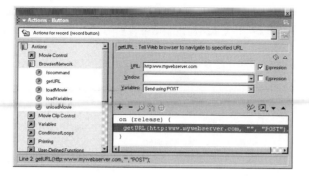

Figure 8.27 You can also use the `loadVariables` action to communicate with middleware and databases.

> **Tip**
>
> You must have the `aboutme.swf` file in the same directory as the `Honeycomb.fla` movie for the `loadMovie` action to work.

9. Exit the Flash Player and save the movie as `Honeycomb.fla`; then save the `aboutme.fla` file with the new form. If you want to compare your Honeycomb site with a movie that is completed up to this point in the book, open the `08Honeycomb.fla` file located in the `Seminar08/Samples` directory on the CD-ROM that accompanies this book.

Troubleshooting the Form

The transfer of data between a form and the Web server can work perfectly, but sometimes you need to troubleshoot your form to figure out why data is not being transferred correctly. The following list describes common errors that can occur when you're working with forms:

- Check that you have your input text fields set up correctly. A common error is to have them set up as static text block or dynamic text fields.

- Check that your URL is set up correctly as per your ISP. A common error is to omit the `http://` from the URL. Be sure that the URL is assigned a string value, not an expression.

- Check that you have instance and variable names exactly matching the database fields or text file fields. A common error is not to have the spelling the same or have the case of the letters match; uppercase and lowercase letters must match.

- Check that you have the correct method set for sending or receiving vari
  ables; for example, be sure you use the POST or GET method set based on the
  type of form that you are using.

Tip

You must specify how you want to load input text field values used in a form. Use the GET
method for a small number of values because this method appends the field values to the
end of the URL. Use the POST method for long strings of variables because this method transfers the values in a separate http header.

Seminar Summary

This seminar covered the basics for setting up a form in Flash. You learned how to
create both an input and a dynamic text field. You learned how to set up the font
attributes for these boxes and how to embed a font outline. Instance names were
assigned to each input text field so that communication could occur between the
form and the back-end database or middleware application. You also used components for drop-down menus and radio buttons from the Component panel of Flash
MX. You configured the variables and values of the component instances and then
assigned an instance name to these objects. You added a Record button to the form
and created a fictitious URL for communicating with a database on the hosting Web
server. If you are familiar with form development with HTML, you are probably seeing that forms in Flash are very similar in both form objects and form communication methods. You should have a good idea of how to create a form in Flash and how
to use the Flash UI components.

The next seminar covers more about ActionScript and teaches you how to use preloaders for controlling access to the main site until all the information of the main
site has been loaded. You will create a conditional if...then loop and then test your
movie in the Flash Player Testing Mode using the built-in Bandwidth Profiler.

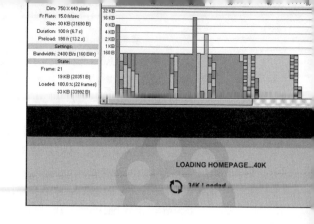

LOADING HOMEPAGE...40K

34K Loaded...

Seminar 9

Using Preloaders and Conditional Loops

In this chapter

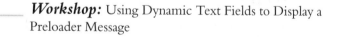

Workshop: Using Dynamic Text Fields to Display a Preloader Message

Overview of Preloader or Gate Page

For you to view a Macromedia Flash Web site over the Internet, the site needs to download or stream to the end-user's machine. Depending on the size and complexity of the movie, this could be a matter of seconds or minutes. Today, many Flash developers use a preloader to entertain the site visitor while the rest of the site streams down in the background. The preloader lets the visitor know that the site hasn't locked up and that he will soon be into the site. The preloader acts as a gate page, to disallow the visitor into the site until enough of the movie has streamed down, ensuring that the movie plays without glitches or unassigned delays. The site is experienced as it was designed. This seminar focuses on the creation of a preloader.

Preloader functionality can be composed of a short animation that plays continuously until enough of the site has streamed down to the end-user's machine, or it can be just ActionScript that occurs behind the scene for checking to see how much of the site is downloaded to the end-user's computer. A preloader is composed of a conditional loop that evaluates the streaming of the site and, based on whether the site is downloaded, determines when the rest of the movie can be played. ActionScript is used to create the conditional loop for this functionality.

Tip ——————————————————————————————————————

In a preloader, you can set the exact amount of the movie that needs to be downloaded. This could be a frame somewhere in the middle of the movie or the very last frame in the movie's Timeline.

Creating a Preloader

To create a preloader, you first need to understand a little more about ActionScript and how to create script. With the release of Flash 5, a new *syntax* was introduced for ActionScript—the Dot syntax. Syntax refers to the rules of grammar or punctuation for script. This syntax replaced the Slash syntax of previous Flash versions. The Slash syntax was a scripting technique that used menus for creating ActionScript. Although this form of scripting provides consistency in how script is developed, it creates limitations for getting higher-power results. Dot syntax is the new method for creating ActionScript that targets objects, properties, methods, and values and is closer to other programming languages, such as JavaScript. You will learn more about each of these features of ActionScript throughout this seminar and the rest of the book.

As you know from Seminar 7, "Site Interactivity and Button Functionality," two modes are available in the Actions panel for creating ActionScript: the Normal Mode and the Expert Mode. The Normal Mode of the Actions panel ensures that your code is developed with the correct syntax because you must develop your code through the various action category choices in the Actions list to the left of the panel. Then, you set the predefined parameters for the selected action on the right of the Actions panel. Keep in mind that the Normal Mode ensures only correct syntax, not correct script. You can still create ActionScript that does not function correctly or at all in the Normal Mode.

The Expert Mode of the Actions panel enables you to create your script by typing directly into the Actions panel. The Action categories are accessible if you need them, but you can also just type the code based on your knowledge of ActionScript and actions. You will use the Expert Mode from this point on in the workshops of this book. Other, various features help to analyze and identify errors in your script in the Expert Mode. You will learn more about these features in the following workshop and in Seminar 11, "Communicating with the End-User."

What Is a Conditional Loop?

To summarize the functionality of a conditional loop, you need to determine the condition that must be met and then tell Flash what to do when the condition is met and what to do when it is not. In the case of a preloader, you can use English to describe this functionality, as shown in the following paragraph:

> "If the movie has downloaded up to 90% to the end-user's machine, play the movie. But if the movie has not loaded up to 90%, go back and reevaluate the original condition of determining if the movie has downloaded to the end-user's machine. Repeat this evaluation until the condition of 90% has been reached."

In the example of a preloader, the condition is "if the predetermined percentage of the movie has streamed down to the end-user's machine." If the condition is not met (called `false` in ActionScript), a loop is created to go back to the condition again and check to see whether the condition is met (seen in ActionScript as `true`). The looping repeats until the condition is true, and then the movie is instructed to continue to play. This might sound complicated at first, but it can be easily implemented through the use of the `getBytesTotal` and `getBytesLoaded` actions, frame labels, variables, and a simple `if` statement. Figure 9.1 shows an example of the

ActionScript, the Timeline structure, and the labels needed to create a preloader that uses a conditional loop.

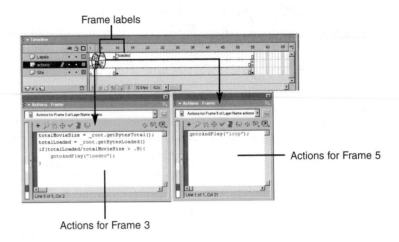

Figure 9.1   The Actions in this figure make a conditional loop by using simple logic and the gotoAndPlay action.

To understand the ActionScript of a preloader, you need to look at all the various pieces that make up this functionality—labels, variables, and the construction of the condition in ActionScript.

Attaching Labels

Labels are key features used when programming with ActionScript. Labels can be attached to a keyframe to enable the Flash developer to accurately designate and call certain areas of the Timeline for creating the interactivity in the movie. Using labels, you mark certain areas of the Timeline. Because the label is attached to a keyframe, if the Timeline is modified, the label moves with the new frame sequence of the Timeline still accurately identifying the area. You attach a label by selecting a keyframe and then assigning a label name in the Property Inspector.

When creating a preloader, you need to label a frame that identifies the point in the movie's Timeline for the conditional loop to begin and another point in the Timeline when the movie can begin to play again. As illustrated in Figure 9.2, labels are attached to keyframes in Frames 3 and 10 in the Labels layer. Frame 3 is labeled the loop frame, and Frame 10 is labeled loaded.

Label name

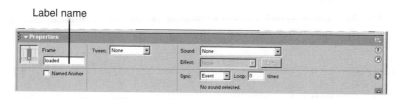

Figure 9.2   It's a good idea to have a layer named `labels` that holds all the labels in the movie.

By selecting a keyframe and then typing a label name in the Property Inspector, you can attach a label to any location in the Timeline. As a visual indicator that a label is attached to a keyframe, a small red flag displays in the keyframe where the label is attached (see Figure 9.3).

Attached label to a keyframe

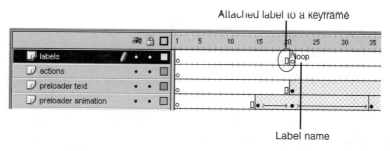

Label name

Figure 9.3   A label name extends to the right of a keyframe only if there are static frames to the right of that keyframe.

Two features of labels visually help you identify them in the Timeline—the label name and a little red flag. A blank keyframe with a label attached displays a small red flag, but it does not always display a label name. A label name displays to the right as long as there are static frames to the right of the attached keyframe. For instance, if you attach a label to the last frame of a movie, the label name does not display even though the label still exists in the keyframe, as indicated by the little red flag. Because the keyframe has the little red flag, you visually know that a label exists in this frame even though you can't see the actual label name. Being able to identify your labeled frames in the Timeline is important when programming with ActionScript. This enables you to better plan your interactivity and accurately implement your ActionScript. You will attach and call label names in the preloader you created for the workshop project in this seminar.

Creating the Variable Values for the Condition

Setting the condition for the conditional loop of a preloader requires using the `getBytesTotal` and `getBytesLoaded` methods of ActionScript and assigning these values to variables. By creating variables, you can assign a value to them for the total movie file size and for determining the amount of the movie that has streamed down. The `if` statement is then used to evaluate the variables and direct Flash to the next action. To understand this better, look at the following script:

```
totalMovieSize = _root.getBytesTotal();
totalLoaded = _root.getBytesLoaded();
if(totalLoaded/totalMovieSizes> .9){
    gotoAndPlay("loaded");
}
```

To understand the script, let's break it down. The first line of script sets a global variable and its value:

```
totalMovieSize = _root.getBytesTotal();
```

The variable name is `totalMovieSize`, and this is followed by an equal sign. The equal sign in ActionScript is used to assign a value to a variable. You can think of a variable as a container for storing data. A variable value can be a number or a string value. The value of any variable is always to the right of the equal sign. The `totalMovieSize` variable is therefore set to a value of the expression `_root.getBytesTotal();`.

An expression always returns a value, and in this script, the `_root` script directs Flash to the main movie; then Flash's built-in method of `getBytesTotal()` evaluates the SWF file to establish the file size. You can find the `getBytesTotal` action in the Objects, Movie, MovieClip, Methods category of the Actions panel.

> **Note**
>
> A semicolon is required to end a statement or line of script. This creates the correct syntax for Flash to evaluate a statement.

> **Note**
>
> You can name a variable anything you want as long as it is one word and does not use any special characters, such as `.`, `,`, `_`, and so on, in the name. To be consistent with other methods and syntax of ActionScript, it is useful to start the variable name with a lowercase letter; any other word(s) that makes up the variable name can begin with uppercase, such as `myVariable`, `todaysDate`, `fishColor`, and so on. This makes identifying your variables easier.

The next line of script also sets a new variable and its value:

```
totalLoaded = _root.getBytesLoaded();
```

The variable is named `totalLoaded`, and its value is set to how much of the movie has been loaded at that point. Flash again has a built-in action for determining this value: the `getBytesLoaded` action. Just as you needed to direct Flash's attention to the main movie for the `getBytesTotal` action, the `_root` script must be used prior to the `getBytesLoaded` action using the Dot syntax. This action evaluates how much of the main movie has loaded when the movie progresses to Frame 3 and assigns that value to the `totalLoaded` variable.

Setting the Condition

When your variables are established, they can be used in statements and expressions. The next line of script uses an `if` statement and an expression that sets the condition for the preloader:

```
if(totalLoaded/totalMovieSize > .9){
    gotoAndPlay("loaded");
}
```

An `if` statement has either a `true` value or a `false` value. In this preloader example, the `if` statement takes the total of the movie loaded so far and divides it by the total movie file size. This number is then evaluated to see whether it is greater than 90%, or .9.

> **Note**
>
> The greater than sign (>) is called an *operator* in ActionScript. Other operators are +, -, <, >=, <=, /, and *. They enable mathematics to be applied to objects, data, and variables.

What Happens When the Condition Is True?

The correct structure of an `if` statement is to first set the condition within the parentheses and then place the action to be performed if the condition is true within the curly brackets. The curly brackets wrap the action for Flash to perform when the `if` statement is true. In this preloader example, Flash is instructed to go to and play the frame labeled `loaded` when the movie has loaded up to 90%. The value used for the condition of "how much of the movie is loaded" is entirely up to the developer—70% might be a good amount, or even 100%.

What Happens When the Condition Is False?

If the condition is not met, Flash automatically skips the action in the curly brackets—the `gotoAndPlay("loaded");` statement—and proceeds to the next frame. The keyframe in Frame 5 has another line of script:

```
gotoAndPlay("loop");
```

This script sends Flash back to a frame labeled `loop` attached in Frame 3. The ActionScript in Frame 3 is again initiated, evaluating how much of the movie has been loaded. A loop is created between Frame 3 and Frame 5 that can't be broken until the condition is met, allowing the movie to continue to play through the

Timeline. To see an example of this preloader, open the `loop.fla` located in the `Seminar09/Samples` directory on the CD-ROM that accompanies this book.

Using the Bandwidth Profiler

To see the preloader and the conditional loop at work, you can test your movie in the Flash Player testing mode. The Flash Player testing mode has a beneficial feature called the Bandwidth Profiler that evaluates your movie's performance as the end-user would see the movie. You can turn on the Bandwidth Profiler while in the Flash Player testing mode by selecting View, Bandwidth Profiler (see Figure 9.4).

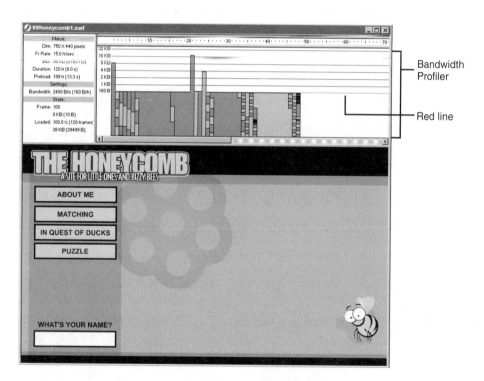

Figure 9.4 The Bandwidth Profiler enables you to see many statistics and analyses of your movie, such as total file size of the SWF file.

You can learn a lot about your movie from the Bandwidth Profiler. It shows any frames that will cause a delay based on the chosen modem connection speed in playback—these are the bars that appear above the horizontal red line. You can determine what the connection speed is by selecting Debug and then selecting from one of the six preset modem connection speeds. The Bandwidth Profiler also contains many statistics about your movie, such as the Stage dimensions, frame rate of the movie, and duration of the movie.

> **Tip**
>
> You can also customize the connection speed options under the Debug menu by selecting Debug, Customize. The Custom Modem Settings dialog box displays and enables you to set your own connection settings.

The Bandwidth Profiler also enables you to see the streaming of the movie as it would download at the chosen connection speed. You can turn streaming on in the Flash Player testing mode by selecting View, Show Streaming (Command-Return)[Ctrl+Enter] (see Figure 9.5).

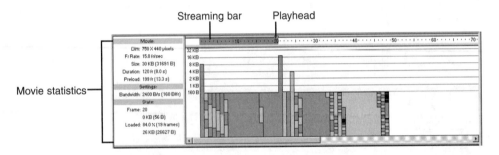

Figure 9.5   Each bar in the Bandwidth Profiler represents each frame in the movie.

The streaming bar shows the progress of the movie downloading or streaming, whereas the playhead shows the progression of the movie through the Timeline. If you have a conditional loop in a preloader, you will see the playhead loop between frames until the streaming bar reaches the download percentage you specify in ActionScript for the preloader. The movie then advances to the specified frame to continue playing the rest of the movie. You will use this feature in the workshop of this seminar to test The Honeycomb site.

Overview of Scenes

A scene is sometimes used to hold a preloader while the rest of the site is contained in another scene or multiple scenes. Scenes are beneficial when you need to break a very large Flash movie into manageable parts. For instance, scenes can be used to contain the information that makes up each page of a Web site: a Company Information page, a Services page, or a Contact Us page. In the case of a preloader, the preloader functionality and its animation can be a held in one scene while the rest of the movie is held in another scene. In either example, each scene would contain the images and functionality for that page or part of the site. This enables a very large site to be broken into its individual areas or pages, making it easier to work with each individual area.

By default, when you create a new movie, you are in Scene 1. Scene 1 is listed on a tab in the upper-left corner of the Stage. Other scenes can be added to a movie by selecting Insert, Scene. When a new scene is created, the Scene 1 tab in the upper-left corner of the Stage changes to Scene 2 (see Figure 9.6). The Timeline and Stage for this new scene are cleared and ready for you to create the new scene content. Using the Timeline and Stage, you can create the next part of the movie that you want represented in Scene 2.

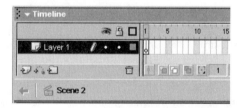

Figure 9.6   When you create a new scene, the Timeline is set back to the default layout of having just one layer and a blank keyframe in Frame 1.

You can work with multiple scenes through the Scene panel (see Figure 9.7). All scenes in a movie are held in the Scene panel, which you can view through the Window, Scene menu command.

Flash plays a movie that has multiple scenes starting with the top scene in the Scene panel and progresses down through the scene list. For instance, the movie represented in Figure 9.7 would start with the Company scene, progress to the Services scene, and end with the Contact Us scene. You can reorganize the order to cause a different scene to play before another scene by clicking and dragging a scene to its new position in the scene list. If you need to rename a scene so its name makes more sense with the content it contains, you can double-click the scene name in the Scene panel and type a new name. To work with scenes—the Timeline and Stage content in that scene—double-click the scene icon in the Scene Panel. This switches to that scene displaying the Timeline and Stage content for Frame 1 of the Scene. All these techniques allow you the flexibility you might need to organize and manage your movie content that is broken into scenes.

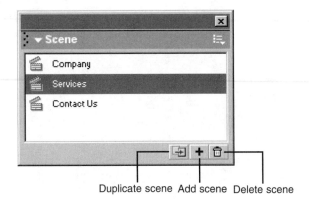

Duplicate scene Add scene Delete scene

Figure 9.7   The Scene panel contains all the scenes used in the movie.

As you become more skilled in your Flash development, you will find that scenes are not always the best solution for your movies. There are some disadvantages to using scenes. Because each scene is composed of its own Timeline, you can't see your entire movie represented by the Timeline at one time. Also, an object instance in one scene can't talk to an object instance in another scene. Another disadvantage of scenes in a movie is that you are limited in the type of transitions you can create as your movie progresses between scenes.

Many Flash developers have moved away from scenes and now use a modular approach for developing their movies. This requires using the main movie Timeline but designating different areas of the Timeline for different movie parts. Using this modularized approach allows for a more streamlined movie that is smaller in file size to what can be created using scenes. Your movie's transitions are smooth and integrated with the other movie areas. You can cause one object to fade out and another to fade in while keeping the rest of the movie intact and playing. Also, because you are using one Timeline, all object instances can talk to each other no matter where they exist in the movie structure. The following workshop provides hands-on practice creating a modularized Timeline for integrating a preloader into The Honeycomb Web site.

Good ActionScript Practices

To communicate your site message effectively and dynamically, ActionScript is used to control and talk to Stage objects so that you can create the interesting and engaging effects, animation, and functionality the site needs. Up to this point in the book, you have created quite a bit of ActionScript for The Honeycomb movie functionality. The remainder of the book focuses on other ActionScript actions and functionality for finalizing the site. So, knowing more about ActionScript and how to troubleshoot your script becomes a must. If the script doesn't function, the message will not be as effective and sometimes will be completely missed or ignored by the visitor.

Flash MX has added several features to check your ActionScript for errors in both the Flash Authoring Mode and Flash Player Testing Mode. You now have new features in the Actions panel, as well as in the Output dialog box and the Debugger panel.

Troubleshooting Features of the Actions Panel

The Actions panel now has more features than ever for working with script. Flash can now identify errors in the script's syntax and functionality. Figure 9.8 shows the various features of the Actions panel in Expert mode.

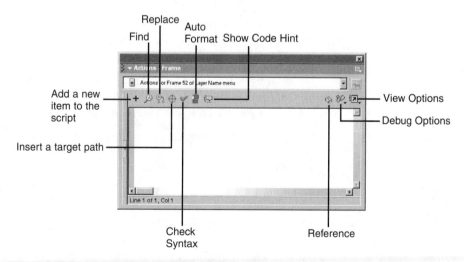

Figure 9.8 If your Actions panel is in Normal mode, these features of the Actions panel are still accessible but are located in different locations based on the Normal Mode display of the panel.

The Actions panel is now even more helpful when it comes to creating script. Taking a closer look at the new features of the Actions panel is beneficial, so Table 9.1 provides information on these features. You also will use many of these features in the following workshop, as well as throughout the rest of this book.

Table 9.1   Features of the Actions Panel

Feature	Description
Add a new item to the script	Allows actions to be added to the Scripting panel of the Actions panel.
Find/Replace	Enables locating and, if needed, replacing specified actions or script.
Insert a Target Path	Opens the Insert Target Path dialog box that enables you to create a path for targeting all named objects in a movie in your script. You can create both relative and absolute paths.
Check Syntax	Select the object or frame with the ActionScript that you want to check for errors, and click the Check Syntax button. Flash examines your script for errors. If it finds errors, it displays them line by line in the Output panel.
Auto Format	Automatically formats code with correct indents.
Show Code Hint	Enables a pop-up menu of actions or a sample of script that shows the syntax and necessary parameters for an action as you are developing your script.
Reference	Opens the Reference panel. This panel was introduced in Seminar 7. It enables a quick reference on any action in both syntax and required parameters.
Debug Options	Allows you to set breakpoints in your script. Breakpoints stop the movie when they are encountered. This can be a troubleshooting technique for testing a complex script. You can break it down by setting a breakpoint at various points in the script, allowing a section of script to be executed and analyzed.
View Options	Allows you to switch between Normal and Expert Mode. You also can view line numbers for your script in the Scripting pane.

Color-Coding of Syntax in the Actions Panel

The Actions panel also provides visual clues for developing your ActionScript. Flash color-codes the syntax in the ActionScript. You might have noticed that certain commands are color-coded differently from other commands in the Actions list of the Actions panel. This color-coding can help you identify errors in your script. Now with Flash MX, you can customize the colors you want the various actions and object references in ActionScript to display. Color-coding identifying the various features of your script as you are creating the script. If you want to customize the colors used for your script, select the Actions pop-up menu in the upper-right corner of the Actions panel and select Preferences from the menu. This displays the ActionScript Editor Preference panel of Flash MX (see Figure 9.9).

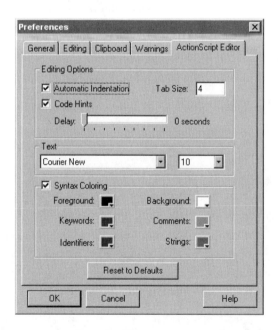

Figure 9.9   You can customize the colors for your script using any of the colors in the Flash movie color palette.

Note

Color-coding of script in the Actions Panel sometimes can be sporadic; therefore, it's always a good idea to use the correct syntax for the script—lowercase for the first word of the script and uppercase for the first letter of any additional words that make up the script.

Checking Your Syntax

You should always check your script for syntax errors before exporting or publishing a movie. If you publish a movie with errors in the script, the Output window displays, listing the lines of code that might have errors in them. Flash will still export the movie, but it will skip over any script it can't understand, which will cause the movie to be only partially functional.

You can create complex actions through the various event handlers, actions, and logic of ActionScript. One of the first areas to check when you run into a problem with your script is your script structure. Certain actions can be wrapped or can enclose multiple statements, as you learn in Seminar 10, "Using ActionScript to Control Objects." Functions, on the other hand, handle parameters or multiple parameters and require parentheses surrounding those parameters. Look at the following script for an example of opening and closing brackets and parentheses:

```
on (release){
    if(eval(this._droptarget) == _parent.ocean){
        alpha = 50;
    } else {
        _visible = 0
    }
}
```

Always check that you have opening and closing brackets ({ }) and parentheses (( )) in your script. A rule of the Flash syntax is that any opened expression must be closed. Many developers count the number of opening brackets/parentheses and compare that to the closing brackets/parentheses. Another technique used by developers is to create the opening and closing brackets at the same time, and then go back to the script and create the statements required. For example, if you wanted to create an if statement, you would first type the following:

```
if(){
}
```

Then you would go back to the script and create the conditional and the contents between the curly brackets.

Another common error is forgetting to use a semicolon to close a statement. Just as a sentence in English must end with a punctuation mark, in ActionScript, a statement must end with a semicolon.

Note

If you test a movie that contains ActionScript errors, the Output window displays, listing all the errors. It gives specific line numbers and displays the line of script that is incorrect. You can turn on the line numbers for your Actions panel by clicking the View Options button and selecting View Line Numbers. You will learn about the Output window next.

Using the Output Window

The Output window displays when you test a movie that has errors or when you check the syntax of the script in the Actions panel. This panel lists, line by line, the script that is wrong, helping you troubleshoot this script (see Figure 9.10). You might have noticed this as you have been testing your movie in the workshop section of the book. If you have errors in the script, this window displays in the Flash Player testing mode.

Figure 9.10   You can open the Output window at any time in Flash Player mode by selecting Window, Output.

Using trace

Flash 4 introduced the trace action, which enables you to send information or comments to the Output window. You can attach this action to an object or a frame in the Timeline by selecting the Actions category in the Actions panel and then selecting the trace action. Then type the message you want to display in the Output window as a string by surrounding it in quotes.

For example, if you want to know when the movie clip with an instance name of girl loads in the movie, you could attach the trace action. This script would look like the following:

```
OnCipEvent(oad){
    trace (_name + " is loaded.");
}
```

When the movie is tested in the Flash Player, if the script is correct, the Output window appears and displays the message girl has loaded. If the script breaks before the girl movie clip loads, the trace action is not executed and therefore does not display the message in the Output window. The trace action is often used by Flash developers to monitor what is happening in the movie, such as seeing when a variable is loaded.

Using the ActionScript Dictionary and the Reference Panel

You might be thinking that you will never master ActionScript because there are too many actions to learn and you can never remember them all, let alone which parameters or syntax they require. Never fear—Macromedia has this covered, too, through the Reference panel and the ActionScript Dictionary.

The Reference panel is a great new feature of Flash MX (see Figure 9.11). You can access this panel by clicking the Reference button in the Actions panel. By selecting an action from the pane on the left of this panel, you can then see information about the parameters required for the action as well as an actual example of script for the action.

Figure 9.11   The Reference panel also includes information on the syntax required for the action and in which version of Flash the action was introduced.

The ActionScript dictionary was introduced in Flash 5. It's a browser-based help system devoted to all the actions of ActionScript. You can access the ActionScript Dictionary by selecting Help, ActionScript Dictionary (see Figure 9.12).

Figure 9.12 The ActionScript dictionary comes with the Flash MX software and is installed locally on your machine.

Using the Movie Explorer

The Movie Explorer is another beneficial feature for analyzing the script used in a movie (see Figure 9.13). It can be accessed by choosing Window, Movie Explorer. This feature allows you to see all the actions used in the movie, as well as to print them. As Figure 9.13 shows, five other buttons can be used to analyze other features of your movie.

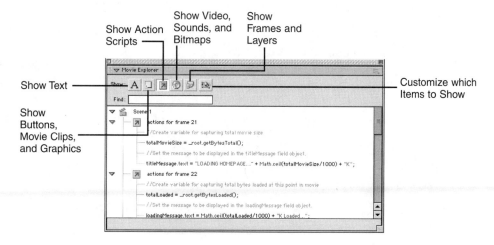

Figure 9.13   You can turn an option on or off by clicking the appropriate button.

Using Code Hints

Code hints are a new feature of Flash MX. There are two types of code hints: a pop-up menu and a ToolTip. Depending on how you are creating your script, one or the other will display. If you are creating an action, a ToolTip displays listing the correct syntax for that action. As you are typing a letter for an event, property, or parameter, a pop-up menu displays, listing all the events, properties, or parameters that begin with that letter. You can enable or disable code hints by clicking the Show Code Hints button in the Actions panel.

> **Note**
>
> When you are working in the Normal mode of the Actions panel, code hints display for parameters and properties but not for events. You will see all three—parameters, properties and events—when working in the Expert mode of the Actions panel.

ActionScript Rules of Thumb

As you become more proficient with Flash and creating movies, you will want to develop good scripting practices. In the areas of ActionScript troubleshooting and authoring practices, these rules of thumb will make your job much easier:

- Be consistent in your naming conventions. For example, you might want to avoid using spaces in words and always use variable and function names that began with a lowercase letter and use a capital letter for each new word. This type of notation is called Camel or Hungarian notation. You can use whatever convention for your script that makes sense to you, but the key is to be consistent.

- Always try to use variable names that make sense within the context of the movie. The name should reflect the content of the variable.

- Get in the habit of using the `trace` action when you run into problems with a script working incorrectly. The `trace` action sends comments to the Output window, so you can easily focus on what script is working and what is not.

- You should use the `comment` action to display comments and instructional notes in the Actions panel. By using comments, you can quickly review what the script is doing if you need to update it later.

- Use the ActionScript Dictionary Reference panel to quickly learn the structure and parameters of new or unfamiliar actions.

You will learn a lot from these features.

Using Dynamic Text Fields to Display a Preloader Message

Seminar 8, "Using Components in a Macromedia Flash Form," introduced editable text fields, both input text fields and dynamic text fields. This seminar takes dynamic text fields to the next level by using them to display information dynamically. Dynamic text fields are different from input text fields because they allow for text responses based on the various interactions or when the movie progresses to a certain point in the Timeline. In the case of the preloader, you can use dynamic text fields to display a message telling how much of the movie is loaded and have it constantly update and show the progression of the movie loading into the end-user's machine. The key to using this type of an editable text field is to name it with an instance name. As a named object, it can be called and controlled through ActionScript (see Figure 9.14).

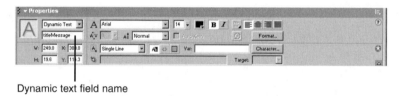

Dynamic text field name

Figure 9.14   Most of the Option settings for a dynamic text field are the same as an input text field.

Adding Preloader Animation and Setting Labels

You will use an existing movie clip symbol from another movie as the preloader animation. This movie clip will visually entertain the site visitor while the movie streams down. It will slowly display on the Stage and then fade out after the condition is `true` and the movie moves past the conditional loop. Follow these steps:

1. Use the `Honeycomb.fla` file you created in Seminar 8, or access or open the `Honeycomb08.fla` movie in the `Seminar09/Samples/` directory and save this file as `Honeycomb.fla` in the directory with your other Honeycomb site files.

2. Insert a new layer above the `Guide.buzzy bee` layer and name it `preloader animation`. Insert a keyframe in Frame 15 of this layer. This is the starting position for the preloader animation.

3. Open as a Library the preloader.fla movie located in the Seminar09/Samples/ directory.

4. With Frame 15 of the preloader layer selected, drag an instance of the preloader symbol from the preloader.fla Library onto the Stage. Position it in the center of the hexagon shape (see Figure 9.15).

Figure 9.15 The instance of the preloader symbol displays after the header and footer appear in the movie.

> **Tip**
>
> To keep the movie Library panel organized, create a new folder named **preloader animation** and drag the symbols for the loader arrow, preloader, and spinning arrows, which comprise the preloader animation, into this folder.

5. Select Frame 21 in the preloader layer and insert another keyframe. To create the fade-in effect for this instance, click the keyframe in Frame 15 and click the preloader instance on the Stage. Set the Alpha effect for this instance to 0% in the Property Inspector. Create a motion tween between the keyframes in Frames 15 and 21. This causes the preloader instance to slowly display in the movie.

6. Now create the preloader animation as it fades out. Click Frame 35 in this layer and insert another keyframe. Select the instance of the preloader symbol on the Stage for Frame 35. Set the Alpha effect for this instance to 0%. Create a motion tween between the keyframes in Frames 21 and 35.

7. To implement a conditional loop for the preloader, labels need to be added. Create a new layer above the actions layer. Name this layer labels.

8. Now create the labels for a conditional loop. Click Frame 21 in the labels layer, and type loop in the frame box of the Property Inspector. Press Enter to set this label name. You will see a red flag in the Timeline and the label name extending to the right (see Figure 9.16).

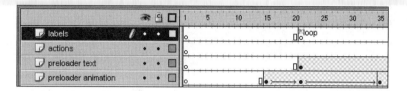

Figure 9.16   Frame 21 is the start of the conditional loop.

9. Click Frame 24 in the labels layer and insert a keyframe. Attach a label to this frame of start (see Figure 9.17).

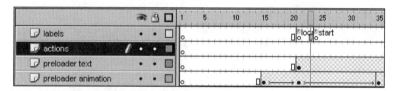

Figure 9.17   A red flag appears in Frame 24, and the label name extends to the right.

10. Test your movie to see the preloader animation.

Creating the Dynamic Text Fields

Next, you'll set up the dynamic text fields that will display the messages on the total movie size and how much of the movie has loaded. To do this, follow these steps:

1. Insert a new layer above the preloader animation layer and name this layer preloader text. Select Photoframe 21 and insert a keyframe. The two messages will display at this point in the Timeline.

2. Click the Text tool and click the Stage to set a text block about 300 pixels wide and 20 pixels tall. In the Property Inspector, make the text block a dynamic text field with the settings that Figure 9.18 indicates. In the Instance Name box, name the dynamic text field titleMessage.

Figure 9.18   Do not set the width and height of this dynamic text field through the Height and Width boxes in the Property Inspector. This causes the text in the field to be distorted in proportion.

3. Next, you must embed the Arial font that was set for this dynamic text field. By embedding a font, the dynamic text field always displays the message in Arial font. In the Property Inspector, click the Character button to display the Character Options dialog box; then select the All Characters option (see Figure 9.19).

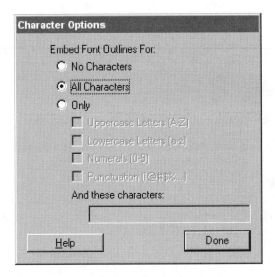

Figure 9.19   By selecting All Characters, you will be able to display a message composed of both letters and numbers.

Note

In the real world of Web development, Arial is a common font that everyone usually has, so step 3 is not really necessary. But due to a wide audience of readers, this was the chosen font for The Honeycomb site because most people would have access to it, and this feature of embedding a font should be covered. You typically would embed a font that is less common—one that you expect most people would not have on their systems.

4. Position the text block above the preloader instance as Figure 9.20 indicates.

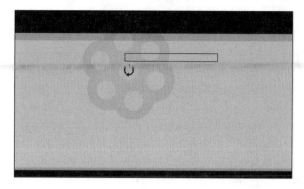

Figure 9.20   The dynamic text fields will appear when the preloader instance displays with the 100% alpha effect of the motion tween

5. Create another dynamic text field about 230 pixels wide and 20 pixels tall. Set the same Property Inspector settings as the `titleMessage` field object, except set the instance name of this dynamic field to `loadMessage`. Again, embed the Arial font for All Characters.

6. Position the `loadingMessage` field object as Figure 9.21 indicates. Your dynamic text fields are developed and have been assigned an instance name. The fields are now seen as objects, enabling them to be called and controlled with ActionScript.

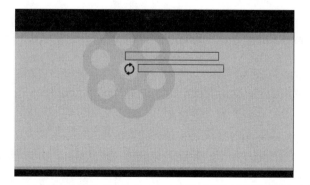

Figure 9.21   These two dynamic text fields communicate the movie file size and dynamically update how much of the movie has loaded when the conditional loop executes.

7. Save the movie. If you would like to see a movie developed up to this point in the workshop, open `Honeycomb1.fla` located in the `Seminar9/Samples` directory on the CD-ROM that accompanies this book.

Capturing Total Movie Size Value and Displaying a Message

With the preloader animation set, labels added to the Timeline, and dynamic field objects created, you can now cause a message to display and indicate the total movie size. You will use the `getBytesTotal` action and add this functionality to the `actions` layer at Frame 21. You will set the condition to be if `99 percent of the movie has loaded`. Another new feature you will use is comments. *Comments* are lines of script ignored by Flash as it compiles the script. They are intended for the programmers' benefit. Comments provide information on what the script is doing so that later, if you need to rework the script, you can get quickly up to speed on the script functionality. You should comment your script as you create it.

Now would be a good time to set the Actions panel to the Expert Mode. Creating ActionScript will be easier if you type in the script directly. This also will help you begin to learn the syntax and actions of ActionScript. To set up this functionality, follow these steps:

1. Open the Actions panel and click the Actions pop-up menu in the upper-right corner. Select Expert Mode from the list.

2. Click Frame 21 of the `actions` layer and insert a keyframe. Frame 21 will display the message of the movie total file size.

3. Add a comment to the Actions panel to explain the script. Comments start with two slashes (`//`). This notation tells Flash that you are creating a comment. Click in the Actions panel to set your cursor, and then type the following (all on one line):

   ```
   //Create variable for capturing total movie size.
   ```

> **Tip**
>
> You can create a comment that can cover multiple lines by using a `/*` notation at the beginning of the comment instead of `//`. To end the comment, you must use a notation of `*/`. This breaks out of the comment and enables you to create other script as needed.

1. Press (Return)[Enter] to create a new line of script. Next, you will set a variable for capturing the total movie file size at Frame 21. In the Actions panel, type the following:

```
totalMovieSize = _root.getBytesTotal();
```

When you type the _root., a code hints menu displays. In the Expert Mode, whenever you type a . (period) or an opened parenthesis ((), Flash is set by default to display code hints in a pop-up menu. With the code hints menu displayed, you can scroll through the list of actions and select the one you want from the list. You can turn this feature on or off by clicking the Show Code Hints button above the Scripting pane of the Actions panel.

Note

There are two styles of code hints for the Expert Mode of the Actions panel. ToolTip-style hints display after an open parenthesis that follows an action name. This type of code hint provides the correct syntax while you are scripting. You can enter a parameter, or if you need to enter multiple parameters, you can use a comma between each parameter. The other type of code hint is the menu-style hint. Whenever a dot is typed after an object name or an open parenthesis is typed after an event handler, a menu-style code hint displays, enabling you to select an action from the list.

Note

You can also select the `getBytesTotal` actions from the Objects, Movie, MovieClip, Methods category in the Actions Toolbox of the Actions panel.

5. Press (Return)[Enter] to create a new line of script. Next, you'll create a message for the `titleMessage` dynamic text field that indicates the total movie size. Create a comment explaining this by typing the following (all on one line):

```
//Set the message to be displayed in the titleMessage field
object.
```

6. Press (Return)[Enter] to create a new line of script. Type the line of script shown in Figure 9.22 into the Scripting pane of the Actions panel.

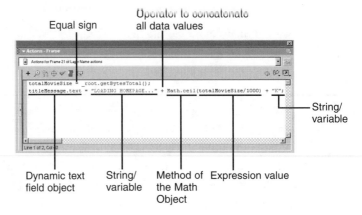

Figure 9.22   This statement introduces many new features and syntax for creating interactivity in a movie.

Note

You can use the various code hint features that display to create this line of script.

Take a moment to examine this script because a few new features have been introduced.

```
totalMovieSize = _root.getBytesTotal();
titleMessage.text = "LOADING HOMEPAGE…" + Math.ceil(totalMovieSize/1000) + "K";
```

To understand the script, it needs to be broken apart:

- The first line sets a variable named `totalMovieSize` and assigns the value of the total bytes for the main movie.

- The `titleMessage.text` directs Flash to the dynamic text object with the same instance name. By following this with `.text`, Flash is directed to display a value in the text object. The value follows the equal sign. In this script, the value is composed of both strings and an expression.

- Next, the statement of script sets the value for the field. The quotation marks in `"LOADING HOMEPAGE..."` sets the text to appear first in the message for the dynamic text field. The quotation marks signify that the text between them is to be treated as a string value. Strings are just characters to Flash; they have no numeric value. Notice that a second string value, `K`, is at the very end of the statement.

- Next is a + operator. Using a plus sign enables you to concatenate different or the same types of data values. You use this to add the numeric value of the expression `Math.ceil(totalMovieSize/1000)` to both the string values of `"LOADING HOMEPAGE..."` and `K`.

- `Math.ceil` is an action of the built-in Math object in Flash. The Math object is used to access and manipulate mathematical functions and constants. The `Math.ceil()` method rounds a specified number to the nearest whole integer that is more than the value specified. In The Honeycomb script, the `Math.ceil` rounds up the value of the `totalMovieSize` variable value divided by 1,000. Finally, a `K` is added to the whole dynamic text field value, causing the total message displayed in this field to be `LOADING HOMEPAGE....` `(a number)K`.

- Save the movie, and then test it. The script is correct if it captures the total movie size and displays the `titleMessage` of `LOADING HOMEPAGE...40K`. Close the testing mode for the Flash Player.

If you would like to see a movie developed up to this point in the workshop, open `Honeycomb2.fla` located in the `Seminar9/Samples` directory on the CD-ROM that accompanies this book.

Creating the Condition for the Conditional Loop

Next, you will set the conditional loop, which will be `if 99% of the movie is loaded`. If this condition is met, Flash will continue playing the movie at the frame labeled `start`; if the condition is not met, Flash will loop around to the frame labeled `check` and test the condition again. Follow these steps to set this conditional loop:

1. To begin the script for a conditional loop, first determine the position in the Timeline at which the loop will be initiated. In the `Actions` layer, click Photoframe 22 and insert a keyframe. This is the point at which the preloader message displays in the movie.

2. Now you will attach ActionScript to the new keyframe that you created for the `actions` layer. Start by commenting your script. Add a comment explaining the script by typing the following (all on one line):

   ```
   //Create variable for capturing total bytes loaded at this
   point in movie.
   ```

3. Press (Return)[Enter] to create a new line of script, and then type

   ```
   totalLoaded = _root.getBytesLoaded();
   ```

This sets a new variable of `totalLoaded` and assigns the amount of bytes that have been loaded in the movie at that point in the Timeline as the value of the `totalLoaded` variable.

4. Press the (Return)[Enter] key to create a new line of script. Then add another comment by typing

   ```
   //Set the message to be displayed in the loading Message
   field object.
   ```

5. Create the message to display in the `loadingMessage` field object on the Stage. Similar to the `titleMessage`, you will use both types of data values—string and expression—as the value for this field object. Type the statement shown in Figure 9.23.

Figure 9.23   The expression evaluates the total amount loaded and divides this number by 1,000 so that it displays in kilobytes.

6. Next, you need to create the conditional loop. You use an `if` statement and set the condition to be a value greater than 99% of the movie loaded. Create a new line of script and type the comment and statement shown in Figure 9.24.

Figure 9.24   The condition takes the value of the `totalLoaded` variable divided by the value for the `totalMovieSize` variable and compares this new value to see whether it is greater than .99.

7 Create a new line of script by pressing (Return) [Enter], then complete the if
statement by creating the statement that tells Flash what to do if the condition is true. Type the comment and statement shown in Figure 9.25.

Figure 9.25   The gotoAndPlay action directs Flash to the Frame labeled start.

> **Note**
>
> It is up to the developer to decide the actual percentage set as the condition. This could be
> 100% or any other number less than this percentage.

8. To complete the conditional loop, you need to tell Flash what to do if the
   condition is false. This means looping back to check the condition again.
   You will use built-in Flash functionality for the Timeline to create this loop.
   Flash automatically moves on to the next line of script or to the next frame if
   it does not understand or receive a value for a statement. Therefore, you will
   create a new statement in Frame 24 of the Actions layer that directs Flash to
   go to the frame labeled loop. Click Photoframe 23 in the Actions layer and
   insert a keyframe.

9. In the Actions panel, type the following statement to direct Flash back to the
   frame labeled loop:

   ```
   gotoAndPlay ("loop");
   ```

10. Test your movie in the Flash Player testing mode. Notice how nicely objects
    display and transition as the movie plays. You have integrated a preloader
    into the actual flow of the movie. Leave the Flash Player testing mode open
    for the next topic.

Tip ───

To increase the efficiency of a conditional loop, some Flash developers cause the condition to be checked twice before the loop is initiated. This is accomplished by adding another keyframe between the keyframe that contains another **if** statement with the condition and looping frame. To see an example of this functionality, open the **09Honeycomba.fla** file in the **Seminar09/Samples** directory on the CD-ROM that accompanies this book.

Using the Bandwidth Profiler to Test the Preloader Scene

To test your movie's performance based on the various types of modem connections the end-user might have, you can use the Bandwidth Profiler. You can test the streaming of this movie based on many modem connection speeds. To test your movie, do the following:

1. With the movie opened in the Flash Player Testing Mode, select Control, Stop to stop the movie. Maximize the Flash Player Window so you can see the entire movie Timeline.

2. Open the Bandwidth Profiler by selecting View, Bandwidth Profiler.

3. Set the connection speed to be 28.8 by selecting Debug, 28.8 (2.3 KB/s).

4. Turn the streaming feature on by selecting View, Streaming. The green streaming bar appears in the Timeline, and the playhead begins to move indicating the progression of the movie through its Timeline (see Figure 9.26).

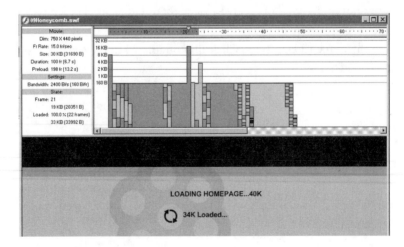

Figure 9.26   The playhead will loop between Frames 21 and 23 until the condition is met.

5. Close the testing mode of the Flash Player.

6. Notice that there is one small problem. The dynamic text objects stay on the Stage throughout the entire movie. After the condition is met, these message boxes are no longer necessary. To cause them to disappear from the movie at Frame 24 of the Timeline, in the `preloader text` layer insert a blank keyframe in Frame 35 (see Figure 9.27).

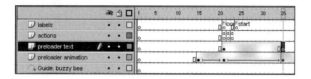

Figure 9.27 Your Timeline should resemble the Timeline in this figure for the top four layers.

7. Test the movie again to see the text messages disappear from the Stage. Exit the Flash Player testing mode and save the movie as `Honeycomb.fla`. If you want to compare your Honeycomb site with a movie that is completed up to this point in the book, open the `09Honeycomb.fla` file located in the `Seminar09/Samples` directory on the CD-ROM that accompanies this book.

Seminar Summary

This seminar covered creating a preloader with ActionScript for a conditional loop. Creating and using scenes was also discussed, as were some of the disadvantages of scenes. Instead of using scenes for The Honeycomb movie, you learned how to modularize the movie to re-create the functionality of scenes. This keeps all the movie's contents in one Timeline and enables the movie to transition smoothly from one area to another. You will use this modularization of the Timeline for other movies you create to enable smooth transitions through the various areas of the Timeline.

You also learned how to add labels to your movie and call those labels in ActionScript. An `if` statement was used to create a conditional loop for determining how much of the movie has streamed down to the end-user's machine. You created two new variables for capturing the values generated by two of Flash's built-in methods—`getBytesLoaded` and `getTotalBytes`. If the condition is true, you set the movie to begin playing. Conversely, if the condition is false, you looped the movie back to the frame containing the if statement. Although this might have seemed daunting at first, the functionality of a conditional loop is very straightforward. You can easily customize this functionality for any of the movies you develop in Flash.

The next seminar covers how to create the host character communication. Seminar 11, "Communicating with the End-User," covers making Buzzy Bee communicate instructions for each activity button, as well as sets up the login functionality for The Honeycomb site. You again will use the Dot syntax of ActionScript to create much of this interactivity.

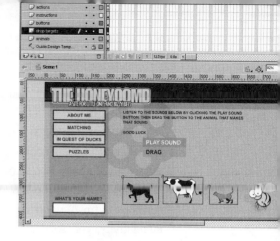

Seminar 10

Using ActionScript
to Control Objects

In this chapter

Workshop: Using Movie Clips to Create the
Matching Activity

Overview of ActionScript

One of the most valuable features of Macromedia Flash is the capability to have multiple objects and movie clips all running and acting independently of each other but still with the power to communicate with each other. But with this power to communicate and control comes somewhat of a strict convention for doing so. This seminar focuses on ActionScript and interactivity between Stage objects. To create this interactivity, you need a few more tools in your ActionScript development. This seminar covers relative and absolute paths for targeting objects and then provides information and hands-on practice using new actions—mainly the onClipEvent action and the if and else statements.

ActionScript is a powerful programming language, and understanding a little more about how it is structured is beneficial for working at a deeper level in Macromedia Flash. In ActionScript, information is arranged in groups that are called *classes*. Each class can have multiple instances that are called *objects*, which can be called and controlled in an action. Predefined classes are available in Flash, or you can create your own.

A class is composed of *properties* or characteristics, as well as *methods* or behaviors, which are generically called actions in Flash. All properties and methods can be applied to an object created from the class.

A predefined class called movie clip is available in Flash, and all movie clips you create in your movies are part of the movie clip class. They are composed of predefined properties and methods. The following is a list of some of the predefined properties for the movie clip class:

- _alpha (Alpha)
- _height (Height)
- _name (Name)
- _rotation (Rotation)
- _visible (Visibility)
- _width (Width)
- _x (X position)
- _xscale (X scale)
- _y (Y position)
- _yscale (Y scale

The methods or the object behaviors of the `movie clip` class are created through the various actions of ActionScript, conditional statements, and operators. Through ActionScript, you can identify an object and control a property of that object or command the object to do something.

> **Note**
>
> The properties for many of the objects in the `movie clip` class are controlled through Boolean values. Boolean values are composed of two results: true or false. True can be represented as **1**, and false can be represents as **0**. You will use Boolean values in the workshops throughout the remainder of the book.

To develop accurate script for more interactivity in your movie, a closer look at ActionScript and its structure, syntax, and protocol is necessary. Then, you will be introduced to the very powerful `onClipEvent` action and how to create logic with ActionScript.

The Structure of ActionScript

ActionScript has a set syntax that is somewhat rigid, both in its characters and its structure. Typically, any action that is made up of more than one word begins with lowercase and then any attached words use uppercase for the first letter. For instance, the `gotoAndPlay` command is composed of three words with the last two words beginning with uppercase. If you do not type this action with this syntax, the command will not work. So, if you were to type `GotoandPlay` for the `gotoAndPlay` action, Flash would not recognize it and would therefore ignore it.

> **Tip**
>
> You should name an instance using the same syntax as is used with actions: lowercase for the first word and uppercase for the first letter of any additional word.

> **Note**
>
> A *statement* is a combination of actions, methods, and conditions. A statement ends with a semicolon.

The Dot syntax of ActionScript enables you to create paths or targets to certain objects on the Stage. After you identify an object, you can control a property of it or tell it what to do. You have seen this form of control in Seminar 9, "Using Preloaders and Conditional Loops," when you directed Flash to a dynamic text field and caused the field to display a value of a variable.

Two types of paths can be called in Flash—relative and absolute. So far in this book, you have used absolute paths, but this seminar introduces you to the relative path and how to use it. This seminar also shows you how to use the _parent reference in your script, which gives you more flexibility when creating interactivity.

Absolute Versus Relative Paths

You must refer to the movie clip or object you want to control using a path. For example, perhaps you have a movie clip instance named fish nested inside a movie clip instance named ocean. Ocean is nested inside a movie clip instance named earth, which is placed on the main Timeline of your movie. You decide you want to hide only the fish by calling the fish's _visible property from a frame action on the main Timeline. You could use either of the following lines of script:

```
_root.earth.ocean.fish._visible = 0; (Absolute Path)
earth.ocean.fish._visible = 0; (Relative Path)
```

Both of these lines of script look very similar, and both accomplish the same thing, but there is a very distinct difference between the two. One starts with the expression _root to ensure Flash knows that you want to start from the very top or the main movie Timeline and work your way into the movie until you find the object you want to change or control.

The second line of script omits the _root expression. Flash accepts this because the line of script is placed on a frame action on the main (_root) Timeline. Flash automatically assumes you are looking first for an instance named earth on the current Timeline.

To understand these two types of paths, look at the previous fish in the ocean, on earth example. Suppose you want to still hide the fish MC using the _visible property, but now you want to execute this line of script from a frame action on the ocean movie clip Timeline. You could once again use either of the following:

```
_root.earth.ocean.fish._visible = 0; (Absolute Path)
fish._visible = 0; (Relative Path)
```

Again, both lines of script get you where you want to go, but you can see that the relative path version is much simpler and more straightforward. The absolute path works just the same as before. It doesn't consider where the action is coming from; it simply jumps from wherever it is, starts at the main movie (_root), and works its way into the movie until it finds the object whose property it is instructed to control.

The relative path version works in the same manner as the longer version of the relative path shown earlier, but it seems simpler this time. Remember: The line of script is now being placed in a frame action on the ocean movie clip's Timeline, not the _root Timeline. The ocean movie clip already knows that it exists inside a movie clip named earth, which is placed on the main Timeline, so by directly calling the fish movie clip instance, the script looks only for movie clips named fish, which exist directly on the ocean Timeline.

An absolute path of any given movie clip is always the same, no matter where you call that movie clip instance from, but a relative path changes depending on where you call it—hence, the term *relative*. You will begin using relative paths in the workshop of this seminar as well as throughout the remainder of this book.

> **Tip**
>
> Whenever possible, you should use a relative path because it will make your ActionScript coding go much more quickly, your script will be easier to read, and the movie will play more quickly.

Using the _parent Reference

Now that you have a fairly good grasp on using relative and absolute paths to call and control movie clips, another new expression enables you to make relative path calls to the movie clips that exist above the current movie clip in the hierarchy. This is the _parent reference, which basically calls the movie clip in which the current movie clip resides or is nested. Looking again at the earth, ocean, fish example, earth has a parent of _root, ocean has a parent of earth, and fish has a parent of ocean. Each movie clip will and can have only one parent movie clip.

> **Note**
>
> _parent is a built-in expression of Flash, and if you have your Actions panel set at the default syntax coloring, it appears blue when typed into a line of ActionScript, just like _root will. As you learned in Seminar 9, you can change the syntax coloring in the ActionScript Editor tab of the Preference dialog box.

Suppose you wanted to change the height of the ocean movie clip to 200 pixels through a frame action within the fish movie clip. You could always resort to the trusty absolute path by typing the following:

```
_root.earth.ocean._height = 200;
```

You can also use the _parent expression by typing the following script:

```
_parent._height = 200;
```

You could not, however, use this script:

```
ocean._height = 200;
```

This would tell Flash to look for an instance named ocean inside the fish movie clip. Because an instance named ocean does not exist in the fish Timeline, nothing would happen.

Taking this new _parent reference one step further, if you wanted to change the height of the earth movie clip to 400 from a frame action within the fish movie clip, you could still use the absolute path, or you could use the _parent expression. You would use it twice, calling the parent of a parent. The following script is an example of this double _parent reference:

```
_parent._parent._height = 400;
```

Each time you use the _parent expression, you are jumping up one level in the movie.

Understanding the Power of Relative Paths and _parent Referencing

The power of a relative path and _parent referencing is seen when you need to modify the interactivity of a movie. Suppose for some reason, deep into development, you decide to nest the earth movie clip inside a new movie clip named universe. Had you used an absolute path to call anything contained inside the universe movie clip, all your script would break and you would have to adjust every path name to include the universe movie clip instance.

Your script would have to change from

```
_root.earth.ocean.fish._visible = 0;
```

to

```
_root.universe.earth.ocean.fish._visible = 0;
```

However, had you planned ahead and used relative paths, none of your script would have to change:

```
fish._visible = 0;
```

As you have already seen with Flash MX, you usually have a few different ways that you can accomplish the same end result. Relative and absolute paths are good examples of two different techniques that produce the same result. If you are working on a small, self-contained application or Web site—something that has a clear ending point—it might be fine to use absolute paths. However, if you want to be a good programmer and create interactivity in a way that is flexible, no matter how large or small the scope of the project, you should use relative paths to communicate from object to object.

Using the onClipEvent Action

Up to this point in the book, you have created a few basic actions. You used the on action to apply script to a button in Seminar 7, "Site Interactivity and Button Functionality." The on action requires an event handler, such as (release). This event is the trigger for the button. This seminar introduces a new action, the onClipEvent action, which is similar to the on action but is attached to a movie clip instead of a button. The onClipEvent action is used often in Flash development to control and communicate with other objects.

Similar to the on action, the onClipEvent action requires an event handler for triggering a movie clip. The main difference between the on and onClipEvent actions is what happens when the end-user interacts with the movie through his mouse.

For the on action to work, the end-user must perform a mouse action directly to the button. The on action is attached to just that button. The onClipEvent, on the other hand, is more powerful because it looks at the whole movie and the Timeline of the movie clip that it is attached. For example, if the user clicks outside a button, the on action does not see the click. But if the user clicks outside a movie clip instance on the Stage, the onClipEvent sees the click because it looks at the entire movie.

The onClipEvent must be attached directly to a movie clip instance. To attach the onClipEvent, select it from the Actions, Movie Clip Control categories in the Actions toolbox of the Actions panel.

The onClipEvent action is structured similarly to the on action (see Figure 10.1). It requires a statement enclosed in curly brackets for what to do when the event occurs to trigger the movie clip. You can use many ActionScript statements to create the functionality that is to occur.

Figure 10.1   The default handler for the onClipEvent event is (load).

The onClipEvent action has multiple event handlers, just like the on action. However, unlike the on action, which can have multiple handers in the actual script, onClipEvent allows just one handler. The default event handler is load, which refers to when the movie clip is loaded on the Stage. Table 10.1 lists all the available event handlers for the onClipEvent action and a description of each.

Table 10.1   Event Handlers for the onClipEvent Action

Event Handler	Description
load	Executes the actions or statements enclosed in the curly brackets when the movie clip loads on the Stage for the first time. This event handler triggers only once, when the movie clip loads on the Stage.
unload	Executes the actions or statements associated with onClipEvent in the first frame after the movie clip is removed from the Stage. Any actions enclosed in the curly brackets of the removed movie clip instance play first, prior to any actions attached to the next frame in the movie.
enterFrame	Executes the actions or statements associated with the onClipEvent action repeatedly every time the playhead of the movie clip instance enters a frame.

Event Handler	Description
mouseMove	Executes the actions or statements associated with onClipEvent every time the mouse is moved.
mouseDown	Executes the actions or statements associated with onClipEvent every time the left mouse button is pressed.
mouseUp	Executes the actions or statements associated with onClipEvent every time the left mouse button is released.
keyDown	Executes the actions or statements associated with onClipEvent every time a key is pressed. You can use the Key.getCode action to specify a certain key for this handler.
keyUp	Executes the actions or statements associated with onClipEvent every time a key is released. Again, you can use the Key.getCode action to specify a certain key for this handler.
data	Executes the actions or statements associated with onClipEvent when data is received in either the loadVariables or loadMovie action.

You will use the onClipEvent action later in the workshop of this seminar and throughout the remainder of the book.

Using Advanced Conditionals

You should be somewhat familiar with using conditionals at this point. You used a simple if statement in Seminar 9 to evaluate how much of the movie was loaded for a preloader. This seminar introduces the else and else if expressions. As you become more comfortable in your development with ActionScript, you'll find conditionals extremely helpful, and they will quickly become very common in your ActionScript code.

Working with the if Statement

To understand the logic behind a conditional, you can look at life itself. In our daily lives, almost any question can be answered with yes or no, true or false, greater than or less than. ActionScript can mimic life in determining the answers to many questions. For example, in Flash, a submitted password is either valid or invalid, a numeric value is likely to be either too large or too small, and an event is either too soon or too late. Using if statements, you can tell Flash to behave in certain ways depending on the answers to these questions at any given time.

Basically, the if statement is structured in the following syntax:

```
if (theQuestion){
        cause something to happen
}
```

The first line of script sets the objects to be evaluated. If the results of the evaluation are true, the if statement moves to the next line of script that causes something to occur. For example, the following script quickly checks to see whether the user has submitted a username equivalent to administrator. If the user has, she is given a message telling her so; otherwise, the code that assigns a text string to the variable alert is completely ignored. Here's the code:

```
if(username == "administrator"){
    alert = "access granted.";
}
```

This script introduces a new operator: the two equal signs in the first line of script (==). This is an operator called the equality operator, and it is different from the assignment operator (=) that you have used up to this point in the book. The equality operator tests for equality between the two expressions, whereas the assignment operator assigns expression 1 the value of expression 2.

Tip

Be sure all your **if** statements use **equality**, rather than **assignment**, for the condition (the question).

Using else and else if Statements

With a simple conditional, you tell Flash to do something if a certain condition is true. But sometimes you want to tell Flash to do something else if it is not true. To summarize this in English, you would say "If this, do this; otherwise, do that."

To see actual script, look at the following example:

```
if(username == "admin"){
        alert = "Access granted.";
    }else{
        alert = "Access denied.";
    }
}
```

This script causes an alert message to display telling the user that the access has been granted if the username submitted is equivalent to admin. However, if the username equals anything else, the script causes another alert message to display telling the user that access is denied. You can take this further by adding a third clause saying, "If this, do this; if that, do that; if anything else, do something else."

Look at the following example:

```
if(username == "admin"){
    alert = "Access granted.";
}else if (username == "oldAdmin"){
    alert = "Access Expired";
}else{
    alert = "Access denied.";
}
```

This example is similar to the previous example, except that there are now two specific conditions that will receive specific responses and a third condition that will catch everything else.

You can have as many else if statements as you like. For example, suppose you have 10 users. For this situation, you would need one if statement, nine else if statements, and a final else for anything other than the 10 usernames.

You will use an else statement in the workshop of this seminar.

Using Movie Clips to Create the Matching Activity

The matching activity of The Honeycomb site is an activity that allows the end-user to listen to three different animal sounds by pressing three different buttons. Then, the end-user can drag the button to the animal that makes the sound. If the end-user is correct, the button disappears; if she is wrong, the button returns to its starting position.

This interactivity is reliant on a movie clip object and the `onClipEvent` action. You will need to implement some logic that compares the location of the movie clip with the correct target area for determining whether the correct animal was matched with the movie clip object. To create the logic for the comparison, you use `if` and `else` conditional statements.

Creating the Layers

To begin developing the matching activity of The Honeycomb Web site, you first must set up layers for holding the Stage content that will be used in this movie. It is beneficial to again create a guide layer and use the `design_template.jpg` image as a design guide for positioning your matching activity on the Stage. To create your layers, follow these steps:

1. Open `matching.fla`, which you created in Seminar 7, or open the `matching.fla` file in the `Seminar10/Samples/Honeycomb09/` directory. Save this file in the same directory as your `Honeycomb.fla` file.

2. Rename the movie layer to `animals` and delete the text block on the Stage with the word `Matching` in it.

3. Insert a new layer above the `animals` layer and name this new layer `drop targets`. Create three more layers, and name them as indicated in Figure 10.2.

4. Lock the `Guide:Design Template` layer so it is no longer modifiable.

5. You must create the instructions that are displayed when the matching activity loads into the Honeycomb movie. Click the keyframe in Frame 1 of the `instructions` layer to make it active. Select the Text tool, and on the Stage, click and drag a text block 400 pixels wide (see Figure 10.3).

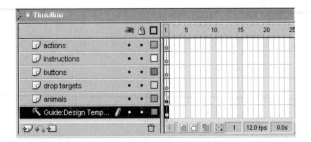

Figure 10.2   The matching movie is composed of these layers.

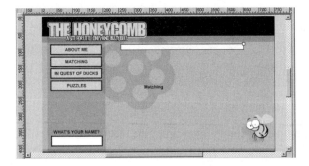

Figure 10.3   The Flash rulers can be used to accurately set your text block.

6. Set the text block settings in the Property Inspector to a Text Type of Static, a font of Arial, a font size of 12, and a font color of black. Then, select both the Bold and Auto Kern options. Type the following text in uppercase:

```
LISTEN TO THE SOUNDS BELOW BY CLICKING THE PLAY SOUND BUTTON.
➥THEN DRAG THE BUTTON TO THE ANIMAL THAT MAKES THAT SOUND.
GOOD LUCK!
```

7. Position the text block so that it is at the top of the activity area for the activity. Do not overlap any of the other Stage content as displayed in the design template (see Figure 10.4).

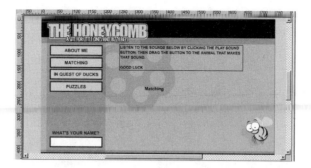

Figure 10.4   The matching game will be displayed below the instructions.

8. Click the `actions` layer and add the `stop` action to the keyframe in Frame 1 of this layer by typing the following script into the Actions panel:

```
stop();
```

The `stop` action causes this matching activity to stop playing at Frame 1. You next need to create the matching activity through the use of movie clips and ActionScript. All the functionality for the matching activity occurs in one frame for this `matching.fla` movie. You create this interactivity by using movie clip symbols that communicate and control other Stage objects.

Adding the Animals for the Matching Activity

To add the objects for this activity, you borrow them from another movie. This saves time not having to re-create these images from scratch. You drag instances of these graphics symbols from the `animals.fla` library and use them in the matching movie. To do this, follow these steps:

1. Open, as a library, the `animals.fla` movie in the `Seminar10/Samples` directory of the CD-ROM that accompanies this book.

2. Click the `animals` layer to make it active, and from the `animals.fla` library, drag instances of the `cat`, `dog`, and `cow` graphics symbols onto the Stage. Position them with the dog on the left, the cow in the middle, and the cat on the right (see Figure 10.5). Use the Align panel to evenly distribute your animal instances with each other and to align them from their bottom edges.

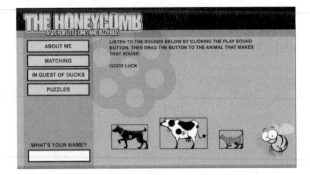

Figure 10.5   These animals will be used for matching the correct sound that the animal makes.

3. You need a few more symbols for this activity, so you'll again borrow from the animals.fla library. Because you will use these symbols a little later in this workshop, drag instances of these symbols to the matching.fla library. Click and drag the drag button, play sound button, catcry.mp3, cow.mp3, and dog.mp3 symbols directly into the matching.fla library. This adds these symbols to the matching movie without placing them on the Stage.

4. Lock the animals layer so that you do not modify these instances as they are positioned on the Stage. Close the animals.fla library by (Control-clicking)[right-clicking] the animals.fla Library panel title bar and selecting Close Panel from the shortcut menu.

You have the symbols and graphics necessary to create the matching activity. Next, you'll create the movie clip symbol that will be converted to a movie clip for the matching functionality of this activity.

Creating the Matching Activity Functionality

The matching activity is created through a new movie clip symbol and ActionScript. The movie clip symbol will have instances of the drag button and the play sound button symbols nested inside it. Each of these buttons will have its own functionality. On the Stage, when the Play Sound button is clicked, the associated animal sound plays. The end-user can then drag the Drag button to the animal that makes the sound. If the match between sound and animal is correct, the movie clip disappears from the Stage. If the match is incorrect, the movie clip returns to its starting position on the Stage. This functionality is all created in the movie clip symbol. You will first create a movie clip instance for the matching with the cat. To create this functionality, you use ActionScript and the methods of startDrag and stopDrag, as well as if and else statements. To create the cat movie clip instance for the matching activity, follow these steps:

1. To begin creating this matching functionality, you need to create a new movie clip symbol. Select Insert, New Symbol. Name the symbol cat_MC and give it a Movie Clip behavior. Click OK to close the dialog box and launch the Symbol-Editing Mode.

2. In the Symbol-Editing Mode, rename Layer 1 to sound. Insert four more layers above the sound layer and name them as Figure 10.6 indicates.

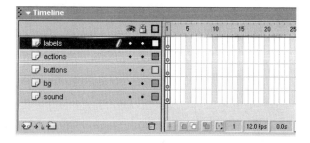

Figure 10.6 You use the movie clip Timeline to develop much of the functionality of the matching activity.

3. Click the keyframe in Frame 1 of the buttons layer and drag an instance of the drag button and the play sound button onto the Stage. They are now nested in the cat_MC symbol. Position the Play Sound button directly above the Drag button and align them by their left edges, as well as from the bottom and top edges so that they are flush to each other (see Figure 10.7).

Figure 10.7 The Play Sound button is programmed to play an animal sound when clicked. The Drag button enables the user to drag the cat_MC movie clip to an animal that makes the sound.

4. Align these two buttons to the registration point in the center of the Stage. Select both buttons so that they both are active; in the Property Inspector, set the x and y coordinates to 0. This moves both buttons to align from the upper-left corner of the Play Sound button.

5. Exit Symbol-Editing Mode to return to the main movie.

6. Click the buttons layer and drag an instance of the new cat_MC symbol onto the Stage. Position it anywhere on the Stage for now. If you need to access a copy of the movie at this point in its development, open matching1.fla located in the Seminar10/Samples directory.

Creating Drag-and-Drop Functionality

Next, you will create the script that enables the cat_MC movie clip to be moved by the end-user. This is accomplished through an event handler and the Flash MX built-in methods of startDrag and stopDrag. To create this functionality, do the following:

1. To create the drag-and-drop functionality, you need to attach ActionScript to the drag button symbol nested inside the cat_MC symbol. To access this button, launch the Symbol-Editing Mode for the cat_MC symbol.

2. In Symbol-Editing Mode, click the Drag button on the Stage to make it active. Open or display the Actions panel in Expert Mode, and click in the Scripting pane to make it active.

3. To start this script for the interactivity, an on action and an event handler must be added. This sets the trigger for the button. You want users to be able to drag the button, so you need to use the press event handler of the on action. Type the following line of script:

```
on(press){
```

4. Now, create a comment that explains the drag feature. Type the following script:

```
//start dragging this entire movie clip
```

Tip

You should use comments throughout your script because they provide a reference for what the script is doing. This aids in communicating your script clearly and accurately in case other developers need to work with it or as a reminder to yourself about the functionality of the script.

5. The on action requires additional script enclosed in the curly brackets to tell Flash what to do when the button is pressed. Create a new line of script by pressing (Return) [Enter]. From the Actions toolbox, click the Actions category, and then click the Movie Clip Control subcategory. Locate the startDrag action, and double-click it to add it to your Actions panel (see Figure 10.8).

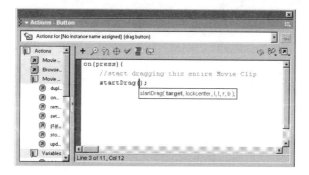

Figure 10.8   A code hint displays showing the additional parameters that can be used in this action.

6. You can target any object with the startDrag action, but you want to target the cat_MC movie clip in which the Drag button is nested. To set the target for this action, use a new expression, the this expression. Type this between the parentheses. The target of this directs Flash to the cat_MC symbol in which the Drag button is nested. This is the only parameter for the startDrag action that you need because you are targeting the cat_MC symbol.

7. Move your cursor to the end of the statement and press (Return) [Enter] to create a new line. Type a closing curly bracket to close this script (}). Your script should be the same as in Figure 10.9.

Note ———————————————————————————————

Notice that even though you typed the ending curly bracket indented to the right in the Scripting pane, it automatically moves to the far left edge of the Scripting pane. Flash automatically understands that the curly bracket closes the script, and the new Auto Format feature of the Actions panel is initiated, causing the curly bracket to move to the left. You can turn the Auto Format feature on or off through the Actions pop-up menu in the upper-right corner of the Actions panel by selecting AutoFormat.

Figure 10.9   This ActionScript enables the end-user to start dragging this movie clip when the Drag button is pressed.

8. Test your movie in Flash Player Testing Mode. Click and drag the Drag button. Notice that after you click this button, it attaches to your mouse and allows you to drag it anywhere on the Stage. Also note that you can't cause it to stop dragging. Next, you'll create the script to cause the Drag button to stop dragging. Close Flash Player Testing Mode and return to the movie.

9. You should still be in the Symbol-Editing Mode for the cat_MC symbol; if you aren't, double-click this symbol from the movie library to return to the Symbol-Editing Mode.

10. Click the Drag button instance on the Stage and access the Actions panel. Click to place your cursor at the end of the script, after the curly bracket (}).

11. Press (Return) [Enter] to create a new line of script. The stopDrag action is used to stop the dragging of the button. You again need to use the on action to set a new response to a mouse event for the Drag button, but this time you will set the event handler to (release). Type the following statement into the Scripting pane:

```
on(release){
```

12. Add the action to be performed if the mouse button is released by using the built-in action stopDrag. Then, create a new line of script by pressing (Return) [Enter], and from the Actions, Movie Clip Control categories, double-click the stopDrag action. Notice that the script hint does not display. This is because the stopDrag action does not require a target; it knows to stop dragging any and all objects when the end-user releases her mouse button.

13. Finish the script by creating a new line of script and typing a closing curly bracket. Your Actions panel should resemble Figure 10.10.

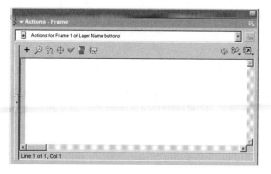

Figure 10.10   This ActionScript enables the end-user to stop dragging this movie clip when the Drag button is released.

14. Exit Symbol-Editing Mode and test your script in Flash Player Testing Mode. Drag the Drag button on the screen, and then release your mouse button to stop dragging the button. If the button stops dragging, the stopDrag action is working.

15. Exist the Flash Player Testing Mode and save your movie.

With the drag-and-drop functionality created for this movie clip, you can now set a target for where the cat_MC can be dragged on the main movie Stage. If you need to access a copy of the movie at this point in its development, open matching2.fla located in the Seminar10/Samples directory.

Creating a Condition for the Matching Activity

With the drag-and-drop interactivity set, you need to create the conditional statement for comparing whether the button is dropped on the correct animal. This requires the if and else statements. This creates logic for Flash to analyze whether the cat_MC instance is on the correct animal and what to do if it is true, as well as what to do if it is false. To create this logic, do the following:

1. Open the cat_MC symbol in the Symbol-Editing Mode. Click the Drag button on the Stage and open or access the Actions panel.

2. Create a new line of script below the stopDrag action. This creates a blank line between the stopDrag(); script and the closing curly bracket. Next, you will wrap the if statement inside the on(release) action. This statement evaluates a condition when the Drag button is released to see whether it is true or false.

3. Before you create the conditional statement, create a comment for explaining the next lines of script. Type the following:

```
//check to see if the user releases the Drag button over the
correct animal.
```

4. Create another line of script; then, create an `if` statement to evaluate the drop target by typing the following:

```
if(eval(this._droptarget) ==_parent.cat){
```

5. Create a new line of script and add another comment by typing the following:

```
//if the target is correct, hide this movie clip.
```

6. To cause the `cat_MC` instance to disappear when the instance touches or overlaps the correct drop target, you set the visible property for the `cat_MC` instance to `0`. Type the following script:

```
_visible = 0;
```

Tip ———————————————————————————————————

You can turn many properties of the movie clip object on or off using `1` or `0`.

7. Now set up the logic by adding an `else` statement that tells what Flash should do if the target is incorrect. Create a new line of script and type the following script:

```
} else {
```

8. Create another new line of script and add a comment by typing the following:

```
//if the target is incorrect return this movie clip to its
➥starting x and y position.
```

9. Now set the x, y coordinate for returning the instance of `cat_MC` symbol to its starting or original position on the Stage. This script references two variables that have not yet been created: `homeX` and `homeY`. You will create these variables a little later in this workshop. Type the following lines of script to complete the `if else` script.

```
_x = homeX;
_y = homeY;
```

10. Create a new line of script and close the `else` statement by typing a closing curly bracket. The Actions panel should resemble Figure 10.11.

```
on(press) {
    //start dragging this entire Movie Clip
    startDrag(this);
}
on(release) {
    //stop dragging this entire Movie Clip
    stopDrag();
    //check to see if the user releases the Drag button over the correct animal.
    if(eval(this._droptarget)==parent[target]) {
        //if the target is correct, hide this movie clip.
        _visible = 0
    } else {
        //if the target is incorrect return this movie clip to its starting x and y position.
        _x = homeX;
        _y = homeY;
    }
}
```

Line 16 of 25, Col 3

Figure 10.11   The `if` statement evaluates whether the button is dropped over the correct drop target. If the `if` statement is not true, the `else` statement kicks in and sends the button back to its original starting position on the Stage.

To better understand the script in step 4, let's break it down:

- The `if` statement requires a parameter to be identified so that it can be evaluated.

- The `if(eval` script tells Flash to evaluate the expression inside the following parentheses—`(this._droptarget) == _parent.cat)`.

- The expression `(this._droptarget)` directs Flash to the `cat_MC` movie clip.

- The `==` establishes equality with the two objects on either side.

- `_parent.cat` is an expression set through a relative path that directs Flash to the parent of this movie clip, which is the main movie because the `cat_MC` exists on the main movie Timeline. By calling `.cat`, you direct Flash to the drop target, which you will create around the cat animal later in this workshop.

If you want to see an example of the movie at this point in its development, you can view the `matching3.fla` file that is completed up to this point in the book. This file is in the `Seminar10/Samples` directory on the CD-ROM that accompanies this book.

Creating the Functionality for the Play Sound Button

To finish the functionality of the cat_MC symbol, you need to develop the movie clip's Timeline and add a cat sound for the Play Sound button to play. To finish developing the cat_MC symbol, follow these steps:

1. Open the cat_MC symbol in Symbol-Editing Mode.

2. Click the playhead in the movie clip Timeline so that you do not have anything active on the Stage. Then, insert a frame by pressing F5. This causes all the layers to extend to Frame 2. Press F5 twice more to add two more frames for all layers so the movie extends to Frame 4 (see Figure 10.12).

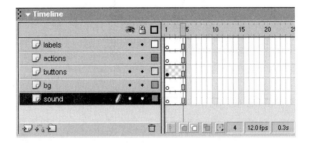

Figure 10.12   You could also have selected Photoframe 4 for all layers by Shift-clicking and then inserted a frame through the Insert, Frame menu command.

3. Click Frame 2 of the sound layer and insert a keyframe.

4. Open or access the library for the movie and drag an instance of the catcry.mp3 sound symbol onto the Stage. The sound attaches to the keyframe in Frame 2 (see Figure 10.13).

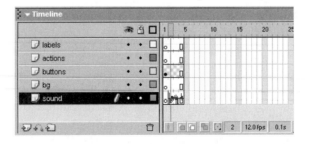

Figure 10.13   Although the sound symbol was dragged onto the Stage, the sound is actually attached to the keyframe as indicated by the waveform in the sound layer of the Timeline.

Note

You will learn more about sound in Seminar 12, "Adding Sound to Enhance a Site."

5. Click the Play Sound button on the Stage to make it active.

6. Open the Actions panel. It should be labeled Actions–Button, indicating that the Play Sound button is the object to which the script will attach.

7. Next, you will create the script to cause the Play Sound button to go to Frame 2 of the movie clip Timeline, where the sound is attached. To make the Play Sound button play a sound, type the following script:

```
on(press){
    gotoAndPlay(2);
}
```

8. The final action that needs to be added is a stop action attached to Frame 1 of the actions layer. This stops the movie clip at Frame 1, allowing the two buttons to be clicked. The Play Sound button causes the movie clip to advance to Frame 2 of its Timeline, playing the attached sound.

9. Exit Symbol-Editing Mode and test your movie in Flash Player Testing Mode. Click the Play Sound button to hear the sound. Because of the ActionScript in the cat_MC movie clip that sets the homeX and homeY variables that do not exist yet, do not test the Drag button. It will not function correctly until a drop target is set in the main movie.

If you want to see an example of the movie at this point in its development, you can view the matching4.fla file that is completed up to this point in the book. This file is in the Seminar10/Samples directory on the CD-ROM that accompanies this book.

Setting the Drop Target Objects on the Stage

Now you need to create the drop target for each animal instance by using _droptarget, which is a built-in object of Flash. You will create a rectangular area that surrounds each animal instance and set this as the drop target area that the if and else statements of the cat_MC instance evaluate. When the end-user drags the cat_MC instance to an animal, a comparison occurs and determines whether this is the correct animal for the cat_MC instance. The rectangular area is the area that is compared to see whether the match is correct. You will use the rectangle symbol in the matching movie library and apply an Alpha effect of 0% to it so that the area is invisible but still exists on the Stage. This allows the animal that it covers to be visible, but it still

defines an area around the animal for the drop target. To create this drop target, do
the following:

1. In the main movie Timeline, click the drop targets layer to make it active,
   and from the library, drag an instance of the square symbol onto the Stage.
   Resize this instance so that it covers the cow image.

2. Apply an Alpha effect of 0% to the square instance. This causes this instance to
   become transparent. To work with this for the rest of the instruction, turn on
   the Show Outline feature for the drop targets layer by clicking the rectangle
   in the Show All Layers As Outlines column of the layers area of the Timeline
   (see Figure 10.14).

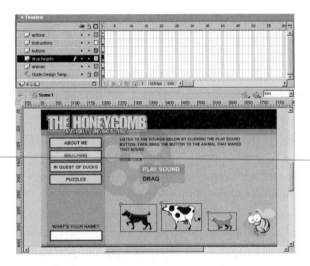

Figure 10.14   You can see the outline of the transparent rectangle with the Show All
Layers As Outlines feature turned on for the drop targets layer.

3. Copy and paste two more instances of the square instance, and position them
   over the dog and cat graphics. Resize them as needed to surround each animal (see Figure 10.15). This instance is used only to set an area around the
   animal.

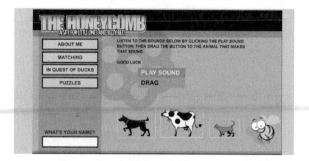

Figure 10.15 Although the instance is transparent, you can still attach instance names and ActionScript to it because it is still an object on the Stage.

4. Each drop target instance needs to have a unique instance name. Open or access the Property Inspector, and select the drop target instance for the dog. Name this instance dog, name the cow drop target cow; and name the cat drop target cat.

Duplicating the cat_MC Movie Clip

To complete the matching activity functionality, you need to have two more movie clips added to the matching.fla movie. You can use the Library panel Duplicate menu command to duplicate the cat_MC movie clip to create a movie clip for each of the other two animals. Then, all you need to do is replace the sound in each of the duplicated movie clips with the correct animal sound for the remaining two animals and change the expression for the relative path to target either the cow or the dog. To do this, follow these steps:

1. Open the main movie library and (Control-click) [right-click] the cat_MC movie clip. From the shortcut menu, select Duplicate to open the Duplicate Symbol dialog box.

2. Rename the movie clip symbol dog_MC and click OK. A new movie clip displays in the library.

3. Repeat steps 1 and 2 to create the cow_MC movie clip.

4. With the two new movie clips created, you need to change the sound for the Sound button in each movie clip. The Sound button is accessible in the Symbol-Editing Mode for each of these movie clips. From the library, double-click the dog_MC movie clip to launch the Symbol-Editing Mode.

5. Click the keyframe in Frame 2 of the Sound layer. Then, in the Property Inspector, click the arrow to the right of the Sound option and select the dog.mp3 sound from the pop-up menu (see Figure 10.16).

Figure 10.16   Because you already attached a sound to this keyframe, you can easily switch the attached sound with another sound you have imported into your library.

6. Double-click the cow_MC movie clip to display this movie clip in the Symbol-Editing Mode, and repeat step 5 to switch the catcry.mp3 sound with the cow.mp3 sound.

7. Exit the Symbol-Editing Mode and return to the main movie. On the button layer, place the instances of the two new movie clips on the Stage. Position an instance of the dog_MC movie clip to the right of the existing cat_MC instance, and position an instance of the cow_MC to the right of the dog_MC instance (see Figure 10.17).

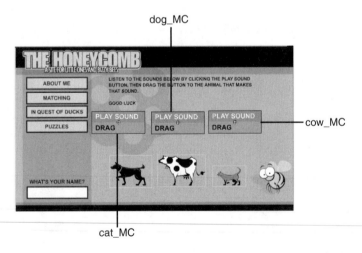

Figure 10.17   Do not worry about aligning these instances yet. You will modify them further in the next step.

8. These animal movie clip instances are a little large. Reduce them in size through the Transform panel. Open the Transform panel by selecting Window, Transform. Then, select all three animal movie clip instances on the Stage so that they all are active. In the Transform panel, set the Width and Height boxes to 70% (see Figure 10.18).

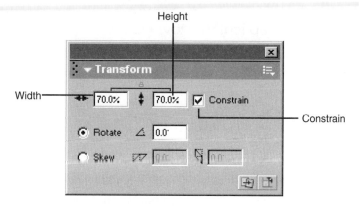

Figure 10.18　If you select the Constrain option, you only need to type 70% into either of the Width or Height boxes; the other box will reflect the same number.

9. Close the Transform panel and open or access the Align panel. Position the movie clip instances centered above the animal below it, as Figure 10.19 indicates.

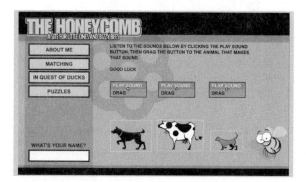

Figure 10.19　You could also have aligned these movie clip instances from their bottom edges or top edges.

All the pieces and much of the functionality are in place for the matching game. Next, you will add the final touches to make the matching game function as intended. One of the missing pieces of this functionality is to customize the target called in the Drag button ActionScript for all three movie clip instances. You'll do this next.

Customizing the Duplicated Movie Clips

With your drop targets created and named, you now need to set the correct relative path to the drop target instances on the Stage. This completes one of the missing pieces of information for the if statement script in each of the animal movie clips. To do this, follow these steps:

1. Click the buttons layer to make it active and (Control-click) [right-click] the cow_MC movie clip instance on the right. Select Edit in Place from the shortcut menu to launch the Symbol-Editing Mode and cause the Stage to dim.

2. Click the Drag button to make it active and open the Actions panel.

3. In the Scripting pane, change the _parent reference in the relative path from _parent.cat to _parent.cow (see Figure 10.20).

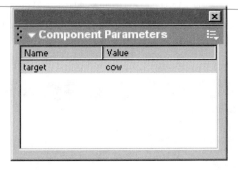

Figure 10.20   The drop target is now set for the cow drop target instance on the Stage.

4. Repeat steps 2 and 3 for the dog_MC instance to set its relative path to the dog drop target.

5. Exit the Symbol-Editing Mode and return to the main movie.

The script for the comparison in the if statement is now set. By setting a specific target, the if statement compares whether the movie clip instance is touching or over the specified target. If it is, it disappears. But if it isn't presently, it remains on the Stage where the end-user drops it. Next, you will create the script for telling the animal movie clip instances to go back to their starting positions, which is the final piece of interactivity required for the else statement.

If you want to see an example of the movie at this point in its development, you can view the matching5.fla file that is completed up to this point in the book. This file is in the Seminar10/Samples directory on the CD-ROM that accompanies this book.

Using the onClipEvent Action

You need to create the homeX and homeY variables for each of the movie clip instances on the Stage. This is the final piece of script required for the matching activity functionality. These two variables store the x and y coordinates for each of the movie clip instances. You will use the onClipEvent action with the (load) event handler to capture this data for the variable values. These two variables store the x and y coordinates for each of the animal movie clip instances when these instances load on the Stage. The variable can then be called in the script for each movie clip symbol for which, up to this point, these variables have not been defined. To create these variables for each animal movie clip instance on the Stage, follow these steps:

1. Click the instance of the cat_MC symbol on the Stage to make it active, and open the Actions panel. Click to set your cursor in the Scripting panel of the Actions panel.

2. First create a comment explaining the script. Type the following comment:

   ```
   //Initiate the following script when this MC appears on the Stage
   ➥for the first time
   ```

3. Create a new line of script and from the Actions, Movie Clip Control category, select onClipEvent. Select load from the Code Hints pop-up menu that displays, setting the event handler for this movie clip instance.

4. Create a new line of script after the opening curly bracket following the onClipEvent action, and again add a comment explaining the next script. Type the following comment:

   ```
   //save the starting x position of this movie clip.
   ```

5. Now you need to establish a variable named homeX that will save the starting x position of the cat_MC instance on the main movie Stage. Create another new line of script and type the following script:

   ```
   homeX = _x;
   ```

Your script should resemble Figure 10.21.

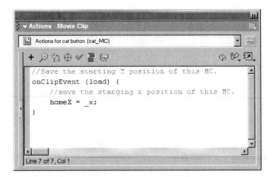

Figure 10.21   By using the x for the value of the variable, you are directing Flash to the main movie Timeline and storing the x coordinate for the cat_MC instance on the Stage.

6. Create a new line of script and add another comment explaining the next script. Type the following:

    ```
    //save the starting y position of this movie clip.
    ```

7. Now set the variable homeY to be the starting y position of the cat_MC instance. Type the following script:

    ```
    homeY = _y;
    ```

8. Create a new line of script and type the closing curly bracket for the onClipEvent action. Your script should resemble Figure 10.22.

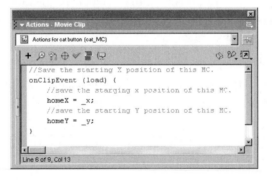

Figure 10.22   The two variables homeX and homeY are used to store the starting x and y coordinates for the cat_MC instance on the Stage.

9 Select all the script in the Actions panel, and copy this information by pressing (⌘C) [Ctrl+C]. Click the dog_MC instance, and in the Actions panel, click in the Scripting pane to set your cursor. Paste the copied script by pressing (⌘-V) [Ctrl+V]. This attaches the script to the dog_MC instance.

10. Click the cow_MC instance and again paste the script in the Script pane of the Actions panel for this instance. By copying and pasting, you are being very accurate and quick in your scripting. Copy and paste ensures accurate script for each movie clip instance.

11. Close the Actions panel and save your matching.fla movie. If you used a file from the CD-ROM as you worked through this workshop, save the file as matching.fla without any of the number references to the different sections of the workshop.

Warning ───

When you're copying and pasting script in the Actions panel, the Edit menu commands Copy and Paste do not always work. For consistent functionality, you must use the keyboard shortcuts. Always click first in the Scripting pane of the Actions panel before using the Copy and Paste commands. If you do not click first in the Scripting pane, you will paste the copied script on the Stage for the active layer.

Testing the Matching Activity

To view the functionality of the matching activity, you must test the movie in the Flash Player. To do this, follow these steps:

1. Select Control, Text Movie to launch the SWF movie in the Flash Player.

2. Click the Play Sound button, and you will hear an animal sound. In Seminar 12, you will learn more about sounds and the compression of sounds.

3. Drag the Drag button for one of the movie clip instances to an animal. If this is the matching animal, the button disappears. Conversely, if it is not, when the user releases his mouse button, the button goes back to its starting x, y coordinate position.

4. Save the movie as matching.fla, and close the movie in both the Flash Player Testing Mode and the Flash MX Authoring environment. If you want to compare your Honeycomb site with a movie that is completed up to this point in the book, open the 10Honeycomb.fla file located in the Seminar10/Samples directory on the CD-ROM that accompanies this book.

Seminar Summary

In this seminar, you learned many new actions and how to attain new ActionScript functionality for calling and controlling objects in your movie. You learned how to use relative paths and the _parent reference. You also learned to how to create an else statement for creating logic. You will use the if and else statements often in your Flash development for creating logic. You also should try to use relative paths as often as possible. They keep your script flexible and save on file size because not as many objects need to be identified when the script is compiled.

You also learned how to create your own custom movie clip. Through the clip parameters, you can customize the movie clip for your movie. Keep movie clips in mind as you create other Flash movies, and use them when you need to encapsulate script for a movie clip that you will use often in the movie.

You also learned a little more about ActionScript and working with the movie clip class by controlling properties of the movie clip. You will take this control further in the next seminar. In the workshop of this seminar, you developed the matching activity of The Honeycomb site. The onClipEvent was used to capture the homeX and homeY variables of each of the movie clip instances used in The Honeycomb site. All this functionality can easily be used in other Flash movies, and you will find that you will use variations of it often.

Next, you will take the features of the dynamic and input text boxes further by starting to call them in ActionScript and manipulating the end-user data for these boxes. You will also begin to control some of the built-in movie clip properties for a movie clip instance on the Stage through the Dot syntax of ActionScript.

Seminar 11

Communicating
with the End-User

In this chapter

Communicating information is usually the main purpose of a Web site. Using Flash for Web development provides some fun and entertaining ways to communicate information to the end-user. As you have seen with previous seminars, dynamic and input text fields enable you to display text messages based on end-user interaction. By integrating creative graphics with these text fields, the message becomes more interesting and can have a bigger impact on the end-user.

That is, as long as the end-user can see the screen clearly.

Accessibility of computers and Internet content is being looked at very seriously today by law makers, companies, and individuals. In previous releases of Flash, accessibility was an issue because the movie information was limited to strictly visual interpretation. You could add sound to further enhance and verbally communicate messages, but this could greatly increase the file size of the movie as well as not effectively helping a person who has impaired vision navigate and understand the site structure. New with Macromedia Flash MX is the Accessibility feature. This new feature allows a Flash MX movie and the various objects that make up the movie to be verbally communicated to the user. This seminar focuses on how to create engaging ways to communicate and capture end-user information, as well as how to make the entire site accessible to all visitors, young and old, sighted or not.

Accessibility in Macromedia Flash MX

The Accessibility feature enables a screen reader application to provide an audio description of the movie contents, object by object. Many screen reader applications are available today, and they all have different features and functionality for interpreting the screen content. Screen readers typically are used to help a user navigate through a screen. The user can click different areas of the screen to cause the screen reader to verbally communicate any of the written text in that area or a description of the area. Flash MX's Accessibility feature can make the following five objects accessible to a screen reader:

- Text
- Buttons
- Input text fields
- Movie clips
- The entire movie

When you first create a new **Flash movie** or document, the Accessibility feature is enabled. All static text blocks that you might use in a movie are automatically accessible to a screen reader. This includes all static text blocks used for button labels, as well as any assigned instance names that you might have added to a Stage object. If you do not assign an instance name to an object, Flash will generically create one. For instance, a button without a label or an instance name will be interpreted as "button". Through the Accessibility feature, a user can click the various areas of the movie to get a description of the movie content through her screen reader.

Note

Screen readers have different methods for interpreting and speaking the screen contents. They each have their own technique for translating written content into speech. Therefore, there is no way to be absolutely sure how the movie will be presented to the end-user because this is dependent on the screen reader application the user has installed.

Note

You can also make two different formats of a movie, one that is built for accessibility and another that is built for the general sighted public. New with Flash MX is the `System.capabilities` object; by using `System.capabilities.hasAccessibility`, you can have Flash check to see whether a screen reader is present on the end-user's machine. If it is present, Flash plays the movie designed for accessibility. Otherwise, the other movie is played.

In Flash, you can customize the accessibility of the five accessible objects through the Accessibility panel (see Figure 11.1). You can open the Accessibility panel either through the Window, Accessibility menu command or by clicking the Edit Accessibility Settings button in the Property Inspector.

Figure 11.1   The Accessibility button is easily found in the Property Inspector.

Depending on whether you have selected the entire movie or an accessible object in the movie, you will get different option settings in the Accessibility panel. You can set the accessibility options for the entire movie by opening the movie and, with nothing selected on the Stage, opening the Accessibility panel (see Figure 11.2).

Figure 11.2   By not having objects or frames selected, you are directing Flash to provide accessibility for the movie, not an object.

You can turn on or off the Accessibility features that you want to apply to the entire movie, as well as provide a custom name and description of the movie. Table 11.1 provides a description of each option.

Table 11.1   Descriptions of Accessibility Options

Option	Description
Make Movie Accessible	Toggle check box that turns the Accessibility features on or off. By default, this option is turned on when you create a new movie.
Make Child Objects Accessible	Toggle check box that enables any nested objects in the active accessible object to also be accessible to a screen reader.
Auto Label	Toggle check box that enables the automatic labeling that Flash uses for the accessible objects to be turned on or off. Depending on the site you are developing, you might want to toggle this feature off, forcing Flash to use only the names you type into the Accessibility panel for an object.
Name	The Name property is the most important feature of this panel because it enables you to assign a custom name to the object that becomes accessible to the screen reader.
Description	The Description property enables a full description to be assigned to the active object.

If you make a movie accessible, you can go even further by setting individual objects to be accessible or not. If you have an accessible object selected on the Stage, when the Accessibility panel is opened, it displays the accessibility features for just that object (see Figure 11.3).

Figure 11.3   You can choose to make an object accessible or not through this panel.

This panel enables you to turn off the accessibility of the active object through the Make Object Accessible option. You might want to do this if you set an accessibility Name property for the active object that already has an assigned instance name. This would cause the screen reader to read both names—the accessibility name and the instance name—which could be confusing for the end-user to hear. To prevent this confusion, you can turn off the Auto Label option for the entire movie and force Flash to use only the name set in the Name property box of the Accessibility panel. Another example of when you might want to turn off the Auto Label option is if you wanted to apply a different name and description for the active object. You will use the Accessibility feature in the workshop section of this seminar to make The Honeycomb site content accessible to a screen reader.

Note

The Name property box of the Accessibility panel is not readable by ActionScript. You must use instance or variable names for text fields and still use instance names for buttons and movie clips when using ActionScript to control these objects.

Overview of Login Functionality

The trick to effective communication is making the communication as personal as possible to the end-user. What better way to do this than to capture the end-user's name and then use that name combined with the various messages throughout the site.

Two types of login functionality can be created for a Web site—a local login and a global login. When you create a *local* login, you do not have to worry about any of the back-end connectivity that you need to keep track of end-user information. The login exists for the duration of the end-user involvement with the site, and it expires when the visitor leaves the site to go to another URL or closes or quits out of his browser application. This type of login is a temporary login and helps provide a friendly and dynamic way to communicate with everyone who accesses the site.

A *global* login requires a database for storing various information about the site visitor. This usually pertains to at least his login name and password, and it can include other personal and business information you might want to capture.

The workshop in this seminar covers how to use an input text field to capture the end-user's name to create a local login.

Note

The global login issues are beyond the scope of this book. You can find more information and resources for learning about ColdFusion, XML, or ASP connectivity technologies at New Riders Publishing's Web site (`www.newriders.com`).

Communicating with The Honeycomb Site Visitor

Now that you have a little experience working with ActionScript to create interactivity and control movie clips, you will make Buzzy Bee communicate with the end-user. He will do this through a dialog bubble that displays when the end-user clicks or rolls over one of the Activity buttons. Because the Activity buttons are instances of the button symbols, you must use the on action with the appropriate event handler to trigger the button. You also must combine this action with other ActionScript statements that are directed at controlling the bubble movie clip instance. Remember: All movie clips are objects within the Movie Clip class and have built-in properties that can be controlled.

Setting Up for the Buzzy Bee Communication

First, you will make a symbol that has both Buzzy Bee and the dialog bubble. The dialog bubble is used to communicate information to the end-user; it will display and hide based on the end-user's interaction with the movie. Follow these steps to create this symbol:

1. Use your Honeycomb.fla file from Seminar 10, or open 10Honeycomb.fla from the Seminar11/Samples/ directory. Save this as Honeycomb.fla in the directory in which you are saving all the files for The Honeycomb Web site.

2. To create a new symbol of Buzzy Bee that has both the bubble and buzzy symbol in it, select Insert, New Symbol. Name the symbol buzzy_MC and give it a Movie Clip behavior; then, click OK.

3. A new symbol opens in the Symbol-Editing Mode. From the library, drag an instance of the buzzy bee symbol in the buzzy bee symbol folder onto the Stage. Using the Align panel, center this instance both vertically and horizontally to the Stage. Rename Layer 1 to buzzy.

4. Create a new layer above the buzzy layer and name this layer bubble dialog. Then, drag an instance of the bubble symbol onto the Stage. Position it as Figure 11.4 indicates.

Figure 11.4   Be sure you have the buzzy bee instance centered at this new symbol reference point.

5. Click the bubble instance on the Stage to make it active, and in the Property Inspector, assign the instance name of bubble.

6. Click the buzzy bee instance on the Stage, and in the Property Inspector, assign the instance name of bee.

7. Exit the Symbol-Editing Mode by selecting Edit, Edit Document and return to the main movie. You have nested both the buzzy bee instance and the bubble instance inside the buzzy_MC movie clip symbol and assigned each an instance name.

Note

To keep your movie's library organized, place the **buzzy_MC** symbol inside the **buzzy bee symbol** folder.

8. Click and unlock the buzzy layer to make it active, and insert a blank keyframe in Frame 98. Drag an instance of the buzzy_MC symbol onto the Stage. This buzzy_MC instance replaces the buzzy bee movie clip in the previous keyframe.

9. Unhide the Guide: Design Template layer and position the buzzy_MC instance for the keyframe in Frame 98 as the guide indicates. This should be the same location as the buzzy bee movie clip instance in Frame 97. Hide the Guide:Design Template layer again.

Tip

You could also use the onion skin feature to position the `buzzy_MC` instance on the Stage for Frame 98 if you adjust the onion markers to show Frames 97–98. By turning on this feature, you can see all the content on the Stage for Frame 97 and accurately position the new `buzzy_MC` instance for Frame 98 in the same location as the `buzzy bee` instance. Seminar 6, "Animation and Special Effects for Flashing Up the Site," covers the onion skin feature of Flash MX.

10. In the Property Inspector, assign the instance name of `buzzy` to the `buzzy_MC` instance in Frame 98.

Note

The absolute path to the dialog bubble would be `_root.buzzy.bubble` because the `buzzy_MC` is on the main movie Stage and this instance is named `buzzy`. The `bubble` instance is nested inside the `buzzy MC` symbol and has an instance name of `bubble`.

11. Test the movie and notice that the first appearance of Buzzy Bee as he flies onto the Stage is without a dialog bubble. When the movie reaches Frame 98 and Buzzy Bee has reached his resting position, the dialog bubble displays.

Save your file. If you want to see a movie developed up to this point in the workshop, open `11Honeycomb1.fla` located in the `Seminar11/Samples` directory on the CD-ROM that accompanies this book.

Creating a Dynamic Text Block

To cause the dialog bubble to display different communications based on the enduser interaction with the movie, you need to create a dynamic text field in the bubble. By assigning a variable name to this dynamic text field, it can be called in ActionScript and manipulated to display different messages. To do this, follow these steps:

1. Open the `bubble` symbol in the Symbol-Editing Mode. Create a new layer above the `bubble` layer, and name this layer `#text#`.

Tip

It is a good idea to name any layer that has a dynamic text field or an input text field with a layer name that is surrounded by # #. This visually helps you see that this layer contains a text field.

2. With the #text# layer active, click the Text tool; in the Property Inspector, set the Text Type option to Dynamic, with a font type of Arial, a font size of 14, a font color of black, and a normal position. Set the Paragraph attributes to be left justified, and set the Line Type option to Multiline.

3. Embed the font by clicking the Character button to display the Character Options. Select All Characters to embed all the characters of the Arial font into this dynamic text field.

Note

When you embed a font outline in a movie, you increase the movie size about 20KB. Use this option only when you want inputted text to match the fonts used throughout the movie.

4. Click and drag a dynamic text field inside the bubble area on the Stage (see Figure 11.5).

Figure 11.5   To adjust the size of the dynamic text field, drag the handle of the text block to set a new size.

5. With the Arrow tool, click the text block to make it active, and in the Property Inspector, assign the instance name of buzzyMessage for the text field. You have now nested a dynamic text field that is assigned the instance name of buzzyMessage inside the bubble symbol.

Note

To target this text block, you call the absolute path to this text block. First, start with the main movie by calling _root; then you call the buzzy instance, then the bubble, and then the text block (that is, _root.buzzy.bubble.buzzyMessage.text).

6 Exit the Symbol Editing Mode and return to the main movie. Test your movie; you will see buzzy appear on the Stage and then the dialog bubble displays without a message. You will create this communication next.

Making the Dialog Bubble Display a Message for the Button

With the buzzy_MC movie clip symbol created and a dynamic text field nested inside the bubble instance, you can create the ActionScript to cause the dialog bubble to display a text message when the end-user rolls over an activity button. You will control the visibility property of the bubble instance causing it to appear and display based on the end-user interaction. All Movie Clip objects have a built-in property of _visible that can be controlled. To create this ActionScript, do the following:

1. Open the menu symbol in the Symbol-Editing Mode. Click the About Me button on the Stage, and then open the Actions panel in the Expert mode. Notice that your previous on action is already attached to this button, and it is set to trigger through the Release event handler.

2. You want the bubble to display the Buzzy Bee communication when the end-user hovers over the button, so you will add another on action with the rollOver event handler to the existing script. Set your cursor after the ending curly bracket of the on (release) { line of script and press (Return)[Enter] to create a new line of script below the existing script.

3. To start creating this script, first create a comment that describes the script functionality. Type the following comment:

   ```
   //when the user rolls over the button
   ```

4. Press (Return) [Enter] to create a new line and then type the following:

   ```
   on(rollOver) {
   ```

5. Create a new line and type another comment:

   ```
   //make buzzy's dialog bubble visible
   ```

6. Create a new line, create the path to the bubble instance on the Stage, and set the visibility property of the dialog to visible. Type the following script:

   ```
   _root.buzzy.bubble._visible = 1;
   ```

7. Create a new line and create another comment by typing the following script:

```
//assign the specified copy to buzzy's dialog bubble
```

8. Create a new line and then create the ActionScript that causes the dynamic text field assigned the instance name of text to have a message. Type the following script all in one line of script and use all uppercase for the actual message that is the string value:

```
_root.buzzy.bubble.buzzyMessage.text = "IN THIS ACTIVITY YOU CAN
➥RECORD INFORMATION ABOUT YOURSELF BY KEEPING A JOURNAL ENTRY ON
➥A DAILY BASIS.";
```

9. Create a new line of script and then end the on(rollOver) action by typing a closing curly bracket. Your Actions panel should look like Figure 11.6.

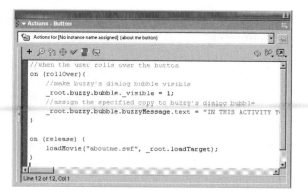

Figure 11.6   Two on actions are attached to the About Me button.

10. Test the movie in the Flash Player Testing Mode and roll over the About Me button. Notice that when you roll off the button, the dialog bubble stays visible. You want it to disappear. You will fix this in the next topic.

Save your file. If you want to see a movie developed up to this point in the workshop, open 11Honeycomb2.fla located in the Seminar11/Samples directory on the CD-ROM that accompanies this book.

Using Event Handlers to Control the Visibility of the Dialog Bubble

To make the dialog bubble disappear when the end-user's cursor moves away from an Activity button, you use ActionScript similar to making the dialog bubble display. However, you use the on action with event handlers of rollOut and dragOut. Then, you set the visibility property for the bubble instance to 0 or false. To do this, follow these steps:

1. Open the menu symbol in the Symbol-Editing Mode. Click the About Me button on the Stage, and open the Actions panel in the Expert Mode.

2. Position your cursor to the right of the ending bracket (}) for the on(rollOver){ script. Create a new line and create the on action by typing the following:

```
on(rollOut, dragOut){
```

3. Create a new line and then type the following comment:

```
//make buzzy's dialog bubble invisible
```

4. Next, you target the bubble and set its visibility property to **0**. Create a new line and type the following:

```
_root.buzzy.bubble._visible = 0;
```

5. End the script by creating another new line and typing the closing bracket. Your Actions panel should look like Figure 11.7.

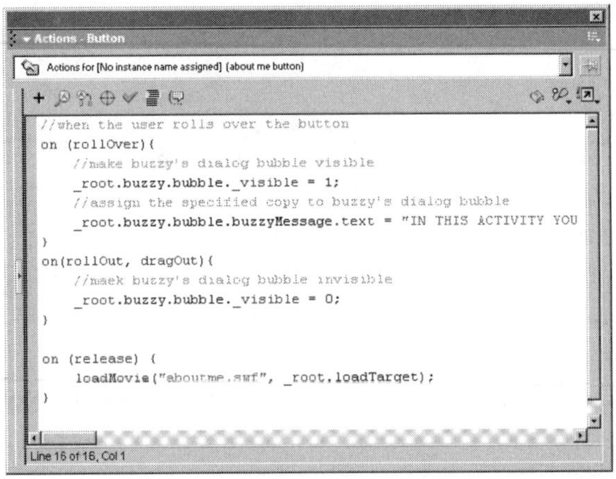

Figure 11.7 By using rollOut and dragOut, you cover your bases on all mousing actions that the end-user can perform to trigger this button.

6. Exit the Symbol-Editing Mode and test your movie. Roll your mouse over and off the About Me button to see the bubble display and disappear.

Save your file. If you want to see a movie developed up to this point in the workshop, open 11Honeycomb3.fla located in the Seminar11/Samples directory on the CD-ROM that accompanies this book.

Communicating Between the Other Activity Buttons and the Dialog Bubble

The next step is to make the other Activity buttons—Matching, Puzzles, and In Quest of Ducks—have a different text message display for Buzzy Bee's bubble dialog. You can copy and paste the ActionScript from the Actions panel for the About Me button to create the dialog bubble text needed for the other buttons. To do this, follow these steps:

1. Open the menu symbol in the Symbol-Editing Mode.

2. Click the About Me button on the Stage and open the Actions panel in the Expert Mode.

3. Highlight the ActionScript for the first on(rollOver) action through the second on(rollOut, dragOut) action (see Figure 11.8).

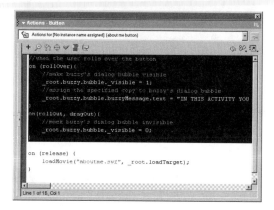

Figure 11.8   Do not highlight the on(release) action.

4. Copy the script by (Control-clicking) [right-clicking] the highlighted script and selecting Copy from the shortcut menu.

5. Click the Matching button on the Stage to make it active.

6. In the Actions panel, create a blank line after the closing bracket for the on(release) action. Paste the copied script below the on(release) action by (Control-clicking) [right-clicking] the Scripting pane and selecting Paste from the shortcut menu.

7. Highlight the string message in the script that is inside the quotation marks, and change this to the following message by typing it in uppercase and in one line of script:

```
TRY YOUR LUCK AT MATCHING ANIMAL SOUNDS WITH THE ANIMAL THAT
➥MAKES THAT SOUND! SILLY NOISES AND FUNNY LOOKING ANIMALS
➥PERFORM DAILY.
```

8. Repeat steps 3–8 for the In Quest of Ducks button and replace the string value for the buzzyMessage with the following message (use all uppercase letters and line of script):

```
PLAY A COUNTING GAME WITH DUCKS. VIEW A MOVIE OF THE DUCKS AND
➥THEN COUNT THEM! ITS FUN!
```

9. Repeat steps 3–8 for the Puzzles button and replace the string value for the
   `buzzyMessage` with the following message (use all uppercase letters and one
   line of script):

   > TEST YOUR SKILLS BY ARRANGING NINE NUMBERS IN THEIR CORRECT ORDER
   > ➥IN THIS SLIDER PUZZLE.

   Warning
   Be sure you type all text messages to be displayed in the dialog bubble in one line and that
   these text messages are enclosed in quotation marks, indicating to Flash that they are to be
   treated as a string.

10. Exit Symbol-Editing Mode and test your movie. Roll your mouse over and
    off of each of the activity buttons to see the different messages display and the
    bubble appear and disappear as you roll over and off each button.

Save your file. If you want to see a movie developed up to this point in the workshop, open `11Honeycomb4.fla` located in the `Seminar11/Samples` directory on the
CD-ROM that accompanies this book.

Creating a Site Login for The Honeycomb Site

Next, you'll create the site login for The Honeycomb site. This login is a local login,
meaning that when the end-user logs in, this login is good only for the session during which she is logged in to the site. If she goes to another URL or exits the
browser, the login information is lost. The end-user must log in again to re-create
this information. The login is not password based for accessing the site.

Note
Creating a login that is permanent requires linking to a database using a middleware application like ColdFusion, ASP, PHP, JSP, or XML. This process is outside the scope of this book.

Setting Up for the Site Login

To create this local login for The Honeycomb site, you first need to create instructions that tell the user how to log in to the site. In Seminar 4, "Using Symbols in a
Movie," you create the login area. When the menu bar and login box display in the
movie, you will need to stop the movie, allowing the end-user to type her name into
the login box. At this point in the movie, you need to display instructions that tell

the end-user what to do to log in to the site. To display instructions for logging in to the site, follow these steps:

1. Drag the playhead to scrub through the movie until you see both the menu and the login box display in their resting positions in the movie. Notice that this is at Frame 63. You want to stop the movie a few frames after this point. In the actions layer, insert a keyframe at Frame 65 and attach the stop action to this frame by typing the following script in the Actions panel:

   ```
   stop();
   ```

2. Insert a new layer above the user login layer, and name this layer login prompt. Insert a keyframe in Frame 65 of this new layer.

3. On the login prompt layer, create a static text block about 400 pixels wide and set the Property Inspector with the character attributes of a font type of Arial, a font size of 14, a font color of black, a font style of bold, AutoKern selected, a position of normal, and left justification. Type the following message in uppercase:

   ```
   WHAT'S YOUR NAME? PLEASE TYPE IT IN THE LOGIN BOX BELOW!

   WHEN YOU ARE DONE, PRESS THE ENTER KEY AND YOU CAN START PLAYING
   THE FUN ACTIVITIES HERE IN THE HONEYCOMB.
   ```

4. Position this text block as Figure 11.9 indicates.

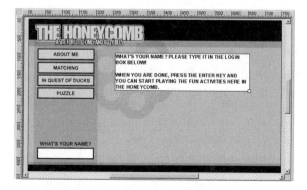

Figure 11.9   At this point in the movie, the buttons on the menu bar are still active.

5. With Frame 65 of the login prompt layer still selected, select File, Open As a Library and open the `login.fla` movie as a library from the `Seminar11/Samples/` directory of the CD-ROM that accompanies this book. Drag an instance of the `input prompt arrow` symbol onto the Stage. Position it to the right of the `login` instance (see Figure 11.10).

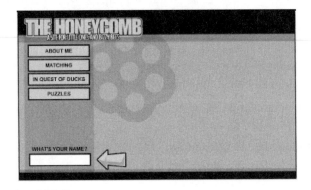

Figure 11.10   This arrow directs the end-user's attention to the login box.

6. Close the `login.fla` library by (Control-clicking) [right-clicking] the title bar of this panel. Select Close Panel from the shortcut menu.

7. Test your movie and notice that it progresses up to Frame 65 and stops. You can still press the activity buttons on the menu bar and cause the activity SWF files to load into the movie. Notice, however, that they do not load at the correct position at this point in the movie. That is because the movie clip you set up for a drop target has not loaded into the movie yet. It is added at Frame 73, and presently the movie stops at Frame 65. You'll fix this small problem next by disabling the activity buttons at this point in the movie.

Disabling the Activity Buttons

You do not want the activity buttons to be triggered before the end-user logs in to the site. Therefore, you need to disable them. To do this, you can use a transparent button to cover them on the Stage. The transparent button will not have actions attached to it; it simply is used to cover the activity buttons and disable them until the end-user logs in. You will also use Flash MX's new ActionScript `useHandCursor` false to cause the button not to display the hand symbol used for clicking a button when the cursor comes in contact with the button. To create this functionality, follow these steps:

1. Insert a new layer above the menu layer and name this layer disable menu.

2. Now create a transparent button. As was covered in Seminar 7, "Site Interactivity and Button Functionality," a transparent button is a button that has Stage content only in the Hit state. Create a new symbol and name it transparent button. Give it a Button behavior. Click OK and the Symbol-Editing Mode opens.

3. Drag an instance of the square symbol onto the Stage and center it vertically and horizontally. The Up state of the button currently holds the square symbol.

4. Drag the keyframe in the Up state to the Hit state for this button (see Figure 11.11). Exit the Symbol-Editing Mode to return to the main movie.

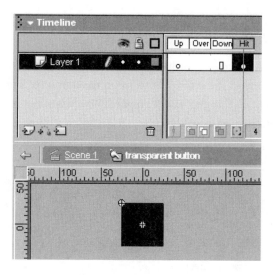

Figure 11.11   Having the square on the Stage for the Hit Mode defines the hot spot area for this button. This is similar to an imagemap in HTML.

5. At Frame 35, the menu instance enters the Stage and the activity buttons are active at this point. The transparent button needs to be added at Frame 35, too, to limit the activity buttons from being triggered. Insert a keyframe in Frame 35 of the disable menu layer and drag an instance of the transparent button onto the Stage.

6. Because the menu Is not In Its final resting position at this point in the Timeline, unhide the `Guide: Design Template` layer so that you can see the final resting position of the menu. Position and resize the `transparent button` so that it covers all the activity buttons (see Figure 11.12).

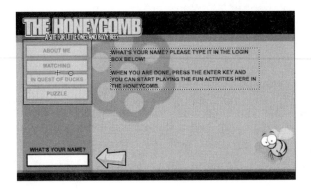

Figure 11.12 The `transparent button` displays on top of the buttons because it resides in a layer that is above the menu layer.

7. Test your movie and notice that it progresses up to Frame 65 and stops. You can't trigger any of the activity buttons on the menu bar until the login takes place. Also notice that the hand cursor displays when the mouse is positioned over the button because of the inherent nature of a button. This can be confusing for the end-user to see the hand symbol and know that a button exists but be unable to make anything happen. You will eliminate this confusion next through a new action for Flash MX.

8. Exit the Flash Player Testing Mode and return to the Flash Authoring Mode. Click the transparent button you just created on the Stage to make it active.

9. You need to assign the button an instance name. In the Property Inspector, type `disableButton` in the Instance Name box.

10. Now, open the Actions Panel and type the following script:

```
on(rollOver, press){
    //Disable the hand cursor from displaying when the user
    ➥comes in contact with the button
    disableButton.useHandCursor = false;
}
```

11. Test the movie again. When the movie stops, move your mouse over the activity buttons. Notice that this time, the hand cursor does not display. By using the event handlers of `rollover` and `press`, you cover your bases for the actions that the end-user will perform when coming in contact with the transparent button. Because you do not want the hand cursor to display, you use the new Flash MX action of `useHandCursor` and set this to `False`. Pretty neat action!

12. Exit the Flash Player Testing Mode.

Save your file. If you want to see a movie developed up to this point in the workshop, open `11Honeycomb5.fla` located in the `Seminar11/Samples` directory on the CD-ROM that accompanies this book.

Creating the Login Functionality

To begin to create the login functionality, you will start with a new instance of a transparent button symbol. When you use a button symbol, it can be assigned the `enterKey` event handler. This event handler is triggered when the (Return) [Enter] key is pressed, causing the movie to continue to play. This new transparent button is placed in the work area outside the movie; therefore, it does not actually exist on the Stage but still responds to the end-user interaction with the movie. To begin creating the login functionality, follow these steps:

1. Click the `login prompt` layer and click the keyframe in Frame 65 where the other login prompt information displays.

2. Drag an instance of the `transparent button` symbol onto the Stage and position it in the work area outside the Stage area next to the login instance (see Figure 11.13).

3. Through the Actions panel in the Expert Mode, attach the following script to this `transparent button` instance:

```
//when the end-user presses the Enter key
//the movie begins to play
on (keyPress "<Enter>") {
        play();
}
```

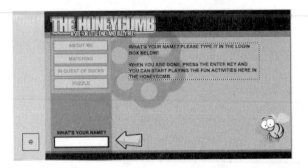

Figure 11.13   By positioning the transparent button outside the Stage area, it will not be accessible in the movie but will still be part of the movie.

4. Test your movie and notice that it progresses up to Frame 65 and stops. Press the Enter key and the movie continues to play to the end. You have created the trigger for advancing the movie. Next, you will create an input text field for capturing the end-user name.

Capturing Login Text for Buzzy Bee's Communication Bubble

To capture the end-user's name and then display it as a message in the bubble dialog of Buzzy Bee, you need both an input text field with an instance name and ActionScript that calls this instance name. You'll create another input text field and nest it in the login symbol, just as you nested the dynamic text field in the `bubble` symbol. The input text field will have an instance name of `name` assigned to it. The instance name of `name` is then called in the ActionScript for displaying the end-user's login name. To create this login functionality, follow these steps:

1. Open the `login` symbol in the Symbol-Editing Mode. Name `Layer 1` to `login box`. Insert a new layer above the `login box` layer. Name the new layer `#name#`.

2. On the `#name#` layer, create an input text field that fits inside the login box of the instance of the `login` symbol. Set the Property Inspector with these character attributes: a font of Arial, a font size of 14, a font color of black, bold, a position of Normal, Center justification, and a line type of Single Line. Again, embed the Arial font outline into this field by clicking the Character button and selecting the All Character option.

3. With the new input text field positioned and its character settings set, in the Property Inspector, assign an instance name of `name`.

4. To have text initially display in this field when the movie loads so that the site visitor visually is clued in on what to do next, click the name input text field on the Stage to make it active; then, type KIDDO. KIDDO will be a generic name for all visitors who access the site. They will need to change this generic name to their name to complete the login process.

5. Exit Symbol-Editing Mode. You have set up the input text field and assigned it an instance name of name. Next, you will call the input text field instance name in ActionScript to make the dialog bubble display the end-user's name.

Note ───────────────────────────────
Remember that the buzzy_MC symbol contains the bubble instance, which has been named bubble. Inside the bubble instance is a dynamic text field named buzzyMessage.

6. Click the user login layer and click the keyframe in Frame 52. Assign the instance name of login to the login symbol that is positioned in the work area below the Stage. Click the keyframe in Frame 63 and again assign the same login instance name to the login symbol. This keyframe contains an instance of the login symbol in its final resting position for the movie.

Warning ─────────────────────────────
If you name an instance that has a motion tween applied, be sure you name both instances of the object—the first one in the starting keyframe of the motion tween and the next instance in the ending keyframe of the motion tween. Flash needs to have both instances named with the same name for any ActionScript calling that instance to work.

Note ────────────────────────────────
The absolute path to the input text field nested in the login instance would be _root.login.name.text.

7. To create the ActionScript for the dialog bubble to display the welcoming message using the end-user's name, open the buzzy_MC symbol in the Symbol-Editing Mode. Double-click the bubble instance to open this nested symbol in the Symbol-Editing Mode.

8. Create a new layer above the #text# layer and name it actions. Click the keyframe in Frame 1 of this layer, and in the Actions panel, attach the following script:

```
//create a variable name of userName for the name input text
➥field
//convert the inputted text to uppercase
userName = _root.login.name.text.toUpperCase();
```

Note ───

You established a new variable in this code: the variable of **userName**. This variable is assigned the value of the input text field with the instance name of **name**. By attaching the property of **.toUpperCase();**, you cause the value of the name variable to always display in uppercase.

9. To create a message that displays in the dynamic text field named buzzyMessage in the bubble symbol, create a new line under the script you just created in the Actions panel. Type the following:

```
//display the user's name, along with the rest of the opening
➥message
buzzyMessage.text = "HELLO, " + userName + ". WELCOME TO THE
➥HONEYCOMB.";
```

10. Your Actions panel should look similar to Figure 11.14.

Figure 11.14 The text message needs to be contained all on one line for that line of script, as this figure indicates.

11. Test your movie. Type your name into the login area and press Enter. The movie advances and Buzzy Bee enters the Stage welcoming you to the site. There are still a few problems, though, such as the fact that the login instructions stay on the Stage and the buttons remain inaccessible. Close the Flash Player to return to Flash Authoring Mode.

12. Click the login prompt layer, click Frame 66, and insert a blank keyframe to clear that layer's content from the Stage.

13. Click the `disable menu` layer, click Frame 66, and insert a blank keyframe to clear that layer's content from the Stage.

14. Test your movie again. Type your name in the login box and press Enter. The login works, and Buzzy Bee addresses you by your login name. Roll over the activity buttons and view the various host character messages that are displayed.

Making The Honeycomb Site Accessible

The Honeycomb site will be viewed mainly by children of various ages. Some of those children might be visually impaired and might have a screen reader application installed on their computers. Therefore, The Honeycomb site needs to be accessible to a screen reader.

Creating an Accessibility Movie Description

Next, you will use Flash MX's new Accessibility feature to make The Honeycomb site, its buttons, and its messages accessible to a screen reader. Because you used a graphic for the site logo, this can't be read by a screen reader. Therefore, you will add a title for the site and a description of the site that the screen reader application can read. To do this, follow these steps:

1. With the playhead in Frame 1 of the movie, click it so that nothing is active on your Stage.

2. In the Property Inspector, click the Accessibility button to open the Accessibility panel.

3. In the Name property box of the Accessibility panel, type `The Honeycomb`.

4. In the Description property box, type `A site for little ones and busy bees`.

5. Keep the three default options selected (see Figure 11.15).

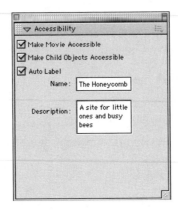

Figure 11.15   With the Auto Label option selected, all static text objects that you used for communicating information will be accessible to a screen reader; this includes all static text blocks and button labels.

6. Test the movie in the Flash Player Testing Mode. Now when the movie is played in a browser, most screen readers will say aloud the movie name and description. Because you kept the Auto Label option active, most screen readers will read any of the objects you have labeled and will read the static text blocks when that object is clicked.

7. Save the movie as Honeycomb.fla. If you want to compare your Honeycomb site with a movie that is completed up to this point in the book, open the 11Honeycomb.fla file located in the Seminar11/Samples directory on the CD-ROM that accompanies this book.

Seminar Summary

This seminar covered many topics related to communication in a Web site. You put practical application behind the seminar discussion in the workshop by creating interactivity in The Honeycomb site that displays messages based on the end-user interaction in the site. You learned how to use a dynamic text field and attach a text message to display in this box. You nested symbols inside other symbols and used both absolute and relative paths to control the nested symbols.

Local login functionality was also covered in this seminar. You used an input text field to capture the end-user's name and, by assigning a variable name to the input text box, you called this variable in ActionScript. You created and used transparent buttons to complete the login functionality and limit the accessibility of the activity buttons. You have begun the journey into the area of interactivity through ActionScript.

You also made the movie accessible to a screen reader. By creating a description name and description for the entire movie, you will now cause a screen reader to read a description of The Honeycomb site when it first loads into a browser. You can easily make all your movies accessible through this new accessibility feature.

The next seminar covers sound in Flash. You will learn how to add both an event and a streaming sound to a Flash movie. Many features for customizing sounds are also covered.

Seminar 12

Adding Sound to Enhance a Site

In this chapter

Workshop: Adding Sound to the Site

Basics of Sound

Sound can add the additional punch you need for communicating a message. People tend to take notice of what is happening in a site if it has engaging music or sound effects. Their attention is drawn to the site, following the progression or flow of the site and message.

Two types of sounds can be used in Macromedia Flash: *streaming sounds* and *event sounds*. Streaming sounds typically are used as background music and are usually longer in duration than event sounds. Event sounds are short in duration and are used for buttons or events that occur based on end-user interaction with the site.

> **Warning**
>
> Sound files can be very large in physical file size. If you are developing for Web use, add sound to the site only if it truly enhances the site.

Importing Sounds

To add sound to a site, you import it just as you would a graphic, through the File, Import command. When you import a sound, it is added to the movie's library (see Figure 12.1).

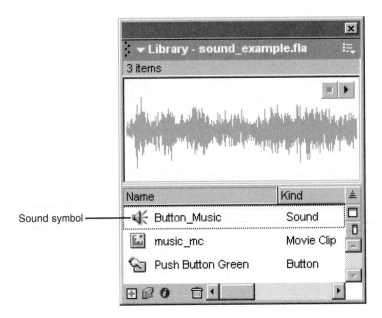

Figure 12.1   The library uses a sound icon to visually represent all sound files in a movie.

As with any symbol, you need only one sound symbol in the movie's library, and you can add as many instances of the sound as you need in your movie.

Flash can import different sound files based on whether you are using a Macintosh or a PC. Both systems can import MP3 files, and if you are using a Macintosh, you can also import AIFF. The WAV format can be imported if you are using a PC. Additionally, if you have QuickTime 4 or above installed on your system, you can import the additional sound formats indicated in Table 12.1.

Table 12.1 Additional Sound Formats Available with QuickTime Installed

Format	Macintosh	PC
Sound Designer II	X	
System 7 Sounds	X	
Sound Only QuickTime Movies	X	X
Sun AU	X	X
AIFF	X	X
WAV	X	X

Tip
You can also use sounds from another Flash movie. Open the movie as a library and drag the sound into your movie or the movie's library.

Flash is not a sound editing application. Therefore, always make sure you have the sound created in the format you need prior to importing it into the Flash movie. MP3 files already have a sound compression format applied to them upon import. If you import WAV or AIFF files, you should import 16-bit, 22KHz mono sounds. You can convert sounds to lower sample rates when you export your movie.

Tip
Sound files can be very large in file size. Just as with a graphic, edit your sound clip so it is short in duration and is set at the quality settings needed before you import it into the movie. You can always lower the quality settings for a sound when you export the Flash movie to SWF format.

Adding Sound to the Movie

After you import sound into a movie, you can attach the sound to either the Timeline or a button. If you attach a sound to the Timeline, it can be set to stream along with the Timeline synchronized with the Stage content, or it can be independent of the Timeline. The Timeline could be for the main movie or for a movie clip. When you attach a sound to a button, you can play the sound in the Up, Over, or Down state of the button.

Attaching Sound to a Timeline

To attach a sound to the Timeline, you simply create a keyframe in the frame that you want the sound to begin to play and then drag an instance of the sound onto the Stage. You will not see any representation of the sound on the Stage, but you will see either a waveform of the sound in the Timeline or a straight line (see Figure 12.2).

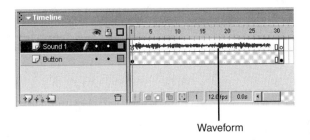

Waveform

Figure 12.2   The waveform displays in the Timeline indicating the number of frames the sound will play.

Just as you should create a layer for all the movie's actions, you also should create a layer for each sound added to the Timeline. By using a new layer for Sound, you can easily identify the sound. When you add multiple sounds to a Timeline, if you want the sounds to overlap, you have to put each sound in its own layer. Otherwise, if they are all in the same layer, the first sound is cut off when the movie progresses to the keyframe holding the second sound. This can make for an abrupt transition.

Attaching Sound to a Button

Event sounds are attached to buttons by attaching them to a button state. This requires the button symbol to be opened in the Symbol-Editing Mode. By inserting a keyframe in one of the button states, you can then drag an instance of the sound symbol onto the Stage and cause the sound to attach to the keyframe (see Figure 12.3).

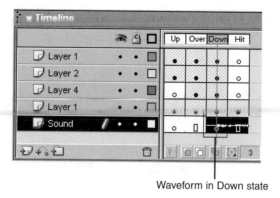

Waveform in Down state

Figure 12.3 A sound waveform will flow into any adjacent frames, as is shown in this figure. The sound in the Down state flows into the Hit state.

Note

Sounds can be attached to the Up, Over, and Down states of a button. The Hit state can't have a sound attached to it because it designates the hot spot area for the button.

Modifying Sounds

After a sound is attached to the Timeline or a button, it can be modified. By selecting the keyframe or any frame that holds the waveform, you can access the sound settings in the Property Inspector (see Figure 12.4). Flash is not a sound editing application, but it can perform minor modifications to a sound.

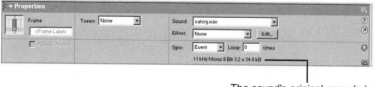

The sound's original recorded settings

Figure 12.4 The Edit button enables the customization of the waveform of the sound.

The Property Inspector enables modification of the Sync and Effect settings as well as setting the number of times the sound will loop. You learn more about these setting in the next section and get hands-on practice in the workshop section of this seminar.

Setting Sound Sync Settings

The Sync option of the Property Inspector allows different types of synchronization of a sound with a Flash movie. The following list describes each Sync setting:

- **Event**—This option creates an event sound by synchronizing a sound to an event, such as the clicking of a button or the progression of the movie to a certain frame in the Timeline. Event sounds play for the duration of the sound unless the event is initiated again before the sound can complete playing. This causes the sound to repeat and cuts off the first sound before it finishes playing.

- **Start**—This is an additional setting that can be applied to an event sound. This option causes the sound to always finish playing before another event sound can be played.

- **Stop**—When Stop is set, an event or start sound stops playing when the movie progresses to the next keyframe in the layer in which the sound resides.

- **Stream**—This option synchronizes a sound to the Timeline, setting it to stream with the Stage content. A streamed sound stops playing when the movie progresses to the end of the Timeline.

Warning

Streaming sounds take precedence over animation, meaning that if the end-user's system does not have enough processing power to compile both the sound and the animation at the same time, the processor focuses on playing the sound first. This causes animation to appear jerky and skip frames so that the sound can play clearly.

Note

The only time the Timeline takes precedence over a streaming sound is when the movie progresses to the end of the Timeline. The streamed sound stops playing no matter where it is in the playback when the end of the Timeline is reached.

Modifying Sound Effect Settings

Flash offers eight basic effects that can be applied to a sound. If you click the Effects option on the Property Inspector, you can set a basic effect. For instance, if you wanted a sound to slowly fade in, you could select the Fade In effect. The basic effects are explained in Table 12.2.

Table 12.2   Flash Sound Effects

Effect	Description
None	Removes any previously applied sound effect and does not apply an effect to the sound.
Left Channel/Right Channel	Applies the sound to only the left or right channel.
Fade Left to Right/Fade Right to Left	Fades sound from channel to channel.
Fade In/Fade Out	Gradually increases or decreases the volume of the sound over its duration.
Custom	Controls your own in and out points of a sound. This setting requires using the Edit Envelope dialog box, which is described shortly.

Looping Sounds

A sound file can be looped numerous times in a Flash movie. To set the number of times to loop a sound, simply type the number in the Loop box of the Property Inspector. You can't set a sound to loop infinitely, but you can simulate infinity by looping a sound set to its the maximum setting of 99,999,999 times. When a streaming sound is looped, it increases the movie file size by the additional frames that Flash automatically adds to the Timeline to enable the sound to play through the loops. Always have a good reason for looping a streaming sound because the movie file size is increased with each loop set.

Customizing Sound Effects

You can further customize a sound effect applied to a sound through the Edit Envelope dialog box. By clicking the Edit button in the Property Inspector, you open the Edit Envelope dialog box (see Figure 12.5).

The Edit Envelope dialog box is made up of two channels: the left and the right channel. Each channel is assigned to either the right or the left speaker of the end-user's computer. The Effect menu can be used to apply one of eight basic sound effects. If you select the Fade Left to Right or Fade Right to Left option, you can create the illusion of the sound being heard in one ear and then the other. You can customize each channel by adjusting the handle on the control line; this changes the Effect menu to Custom because you are now creating a custom effect.

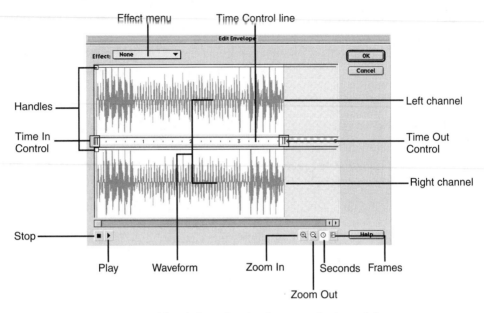

Figure 12.5   Test your sound by clicking the Play button in the lower-left corner.

Viewing Frame Length or Time Duration of a Sound

You can zoom in and out on the waveform by clicking the Zoom In or Zoom Out button in the lower-right corner of the Edit Envelope dialog box. This enables you to see the full waveform or to zoom in on a certain area of the waveform. The Seconds and Frame buttons enable you to change the view of the waveform to either display in relation to the number of seconds it plays or to the number of frames it plays. If you set your sound to loop, you will see the additional waveforms representing each loop (see Figure 12.6).

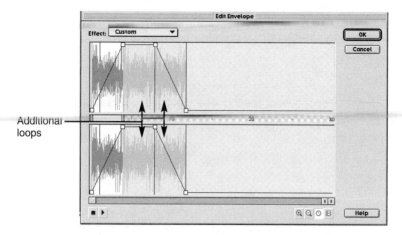

Figure 12.6 You can click the control line to add more handles for each channel of the sound. This figure shows a sound that fades in on the first loop of the sound and then fades out on the third loop of the sound.

Controlling the Sound Duration

The Time In and Time Out Controls allow for minor adjustments when the sound begins to play and when it ends. By dragging these controls on the Time Control line, you can cause the sound to begin and end at different points in its duration. A rule to follow when working with sound is to always import the sound edited to the exact duration as you need in the Flash movie. Use a sound edit application to cut out any parts of a sound you do not want to be part of the final sound file. This cuts down the file size of the sound file and, therefore, the Flash movie.

Compression and Sound Files

After you have the sound effects added to your movie, you can then set the type and amount of compression for all sounds in the movie. Flash applies different compression formats to sounds and images when the movie is published or exported. Five compressions formats exist for sound—Default, ADPCM, MP3, Raw, and Speech. When you export or publish the movie, you apply one of these formats to all the sounds used in the movie either individually or globally. The generated SWF file of the movie now has a compressed version of all the sounds in the movie based on your compression settings.

To apply a compression format to an individual sound, you open the Sound Properties dialog box by double-clicking the sound symbol in the movie's library (see Figure 12.7).

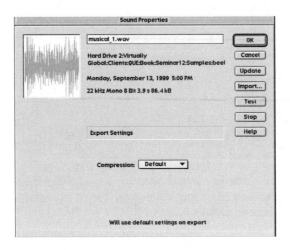

Figure 12.7   You can update and reimport the sound file of the sound symbol through the buttons on the right of this dialog box.

Sampling and Sound Quality

Through the five formats for sound compression, you can set the sampling and sound quality of a sound when the movie is exported or published. To control the compression for individual sounds in your movie, click the Compression option and select one of the five choices: Default, ADPCM, MP3, Raw, or Speech.

Based on the Sync setting of sound, whether the sound is an event sound or a streaming sound, you should set the compression for that Sync type. Most streaming sounds are exported with an MP3 compression, whereas an event sound is usually exported with an ADPCM compression. When you choose any of these compression settings, you access new options for configuring the sampling and sound quality based on the chosen compression setting. You will have hands-on practice adding sounds and setting compression in the workshop section of this seminar. The next section covers each of these compression settings to provide an overall knowledge of when to use them for your movie sounds.

Applying the Default Compression

The Compression option of Default is the default setting for all sounds imported into a movie. This setting allows a sound to conform to the compression settings set in the Publish Settings dialog box. You can globally set a compression setting for both streaming and event sounds in the Publish Settings dialog box. More is covered on this topic and the Publish setting dialog box in Seminar 16, "Publishing and Testing the Site."

Applying ADPCM Compression

As mentioned previously, an event sound usually has a compression format of ADPCM. To access this setting, click the Compression option and select ADPCM from the menu. You now have access to options for setting the sampling and quality of the compressed version of this sound (see Figure 12.8).

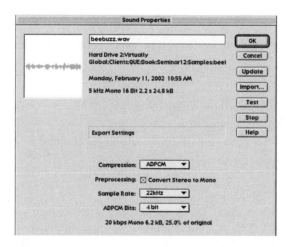

Figure 12.8 Flash lets you know the amount of compression that is applied to the sound at the very bottom of this dialog box.

If you click the Convert Stereo to Mono option, you convert a stereo sound to a mono sound. This reduces the sound file's size by half. It is recommended that all sounds in a Web site be mono sounds. The Sample Rate option enables you to see the sampling for the sound. These settings are in *kilohertz (KH)*, and the smaller the setting, the lower in file size the compressed sound will be. However, it also loses sound quality or fidelity. Table 12.3 explains each of the ADPCM sample rates.

Table 12.3   ADPCM Sample Rates

Sample Rate	Description
5KHz	This setting is barely acceptable for speech but produces a file small in physical file size.
11KHz	This setting is the lowest quality for a short segment of music. Again, the compressed file is small in physical file size.
22KHz	This setting is the recommend choice for Web sites delivered on the Internet. It is half the standard CD rate. Sound fidelity and quality are better, and the file is larger in physical file size.
44KHz	This setting is the recommend choice for standard compact disc (CD) playback. Sound fidelity and quality are high as is the physical file size of the sound file. When the movie is exported, some compression will be applied to all sounds. Therefore, a Flash movie sound set at 44KHz does not have quite the quality of a CD when played back.

The ADPCM Bits option enables you to set the number of bits to be used in the ADPCM encoding for compressing the sound. 2-bit is the smallest and lowest-quality option, whereas 5-bit is the largest and best-quality option. You can test your sound based on the ADPCM compression settings you select by clicking the Test button. Flash plays the sound as it will be heard with these compression settings applied. This allows for adjustments to the settings to obtain the best sounding sound with the lowest physical file size.

Tip

Flash can't improve the quality of sounds. If a sound is recorded at 11KHz mono, Flash continues to export it at 11KHz mono even if you change the sampling rate to 44KHz stereo. To improve the quality of a sound, you must edit the sound in a sound-editing program and reimport the sound into the Flash movie.

Tip

Keep your sounds small by importing 22KHz 16-bit mono sounds whenever possible (importing a stereo sound doubles the data).

Applying MP3 Compression

Most streaming sounds are long in duration and it is smart to use MP3 compression. You set MP3 compression through the Sound Properties dialog box. When you select MP3 from the Compression option in this dialog box, you again access a new set of sampling choices based on MP3 compression (see Figure 12.9).

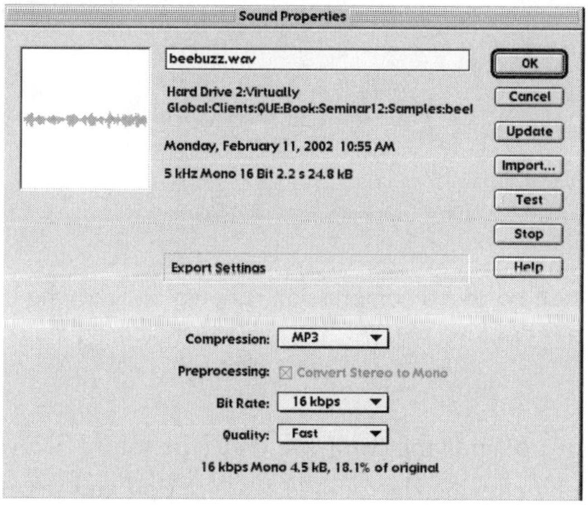

Figure 12.9   You can convert a sound recorded in stereo to mono by selecting the Preprocessing option.

The Bit Rate option enables you to set the maximum bit rate for the sound when played by the MP3 encoder. This option allows you to choose bit rates between the settings of 8Kbps and 160Kbps (kilobits per second). The lower the setting, the lower the sound quality. Many developers recommend that a 16Kbps or higher setting be used for any exported music.

The Quality setting has three choices: Fast, Medium, and Best. The Fast choice applies faster compression, but the sound quality will be low. Medium applies slower compression with better sound quality, and Best applies the slowest compression, which produces the best sound quality. Many developers recommend using Fast for Web-delivered movies.

Applying Raw Compression

If you want to export a sound without any sound compression applied, select the Raw option from the Sound Properties dialog box (see Figure 12.10).

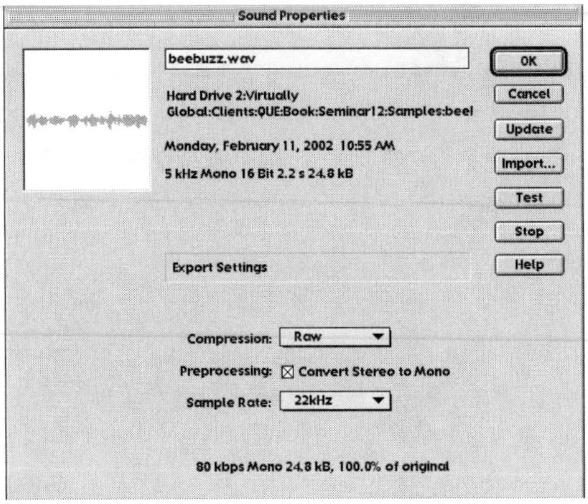

Figure 12.10   Because no sound compression is being applied, the bottom message of this dialog box always displays `100.0% of original` indicating the compression settings.

Even though you are not applying compression to the sound file, you can still set different sample rates by clicking the Sample Rate option and selecting the rate. The higher the sample rate, the better the sound quality. Conversely, the lower the sample rate, the lower the sound quality.

> **Tip**
>
> If you need very good sound quality, using Raw really isn't the best solution. Try experimenting with higher rates using MP3 or other compressions. This will probably reduce the file size.

Applying Speech Compression

The Speech compression setting is new with Flash MX (see Figure 12.11).

You again have choices for controlling the sample rate of the speech sound. These settings set the sound fidelity and file size. The lower the setting, the smaller the file size, but the sound degrades in sound quality. The higher the setting, the larger the file size, but the better the sound quality. You will need to weigh the balance between sound quality and file size for determining the best compression setting.

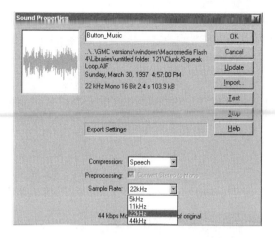

Figure 12.11   This setting is specially designed for compressing sound that is speech.

Testing Sounds

As mentioned earlier in this seminar, you can test all sounds for which you set individual compression settings by one of two methods—through the Test button in the Sound Properties dialog box or by exporting the movie to SWF format. If the sound quality is not at the caliber you need, you can adjust the compression settings to obtain the result you need for your movie.

Using a Sound Toggle Button in a Movie

If you are a Web surfer, I am sure you have visited a site that has background music that continues to play and play and play—basically annoying you and causing a quick exit from the site. You should always use a sound toggle button in any movie that has streaming background music. This button enables the visitor to turn the music off, thus giving him control over his viewing experience and keeping him at the site.

Through the use of buttons and movie clips, a sound toggle button can be implemented in a movie. To view an example of a sound toggle button, from the CD-ROM that accompanies this book, open the file `sound_example.fla` in the `Seminar12/Samples` directory. When this movie opens, there is a button on the Stage. Test the movie and notice that when the movie loads, a sound is playing. If you click the button that is now labeled Music Off, the sound stops. The button label changes to indicate that if pressed again, you can turn the music back on. Click the button again and the music begins to play again. This is a toggle button for turning the music on or off. Exit the Flash Player to return to the movie in the Flash Authoring Mode.

To understand the functionality of this sound toggle button, you need to open the music_MC movie clip symbol in the Symbol-Editing Mode. The button instance is actually a button nested inside a movie clip symbol: If you double-click the button, you drill down into the nesting order to the Push Button Green button symbol (see Figure 12.12).

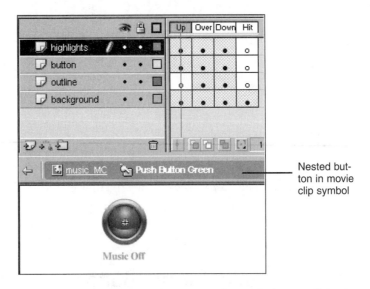

Nested button in movie clip symbol

Figure 12.12   By nesting a button instance inside a movie clip symbol, you still get button functionality but you can now work within the Timeline of the movie clip symbol.

The key to a sound toggle button is a combination of the Timeline of the movie clip symbol, the Sync settings of Start and Stop in the Property Inspector for the sound, and ActionScript.

The following workshop section of this seminar covers the actual steps for creating this functionality.

Adding Sound to the Site

This workshop covers adding both streaming and event sounds. In the Honeycomb movie, you will add a buzzing noise to Buzzy Bee when he makes his entrance onto the Stage. First, you will lay down this sound in a layer on the main movie; then you will create a sound toggle button that allows the end-user to turn this buzzing noise on and off. In Seminar 10, "Using ActionScript to Control Objects," you added three animal sounds to a button. You will also set the sound compression rate for these sounds.

Adding the Buzzing Sound to Buzzy Bee

It would be nice if Buzzy Bee could make some noise as he enters the movie. A buzzing sound can be added to the Honeycomb movie Timeline at the point where Buzzy Bee makes his entrance on the Stage. To add this sound to the movie, follow these steps:

1. Use your `Honeycomb.fla` file from Seminar 11, "Communicating with the End-User," or open `11Honeycomb.fla` from the `Seminar12/Samples/` directory. Save the file as `Honeycomb.fla` in the directory with the other Honeycomb files.

2. Click the `Guide: buzzy bee` layer and insert a new layer above it. Name the new layer `buzzing sound`.

3. Add a keyframe to Frame 74 of the `buzzing sound` layer. This is the point in the Timeline at which Buzzy Bee begins to make his entrance onto the Stage.

4. Now import the sound that will be used for the buzzing noise. Select File, Import and navigate to the CD-ROM. Import the `beebuzz.wav` file located in the `Seminar12/Samples/` directory. This sound is now a sound symbol in the movie library.

5. With the keyframe in Frame 74 of the `buzzing sound` layer selected, drag an instance of the `beebuzz.wav` sound symbol onto the Stage. The Timeline reflects the addition of this sound to the movie (see Figure 12.13).

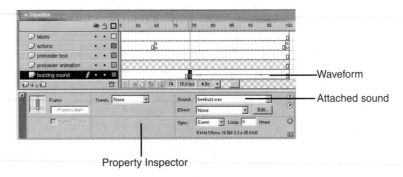

Figure 12.13   The Property Inspector also reflects the name of the sound attached to the selected keyframe.

Test your movie and notice that a buzzing noise is heard when Buzzy Bee enters the movie.

Configuring the Buzzing Sound

Adding the sound to the movie for Buzzy Bee's entrance is a nice effect, but the sound ends when the movie reaches the end of its Timeline. So, Buzzy Bee is still hovering in the lower-left corner of the Stage without any buzzing noise. Next, you will loop this sound so that it continues to play even after the movie reaches the end of the Timeline. This requires configuring the sound settings in the Property Inspector. To configure this sound instance so it plays longer than the Timeline, follow these steps:

1. In the main movie, click the keyframe in Frame 74 of the buzzing sound layer. This keyframe contains an instance of the buzzbee.wav symbol.

2. Open or access the Property Inspector.

3. Click the Sync option and select Start from the pop-up menu. This allows the sound to continue playing through its duration, even after the movie progresses to the last frame of the Timeline.

Note

Only streaming sounds will stop playing when the movie reaches the end of the Timeline.

4. To cause the sound to play longer, you can loop it. Click the Loop box, and type 10. Your Property Inspector settings should resemble Figure 12.14.

Figure 12.14   The Property Inspector also reflects the name of the sound attached to the selected keyframe.

5. Test the movie and notice that the sound plays much longer with these new sound settings. Exit the Flash Player Testing Mode.

Save your file. If you want to see a movie developed up to this point in the workshop, open `12Honeycomb01.fla` located in the `Seminar12/Samples` directory on the CD-ROM that accompanies this book.

Configuring the Sounds in the Matching Activity

In Seminar 10, you added the animation sounds to the Matching Activity. By default, these sounds were set to be event sounds, but because they are very short in duration, Event is the setting you want. They most likely can be set to compress to a smaller file size without sacrificing too much in sound quality. To set the compression for these sounds when the movie is exported, follow these steps:

1. Use the `matching.fla` file you created in Seminar 10, or open `matching.fla` from the `Seminar12/Samples/11Honeycomb/` directory. Save this file in the directory that contains your other Honeycomb files.

2. Open the library and double-click the `catcry.wav` symbol. This opens the Sound Properties dialog box (see Figure 12.15).

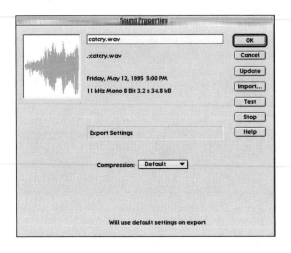

Figure 12.15   This sound was originally recorded at 11KHz mono.

3. Click the Compression option and select ADPCM from the pop-up menu (see Figure 12.16).

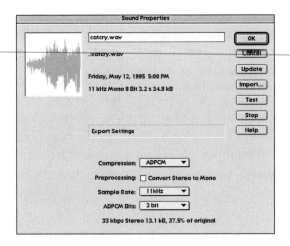

Figure 12.16   The ADPCM compression options are now displayed.

4. This sound clip was recorded in mono, so in this instance it does not matter whether the Convert Stereo to Mono option is selected. However, you always should use mono sound clips when developing for the Internet.

5. Set the Sampling Rate option to 11KHz.

6. Click the Bit Rate option and select 5 Bit.

7. Click the Test button of this dialog box to test the sound quality with these compression settings applied. There is a slight degradation in sound quality but nothing too noticeable.

8. Close the dialog box by clicking OK.

9. Repeat steps 2–8 for the dog.wav symbol and the cow.wav symbol.

10. Test the Matching Activity in the Flash Player by testing the movie. Click the Play Sound button for all three buttons, listening to the sound. Close the Flash Player and save the matching.fla movie. Close the matching.fla movie.

Creating a Sound Toggle Button

You now have the sounds added to the movie for both the main Honeycomb movie and the Matching Activity. As you have been working on the movie, you realize that the buzzing noise might be annoying to visitors of the site. So you decide to create a sound toggle button to turn the sound on and off. To create this button, follow these steps:

1. Open or access the Honeycomb.fla movie or open the 12Honeycomb01.fla file located in the Seminar12/Samples/ directory on the CD-ROM that accompanies this book. Save this file as Honeycomb.fla in your directory that contains all other Honeycomb site files.

2. To begin developing this sound toggle button, you need to start with a button symbol. To save time, you will get this symbol from another movie. Select File, Open As a Library, and open the sound_button.fla movie as a library.

3. Because the buzzing sound begins when Buzzy Bee makes his entrance in the movie, the sound toggle button needs to appear at this point in the movie's Timeline. Insert a new layer above the buzzing sound layer and name it sound toggle.

4. Click Frame 74 of this new layer and insert a keyframe.

5. From the sound_button.fla library, drag an instance of the sound button symbol onto the Stage and position it as Figure 12.17 indicates.

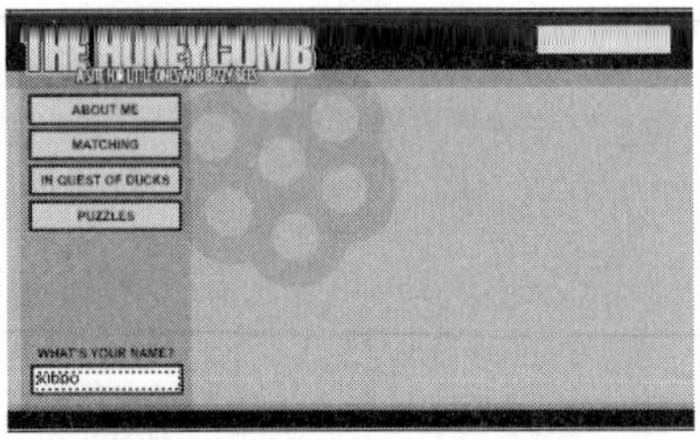

Sound toggle button

Figure 12.17   This button is easily accessible and visible in the upper-right corner of the movie.

6. Now covert the instance of the `sound_button` symbol on the Stage to a symbol by selecting Insert, Convert to Symbol. Name this new symbol `toggle_MC` and give it a Movie Clip behavior. Set a center registration point for the new movie clip symbol. This action nests the `sound_button` inside the new movie clip symbol. Because it's a movie clip symbol, you have a new Timeline independent of the main movie to work with, and because the button is nested, the movie clip will have button functionality, too.

7. Open the `toggle_MC` symbol in the Symbol-Editing Mode by double-clicking it from the library.

8. Rename `Layer 1` to `button` and insert a new layer above this layer. Name the new layer `button label`.

9. Select the Text tool from the toolbar and set the Text Type box to Static. Then, set the following text attributes: a font of Arial, a font size of 18, a font color of black, bold selected, AutoKern selected, and left justification selected. Click the Stage to set a static text block and type (in uppercase) `BUZZING OFF`.

10. Align the text block centered both horizontally and vertically to the Stage.

11. Insert a new keyframe in Frame 2 of both the layers of this movie clip by clicking Photoframe 2 of the `button label` layer and then Shift-clicking Photoframe 2 of the `button` layer and selecting Insert, Keyframe to insert a keyframe in both layers.

12. Click Frame 2 of the `button` layer and change the text block to display `BUZZING ON`. You now have the toggle button developed graphically.

13 Test the movie in the Flash Player Testing Mode. Notice that, because this
button is nested in a movie clip, the movie clip continuously plays its
Timeline, causing the button to display each of the text labels repeatedly. You
will fix this a little later in this seminar.

Next, you will attach the beebuzz.wav file to the Timeline of this movie clip.

Attaching a Sound Clip to the Sound Toggle Button

With the sound toggle button graphically designed, you can attach the sound file to
the Timeline of the movie clip symbol. Through the Property Inspector, you can set
the Sync setting to control how the sound plays for each of the two frames of the
toggle_MC symbol. Follow these steps to add sound to this symbol:

1. The toggle_MC symbol should be open in the Symbol-Editing Mode. If it's
   not, open this symbol in the Symbol-Editing Mode.

2. Insert a new layer above the button label layer and name it sound.

3. Click the keyframe in Frame 1 of the sound layer, and drag an instance of the
   beebuzz.wav symbol onto the Stage. The waveform of this symbol displays in
   the Timeline.

4. Insert a keyframe in Frame 2 of the sound layer, and this time click the Sound
   option in the Property Inspector and select the beebuzz.wav sound from the
   pop-up menu. You have added two instances of the beebuzz.wav symbol to
   the Timeline of this movie clip symbol using two different techniques.

5. Next, you need to configure the Sync settings in the Property Inspector for
   each of these two sound instances. Click the keyframe in Frame 1 of the
   sound layer and open or access the Property Inspector. Select the Sync option
   and select Start from the pop-up menu. Set the sound to loop 10 times by
   typing 10 into the Loop option box. These settings will enable the sound to
   play through 10 times.

6. Click the keyframe in Frame 2 of the sound layer and set the Sync setting to
   Stop. This causes the beebuzz.wav sound to stop playing when the movie progresses through the Timeline and encounters a Stop action in the Timeline.
   Because no ActionScript is attached to the Timeline yet, this Sync setting will
   not function as it should. Next, you will add the ActionScript for making the
   button fully functional.

Save your file. If you want to see a movie developed up to this point in the workshop, open `12Honeycomb02.fla` located in the `Seminar12/Samples` directory on the CD-ROM that accompanies this book.

Adding the ActionScript to Make the Sound Toggle Button Functional

With the sound added to the movie clip symbol, you need to add ActionScript to both of the two instances of the button on the Stage. This ActionScript will set the trigger action of the end-user and what happens next when the button is triggered. You need to add two new layers, one for labels and one for actions. Then, through ActionScript, you can call the different frame labels to cause the button to display for each button state—Buzzing Off and Buzzing On—and to turn the buzzing sound on and off. Follow these steps to make the sound toggle button functional:

1. The `toggle_MC` symbol should be open in the Symbol-Editing Mode. If it isn't, open this symbol in the Symbol-Editing Mode.

2. Click the `sound` layer and insert two new layers. Name the top layer `labels` and the second from the top layer `actions`.

3. Click the keyframe in Frame 1 of the `labels` layer. In the Property Inspector, attach a label name of `buzzing on`. Insert a keyframe in Frame 2 of the `labels` layer and attach another label name of `buzzing off`.

4. To keep the movie clip from playing through its Timeline, you must add two `stop` actions to both Frame 1 and Frame 2. Click the keyframe in Frame 1 of the `actions` layer and attach the `stop` action to this frame (see Figure 12.18).

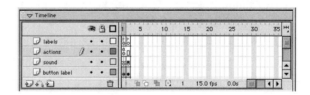

Figure 12.18   The Stop action in Frame 1 of the `actions` layer keeps the movie clip from advancing to Frame 2, allowing the end-user to click the sound toggle button on the Stage.

5. Now insert another keyframe in Frame 2 of the `actions` layer and again attach a `stop` action.

6. Next, you need to add the ActionScript for triggering the button. Drag the playhead to Frame 1 and click the instance of the button symbol on the Stage. Make sure you do not select the text block of the button label layer.

7. In the Actions panel, attach the script to this button instance, as shown in Figure 12.19.

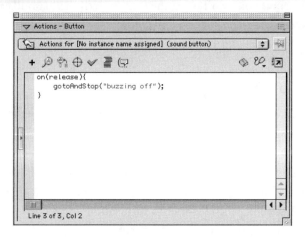

Figure 12.19 This script causes the button, when clicked, to advance to the frame labeled buzzing off.

8. Attach the ActionScript to turn the music back on. Drag the playhead to Frame 2 and again select the button object on the Stage. Attach the script as shown in Figure 12.20.

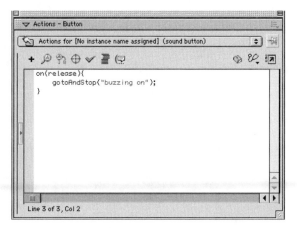

Figure 12.20 This script causes the button to loop back to Frame 1, which is labeled buzzing on.

9. With the sound toggle button now complete with graphics, sound, and ActionScript, you no longer need the buzzing sound layer in the main movie Timeline. Exit the Symbol-Editing Mode and delete the buzzing sound layer by selecting the layer and clicking the Delete Layer icon.

10. Test the movie and try the sound toggle button. You should be able to toggle the buzzing noise on or off using the button. Exit the Flash Player and save the Honeycomb.fla file.

Seminar Summary

This seminar covered adding and using sound in a Flash MX movie. You should feel comfortable adding sound to your movies when you develop in Flash. You also learned how to customize the compression settings for individual sounds in a movie. You will learn how to globally set the compression settings for both streaming and event sounds in Seminar 16. Hopefully, you can see the benefit of adding a sound toggle button for enabling the end-user to turn sound on and off. You will use this type of sound functionality in future movies that you develop.

The next seminar covers more advanced animation and interactivity effects. You will learn how to use a mask for showing only certain objects on your Stage. You also will create a drop-down menu for the Slider button. You'll also get more coverage on ActionScript when you make Buzzy Bee's eyes blink randomly throughout the movie.

Seminar 13

Enhancing the Site Interface and Interactivity

In this chapter

Workshop: Enhancing the Site with Masks, Drop-Down Menus, and Random Animation

Creating Drop-Down Menus Graphically

As you saw in Seminar 8, "Using Components in a Macromedia Flash Form," you can create a drop-down menu in Macromedia Flash MX using two new components—ListBox and ComboBox. These components both create a version of a drop-down menu, but they both are limited in their appearances and therefore might be difficult to integrate in a movie. Many times in Flash development, you'll want to have a custom drop-down menu that integrates with the site design for offering other menu choices. This can be accomplished through the use of buttons, movie clips, ActionScript, and transparent buttons. You will create a drop-down menu in the workshop section of this seminar.

The key to graphically creating a drop-down menu is to nest an instance of a button or buttons inside a movie clip symbol that will be used for the drop-down menu. The buttons are the menu choices of the drop-down menu. You can then simulate the illusion of a menu dropping down and rolling up through the use of motion tweens. Because you used buttons for the menu choices, you can assign ActionScript to them.

To see an example of a drop-down menu, open the dropdown.fla file that is located in the Seminar13/Samples directory on the CD-ROM that accompanies this book. Test this movie in the Flash Player Testing Mode and notice that when you hover your mouse over the Basic Menu Commands menu on the Stage, the drop-down menu displays. When you move outside this drop-down menu, the menu rolls up. To understand this movie, you need to look at the symbols used, the Timeline structure, and the ActionScript of this movie.

Creating the Illusion of the Drop-Down Menu Motion

In the library of the dropdown.fla file, you'll find all the symbols used to create this drop-down menu. The Menu symbol contains the three menu choices of the drop-down menu. Each of these menu choices is a button symbol and is nested in the Menu symbol.

If you examine the Timeline of the dropdown.fla movie, you'll see that there are two motion tweens, one that starts at Frame 2 of the Menu layer and another at Frame 18 (see Figure 13.1).

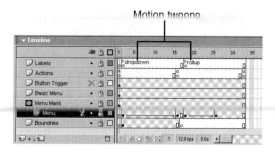

Figure 13.1   These two motion tweens make up the animation for the menu dropping down and rolling up.

The motion tween that occurs in Frame 2 to Frame 15 is the animation for the menu dropping down. Notice that Frame 2 is also labeled dropdown in the Labels layer. The second motion tween occurs in Frame 18 to Frame 33. This is the animation for the menu rolling up. There are fewer frames for this motion tween, so the menu rolling up occurs more quickly than the menu dropping down. Notice that Frame 18 is labeled rollup in the Labels layer.

Understanding the ActionScript for the Drop-Down Menu Functionality

The functionality of the drop-down menu is created through transparent buttons, ActionScript, and labels. Frame 1 of the Basic Menu layer holds the Basic Menu Commands menu under which the drop-down menu displays. This is a movie clip symbol. The layer above this holds a transparent button that covers the same area as the Basic Menu Commands menu. Because this transparent button is a button symbol, you can attach ActionScript to it that tells Flash what to do when it is triggered. Frame 1 of the Actions layer has a stop action attached. This causes the movie to stop at Frame 1 and wait for end-user interaction to trigger it to begin to play again.

The script attached to the transparent button uses the on action with a rollover event handler and directs Flash to go to and play the Frame labeled dropdown, which is also Frame 2 (see Figure 13.2).

Figure 13.2   Frame 2 is where the drop-down menu animation begins.

Because the `gotoAndPlay` action is used, Flash is directed to the Frame labeled `dropdown` and begins to play through the Timeline at this point. Notice that a `stop` action is attached to Frame 15. This is where the motion tween for the drop-down menu ends. The movie again stops at this point, allowing the end-user a chance to view the new drop-down menu choices and make her selection.

To complete the animation of the menu rolling up, another transparent button is used. You'll find this transparent button on the `Button Trigger` layer. This button is sized larger than the drop-down menu object and, in essence, creates an invisible hot spot area around the drop-down menu.

The script attached to the transparent button completes the animation for the drop-down menu (see Figure 13.3).

Figure 13.3   By using the `rollOver` and `dragOver` event handlers, you cover your bases for the two mousing events the end-user could perform when exiting this drop-down menu.

This script directs Flash to go to and play the frame labeled rollup, which is where the animation for the menu rolling up begins. When the playhead reaches Frame 33, one more script is attached to the Timeline. This script directs Flash to return to Frame 1 and stop. Therefore, only the Basic Menu Commands menu exists on the Stage. This completes the functionality of the drop-down menu.

But, one more piece is required to create the illusion of the menu dropping down and rolling up into the Basic Menu Commands menu. A mask is used to set only a specific area for any of the objects on the Menu layer to show. Without this mask, the drop-down menu would also display above the Basic Menu Commands object.

Using Masks

Masks are used often in Flash development because they are a powerful feature for creating the illusions and special effects you want for your movie. Typical of a mask in other graphics applications such as Photoshop, masks in Flash are used to designate an area that will allow other Stage content to be visible. For instance, if you wanted a spotlight to move around a picture showing only the area of the picture in the spotlight, you would need a masking in a circular shape. This masking shape determines the area that will display on the picture.

To create a mask, you start with a special layer called a *mask layer*. This mask layer is always linked or attached to at least one layer—the *masked layer*. In the dropdown.fla movie, the Menu Mask is a mask layer and is set to mask the Menu layer—the masked layer (see Figure 13.4).

The Show Masking feature is automatically enabled when a mask is applied in Flash. This enables you to see the effect of the mask on the masked or linked layer(s). To see the masking object on the mask layer, toggle the Show Masking feature off. To toggle Show Masking on or off, simply click the lock icon in the Lock/Unlock All Layers column of the mask layer. In the dropdown.fla movie, the Menu Mask layer holds the masking shape, which is a rectangular shape that covers the area directly underneath the Basic Menu Commands menu (see Figure 13.5).

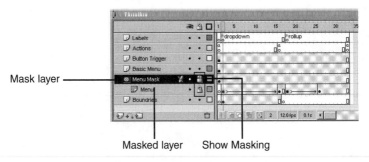

Mask layer ──────

Masked layer   Show Masking

Figure 13.4   When both the Mask and the Masked layers are locked, the show masking feature is enabled in the Flash Authoring mode.

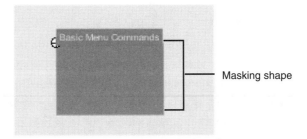

Masking shape

Figure 13.5   The rectangular masking shape determines the area for the linked masked layer that will be visible.

Because the rectangular masking shape is below the menu, the animation of the menu dropping down appears to drop out of the Basic Menu Commands object. Neat trick! You will create a mask in the workshop of this seminar.

> **Tip**
>
> The masking shape can be made up of any fill or stroke because it will never really be visible in the movie; it is strictly a shape for determining an area. Many developers use a fill for the masking shape that really stands out from their site design. This enables them to quickly identify the masking shape when developing the movie.

> **Tip**
>
> You can mask multiple layers by positioning these layers under the mask layer. If you position a layer between the mask layer and the linked masked layer, it automatically becomes a linked masked layer. If, on the other hand, you position the layer below the masked layer, you must convert it to a masked layer through the Layers Property dialog box. Select Modify, Layers to display this dialog box, and then select the Masked option.

The Built-In Math Object

The Math object is a built-in object of Flash that can be used to access and manipulate mathematical functions and constants. As discussed earlier in this book, Flash has many objects. You have been working with the Movie Clip object for much of the interactivity of The Honeycomb site in the workshop of this book. Another object of Flash is the Math object. In Flash, an object can have actions or methods assigned to it, and the Math object is no different. You submit a value to the method, and it returns a result based on that method.

More than 15 actions are attached to the Math object. Table 13.1 describes each of these actions for the Math object.

Table 13.1 Description of Math Object Actions

Panel	Syntax	Description of Actions
Math.abs	Math.abs(x)	By using a number for the parameter represented by x, this action calculates the absolute value of that number.
Math.acos	Math.acos(x)	By using a number from −1.0 to 1.0 for the parameter represented by x, this action calculates and returns the arc cosine of that number.
Math.asin	Math.asin(x)	By using a number from −1.0 to 1.0 for the parameter represented by x, this action calculates and returns the arc sine of that number.
Math.atan	Math.atan(x)	By using a number for the parameter represented by x, this action calculates and returns the arc tangent of that number. The return value is always between positive pi divided by 2 and negative pi divided by 2.
Math.atan2	Math.atan2(x, y)	This method requires a parameter for both the x and y coordinates. The x parameter represents the adjacent side length of a right triangle, and the y parameter is the opposite side length of the right triangle. This action calculates and returns the arc tangent of y/x radians. The return value basically is the angle opposite the opposite angle of the right triangle.

continues

Table 13.1   Continued

Panel	Syntax	Description of Actions
Math.ceil	Math.ceil(x)	By using a number for the parameter represented by x, this action calculates the ceiling of that number; it rounds a number up to the closest integer.
Math.cos	Math.cos(x)	By using a number for the parameter represented by x, with the number being an angle measured in radians, this action calculates the cosine of the angle for that number.
Math.exp	Math.exp(x)	By using a parameter for x that is either a number or an expression, this action calculates and returns a value of the base of the natural logarithm(s) to the power of the exponent of that parameter.
Math.floor	Math.floor(x)	By using a number or expression for the parameter represented by x, this action calculates the value of that number that is the floor of the number. The floor is the closest integer that is less than or equal to the specified number or expression. In other words, it rounds down the specified parameter.
Math.log	Math.log(x)	By using a number or expression that is greater than 0 for the parameter represented by x, this action calculates and returns the natural logarithm for the parameter.
Math.max	Math.max(x, y)	By using a number or an expression for both parameters represented by x and y, this action determines the larger of the two values.
Math.min	Math.min(x, y)	By using a number or an expression for both parameters represented by x and y, this action determines the lesser of the two values.

Panel	Syntax	Description of Actions
Math.pow	Math.pow(x, y)	This method requires a parameter for both the x and y coordinates. The x parameter represents a number to be raised to a power, and the y parameter represents the number specifying the power. This action calculates and returns a value of x to the power of y.
Math.random	Math.random()	No parameters are required for this action. This method returns a value between 0.0 and 1.0.
Math.round	Math.round(x)	By using a number for the parameter represented by x, this action rounds the value of the parameter to the nearest integer, either rounding up or rounding down.
Math.sin	Math.sin(x)	By using a number for the parameter represented by x, with the number being an angle measured in radians, this action calculates the sine of the angle for that number.
Math.sqrt	Math.sqrt(x)	By using a number or an expression that is greater than 0 for the parameter represented by x, this action calculates and returns the square root for that number.
Math.tan	Math.tan(x)	By using a number for the parameter represented by x, with the number being an angle measured in radians, this action calculates the tangent of the angle for that number.

The Math object can be quite powerful and complex or very simple and straightforward—regardless, it's often useful. You might be thinking that some of the Math object actions are a little scary, but they all have their place in ActionScript depending on the result you want. The workshop of this seminar focuses on the Math.floor and Math.random actions.

Math.floor();

This action rounds a specified number to the nearest whole integer that is less than the value specified. Look at the following examples of a value calculated by the Math.floor action:

```
Math.floor(6.2) = 6;
Math.floor(6.9) = 6;
```

This action is useful for staying on the safe side. If you are dealing with a value in which you would rather have too little than too much, you would fire that value through the floor method of the Math object. A good example of this is if you were using a preloader and wanted to return the percent loaded. You would always want to round down, not up, for determining this percentage.

Math.random();

This action is simple and straightforward and can allow you to create some pretty cool effects.

The Math.random action has no arguments; it merely generates a pseudo random number between 0 and 1. Look at the following example:

```
randomNumber = Math.random();
```

This line of code could leave you with randomNumber equaling .02, .134567, or .00000002.

You're probably thinking that because the Math.random action is limited to numbers between 0 and 1, that it might not be so cool after all. You're right—the Math.random action by itself is pretty limited, but there is a way to be more specific about the values and scope of the values you randomly generate. If you wanted to generate a random number between 0 and 10, you would do the following:

```
randomNumber = Math.random() * 10;
```

Now, you might expect a result like 9.3, .12, or 5.33378.

You will use this action in the workshop of this seminar to specify a number between 1 and 100. The generate value simulates a random number and is used to designate a period of time for making Buzzy Bee's eyes blink.

Enhancing the Site with Masks, Drop-Down Menus, and Random Animation

In this workshop, you will create a drop-down menu graphically as well as make Buzzy Bee's eyes blink at random intervals. The drop-down menu requires the use of motion tweening to create the menu dropping down and rolling up, as well as a mask to create the illusion of the menu appearing as if it were rolling out of the Puzzle button. Making Buzzy Bee's eyes blink randomly requires the use of frame-by-frame animation and the Math object actions of random() and floor(). First, you'll create the drop-down menu.

Creating the Drop-Down Menu Symbol

To begin to create this new functionality for the Puzzle button, you need to create a symbol that will be the Puzzle button drop-down menu. This will be the menu that displays when the end-user hovers his mouse over the Puzzle button. This menu will link to just one movie, the Slider Puzzle.

> **Note**
>
> This workshop covers the use of only one menu choice in the drop-down menu, but you can easily modify the following instructions to include as many menu choices as you need for a drop-down menu.

To create the symbol for the Puzzle button drop-down menu, follow these steps:

1. Use your Honeycomb.fla file from Seminar 12, "Adding Sound to Enhance a Site," or open 12Honeycomb.fla from the Seminar13/Samples/ directory. Save this as Honeycomb.fla in the directory in which you are saving all the files for The Honeycomb Web site.

2. Create a new symbol and name it dropdown. Give it a Movie Clip behavior. This new symbol opens in the Symbol-Editing Mode.

3. Rename Layer 1 to slider button.

4. Now you will add a button to be used as the sole menu choice for the drop-down menu. You'll borrow this button from another movie. Select File, Open As a Library and open the puzzles.fla file in the Seminar13/Samples/ directory on the CD-ROM that accompanies this book.

5. On the **slider button** layer, drag an instance of the **slider button** symbol from the `puzzles.fla` library onto the Stage. Center this instance on the Stage. Then, close the `puzzles.fla` library by (Control-clicking)[right-clicking] the title bar of its Library panel and selecting Close Panel from the shortcut menu.

Note ──

When you placed an instance of the **slider button** on the Stage, Flash automatically added this symbol and any other symbol that was used to create the **slider button** symbol to the Honeycomb movie library. You might want to organize your library by placing all the new menu symbols you just added to the movie into the **menu bar** folder.

Converting the Puzzle's Activity Button to a Movie Clip

The Puzzle button of The Honeycomb site will be used to link to many puzzles; therefore, you should use a drop-down menu to display these puzzles choices. To create a drop-down menu, you must first convert the `puzzles button` symbol and the instance on the Stage into a movie clip symbol. To do this, follow these steps:

1. To begin creating a drop-down menu with the `puzzles button` symbol, it needs to have a different behavior. Open the library and select the `puzzles button` in the `menu bar` folder. Click the Properties button in the lower-left corner of the Library panel to open the Symbol Properties dialog box. Change the behavior to Movie Clip, and click OK to set this behavior.

2. Open the `menu` symbol in the Symbol-Editing Mode. Select the instance of the `puzzles button` symbol on the Stage. Then, open the Actions panel and select all the script in the Scripting pane. Cut this script from the panel by (Control-clicking)[right-clicking] the highlighted text and selecting Cut from the shortcut menu. This is the script that communicates the button activity. This script needs to be attached to the instance of the slider button that displays as the drop-down menu displays.

3. Next, you will move the script from the `puzzles button` instance to the `slider button` instance. Open the `dropdown` symbol in the Symbol-Editing Mode. Click the instance of the `slider button` on the Stage, and in the Actions panel, paste the previously cut script into the Scripting pane by (Control-clicking)[right-clicking] the Scripting pane and selecting Paste from the shortcut menu.

4. Now change the behavior of the instance of the `puzzles button` symbol that is nested inside the `menu` symbol. Open the `menu` symbol in the Symbol-Editing Mode. Click the `puzzles button` instance on the Stage, and through the Property Inspector, change the Behavior to Movie Clip by clicking the Symbol Behavior option and selecting Movie Clip from the pop-up menu (see Figure 13.6).

Figure 13.6   When you change the behavior of an instance, you don't affect the behavior of the linked symbol.

Tip

When you change the behavior of a symbol you have already used to create instances on the Stage, the already created instances will not reflect the new symbol behavior. You must change these instance behaviors to the new behavior if you want them to reflect the new behavior and functionality of the modified symbol.

Note

When you change the behavior of an instance on the Stage, any script attached to that instance is deleted.

5. Double-click the instance of the `puzzles button` symbol in the `menu` symbol to open it in the Symbol-Editing Mode. Instead of button states, the symbol now has its own Timeline because its new behavior is Movie Clip (see Figure 13.7).

Figure 13.7   Notice that the layers you previously set up for the `puzzles button` symbol are still represented in the new Timeline. The button states are now represented as keyframes.

Save your file. If you want to see a movie developed up to this point in the workshop, open `13Honeycomb01.fla` which is located in the `Seminar13/Samples` directory on the CD-ROM that accompanies this book.

Creating the Drop Down Menu Animation

You have converted the `puzzles button` instance to have a Movie Clip behavior retaining all the graphics, keyframes, and layers that were used for the original `puzzles button` symbol. Because this symbol is now a movie clip, you can create movement, transitions, and animation that would not be possible with a Button symbol.

The functionality you need to simulate for the new Puzzle activity button is a drop-down menu. This menu is triggered to drop down whenever the end-user hovers her mouse over the button. You also need to create the illusion of the drop-down menu rolling up into the Puzzle button when the end-user ends her interaction with the button. This rolling up of the menu will be faster in the movement than the dropping down of the menu. To do this, follow these steps:

1. If the `puzzles button` symbol is not opened in the Symbol-Editing Mode, open the `menu` symbol in the Symbol-Editing Mode; then double-click the instance of the `puzzles button` symbol to open this symbol in the Symbol-Editing Mode.

2. Create a new layer above the `button label` layer and name this layer `hit area`. This layer will simulate the Hit state of a button. To do this, you use a transparent button on this layer and size the button to be the hot spot area.

3. With the `hit area` layer active, drag an instance of the `transparent button` symbol on the Stage. Position and resize the instance so that it covers the Puzzle activity button image on the Stage. Zoom in so that you can precisely size and position this instance.

4. Add two new layers above the `hit area` layer. Name the top layer `labels` and the other new layer below it `actions`.

5. Click the `actions` layer and add a `stop` action to the blank keyframe in Frame 1. This causes the movie to stop at Frame 1 of this movie clip symbol, allowing the end-user time to click the Puzzle button.

6. In the `labels` layer, insert a keyframe in Photoframe 2. Through the Property Inspector, attach a label of `over` to the keyframe. Insert another keyframe in Photoframe 17 of the `labels` layer. Then, attach another label of `out` to this keyframe. These are the two areas of the Timeline that hold the motion for the drop-down menu.

7. Add a new layer and drag it to the bottom of the layer stacking order. Name this layer `dropdown menu`.

8 Extend the Timeline out to Frame 20 for all layers by selecting Frame 20 in all the layers and inserting a Frame (F5).

9. Insert a keyframe in Frame 2 of the dropdown menu layer and drag an instance of the dropdown symbol onto the Stage. Position this instance as Figure 13.8 indicates. Use the Align panel to center the dropdown instance vertically to the Stage.

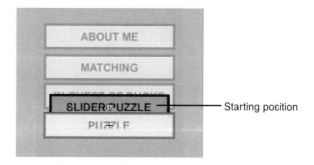

Figure 13.8   This will be the starting position of the drop-down menu.

10. In the dropdown menu layer, click Photoframe 15 and insert a keyframe. Position the instance of the dropdown symbol under the Puzzle button so that its top edge is flush with the Puzzle button's bottom edge (see Figure 13.9). Use the Align panel to center the dropdown instance vertically to the Stage.

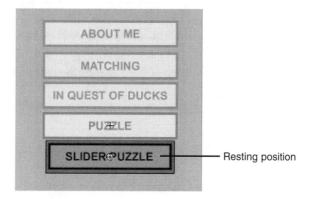

Figure 13.9   This will be the resting position of the drop-down menu when it drops down.

Warning

Be sure you do not have any space between the drop-down menu and the Puzzle button. A space will cause the drop-down menu to behave sporadically or not at all due to a transparent button that needs to be added in the next topic of this workshop, "Making the Drop-Down Menu Interactive." The transparent button will cause the menu to roll up when the end-user moves her mouse into the button area.

11. (Control-click)[Right-click] any frame between the two keyframes in the `dropdown menu` layer and select Create Motion Tween from the shortcut menu. This motion tween creates the movement of the menu dropping down.

12. To create the movement of the menu rolling up, click Frame 17 in the `dropdown menu` layer and insert a keyframe. Click Frame 20 and insert another keyframe. With the new keyframe in Frame 20 active, position the instance of the `dropdown` symbol above the Puzzle button as Figure 13.10 indicates. Center the instance vertically to the Stage.

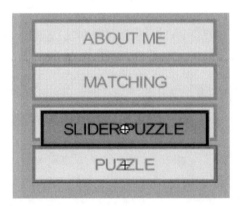

Figure 13.10   This is the resting position of the drop-down menu when it rolls up.

13. Create a motion tween between the keyframes in Frames 17 and 20 of the `dropdown menu` layer. This is the animation for the menu rolling up. Because fewer frames are used between the two keyframes, the rolling up of the menu is much faster than the dropping down of the menu.

14. Test the animation by scrubbing through the Timeline. You should see the menu dropping down and rolling up.

Save your file. If you want to see a movie developed up to this point in the work-shop, open `13Honeycomb02.fla` located in the `Seminar13/Samples` directory on the CD-ROM that accompanies this book.

Making the Drop-Down Menu Interactive

Now you need to make the drop-down menu display whenever the end-user hovers his mouse over the Puzzle button. You also need to make the menu roll up when-ever the end-user rolls off or drags off the Puzzle button. You will create a transparent button and attach ActionScript to the button to handle both interactions. To do this, follow these steps:

1. You should have the `puzzles button` symbol still open in the Symbol-Editing Mode; if you don't, open the `menu` symbol and then double-click the `puzzles button` instance to open this nested symbol in the Symbol-Editing Mode.

2. Click the `hit area` layer and click the transparent button on the Stage. Open the Actions panel and add the following script to direct Flash to go to and play the frame labeled `over`, which is where the drop-down menu animation is located in the movie clip Timeline:

   ```
   on(rollOver){
       gotoAndPlay ("over");
   }
   ```

3. Insert a keyframe in Frame 15 of the `actions` layer and add the `stop` action to this keyframe. This stops the movie at Frame 15 and enables the end-user to select a menu choice on the drop-down menu.

4. Test the movie in the Flash Player Testing Mode. Hover your mouse over the Puzzle activity button; you should see the drop-down menu display. Notice that the menu stays visible and does not roll up when you move your mouse outside the drop-down menu. You'll create the ActionScript for this next.

5. Insert a new layer and name it `rollover area`. Move it to the bottom of the stacking order.

6. Insert a keyframe in Frame 2 of the `rollover area` layer. Drag an instance of the transparent button onto the Stage.

7. In the Property Inspector, resize the `transparent button` instance to the fol-lowing dimensions: a width of 450 and a height of 450. Position the button so that it covers the area of the menu and most of the Stage (see Figure 13.11).

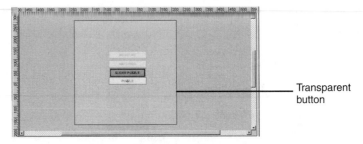

Transparent
button

Figure 13.11   Because this layer is positioned below all the other layers, when the mouse rolls into the area of the transparent button, any script applied to the button is triggered.

8. With the instance of the `transparent button` active on the `rollover` layer, open the Actions panel and attach the following script:

```
on(rollOver, dragOver){
    gotoAndPlay("out");
}
```

9. Exit the Symbol-Editing Mode and test your movie. In the Flash Player Testing Mode, hover your mouse over the Puzzle button; you should see a drop-down menu display. If you move the mouse outside the Puzzle button or the drop-down menu, the menu rolls back up. It's working! But there is one problem—the drop-down menu is visible above the Puzzle button in both its starting and ending positions. You'll fix that next with a mask.

Save your file. If you want to see a movie developed up to this point in the workshop, open `13Honeycomb03.fla` located in the `Seminar13/Samples` directory on the CD-ROM that accompanies this book.

Creating the Mask for the Puzzle Button

A mask is needed to help finish the drop-down menu animation. You will create a new mask layer and link the `dropdown menu` layer. Typically, you would use multiple menu choices for a drop-down menu, so a mask is even more essential. A mask in Flash sets the area that will display for the masked layer. Any other Stage content that is positioned outside the masking object will not display. You want the menu to appear to be dropping down from the Puzzle button, so you need to mask this layer and position a masking object below the button. To do this, follow these steps:

1. Open the menu symbol in the Symbol-Editing Mode. Double-click the instance of the `puzzles` `button` nested in the `menu` symbol to access this symbol in the Symbol-Editing Mode.

2. Click the `dropdown` `menu` layer to make it active and insert a new layer above it. Name the layer `dropdown` `mask`.

3. (Control-click)[right-click] the `dropdown` `mask` layer and select Mask from the shortcut menu. This converts the layer into a mask layer and links the `drop-down` `menu` layer to it as a masked layer (see Figure 13.12).

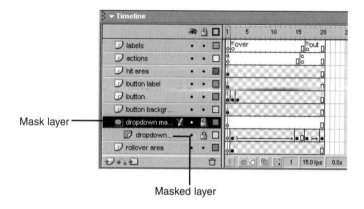

Figure 13.12   Your Timeline for the `puzzles` `button` symbol should resemble this.

4. Unlock the `dropdown` `mask` layer and click Photoframe 2. Insert a keyframe, and then drag an instance of the `square` symbol onto the Stage. This is the masking shape.

5. Resize the `square` instance so that it covers the area below the Puzzle button about the same size as the drop-down menu (see Figure 13.13).

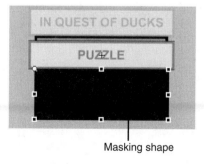

Masking shape

Figure 13.13   The masking shape sets the area that determines what will be visible in the linked masked layer.

6. Lock both the dropdown_mask and dropdown_menu layers and drag the playhead through the Timeline. You'll see the menu display only below the Puzzle button.

7. Exit the Symbol-Editing Mode and test your movie again.

Save your file. If you want to see a movie developed up to this point in the work-shop, open 13Honeycomb04.fla located in the Seminar13/Samples directory on the CD-ROM that accompanies this book.

Creating the Button States for the Puzzle Button

It would be nice if the Puzzle button could gradually highlight when it is selected to allow the menu to display below it as it highlights. You can create this highlight through the Timeline of the puzzles button symbol. To do this, follow these steps:

1. Open the puzzles button symbol in the Symbol-Editing Mode.

2. Hide the hit area layer.

3. Click the button layer to make it active and click the keyframe in Frame 2.

4. Click the button instance on the Stage for the keyframe in Frame 2 of the button BG layer. Apply a Tint effect of white. The button first will quickly display white and slowly fade to a light yellow color as the drop-down menu displays.

5. Drag the keyframe in Frame 3 to Frame 15. Click the button instance on the Stage for the keyframe in Frame 15 and apply a Tint effect with the hexadeci-mal value of #FFFF99 to the button instance.

6. Click in Frame 17 of the button layer and insert another keyframe. This copies the previous keyframe Stage content to this keyframe.

7. Click Frame 20 and insert another keyframe. Click the button instance on the Stage and apply a Tint effect with a hexadecimal value of #FFCE31 to the button instance.

8. Now create motion tweens between Keyframe 2 and 15, and between Keyframes 17 and 20 in the button layer.

9. Exit the Symbol-Editing Mode and test the movie. Trigger the Puzzle button and notice that the button quickly highlights white and then slowly changes to a light yellow as the drop-down menu displays. When the mouse moves off the button, notice that it changes back to its original color as the drop-down menu rolls back into the Puzzle button. Click the Slider button, and the puzzle.swf movie loads into The Honeycomb movie.

Save your file. If you want to see a movie developed up to this point in the workshop, open 13Honeycomb05.fla located in the Seminar13/Samples directory on the CD-ROM that accompanies this book.

Creating the Animation for the Eyes Blinking

To make Buzzy Bee's eyes blink at a random interval, you need to use the Math object with the random method. This action sets a random number between 0.0 and 1.0. You also must use the Math.floor action to round the number to the smallest integer and then multiply it by 100 so that you get a number between 1 and 100. To make the eyes blink, you will also need another movie clip symbol for Buzzy Bee's eyes blinking. To create this functionality, follow these steps:

1. First, you must get the symbol for the bee character's eyes being shut. Select File, Open As Library and open the eyes.fla file as a library from the Seminar13/Samples directory located on the CD-ROM that accompanies this book.

2. Drag the eyes shut symbol into the buzzy bee symbol folder in the Honeycomb.fla Library panel. This places the symbol and any other symbols that create the eyes shut symbol in buzzy bee symbol folder. Close the eyes.fla Library panel by (Control-clicking)[right-clicking] the title bar and selecting Close Panel from the shortcut menu.

3. Open the buzzy bee movie clip symbol in the Symbol-Editing Mode. This symbol is nested inside the buzzy_MC movie clip symbol that is used on the Stage of the movie. You will develop this symbol, and all the new functionality will also be present in the buzzy_MC movie clip because it is nested in this symbol.

4. Insert a new layer above the buzzy layer. Name the new layer eyes.

5. Insert two more layers above the eyes layer and name the very top layer labels, and name the layer below the labels layer actions.

6. Now extend the Timeline for all layers so that it extends out to Frame 7 for all layers by selecting Frame 7 for all layers and inserting a frame (F5).

7. Select Photoframe 2 in the eyes layer and insert a keyframe. Drag an instance of the eyes shut symbol onto the Stage and position it as Figure 13.14 indicates.

Figure 13.14   The eyes opening and closing uses frame-by-frame animation—just as it was used to make the wings flap.

8. Drag the playhead between Frames 1 and 2 to test the movie clip. The eyes appear to blink.

9. To cause the movie clip to stop at Frame 1 so that a trigger can be set to advance this movie clip Timeline to Frame 2, in the actions layer attach a stop action to Frame 1.

10. Now create a label for Frame 2 that can be called when the movie clip is triggered, causing the eyes to blink. Click Frame 2 of the label layer and insert a keyframe. In the Property Inspector, create a label of blink for this new keyframe.

11. Exit the Symbol-Editing Mode and return to the movie.

Creating the Trigger for Randomly Blinking the Eyes

To create a trigger for the bee's eyes to randomly blink, you will use the onClipEvent action with the enterFrame event handler. By attaching this to an instance of the buzzy movie clip symbol on the Stage, you can cause the script to repeatedly execute due to the enterFrame event handler. The enterFrame event handler repeatedly executes every time the playhead enters a frame. Because of the nature of a movie clip symbol, which continuously loops unless directed to stop, you can cause the script attached to the instance of the buzzy movie clip symbol to continuously execute. Then, using the Math object with the floor and random actions, you generate a random number that is then assigned to a variable. The variable is compared to the number 50; if the variable matches this number, you direct Flash to play the frame labeled blink. To create this functionality, follow these steps:

1. Open the buzzy_MC movie clip symbol in the Symbol-Editing Mode.

2. Click the instance of the buzzy movie clip on the Stage and open or access the Actions panel.

3. Start the script with a comment explaining what the attached script does Type the following script:

```
//execute this script continuously to generate a random number
```

4. Next, you generate a random number between 1 and 100. You'll assign this number to a variable named randomNumber. Create a new line of script and type the following script:

```
onClipEvent(enterFrame){
    randomNumber = Math.floor(Math.random()*100);
```

5. Now create another comment explaining the next line of script. Create a new line of script and type the following comment:

```
//if randomNumber equals 50, then make buzzy blink his eyes once
```

6. To create this functionality of making Buzzy blink his eyes, you need to use an if statement. You will compare the randomNumber variable with the number 50. If the randomNumber variable equals 50, you will direct Flash to play the frame labeled blink. Create a new line of script and type the following script:

```
if(randomNumber == 50){
    gotoAndPlay("blink");
}
```

7. Close the open curly bracket of the onClipEvent action that you created first by creating another new line of script and typing a second closing curly bracket (}). The Scripting pane of the Actions panel should resemble Figure 13.15.

Figure 13.15   If the if statement returns a false value, this script continues to execute repeatedly until the randomNumber variable equals 50. Then, the gotoAndPlay action is initiated.

8. Exit the Symbol-Editing Mode and test your movie. You should see Buzzy Bee's eyes blink at random intervals. The script is working.

9. Save the movie as `Honeycomb.fla`. If you would like to compare your Honeycomb site with a movie that is completed up to this point in the book, open the `13Honeycomb.fla` file located in the `Seminar13/Samples` directory on the CD-ROM that accompanies this book.

Seminar Summary

This seminar covered the technique of nesting a button in a movie clip symbol. This provides new functionality that you can't attain with just a button. Because the movie clip has its own Timeline, you can create almost any animation or effect that you can think up. In the workshop of this seminar, you learned how to create a drop-down menu. You will most likely use drop-down menus in other Flash movies that you develop. Just to point out one more time, the movie clip symbol is a very powerful and versatile object in Flash MX.

This seminar also covered the `Math` object and many of the actions that can be performed by it. You learned how to use the `Math.random` object to generate a random number. Then, you used the `Math.floor` object to round this number to an integer. These are common uses for the `Math` object, and you will use both of these new actions, as well as other `Math` objects, in your Flash development.

The next seminar covers dynamic ActionScript for controlling Stage content and creating movement. It also covers ActionScript-based movement. You will take another leap forward in your Flash development from the information in the following seminar. In the workshop of Seminar 14, "Dynamic ActionScript for Controlling Stage Content and Movement," you will create the Slider puzzle for the puzzles activity of The Honeycomb site.

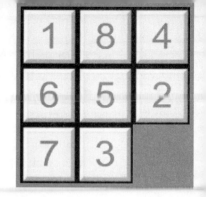

Seminar 14

Dynamic ActionScript for Controlling Stage Content and Movement

In this chapter

Creating ActionScript-Based Movement

Until now, you have used shape tweening, motion tweening, and frame-by-frame animation to animate your graphics in Macromedia Flash MX. These are all quite acceptable ways to animate, but you can also use ActionScript to create animation. This fourth technique enables you to create movement through a very powerful and dynamic approach called ActionScript-based animation. Using the various properties of movie clips—x position, y position, height, width, alpha, and so on, you can animate your movie clips by using math to vary the values of these properties over time.

You might be thinking that this is too complex and you'll never use it, but it's not as scary as it might sound. After you get a good handle on how to exploit the powers of ActionScript-based movement, you will begin thinking and developing in ways you never dreamed.

This seminar covers ActionScript-based movement and is probably the most challenging seminar in the book. Relax, work through the seminar and workshop, and then give yourself some time to assimilate the information in this seminar.

Differences Between ActionScript-Based Movement and Tweening

The theory behind tweening is that you have a symbol and you define a starting point and an ending point—a point "A" and a point "B." After assigning the starting and ending points, you assign a tween to the frames in the Timeline between your starting and ending objects. Flash then fills in the gaps and places appearances, not instances, of the tweened object at various points between the starting and ending points. When the movie is played, it appears as though the object is moving.

Although this might seem very slick and useful, it can also be quite limiting. For example, if you have given the user the control to move an object anywhere he wants on the screen, you do not have a set starting point because it can be different for each end-user. This can be a problem if you later want that object to move from its current location, wherever that might be, to a predefined x, y location.

Sound impossible? Well, with tweening it is, but with ActionScript, you can accomplish this task quite easily. ActionScript enables you to ask yourself a few questions about the movie clip:

- Where is it now?
- Where do you want it to be?
- How fast do you want it to get there?

By writing as little as one line of looping ActionScript, you can create a loop that will take a movie clip object and move it anywhere you want, from wherever it is currently positioned. To accomplish this, you can use the `onClipEvent(enterFrame)` action. This action causes the wrapped actions to execute repeatedly, in a loop, for the duration of that movie clip's existence on the Stage. To disable or break the loop, the movie clip must be removed from the Timeline by either using the `removeMovieClip` action or manually inserting a blank keyframe at the point in the Timeline that you want the movie clip to no longer exist. You will create a loop using the `onClipEvent(enterFrame)` action in the workshop section of this seminar.

Using Increment and Decrement

As you become more familiar with the development side of Flash, you'll find that addition and subtraction are part of everything. You are either adding the distances between two points or objects or calculating an item total in an e-commerce shopping cart.

In Flash development, one of the most common forms of addition and subtraction is to either add or subtract 1 from a value. For example, if you want to slowly move an object across the screen, you might use the following script:

```
onClipEvent(enterFrame) {
    x = _x + 1;
    trace = (x);
}
```

If the object started at an x coordinate of 100, it would then display at position 101 in Frame 2, 102 in Frame 3, and so on. The trace action line of script causes the Output window to display the x coordinate as the movie clip moves across the Stage.

This methodology is pretty simple and straightforward—nothing more than basic math. However, things can get more involved, and this simple task can become quite taxing. For example, if you wanted to add 1 to the following x position, you could start with the following script:

```
_root.firstMC.secondMC.thirdMC.fourthMC._x
```

If you didn't know the current x position of this movie clip, you would be forced to use the following script:

```
_root.firstMC.secondMC.thirdMC.fourthMC._x =
➥_root.firstMC.secondMC.thirdMC.fourthMC._x + 1;
```

Although it's correct in function, this statement is wordy and messy. There is a better way.

Using what is called *incrementing* or *decrementing*, you can add or subtract 1 from any value quickly and easily. Incrementing is created by typing ++, and decrementing is created by typing --. To increment a value, simple type the value you want to increment and then immediately place two plus symbols after the variable name.

Using incrementing, the messy script in the previous example now becomes the following:

```
_root.firstMC.secondMC.thirdMC.fourthMC._x++;
```

This basically says, "Add 1 to the current value of this property or variable."

Decrement works in the same basic way. To decrement a value, simply type the value you want to decrement and then immediately place two minus symbols after the variable name. For example, using the previous example, if you wanted to decrement the x position of the fourthMC, you would use the following script:

```
_root.firstMC.secondMC.thirdMC.fourthMC._x--;
```

Note ───────────────────────────────────

There is nothing functionally better about using increment and decrement as opposed to other scripts; they are just cleaner and easier to use.

Using the Addition and Subtraction Assignment

The *addition assignment* and *subtraction assignment* operators of Flash are used often in ActionScript to add or subtract a given value from an expression. Similar to incrementing or decrementing, the addition or subtraction assignment operators allow you to add more than 1 to any given property or variable. For example, suppose you wanted to add 5 to a variable with an unknown value; you couldn't use incrementing because it adds only 1. But you could use the Dot syntax of Flash to specify the object on the Stage and then add the value as shown in the following script.

If...

```
_root.firstMC.secondMC.thirdMC.fourthMC._x = 30;
```

then...

```
_root.firstMC.secondMC.thirdMC.fourthMC._x += 5;
```

This returns a value of 35. The addition assignment operator adds the value of the expression on the right to the expression on the left and then assigns the expression on the left the total value of both.

A negation assignment subtracts the value of the expression on the right from the expression on the left and then assigns the expression on the left the total value of both. For example, if you wanted to gradually fade an object from the Stage, you could use the subtraction assignment operator. The following script would cause an object to fade to a 10% alpha effect:

```
_alpha -= 10;
```

Other assignment operators are available in Flash, but some are quite complicated and complex in both their function and use. Table 14.1 lists and describes the common assignment operators.

Table 14.1   Assignment Operators

Assignment	Description
=	Assigns a value
+=	Adds the value of the expression on the right to the expression on the left and then assigns the expression on the left the total value of both
-=	Subtracts the value of the expression on the right from the expression on the left and then assigns the expression on the left the total value of both
*=	Multiplies the value of the expression on the right with the expression on the left and then assigns the expression on the left the total value of both
/=	Divides the value of the expression on the right into the expression on the left and then assigns the expression on the left the total value of both

You will use the addition assignment operator in the workshop of this seminar.

Understanding Exponential Movement

Exponential movement is a process of either increasing or decreasing a value by a set increment, with the increment being an expression with a changing value. When you think of exponential movement, think of acceleration and deceleration. A good example of this would be a game of shuffleboard. As soon as the puck loses contact with the shuffleboard stick, it begins to lose speed; over time, it will gradually slow to a complete stop. This is because we live in a world based on friction. In a virtual world such as Flash, friction does not exist, but you can attempt to simulate friction to achieve more realistic movement, which in turn makes for a more realistic end-user experience.

To understand exponential movement better, let's explore the shuffleboard analogy and the puck's movement. The puck has a starting point and a stopping point—a point A and point B. If nothing but friction interferes with the puck as it glides across the court, the puck maintains a perfectly straight path. The distance in feet from the starting point, or point A, and the stopping point, or point B, is 200 feet. You can also assume that it takes 10 seconds for the puck to move from point A to point B, gradually slowing each second, until it reaches both a complete stop and point B simultaneously.

In the first second of the puck's journey, assume for simplicity's sake that the puck travels exactly half the distance to its final resting point, 100 feet. This is a feasible assumption because friction has had little time to take effect. Plus, it makes the theory behind exponential movement easier to understand.

To simplify what is happening, we can say that in this snapshot of time, the puck is currently moving 100 feet per second, and 100 feet is exactly half the distance to the goal. It still has 100 feet remaining and now has 9 seconds to cover those 100 remaining feet.

Friction is beginning to take its toll, so the puck travels only 50 feet in the next second, which coincidentally is exactly half the remaining distance to the goal. In the third second, friction has slowed the puck even more, and it moves only 25 feet closer to the end point. Once again, 25 feet is coincidentally half the distance of the remaining 50 feet.

Are you starting to see a pattern in the movement of this shuffleboard puck? I think it is safe to say that in every second of time that passes, the puck moves exactly half the remaining distance to its goal. This last statement is something that can be used in Flash to build an equation for exponential deceleration.

To see a movie that uses this exponential deceleration movement for animating the shuffleboard puck, open the shuffle.fla movie that is located in the Seminar14/Samples/ directory on the CD-ROM that accompanies this book.

The shuffle.fla movie is composed of one frame and one symbol. Test the movie, and you'll see the puck cross the screen and gradually slow to a stop. This simulates the effect that friction has on real-world objects.

To create this functionality, the following script is attached to the puck instance on the Stage to set two variables: destination and speed:

```
onClipEvent(load){
    destination = _x + 200;
    speed = .5;
}
```

More script is attached to the first frame of the movie clip symbol. Open the puck symbol in the Symbol-Editing Mode and with Frame 1 active, open the Actions panel. You will see the following script:

```
_root.puck.onEnterFrame = function () {
    //the code in this Movie Clip event will execute every frame
    //how far is it from the puck's current location to where it will stop
    remainingDistance = destination - _x;
    //distance to travel during a single frame
    toTravel = remainingDistance * speed;
    //finally, we can move the puck with this script
    _x = _x + toTravel;
};
```

> **Note**
>
> This script uses the Flash MX new Movie Clip object-oriented events, which are covered in Seminar 15, "Adding Digital Video to the Site." Notice that this script begins with `_root.puck.onEnterFrame = function() {` and ends with `};`. You will learn about this in the next seminar.

For exponential movement to occur, the script must be repeated over and over, each time reducing the amount of distance to travel. By using _root.puck prior to this movie clip event, you are directing Flash to the puck instance on the Stage. Then you use the onEnterFrame = function() { movie clip event. (You also could have used the onClipEvent(enterFrame) action and attached it directly to the movie clip instance.) This script causes Flash to repeat the script wrapped inside the curly brackets over and over as long as the movie clip exists on the Stage. Also, notice that some variables are also set in the `onClipEvent(load)` event—the `destination` and `speed` variables. The `destination` variable is assigned the value of the current x position of the movie clip instance plus 200. This establishes the maximum distance the puck will travel. The `speed` variable is set to .5.

With these variables set, the `onEnterFrame = function() {` Movie Clip event can now execute. A new variable is set, `remainingDistance`, which is assigned the value of the `destination` minus the current x position (which would be 200 in this script). Then, by establishing another variable called `toTravel` and assigning it the value of the `remainingDistance` multiplied by the `speed` (or 200×5), you begin to create the exponential deceleration. This produces the result of 100, which then is assigned as the new x position for the movie clip. It moves 100 pixels on the Stage. Because you're using the `onClipEvent(enterFrame)`, this script is executed repeatedly, each time moving the movie clip instance one-half the distance it has to travel to its ending point. This script represents exponential deceleration in Flash.

> **Note** ——————————————————————————————————
> You might be thinking that there is no end to this exponential deceleration because the distance between the puck and its resting position will always be cut in half, never allowing the final resting coordinates to be reached. You are right. But as a programmer, you can use other methods to end this exponential deceleration and cause the puck to move to its resting position. In the workshop, you will create a script that designates a certain number to be reached in the exponential deceleration and then direct the object to be positioned at its resting position, thus ending the deceleration cycle.

> **Tip** ——————————————————————————————————
> To get a slow-motion version of this movement, to help you understand it better, set your frame rate to .1 frame per second.

> **Tip** ——————————————————————————————————
> You should name your movie clip instances, especially the ones you plan to control with ActionScript.

Using and and or to Beef Up the if Statement

You can make your conditional `if` statements more specific in the conditions they test for by using the `&&` (and) operator or the `||` (or) operator. These operators are used when you want something to happen only if one condition is true and another is false, or if you want to allow an action to occur if one of two different conditions is true. For example, suppose you want to ensure that the user has a valid username and password before you grant him permission to certain content. You would use the following condition with the && (and) operator:

```
if(username == "admin" && password == "123456"){
    gotoAndPlay("secure"),
}
```

By breaking down the `if` statement, you'll see that only if both the username and password are correctly entered will the movie play the secure content. If the end-user enters his username correctly as `admin` but accidentally adds a 7 to the end of his password (`1234567`), the conditional will return false because only one of the two required conditions is true. Therefore, the movie will not play `"secure"`. Think of && as saying, "Only if this and this are true, will I do this."

However, if you want to allow an activity if either one or the other is true, you would use the || (or) operator. The following script uses an || operator that allows a valid password as well as a generic password of `guest` to gain entry to `"display"`:

```
if(username == "admin" || username == "guest"){
    gotoAndPlay("display");
}
```

This code allows the end-user to view `"display"` if his username is either `admin` or `guest`. Think of || as saying, "If one of the following conditions is true, then do this." You will use the || operator in the workshop section of this seminar.

Embedding a Conditional Inside a Conditional

You can also embed a conditional inside another conditional. This enables you to test for one condition before you bother to check the next condition. You might think that this approach accomplishes the same results as using &&, but this is not necessarily true. Using && is an all-or-nothing approach. If only one of the two conditionals is true, the conditional returns false and none of the embedded actions execute. To get around having to have two responses be true, you can embed a conditional statement inside another conditional statement. In the login example introduced earlier, you would use a conditional statement embedded inside another conditional statement if you wanted to help the end-user by telling him which part of his login contains the error—the username or the password he submitted with that username.

Look at the following example:

```
if(username == "admin"){
    alert = "Invalid password";
    if(password == "validPassword"){
        alert = "Access Granted";
    }
}else{
    alert = "invalid username";
}
```

To understand this script, it needs to be broken down. If the username equals admin, the action within the curly brackets for the if statement executes. The first thing that happens is that "alert" is populated with a message telling the user that his password is invalid. This might seem odd considering that the password has not been tested for validity yet, but if the password is valid, that message immediately is overwritten by the message telling him that his access has been granted. If his password is not valid, the message remains invalid password, which also initializes this variable to be used later. However, if the username does not equal admin, the bottom else statement kicks in and tells the user that his username was not recognized.

Conditions are common in every programming language. In fact, they are the basis of computers and the binary system: 1 = on, and 0 = off. Conditions can be used to accomplish simple tasks, or they can become very complicated to accomplish more taxing tasks. You embed a conditional inside another conditional in the workshop section that is covered next in this seminar.

Building the Slider Puzzle Activity

Like every project, big or small, you need to determine what the goals of the project are and how you plan to accomplish those goals, all before you begin programming. The slider puzzle activity is a game based on moving numbered tiles into sequential order within a rectangular area. I am sure that many of you are familiar with this concept and have probably played with a real-world version of the game at some point. This will hopefully make the game easier to understand and build.

This game will be played on a 3×3 grid, with 9 total spaces. It will have 8 tiles, numbered 1–8, and an empty slot to allow for the movement of the tiles. The user will move and rearrange the tiles by clicking. When clicked, a tile will move only if the empty space is either to the left, right, top, or bottom of the tile being clicked. All this functionality is created in one frame of the `puzzles.fla` movie that you created in Seminar 7, "Site Interactivity and Button Functionality." You will do this through ActionScript, movie clips, and button symbols.

Creating the Slider Puzzle Objects

To begin creating this slider puzzle activity, you first need to set up the Stage with the object required for the interactivity. This would be the game board for the puzzle and the tiles. To create these objects, follow these steps:

1. Open the `puzzles.fla` file you created in Seminar 7, or access or open the `puzzles.fla` movie in the `Seminar14/Samples/Seminar13/` directory; save this file as `puzzles.fla` in the directory with your other Honeycomb site files.

2. Click the `movie` layer to make it active and rename it `gameboard`. Delete the `Puzzles` text block from the Stage. The `gameboard` layer holds the board that will contain all the tiles or pieces of the puzzle.

3. Add another layer above the `gameboard` layer and name this layer `tiles`. The tiles layer will contain the movie clip object for the eight tiles and the empty slot, which really is an instance of the `tile` symbol with its `_visible` property set to `0`.

4. You will borrow some symbols from another movie's library to begin setting up for this slider puzzle activity. Open, as a Library, the `game.fla` file located in the `Seminar14/Samples/` directory on the CD-ROM that accompanies this book.

5. Click the gameboard layer and drag an instance of the tile square symbol from the games.fla library onto the Stage. Position it anywhere for now. Click the tiles layer and drag an instance of the tile symbol from the game.fla library. Again, position it anywhere for now. Drag the transparent button from the game.fla library into the puzzles.fla library because you will use this symbol later. Close the game.fla library.

6. Click the tile square instance on the Stage to make it active, and in the Property Inspector, set the Width and Height to 220; then set the x coordinate to 275 and the y coordinate to 100. Lock the gameboard layer because you are finished with this layer.

7. Apply a 50% Alpha Effect to the tile square instance on the Stage.

8. Next, you'll set up the tile symbol with a dynamic text field and a transparent button. Open the tile symbol in the Symbol-Editing Mode. Click the tile layer and insert two new layers above this layer. Name the layer at the top of the stacking order hit area and the other new layer number.

9. Click the number layer to make it active and add a dynamic text field. Do this by clicking the Text tool and, in the Property Inspector, setting the following: Text Type option to Dynamic Text, a font of Arial, a font size of 42, a Line Type of Single Line, Bold, and a Position of Normal. Open the Color Mixer and apply a fill color of black with an Alpha effect of 50% for the text in the dynamic text field. Click and set a dynamic text field on the Stage.

10. With the dynamic text block active, embed the Arial font outline by clicking the Character button of the Property Inspector and in the displaying Character Options dialog box selecting Only and then Numerals (0-9). Click Done to close this dialog box.

11. With the dynamic text field settings established and the field set, type the number 8 in the text field. Position and size this text field by dragging the square handle in the lower corner of the field so that it is positioned in the yellow area of the tile object (see Figure 14.1). Do not use the Free transform tool to resize the text field.

Figure 14.1   You have set the number 8 to display in the dynamic text field

12. With the dynamic text field active on the Stage, in the Property Inspector assign a variable name by clicking in the Var box and typing `tileNumber`. You will call this variable in script that you will create later for dynamically updating the numbers for each `tile` instance that will make up the puzzle.

13. Click the `hit area` layer to make it active and drag an instance of the `transparent button` on the Stage. Position and resize the button in the Property Inspector with a Width and Height of `70`, and x and y coordinates of `0`. This precisely sizes the `transparent button` to cover the tile area.

14. Exit the Symbol-Editing Mode and save your file. If you want to see a movie developed up to this point in the workshop, open `puzzles1.fla` located in the `Seminar14/Samples` directory on the CD-ROM that accompanies this book.

This completes the initial setup for this activity. Just as the matching activity you created in Seminar 10, "Using ActionScript to Control Objects," used only one frame for the activity movie, the puzzles activity will need only one frame in the activity movie Timeline. All the functionality occurs through movie clips, buttons, the Timeline, and ActionScript.

Checking for the Empty Tile

To set up the functionality of each tile checking for the empty slot in the puzzle, you attach script to the `tile` symbol. By attaching script to the symbol, it will be part of all the instances you create of this symbol. This is what you want because all tiles will behave the same. To create this checking functionality, follow these steps:

1. You need to modify the `tile` symbol to attach the ActionScript for this functionality. Double-click the `tile` symbol in the `puzzles.fla` library and launch the Symbol-Editing Mode for this symbol.

2. Lock both the number and tile layers; then make the hit area layer active. Click the instance of the `transparent button` symbol on the Stage to make it the active object.

3. Because this is a button, you will attach the `on(press)` action. Open the Actions panel and set the `on(press)` action by typing the following:

```
on(press) {
```

4. Create a new line of script and comment your script by adding the following comment in one line of script:

```
//check to see if the empty tile is either in the row directly
➥above or below this tile
```

5. Now create an `if` statement with a condition that checks for the empty tile in a row above or below the tile. Type the following line of script:

```
if(_parent.empty._y == _y + _height || parent.empty.y == _y -
➥_height){
```

This `if` statement has two conditions because it uses the or operator (`||`). Each of the conditions checks to see whether the empty tile is either in the row above or the row below, as well as in the same column as the instance being pressed. You have not created the empty tile yet but you will shortly.

6. Create a new line of script and again comment your script by adding the following comment all on one line:

```
//check to see if the empty tile is in the same column as this
➥tile
```

7. The next script needs to check to see whether the empty tile is in the same column as the tile instance being pressed. To create this functionality, you again need an `if` statement. Therefore, you nest an `if` statement inside the first `if` statement, with the conditions each checking for the empty tile. Type the following:

```
if (_parent.empty._x == _x){
```

8. Now, complete the second `if` statement by telling Flash what to do if both `if` statements are true. Create a new line and type the following comment and line of script:

```
//set the new y location of this tile, equal to the y location of
➥the empty tile
newY = _parent.empty._Y
//place the empty tile where this tile currently resides
_parent.empty._y  = _y
}
```

If both of the if statements test true, this script tells the current instance being pressed and the empty tile to swap positions.

9. Close the first if statement by creating a new line of script and typing a closing curly bracket. This completes one-half of the functionality you need for the slider puzzle. You also need to check the columns to the left and right of the tile instance being pressed. Your Actions panel should resemble Figure 14.2.

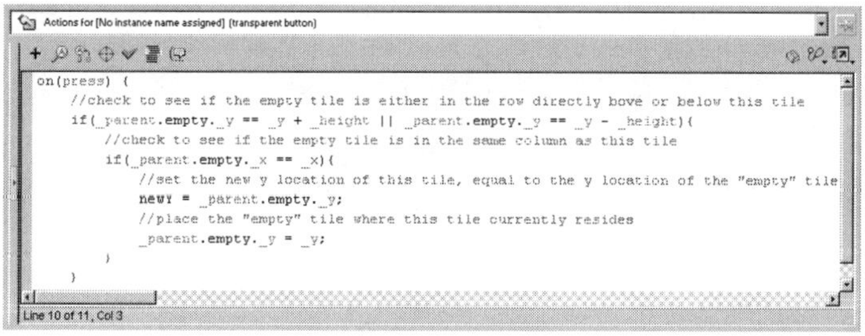

```
Actions for [No instance name assigned] (transparent button)
on(press) {
    //check to see if the empty tile is either in the row directly bove or below this tile
    if(_parent.empty._y == _y + _height || _parent.empty._y == _y - _height){
        //check to see if the empty tile is in the same column as this tile
        if(_parent.empty._x == _x){
            //set the new y location of this tile, equal to the y location of the "empty" tile
            newY = _parent.empty._y;
            //place the "empty" tile where this tile currently resides
            _parent.empty._y = _y;
        }
    )
}
Line 10 of 11, Col 3
```

Figure 14.2   Double-check that all statements of script end with a semicolon and that all opening parentheses and curly brackets are closed.

10. Now you will create the script for checking the columns to the left and right of the instance being pressed. This script is similar to the script that checks for the empty tile in the rows above or below. It uses the same if statements but sets different conditions that check for the empty tile in the columns to the left or right. Type the following:

```
//check to see if the empty tile is either in the column
➥directly to the right or left of this tile
if(_parent.empty._x == _x - width || _parent.empty._x == _x +
➥_width) {
    //check to see if the empty tile is in the same row as this
    ➥tile
    if (_parent.empty._y == _y) {
        //set the new x location of this tile equal to the x
        ➥location of the empty tile
        newX = parent.empty._x;
        //place the empty tile where this tile currently resides
        parent.empty._x = _x;
    }
}
```

Similar to the functionality of the previous script, the first if statement asks, "Is the empty space either in the column to the right or the column to the left of me?" If this is true, it then asks if it is in the same horizontal row. If both of these conditions test true, the code tells the current instance and the empty tile to swap positions.

11. Close the on(press) action you used to begin this script. Then, type a closing curly bracket. The Actions panel should resemble Figure 14.3.

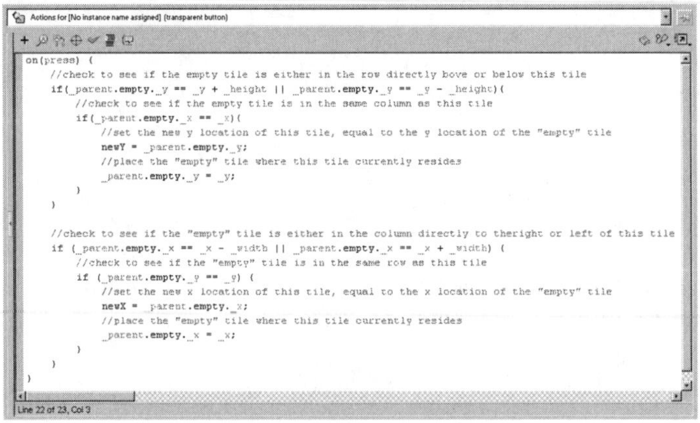

Figure 14.3 Because you're using the on(press) action each time a tile instance is pressed, the wrapped if statements and conditions are evaluated.

12. Save your file. If you want to see a movie developed up to this point in the workshop, open puzzles2.fla located in the Seminar14/Samples directory on the CD-ROM that accompanies this book.

Establishing the Variables for the Movie

First, you will establish and initialize your variables and the values for the variables. These two variables, newX and newY, are used to establish the starting x, y coordinate for each tile as it makes its movement into the empty slot and around the puzzle. These variables will be the goal of each tile instance. If the current y coordinate does not equal the value of newY, the tile instance will move up or down until it does. The newX variable will behave the same. To create these variables, follow these steps:

1 With the tile movie clip selected, open your Actions panel. This script requires the onClipEvent to trigger one time when the movie clip loads on the Stage and then play through all script wrapped in the curly brackets. Type the following script:

```
onClipEvent (load) {
```

2. Now add a comment explaining what the next line of code will do by typing the following:

```
//initialize newY and newY variables assigning the values for
➥each with the starting x and y coordinate of this tile
```

3. Now create the newX and newY variables and assign the starting x and y coordinates for the instance by typing the following:

```
newX = _x;
newY = _y;
}
```

> **Note**
>
> Because you are starting by assigning the value of **newX** the same value as the current x coordinate, the clip will not move left or right—the same goes for the **newY**. If something were to occur to change the value of **newX** or **newY**, the instance would then move.

> **Note**
>
> Because all the tiles will basically behave in the same fashion, you'll develop the one instance of the tile on the Stage and then copy and paste this instance to the game board for all nine tiles. Then, you'll make small modifications to the code for each tile instance.

Creating the ActionScript-Based Movement for Animating the Tile

To create the animation of the tile moving into the empty slot, you use the _xscale and _yscale properties of the Movie Clip object to create the illusion of the tile expanding into the empty slot. Then, through a combination of the variables and incrementing, you create the movement of the tile sliding into the empty slot. To create this animation, follow these steps:

1. With the tile instance on the Stage active, open or access your Actions panel. Create a new line of script after the closing curly bracket of the onClipEvent action. To begin this script, you must set a movie clip event for triggering the tile instance movie clip. You'll use the onClipEvent with an event handler of enterFrame. The enterFrame event handler will cause this script to execute repeatedly until the movie clip is removed from the main movie Timeline. Type the following:

   ```
   onClipEvent (enterFrame){
   ```

2. Begin by commenting your script. Type the following all on one line of script:

   ```
   //increase the width and the height of this tile as it moves from
   ➥x and y location to x and y location
   ```

3. Now you need to add two lines of code that make the instance distort as though to display movement as it moves from location to location. Type the following lines of script:

   ```
   _xscale = 100 + Math.abs (newX - _x)/2;
   _yscale = 100 + Math.abso (newY - _y)/2;
   ```

   The first line of script distorts the instance as it moves left and right across the gameboard. The code is basically saying, "Set the instance xscale (its pro portionate width) equal to 100% of its starting size, plus whatever the distance it has left to travel."

   This might be confusing, but think of it like this: When the instance is moving left or right, it will be wider. If it is 50 pixels away from its destination, the width will be 150% (100 + 50) of its starting width, and this percentage will decrease as the piece gets closer to its goal (newX). When it is 5 pixels away from its goal, it will be 105% (100 + 5), and when the instance gets to its goal of newX, it will be 100% (100 + 0) of its starting size—no larger, no smaller.

   The second line of script does the same thing as the first line, except this line takes effect when the instance is asked to move up or down, instead of right to left.

Note

Also, in these two lines of script, you used the `Math.abs` action. This action is used because an instance could be either to the left or right or to the top or the bottom of the goal, meaning the location might be positive or negative pixels away. The `Math.abs` action returns a positive value. Seminar 13, "Enhancing the Site Interface and Interactivity," covered the `Math` object of Flash MX and provided more information on the `Math.abs` action.

4. Next, you'll create the script causing the `tile` instance to begin to move. Start by commenting this script; type the following comment on one line of script:

```
//set the x and y location of this tile half the distance from
➥where it lies now as its newX and newY values
```

5. Now you'll create the actual script for controlling the `tile` instance movement by typing the following lines of script:

```
_x += ((newX - _x)/2);
_y += ((newY - _y)/2);
```

These two lines of script go hand in hand like the previous two lines of script, except these lines control the movement of the instance, for both its x coordinate and y coordinate. The first line tells the instance to set its x position equal to itself plus half the distance to its goal of `newX`. For instance, if the instance currently resides at an x position of 100, and `newX` equals 200, the instance will move to 150, then 175, then 187.5, and so on until it reaches its goal of `newX`. This creates the illusion of the instance sliding gradually into its new home.

The second line of script does the same thing as the first line, except that it controls the movement along the vertical axis, up and down. The Actions panel should resemble Figure 14.4.

If you would like to see a movie developed up to this point in the workshop, open `puzzles3.fla` located in the `Seminar14/Samples` directory on the CD-ROM that accompanies this book.

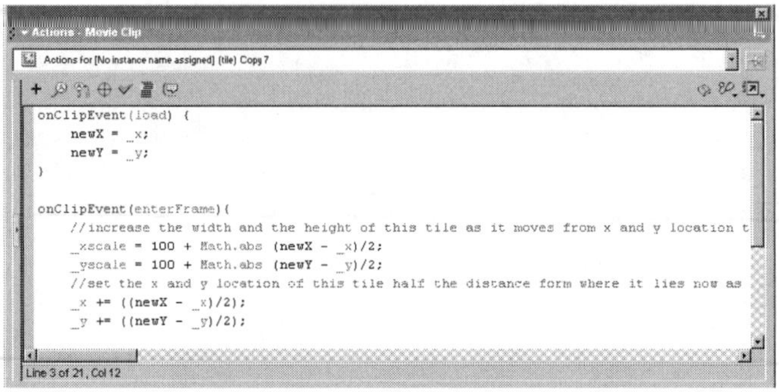

```
Actions - Movie Clip
Actions for [No instance name assigned] (tile) Copy 7
+ ♪ ⊕ ✓ ₤ ⏍                                              ♀ ⅋ ⊠

onClipEvent (load) {
    newX = _x;
    newY = _y;
}


onClipEvent (enterFrame) {
    //increase the width and the height of this tile as it moves from x and y location t
    _xscale = 100 + Math.abs (newX - _x)/2;
    _yscale = 100 + Math.abs (newY - _y)/2;
    //set the x and y location of this tile half the distance form where it lies now as
    _x += ((newX - _x)/2);
    _y += ((newY - _y)/2);

Line 3 of 21, Col 12
```

Figure 14.4   This script creates the illusion of the tile moving.

Setting the New Position for the Tile Instance

Now, stop for a moment and think. If the previous two lines of script continually tell the instance to move half the distance to the goal, it will never reach its goal. It will just keep cutting that distance in half no matter how small a fraction that might be. Because of this, you must write a conditional for each line of script that basically says, "If the distance from the instance's current position to its goal is less than .5 pixels, which is less than the human eye can distinguish, then stop moving the instance in increments of one half." To do this, you simply set the x or y position equal to newX or newY, depending on whether the instance is moving up and down or left and right. To create this script for setting the new position of the tile instance, follow these steps:

1. You should still have the Actions panel open and be attaching actions to the tile instance on the Stage. If not, click the tile instance on the Stage and open or access the Action panel.

2. To begin this script, you again start by commenting it. Type the following comment on one line of script:

   ```
   //If this tile instance is within .5 pixels of its destination,
   ➥newX and newY, move it to its new destination
   ```

3. Begin this new functionality with an if statement that sets the following condition: "If the tile is within .5 pixels of its x coordinate destination." Type the following script:

   ```
   if(Math.abs(newX - _x)<.5){
   ```

In this if statement, the Math.abs action is used because the instance could be either to the left or right of the goal, meaning the distance might be positive or negative. Rather than writing two conditionals to consider for each case, you will convert the number, positive or negative, into a positive value.

4. Next, you create the script that tells Flash what to do when the condition of the if statement is true. Type the following script:

```
_x = newX;
}
```

This script sets the x coordinate to be the value of the newX; therefore, the tile instance moves to its new x coordinate as established in the newX value.

5. Repeat steps 3 and 4 to create the if statement setting the condition for the y coordinate being within .5 pixels of its y coordinate destination. Type the following if statement:

```
if(Math.abs(newY - _y)<.5){
_y = newY;
}
```

6. End this script by closing the onClipEvent action with one more closing curly bracket. Your Actions panel should resemble Figure 14.5.

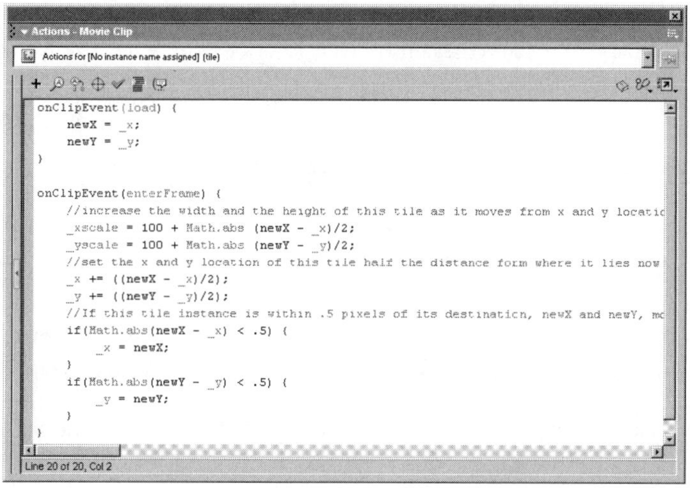

Figure 14.5 The onClipEvent (enterFrame) action is key to this part of the slider puzzle functionaltiy because it repeatedly executes the enclosed script.

> **Tip**
> You can remove any movie clip from a Timeline either by inserting a blank keyframe at the point in the Timeline that you want the movie clip to be removed from the movie or by using the `removeMovieClip` action located in the Objects, MovieClip, Methods categories of the Actions toolbox.

7. Save your file. Because the movie is not complete at this point in the movie's development with the required functionality, there is no reason to test the movie since it will not function as intended for the slider puzzle.

If you want to see a movie developed up to this point in the workshop, open `puzzles4.fla` located in the `Seminar14/Samples` directory on the CD-ROM that accompanies this book.

Setting the Numbers to Display on Each Tile

Next, you'll create the numbers that display on each of the tile pieces. Again, you will use ActionScript to dynamically create these numbers for the dynamic text field that is nested in the tile symbol. First, you need to initiate the value of the variable that was assigned to the dynamic text field. You will do this in the `onClipEvent` (`load`) action. Then, because you want to set the numbers on each tile so that the puzzle begins displaying the numbers for the tile pieces, you need to implement an `if` statement as part of the `onClipEvent` (`enterFrame`) action. The condition that is set for the `if` statement sets a number to be displayed. You will use incrementing to cause Flash to generate this number. Because this script is included in the `onClipEvent` (`enterFrame`) action, the script will fire until the condition is met for the `if` statement.

This text field was assigned a variable name of `tileNumber`. In previous seminars, you assigned an instance name to an input or dynamic text field. In this seminar, however, you will use a variable name because you do not really need to control anything but the numbers displayed. To create the tile numbers, follow these steps:

1. In the main movie, click the instance of the `tile` symbol on the Stage and open the Actions panel.

2. Establish the value for the variable `tileNumber` as 1. Click the third line of script, which is newY = _y; then, create a new line of script by pressing Enter. Type the following line of script:

   ```
   tileNumber = 1;
   ```

This initiates a starting value for the variable tileNumber. The Actions panel should resemble Figure 14.6.

```
▼ Actions - Movie Clip
Actions for [No instance name assigned] (tile)

onClipEvent (load) {
    newX = _x;
    newY = _y;
    tileNumber = 1;
}

onClipEvent (enterFrame) {
    //increase the width and the height of this tile as it moves from x and y location to
    _xscale = 100 + Math.abs (newX - _x)/2;
    _yscale = 100 + Math.abs (newY - _y)/2;
    //set the x and y location of this tile half the distance form where it lies now as it
    _x += ((newX - _x)/2);
    _y += ((newY - _y)/2);
    //If this tile instance is within .5 pixels of its destination, newX and newY, move it to
    if(Math.abs(newX - _x) < .5) {
        _x = newX;
    }
    if(Math.abs(newY - _y) < .5) {
        _y = newY;
    }
}
Line 21 of 21, Col 2
```

Figure 14.6   This script initiates a starting value for the variable tileNumber for this instance of the tile symbol.

When you create all the tiles for the game, you must edit this number to reflect the other numbers for the tile pieces.

Setting Up the Game Board

With the script to create the interactivity required for the tile instance on the Stage complete, you now can use this instance to set up the game board. This requires adding a total of nine instances of the tile symbol to the main movie. To do this, follow these steps:

1. Be sure you have both the gameboard and the guide layers locked. Then, in the main movie, click the tiles layer to make it active; next, click the tile instance on the Stage. In the Property Inspector, set the x coordinate to 280 and the y coordinate to 105. Press Enter after you type each coordinate.

2. Copy this instance and then click anywhere on the Stage to deselect the tile instance. Now paste a new instance of the tile on the Stage. With this new instance active, set the x coordinate to 350 and the y coordinate to 105.

Tip

You can also use the Edit, Duplicate command to duplicate the **tile** instance, which enables you to use just one command instead of two as with Copy and Paste.

3. Click again in a blank area of the Stage to deselect the second tile instance; then paste another instance of the **tile** symbol. Set this tile instance with an x coordinate of **420** and a y coordinate of **105**. This positions the tiles at the top of the game board and vertically centers them in the game board (see Figure 14.7).

Figure 14.7   The tile pieces fit perfectly in the game board area because both the game board and the tile instances are squares and are sized for this fit.

Warning

For the slider puzzle to work, all the tiles must be sized to a 70x70 pixel dimension. Additionally, they all must be aligned vertically and horizontally with all edges flush to each other. Therefore, it is very important to use the x and y coordinates for setting each tile location. There must be 70 pixels between each tile.

4. Select the three **tile** instances to make them all active and copy them. Paste them on the Stage and, with all three tiles selected, in the Property Inspector, set the x coordinate to **280** and the y coordinate to **175**. The second row for the puzzle is now in place.

5. Click to deselect the active tiles, and then paste the copied tiles again. With all three tiles active, set the x coordinate to **280** and the y coordinate to **245** (see Figure 14.8).

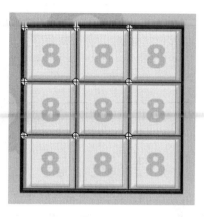

Figure 14.8   The game board is now populated with the `tile` instance.

6. Save your movie and test it in the Flash Player testing mode. Because you have not set up the empty tile, there is no functionality. Also notice that all nine tiles display with the number 1. You'll fix these problems next.

If you want to see a movie developed up to this point in the workshop, open `puzzles5.fla` located in the `Seminar14/Samples` directory on the CD-ROM that accompanies this book.

Setting the Numbers for Each Tile

To establish the numbers from 1 to 8 for each of the tile pieces, you must set a number for each individual tile. You need to modify the script you created for the `onClipEvent(enterFrame)` action. To do this, follow these steps:

1. In the `puzzles.fla` movie, click the tile instance that appears in the top row, middle position and open the Actions panel.

2. Change the `tileNumber = 1;` line of script so that it assigns the numeric value of 8. The script should read as follows:

   ```
   tileNumber = 8;
   ```

3. Repeat step 2 for the other `tile` instances on the Stage, changing the variable value to any number between 2 and 7. Keep track of which numbers you have used so that you do not duplicate a number. The slider puzzle needs to reflect the numbers between 1 and 8 without repeating any of the numbers. Do not set a number for the bottom-right `tile` instance because this tile will be the empty space tile for the puzzle.

1. Save and test your movie. You should see all the tiles display a number between 1 and 8 without any repeating except for the number 1, which is repeated in the lower-right tile. This will become the empty slot for the puzzle.

If you want to see a movie developed up to this point in the workshop, open `puzzles6.fla` located in the `Seminar14/Samples` directory on the CD-ROM that accompanies this book.

Creating the Empty Slot for the Game

With the game board set up, you will now create the empty slot for the slider puzzle. You will do this by setting the `_visible` property for the lower-right instance of the `tile` symbol to `0`, which causes it to display transparent. To create the empty slot for the game, follow these steps:

1. Click the `tile` instance in the lower-right corner of the game board to make it active. This will be the empty slot.

2. In the Property Inspector, give this instance a name of `empty`.

3. Apply an Alpha Effect of `25%` to the instance so you can visually see that this is the empty slot. This step is really not necessary because you will control the `_visible` property of the tile in the ActionScript you create next. But, when working in the Flash Authoring Mode, it is nice to visually distinguish this tile from the others.

4. Now create the ActionScript that will cause this movie clip instance to be invisible. With the `empty` tile instance selected, open the Actions panel and deleted all the script after the first line of script—the `onClipEvent (load) {` script.

5. Create the script to control the visible property of this instance by typing the following script:

   ```
   visible = false;
   ```

6. Close the open curly bracket of the `onClipEvent` action by creating a new line of script and typing a closing curly bracket. The Actions panel should resemble Figure 14.9.

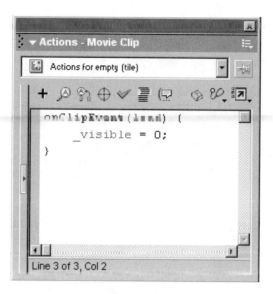

Figure 14.9 The empty tile is called in the script for checking the functionality as well as the script for moving a tile.

7. Save and the test your movie. You should see the game board display with an empty slot in the lower-right corner. Click any tile around the empty slot, and you should see the tile move to the empty slot in the puzzle. It's working.

If you want to see a movie developed up to this point in the workshop, open `puzzles7.fla` located in the `Seminar14/Samples` directory on the CD-ROM that accompanies this book.

Wrapping Up the Slider Puzzle

The final pieces of functionality that need to be added to the puzzle are a `stop` action to Frame 1 of the `puzzles.fla` movie Timeline and setting the speed for the ActionScript-based movement for all the `tile` instances. To create this final bit of interactivity, follow these steps:

1. In the `puzzles.fla` movie Timeline, add a new layer above the `tile` layer and name this new layer `actions`. This layer should be at the top of the layer stacking order.

2. Click the keyframe in Frame 1 and open or access the Actions panel.

3. Set the speed for the tile ActionScript-based movement by typing the following:

```
speed = 2.5;
```

Create a new line of script and add a stop action. The Actions panel should resemble Figure 14.10.

Figure 14.10   You have set the speed for the tile movement to 2.5 seconds.

4. Test your movie. The slider puzzle is working.

5. Exit the Flash Player Testing Mode and save the movie as puzzles.fla. If you want to compare your puzzles.fla movie with a movie that is completed up to this point in the book, open the puzzles.fla file located in the Seminar14/Samples directory on the CD-ROM that accompanies this book.

Seminar Summary

This seminar covered several new skills that were complex and required a stretch in your Flash MX development skills. Don't worry if you are still a little confused by some of the script used in the slider puzzle activity and throughout this workshop. You have been introduced to many new concepts and programming logic, and as you get more comfortable with Flash MX, you can review this puzzle and the script. I would bet that at that time, this puzzle will become clearer in its logic and script.

This seminar covered ActionScript based movement for instances. You learned about using the increment and decrement operators, which are useful for creating concise script that causes an object to move 1 pixel at a time. You will use increment and decrement often in other Flash projects.

The workshop section of this book used ActionScript-based movement to cause the slider puzzle tiles to move around the game board. You learned more about if statements and how to use the addition assignment to establish two conditions that must be true, as well as the subtraction assignment for setting two conditions with only one needing to be true. You used these assignment operators in the slider puzzle. As you become more advanced in your Flash development, your if statements will become more complex.

The next seminar covers the development of the In Quest of Ducks activity. This activity uses video, so you will learn all about video in a Flash MX movie. The capability to embed a video clip in a Flash MX movie is a new feature of Flash MX. The workshop in Seminar 15 also covers many of the ActionScripts that you have learned throughout the book. It is a summary chapter for all skills with an introduction to video. Enjoy!

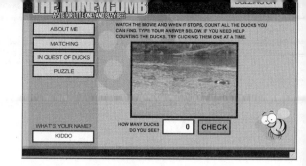

Seminar 15

Adding Digital Video to the Site

In this chapter

Workshop: Creating the In Quest of Ducks Activity

Importing Video into Macromedia Flash MX Movies

Macromedia Flash MX can now import video into a movie. As you learned in Seminar 1, "Macromedia Flash MX and Web Site Development," you can import Macromedia Flash Video (FLV) format files directly into a movie. And if you have QuickTime 4 or later installed on your computer system, you also can import video clips formatted as QuickTime Movie (MOV), AVI, or MPEG. This adds a whole new dimension to Flash development.

> **Note**
>
> If you have DirectX 7 or later installed on a Windows-based computer system, you can also import MOV, AVI, and MPEG video files into Flash MX movies.

Through video, you can quickly and easily communicate key information in a real-world setting. For example, you can now present short instructional video clips for communicating new skills or information to all employees in a company, or to quickly communicate news updates or late-breaking information. In prior releases of Flash, you had to simulate this type of information through animation, text, and graphics. This seminar focuses on the new video capabilities of Flash MX.

Importing a Video Clip

To import a video in Flash MX, you use the File, Import or the Import to Library commands. Using these commands, you can import into the movie library a video clip in one of the supported formats, as well as embed it directly into the movie just as you would any bitmap graphic. You might be thinking, "Cool!," but Macromedia took this functionality one step further by also enabling a link to be created between the Flash movie and an external QuickTime movie. Therefore, rather than embedding the QuickTime movie, you can just link to it, allowing your Flash movie to maintain a lower file size. Flash maintains a pointer or link to the QuickTime movie.

The video import process begins with the typical dialog box for importing any file in Flash. When you begin the import process, you will see two more dialog boxes. The first to display is the Import Video dialog box, which offers a choice of either embedding the video clip into the movie or linking to an external video file (see Figure 15.1). The following section, "Embedding a Video Clip in a Movie," discusses the first option (embedding a video in a Macromedia Flash document), and the section after this, "Linking to a QuickTime Movie Video Clip," discusses the second option (link to an external video file).

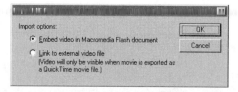

Figure 15.1   You can embed a video clip in the movie or create a link to an external file through this dialog box.

Embedding a Video Clip in a Movie

If you choose to embed the video clip in the movie, it becomes part of the movie, and if you use the Import command—not the Import to Library command—it displays on the Stage for the active keyframe. If you import the video clip to the movie library, it becomes an object of the movie when you drag an instance of the video clip symbol from the library.

If you choose to embed the video clip, a second dialog box displays, the Import Video Settings dialog box (see Figure 15.2). You set the compression settings for the video clip in this dialog box.

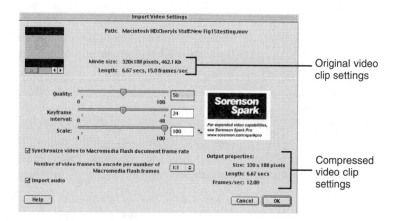

Figure 15.2   You can set the quality, keyframe interval, and scale of the compressed video clip in this dialog box.

Macromedia implemented Sorenson Spark motion video codec into Flash MX, and it's used to compress the imported video clips. Spark is a high-quality encoder and decoder that helps reduce the imported video in physical file size while maintaining a quality picture. Table 15.1 explains each of the options available to you for encoding a video clip.

Table 15.1   Import Video Settings Dialog Box Options

Option	Description
Quality	Set a value for the quality of the compressed video clip. The higher the value, the better the quality of the video image, but the larger the file size. A lower value decreases the image quality but produces a smaller file size.
Keyframe Interval	Set a value to control the frequency of keyframes in the video clip. A keyframe is composed of all the frames required for complete data. For example, if you set an interval of 15, a keyframe with complete data is stored every 15 frames. The frames between the intervals store only the data that changes as the video clip progresses. The smaller the value, the more complete each frame is, but also the greater the file size is.
Scale	Set a percentage value to control the physical dimensions of the video clip. If you reduce the physical dimension of the video clip, you are reducing the overall video file size.
Synchronize Video to Macromedia Flash Document Frame Rate	Toggle button for synchronizing a video clip to match the movie frame per second rate. This option will drop frames or add frames based on the difference between the video clip's frame rate and the movie frame rate. This feature can create a hiccup effect when the video clip is played.
Number of Video Frames to Encode Per Number of Macromedia Flash Frames	This option is available only if you have the Synchronize Video to Macromedia Flash Document Frame Rate option selected. Through this option, you can set the ratio of the imported video frames that play in regards to the main movie Timeline. The default setting of 1:1 plays one frame of the video clip per one frame of the movie.
Import Audio	A toggle button for importing the audio track that might be included in a video clip. If selected, the audio track is also imported into Flash. You'll see a warning message if the audio track in the video clip is not supported by Flash when you click OK to close the Import Video Settings dialog box. If you ignore the message, Flash will import the video clip without the audio track. If you want the unsupported audio track included with the imported video clip, you will need to resave the video clip in a video-authoring application with an audio codec that Flash supports.

When you click OK in the Import Video Settings dialog box, Flash compresses the video clip based on the options you've set. If you chose to embed the video clip into the movie, another dialog box displays if you do not have enough frames developed in the movie Timeline (see Figure 15.3).

Figure 15.3   You can turn this message off by selecting the Don't Show Me This Message Again option.

Flash automatically extends the Timeline of the main movie to the number of frames required for displaying the embedded video clip. The Flash movie increases in file size by the compressed video file size. The video clip becomes a symbol in the movie library (see Figure 15.4).

Figure 15.4   Because the video is a symbol, you can use as many instances of the video as you need in a movie.

You can scrub through the video clip by dragging the playhead through the Timeline. This enables you to view the video playback while in the Flash Authoring Mode. You also can test your movie and view the video clip playback in relation to the entire movie and all other objects of the movie.

Linking to a QuickTime Movie Video Clip

You also can link to a video clip that is in QuickTime Movie format. Flash will create a link between the video clip library symbol and the QuickTime Movie video clip. This enables a video clip with a large file size to be stored in an external location outside the movie. When you link to a QuickTime Movie video clip, only the first frame of the QuickTime Movie video clip is displayed in the Flash Authoring environment. If you want to see more of the video clip, you must extend the Flash movie Timeline.

There is a restriction for exporting a Flash movie that links to a QuickTime Movie video clip. The Flash movie must be exported or published as a QuickTime movie, not as a Flash SWF file. This enables the linked QuickTime Movie video clip to remain in QuickTime format. You will learn more about publishing a Flash movie in QuickTime format in Seminar 16, "Publishing and Testing the Site."

> **Note**
>
> You cannot create a link to a video clip that is saved in any format other than QuickTime Movie, MOV.

In the following workshop, you will import a video clip in AVI format and use it for the "In Quest of Ducks" activity of The Honeycomb site.

> **Note**
>
> If you create a video object in Flash MX, you can create streaming video. This topic is outside the scope of this book but you can find more information on it through Flash Help and the "Working with Imported Video Files" section.

New Movie Clip Event Handlers

New with Flash MX are *movie clip event handlers* that allow you to attach a mouse event action and handler directly to a movie clip so that you don't need to use a button. Now you can use the instances of movie clips to cause traditional button functionality in Flash.

The following script shows how a movie clip causes a movie to go to Frame 10 and begin playing when the end-user clicks the movie clip instance:

```
onClipEvent (load) {
    this.onPress = function() {
```

```
        gotoAndPlay (10);
    };
}
```

Notice that in this script, the first line begins with the `onClipEvent` action with the `load` event handler. You should be pretty familiar with this method for movie clips, but look at the second line of script:

```
this.onPress = function(){
```

This script shows the new action or method for the movie clip class. First, you must direct Flash's attention to the movie clip to which the `onPress` method is directed; in this case, it is `this`, or the movie clip to which the action is attached. Then you must follow `this` with a defined function that will execute when the `Press` event is triggered. Wrapped in the brackets for this action is script that tells Flash what to do; in this example, Flash is directed to go to and play Frame 10. Also notice that the ending curly bracket for this action is composed of both a curly bracket and a semicolon (`};`). This is the correct syntax for ending this new Flash MX feature.

> **Note**
>
> You can also attach the new Movie Clip Event actions to a frame in the Timeline of a movie clip object.

There are many new event handlers for Flash MX. Table 15.2 lists the more common methods and event handlers.

Table 15.2   Flash MX Movie Clip Event Handlers

Movie Clip Method	Description
`MovieClip.onData`	Event handler that triggers when the movie clip receives data from the `loadVariables` or `loadMovie` actions.
`MovieClip.onDragOut`	Event handler that triggers when the end-user clicks directly on a movie clip and then drags outside the movie and then back over the movie clip.
`MovieClip.onEnterFrame`	Similar to the `onClipEvent(enterFrame)` action, this event handler is repeatedly called at the frame-per-second rate of the movie. Any actions associated with this event are compiled first, before any other actions attached to any of the affected frames.

continues

Table 15.2   Continued

Movie Clip Method	Description
MovieClip.onKeyDown/onKeyUp	Event handler that triggers when a designated key is pressed down or let up by the end-user.
MovieClip.onLoad	Event handler that triggers when the movie clip to which it is assigned loads into the movie.
MovieClip.onMouseDown	Event handler that triggers when the end-user presses the left mouse button.
MovieClip.onMouseMove	Event handler that triggers when the end-user moves the mouse.
MovieClip.onMouseUp	Event handler that triggers when the end-user lets up on the left mouse button.
MovieClip.onPress	Event handler that triggers when the end-user clicks directly on the movie clip instance to which this action is attached.
MovieClip.onRelease	Event handler that triggers when the end-user clicks and releases the left mouse button directly on the movie clip instance to which this action is attached.
MovieClip.onReleaseOutside	Event handler that triggers when the end-user presses down the left mouse button directly on the movie clip instance and then releases the mouse button outside the movie clip instance to which this action is attached.
MovieClip.onRollOut	Event handler that triggers when the end-user rolls the mouse pointer outside the movie clip instance to which this action is attached.
MovieClip.onRollOver	Event handler that triggers when the end-user moves the mouse pointer over the movie clip instance to which this action is attached.
MovieClip.onUnload	Event handler that triggers when the first frame plays after the movie clip is unloaded from a Timeline.

You will use this new feature of Flash MX in the workshop section of this seminar.

Creating the In Quest of Ducks Activity

This workshop pulls together many of the features you have learned about Flash throughout this book. You will create the "In Quest of Ducks" activity of The Honeycomb site. To see a preview of the In Quest of Ducks activity, open the ducks.fla file located in the Seminar15/Samples directory on the CD-ROM that accompanies this book. Test the movie in the Flash Player Testing Mode and you'll see a short video clip display showing ducks in a pond. As the instructions indicate, when the clip ends, you are to count the visible ducks. You can either type an answer in the input box below the video clip, or you can manually click each duck to generate a new number in the input box. Click the Check button to check whether the number in the input box is correct. A message displays letting you know whether the number is correct.

You will use the new video import feature of Flash MX to embed a video clip in the movie. Then, through the use of both a dynamic and an input text field and ActionScript attached to buttons or movie clip instances, you will create the counting and confirmation functionality for the activity.

Importing Digital Video Frames into Flash

To begin developing the "In Quest of Ducks" activity, you will first add the video for the ducks movie. You will use the ducks.fla movie that you created in Seminar 7, "Site Interactivity and Button Functionality." Through Flash MX's new video feature, you can now import and compress an AVI file into a Flash movie. The AVI file you'll import is a short video clip of ducks swimming in a pond. You'll also use the new compression feature of Flash MX to compress the file to a workable file size for the movie. This file is then embedded in the ducks.fla movie. To do this, follow these steps:

1. Open the ducks.fla file you created in Seminar 7, or open the ducks.fla movie in the Seminar15/Samples/Seminar14/ directory and save this file as ducks.fla in the directory with your other Honeycomb site files.

2. As you know from developing The Honeycomb site, the ducks.fla file is loaded into the Honeycomb.fla movie. Because the ducks.fla file is a loaded SWF file, it will automatically acquire the same fps rate of 15 fps as the Honeycomb.fla movie. Presently, the ducks.fla movie is set to an fps of 12; change it to a 15 fps rate by using the Property Inspector and the Size option. This will help synchronize the imported AVI video clip to the frame per second rate that is set for the Honeycomb.fla movie.

3. Click the movie layer to make it active, and rename it video. Delete the In Quest of Ducks text block that is on the Stage.

4. With the video layer active, import the quest.avi file located in the Seminar15/Samples directory on the CD–ROM that accompanies this book. This displays the Import Video dialog box (see Figure 15.5).

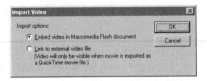

Figure 15.5   You can also embed a QuickTime movie in a Flash MX movie.

5. Click the Embed Video in Macromedia Flash Document option, and then click OK. This opens the Import Video Settings dialog box.

6. Because your target audience most likely will have modem Internet connections, you need to apply some compression to this video clip. Set the Quality to 80 by clicking in the Quality box and typing 80. Set the Keyframe Interval option by clicking in the Keyframe Interval box and typing 29. Scale the movie dimensions to 40% by clicking the box of the Scale option and typing 40. This will reduce the dimensions of the movie to a height of 230.9 pixels and a height of 124.8 pixels.

7. Select the Synchronize Video to Macromedia Flash Document Frame Rate option so that it is turned on. This option synchronizes the video clip to match the same frame per second rate of the ducks.fla movie.

8. If the Number of Video Frames to Encode Per Number of Macromedia Flash Frames option is not set to 1:1, click the arrow and select 1:1 from the pop-up menu. This feature sets the quest.avi video clip to play one frame per the ducks.avi Timeline frame. The Import Video Settings dialog box should resemble Figure 15.6. Click OK to import the video clip.

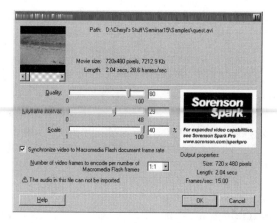

Figure 15.6 The `quest.avi` video clip does not have an audio track. If it did, you would have another option in this dialog box for turning on or off the audio track upon import.

Note ────────────────────

If you set a ratio for the imported movie of 1:2 or 1:3 for the Number of Video Frames to Encode Per Number of Macromedia Flash Frames, this will not drop frames from the video clip. Instead, the video clip displays fewer frames per second, creating a choppy playback of the video clip.

Note ────────────────────

A 1:1 ratio for the Keyframe Interval setting stores a complete frame for each frame of the video clip. It is recommend that you use this ratio setting only when working with small video clip files.

9. Next, you'll see the Importing dialog box showing the progression of the video being imported into the movie. Then a warning displays, letting you know that the video clip requires 31 frames to display in the `ducks.fla` movie Timeline (see Figure 15.7). Click Yes to automatically extend the Timeline for the `ducks.fla` movie.

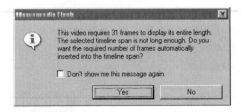

Figure 15.7   If you select No, Flash will not extend the movie Timeline. The video clip will only display its frame-by-frame content for the same number of frames in the main movie Timeline.

10. The quest.avi video clip is imported and embedded into the ducks.fla movie as an instance on the Stage. The Timeline for the video layer is extended to Frame 31. Click Photoframe 31 in the Guide:Design Template layer and insert a frame by pressing F5. This extends the guide layer to Frame 31.

11. Now position the video clip instance on the Stage by clicking the instance to make it active and setting the Property Inspector to an x coordinate of 300 and a y coordinate of 140. This positions the video clip instance so there is room above and below the clip for the other objects required for this activity.

12. You can use one of two techniques to view the video clip. Either play the ducks.fla movie in the Flash Authoring Mode or test the movie in the Flash Player Testing Mode. You'll see ducks in a pond, and then the video clip zooms in on four ducks. These are the ducks that will be counted in the activity.

13. Lock both the guide and the video layer. Save your movie.

If you would like to see a movie developed up to this point in the workshop, open ducks1.fla, located in the Seminar15/Samples directory on the CD-ROM that accompanies this book.

Setting the Instructions for the Activity

Next, you create the static text blocks that communicate the instructions for the game as well as label the input area for the activity. To do this, follow these steps:

1. Create a new layer above the video layer and name it instructions.

2. With the instructions layer active, click the Text tool. In the Property Inspector, set the Text Type option to Static Text, font of Arial, font size of 12 points, black color, Bold and AutoKern selected, left justified. Click the

Stage and drag a text block about 400 pixels wide and type the following in uppercase:

```
WATCH THE MOVIE AND WHEN IT STOPS, COUNT ALL THE DUCKS YOU CAN
➥FIND. TYPE YOUR ANSWER BELOW. IF YOU NEED HELP COUNTING THE
➥DUCKS, TRY CLICKING THEM ONE AT A TIME.
```

3. Position this static text block as Figure 15.8 indicates.

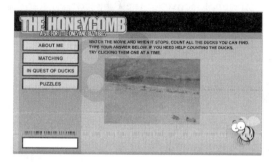

Figure 15.8   The instructions can be read by a screen reader because they're displayed in a static text block.

4. Create another static text block about 75 pixels wide with the same character settings as the previous static text block except for the justification. Set a right justification for this text block, and then type the following all in uppercase in this text block:

```
HOW MANY DUCKS DO YOU SEE?
```

5. Position this text block as Figure 15.9 indicates.

Figure 15.9   This text block is the label for the input box of the activity.

6. Create a new layer above the `Guide:Design Template` layer and name it `border`.

7. Now you'll add a black border to the video clip instance. You will do this by creating a rectangle that's slightly larger than the video clip instance and placing the black rectangle behind the video clip instance. Create a rectangle with just a black fill and no stroke on the `border` layer. Don't worry about the position or size of the rectangle; you'll set these settings next.

8. With the black rectangle active, in the Property Inspector, set the Width to `298`, the Height to `202`, the x coordinate to `295`, and the y coordinate to `135`. This positions the rectangle centered with the video clip instance. Because it's slightly larger, the rectangle appears as a border around the video clip instance. Lock this layer.

9. You will use this rectangular shape for other objects in this workshop, so convert it to a symbol. Name the symbol `rectangle` and give it a Movie Clip behavior. Set the registration point in the center.

10. Save your movie.

Setting Up the Counting Activity Objects

Next in the development of the "In Quest of Ducks" activity, you need to create some of the objects required for the functionality of the activity. This includes some graphical elements for the input text area as well as two editable text fields, one for inputting the count of the ducks and another for displaying a message if they are right or wrong. This will create all the objects needed for the "In Quest of Ducks" activity. To finish setting up the Stage for the activity, follow these steps:

1. Click the `video` layer and insert a new layer. Name this layer `contents`. Click the blank keyframe in Frame 1 to make it active.

2. First, you create the input box graphically on the Stage. Drag an instance of the `rectangle` symbol onto the Stage and resize it by setting a width of `90` and a height of `40` in the Property Inspector. Position it to the right of the HOW MANY DUCKS DO YOU SEE? static text block (see Figure 15.10).

Black rectangle symbol

Figure 15.10   This black rectangle symbol will be the border for the input box area.

3. Copy the `rectangle` instance and paste another copy of the instance on the Stage. In the Property Inspector, set a Tint effect of white for this instance. Size the instance to a width of 84 and a height of 34. Center this inside the black rectangle instance to create the input box area. By using multiple instances of this rectangle symbol, you are keeping the file size very low for this `ducks.fla` file.

4. Now create the graphic for a Check button that will check the answer. Select both rectangle instances that make up the input box area, and copy them. Paste them and move these two objects to the right of the input box area. Click the white rectangle and apply a Tint effect of gray.

5. Now create a label for this button area by adding a static text block with the settings of Arial, 20-point font, black, bold, left-justified to the Stage, and typing `CHECK`, in uppercase. Center this text block in the gray rectangle of the graphical button area (see Figure 15.11).

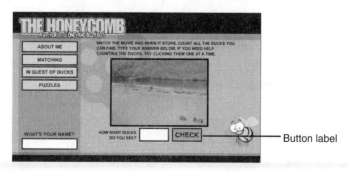

Button label

Figure 15.11   You will put a transparent button over this graphical button area to make this a functional button.

6. Open as a Library the buttons.fla movie that you'll find in the Seminar15/Samples directory on the CD-ROM that accompanies this book. With the contents layer active, drag an instance of the transparent button from the buttons.fla library onto the Stage. Position and size it so that it covers the Check graphical button area.

7. Lock the contents layer because you are finished creating the objects of this layer.

8. Create a new layer above the contents layer and name it fields. Click the Text tool and create an input text field with the settings of a 20-point Arial font, bold and left justified, and a Line Type of Single Line. Set the Maximum Characters box to 2.

9. Create an input text field that is inside the white rectangle instance that makes up the input box area.

10. With the input text field active, embed the Arial font into the text field by clicking the Character button on the Property Inspector. This displays the Character Options dialog box. Select Only, and then select Numerals (0–9) in the Character Options dialog box. Click Done to close this dialog box, embedding the Arial font in the input text field. Your movie should resemble Figure 15.12.

Figure 15.12   This input text field allows the user to type an answer, or it will dynamically count as the end-user clicks each duck in the pond.

11. With the text field active, assign a variable name of totalCount in the Var box of the Property Inspector. This completes the setup for this input text field. You still need to create a dynamic text field for displaying a message letting the end-user know whether she is right or wrong.

12. To create the message text field for this activity, you will use a dynamic text field. Be sure the input text field that you just created is not active. Click the Text tool, and in the Property Inspector, set a Text Type of Dynamic Text and the font settings of a 12-point Arial font, bold and left justified, and a Line Type of Single Line. Click the Stage and drag a text field about 250 pixels wide. Position the text field as Figure 15.13 indicates.

Figure 15.13 This dynamic text field will display one of two set messages, one message communicating that the end-user is correct in her answer and another indicating that the answer is incorrect.

13. With the dynamic text field active on the Stage, embed the Arial font into the text field by clicking the Character button on the Property Inspector and selecting All Characters from the Character Options dialog box. Click Done to close this dialog box, embedding the Arial font in the dynamic text field.

14. Now assign an instance name of message to this dynamic text field in the Property Inspector. You used a variable name for the input text field and an instance name for the dynamic text field. Next, you will communicate with ActionScript to each of these fields.

If you would like to see a movie developed up to this point in the workshop, open ducks2.fla, located in the Seminar15/Samples directory on the CD-ROM that accompanies this book.

Attaching ActionScript to the Timeline

With the editable text fields created and named either an instance name or a variable name, now you can begin to manipulate them through ActionScript. First, you will attach script to Frame 1 of the ducks.fla Timeline. By calling the variable name of `totalCount`, which is assigned to the input text field, you can cause this field to display an initial value as well as set zero as the start value for this variable. You also will cause the movie to stop when it reaches the end of the Timeline by attaching the `stop` action. To create this ActionScript, follow these steps:

1. Create a new layer above the `instructions` layer and name the new layer `actions`.

2. Click the blank keyframe in Frame 1 of the `actions` layer and open or access the Actions panel. Type the following script into the Scripting pane of the Actions panel:

   ```
   //establish the variable of totalCount and set its value to 0
   totalCount = 0;
   ```

3. To stop the movie at the end of the Timeline, the stop action must be attached to the last frame of the Timeline. Insert a keyframe in Frame 31 of the `actions` layer, and attach the stop action to this frame by typing the following in the Actions panel:

   ```
   stop();
   ```

4. Save and test your movie. You should see the video clip play, and then the input text box will display with an initial value of 0.

This completes the setup for the `ducks.fla` movie. The next section shows you how to make it functional.

If you want to see a movie developed up to this point in the workshop, open `ducks3.fla`, located in the `Seminar15/Samples` directory on the CD-ROM that accompanies this book.

Creating Hot Spots with Movie Clip Instances

The In Quest of Ducks activity is a counting activity in which the end-user can either click the ducks in the video clip to count them one at a time or can just type a number for their count into an input box. This functionality makes use of movie clip symbols that mark the hot-spot area for each duck and the `totalCount` input text field. In the previous section, you set a numeric value of zero for the `totalCount` variable, which also displays in the input text field. Now, you will have the number 1 added to this variable each time one of the movie clip instances for each duck is clicked. The new variable value will again display in the input text field. To create this functionality, follow these steps:

1. Click the `video` layer and insert a new layer above it. Name this new layer `counters`.

2. Insert a keyframe in Frame 31 of the `counters` layer. This is the point of the video clip at which all the ducks that the end-user is to count are visible. Notice that there are four ducks in the pond.

3. Add an instance of the `rectangle` symbol to the Stage. Resize and position it so that it covers one of the ducks.

4. With the `rectangle` instance selected, open or access the Actions panel. Type the following script:

```
//increase the count for the totalCount variable by one each
➥time the user clicks a hotspot.
onClipEvent(load){
    this.onPress = function(){
    _parent.totalCount++;
    };
}
```

This functionality enables you to create button functionality with a movie clip instance. By attaching this script to the `rectangle` movie clip instance, you are telling Flash that, when the end-user presses his mouse button on this movie clip instance, go to the main Timeline and add 1 to the `totalCount` variable.

5. Click the `rectangle` instance designating the first hot-spot area around a duck. In the Property Inspector, set an Alpha setting of `0%` to make this instance transparent or a hot-spot area.

Tip

You can turn the Show All Layers as Outlines feature on for the **counter** layer so that you can see each of the transparent **rectangle** movie clip instances on the Stage.

6. With the transparent `rectangle` instance active, copy it, and then paste it on the `counter` layer three more times. Position each instance over one of the remaining three ducks. Resize the `rectangle` movie clips so that they do not overlap each other (see Figure 15.14). Lock this layer because you are finished with it.

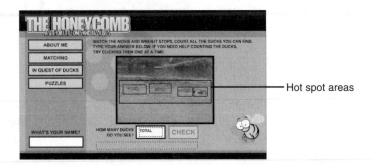

Hot spot areas

Figure 15.14   The rectangle instances work the same as an imagemap in HMTL code.

7. Save and test the movie. Click each duck and notice that the input box reflects the number of clicks.

Now you need to create functionality for the Check button to check whether the number in the input text box is correct. You will do this in the next section.

If you would like to see a movie developed up to this point in the workshop, open ducks4.fla, located in the Seminar15/Samples directory on the CD-ROM that accompanies this book.

Checking the Answer

The "In Quest of Ducks" activity is progressing nicely. Now it needs to have some functionality added to the Check button that checks the number in the input text field to determine whether the end-user has counted correctly. Four ducks are visible in the video clip when it ends—this is the correct number, 4. Through a simple if and else statement, you can create a comparison between the number in the input text field, which really is the number that's currently assigned to the totalCount variable, and compare that to 4. If it matches, a confirmation message displays; if it doesn't match, a message displays indicating that the number is not right. To create this functionality, follow these steps:

1. Click the contents layer and unlock it. Click the transparent button on the Stage that covers the Check button to make it active. Open or access the Actions panel.

2. You'll begin this script with a comment. Type the following:

```
//check to see if the inputted answer equals four.
```

3. Now create the trigger for this button by typing an `on` action with the event handler of `press`:

```
on(press) {
```

4. Create an `if` statement with a condition of the correct number, the number 4, by typing the following script:

```
if(totalCount == 4) {
```

5. Set the action to be executed if the condition is true by typing the following script:

```
message.text = "GOOD WORK, YOU ARE RIGHT!";
```

This statement tells Flash to go to the main movie Timeline and in the `message` dynamic text field, display GOOD WORK, YOU ARE RIGHT!

6. Now create an `else` statement that tells Flash what to do if the condition tests false. Type the following:

```
}else{
message.text = "SORRY, TRY AGAIN.";
```

This statement tells Flash to display the message SORRY, TRY AGAIN in the `message` dynamic text field.

7. Close the open curly brackets for the `else` statement and the `if` statement by typing the following:

```
    }
}
```

Your Actions panel should resemble Figure 15.15.

8. Test your movie, and type an answer into the input text box and click the Check button. The message dynamic text field displays a message. The activity is working as it should, and you have come a long way in your Flash development!

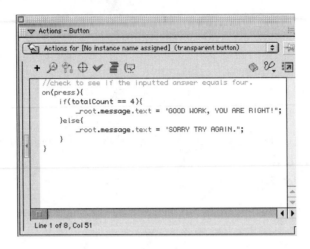

Figure 15.15   By using _root.message.text, you are directing Flash to the message text field.

9. Exit the Flash Player Testing Mode and save the movie. Open the honeycomb.fla file that you completed in Seminar 13, "Enhancing the Site Interface and Interactivity." Test this movie and, when you can, click the In Quest of Ducks button to see the ducks.fla movie loaded into The Honeycomb site.

Seminar Summary

This seminar introduced the new video import feature of Flash MX. You can now import and embed a video clip file into a Flash movie, as well as link to a QuickTime Movie file. Because Internet delivery file size is still an issue, through the import feature of Flash MX, you can also compress the video clip. This opens many avenues for Flash development. You can very quickly communicate information using a video clip. If you have a digital video camera, hopefully you are seeing that the possibilities for Web development with Flash MX have just been expanded.

The next seminar focuses on publishing or exporting a Flash movie and viewing the movie in a browser. You will learn about the Publish Settings feature of Flash MX and how to test your published movie through many different platforms. You're almost finished with the book. Be proud: You have come a long way in your Flash knowledge and development skills!

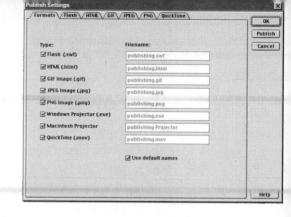

Seminar 16

Publishing and
Testing the Site

In this chapter

- The Power of the Publish
  Command   540

- Exporting Your Movie Using the
  Export Command   552

- Testing the Published Movie   553

- Publishing the Site for Internet
  Access   555

Workshop: Publishing the Site for Internet Access

The Power of the Publish Command

Up to this point in the book, you have been using the Macromedia Flash Authoring Mode and the Flash Player Testing Mode to test your movies. Now you will learn how to publish a movie for Internet viewing. This requires the use of the Publish command of Flash MX: File, Publish. You'll find that this command is very powerful and helpful. As you know from Seminar 1, "Macromedia Flash MX and Web Site Development," for a Flash movie to be viewed in a browser, it should be embedded in an HMTL page or another server-side scripting language. The beauty of the Publish command is that through it, you can generate many different formats of your movie as well as create the HTML page required for playback in a Web browser. This seminar covers how to publish your movie for Internet viewing.

Publishing Macromedia Flash MX Movies

When you have your movie developed, the final step is to publish or export the Flash FLA movie to another format for playback. Throughout this book, you have been testing your movies in the Flash Player testing mode, but to deliver your movie to an audience, you must generate a format of the movie for playback on the platform in which it will be delivered. This requires setting the appropriate publish settings and publishing the movie. You set your publish settings through the File, Publish Settings command. This command opens the Publish Settings dialog box (see Figure 16.1). By default, it is set to generate an SWF file of the movie as well as the HMTL document in which the SWF file is embedded.

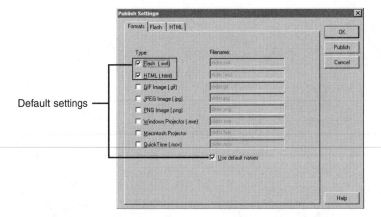

Figure 16.1   The Flash Publish command is designed for presenting the Flash movie on the Internet.

By default, there are three tabs in the Publish Settings dialog box: Formats, Flash, and HTML. Each tab contains settings for publishing your Flash movie. The Formats tab is displayed by default and is used to set additional formats for publishing the movie. If you select the GIF Image (.gif), JPEG Image (.jpg), PNG Image (.png), or QuickTime (.mov) options, another tab displays in this dialog box. Each new tab enables you to customize the setting for exporting the Flash movie to the selected format. In the workshop of this seminar, you will publish The Honeycomb movie with custom settings for Web delivery.

Tip

It's always a good idea to save your Flash FLA movie before you publish it.

Note

In Macromedia Flash 5, you can export and publish your movie to Real Video format, as well as to Macromedia Generator format. These two formats were excluded from the Flash MX version of the Publish and Export commands.

The Formats Tab

As you can see from the Formats tab of the Publish Settings dialog box in Figure 16.1, there are many different file formats for publishing your movie. This tab enables you to start at a global level and set the various formats for your movie. For example, if your method of delivery is the Internet, you would want to select the Flash (.swf) and HMTL (.html) formats, and you also might want to select the GIF Image (.gif) format. The GIF image can be used as an alternative image that's used to replace the SWF image if the end-user's machine does not have the Flash Player plug-in.

Table 16.1 provides a description of the settings that appear on the Formats tab.

Table 16.1   Formats Tab Publish Settings

Format Type	Description
GIF Image (.gif)	Flash generates an image of the first frame of the movie. This image can be used as an alternative image in case the site is being viewed by someone with an older browser that does not have the Flash plug-in.
JPEG Image (.jpg)	Flash generates a JPEG image of the first frame of the movie. A new tab appears in the Publish Settings dialog box that enables you to determine JPEG image settings.

continues

Table 16.1   Continued

Format Type	Description
PNG Image (.png)	Flash generates a PNG image of the first frame of the movie. A new tab appears in the Publish Settings dialog box that enables you to determine PNG image settings.
Windows Projector (.exe)	Flash generates a Windows Projector file of the entire movie. The Windows system's projector can play this file.
Macintosh Projector	Flash generates a Macintosh Projector file of the entire movie. The Macintosh system's projector can play this file.
QuickTime (.mov)	Flash generates a QuickTime movie of the entire movie. A new tab appears in the Publish Settings dialog box that enables you to determine QuickTime movie settings.
Use Default Names	Just like the Test Movie command, which generates an SWF file in the same folder as the Flash FLA movie, the Publish command will generate files in the same folder as the Flash FLA movie. Be sure you have the Flash file in the folder location in which you want your published files to appear.

Tip

If you deselect the Use Default Names option in the Publish Settings dialog box, you can type any name for the file that you want in the appropriate Filename box. You also can designate a directory/folder/file hierarchy by typing in the full path and the filename. For Windows, use a path such as `C:\Folder\filename.swf`. For Macintosh, use a path such as `HardDrive name:Folder:filename.swf`.

Warning

If you create a Macintosh Projector file using a Windows version of Flash, you must convert the Macintosh Projector file to appear as an application file in the Macintosh *Finder*. You can use a file translator such as BinHex to do this conversion. The Windows version of Flash uses an .hqx extension when it names a Macintosh Projector file, which will not work on the Macintosh system. Not all features of Flash MX for standalone projector files are supported by the projectors. You might need to publish using a lower Flash version setting.

The Flash Tab

The Flash Tab is used to customize the Flash SWF movie settings (see Figure 16.2).

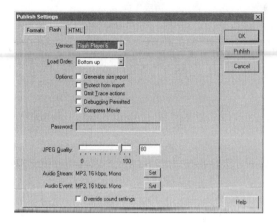

Figure 16.2   The Flash tab enables settings for how the Flash SWF file will be viewed in a browser window.

By selecting the various settings you want to apply to your Flash movie, you can customize how it will display and who can access it. Table 16.2 covers each feature of the Flash tab in the Publish Settings dialog box.

Table 16.2   Flash Tab Publish Settings

Flash Setting	Description
Version	Set the version of the Flash Player in which the SWF file will be published.
Load Order	Designate whether a movie will be displayed by showing the movie layers from the Bottom Up or Top Down. If you use a preloader or gate page in your Flash movie, this option does not apply to your movie because the movie will display as intended due to the preloader functionality.
Generate Size Report	Generate a report with various statistics and data about the final SWF file.
Protect from Import	Protect the Flash SWF so that others cannot import it into a Flash FLA file.
Omit Trace Actions	Causes Flash to ignore any trace actions you might have used in your movie. This prevents the Output window from displaying any trace actions.

continues

Table 16.2   Continued

Flash Setting	Description
Debugging Permitted	Activates the Debugger and enables remote debugging by others. If this option is selected, you also can create a password for accessing this feature.
Compress Movie	A Flash Player 6–only setting that will compress the Flash movie to create a smaller file size SWF. By default, this option is turned on, and it is recommended for movies that have lots of text or ActionScript. If you compress a movie, the SWF file can be viewed only through Flash Player 6. If you publish a movie for the Flash 6 player, this setting is automatically applied.
Password	If the Debugging Permitted option is selected, you can access the Password box, enabling the creation of a password for accessing the movie for remote debugging.
JPEG Quality	Set a quality setting for controlling the compression applied to any bitmaps in the movie. A higher setting creates better image quality but a larger file size movie. A lower setting reduces the image quality but creates a smaller sized file. As discussed in Seminar 5, "Importing Graphics into a Movie," you should import artwork without compression and compress the image through this setting in Flash.
Audio Stream: MP3, 16 Kbps, Mono	Click the Set button to access the Sound Settings dialog box for the movie. You can globally set a compression format for all streaming sounds in your movie through this dialog box. Any streaming sound that you did not individually set with a compression format will use this global setting. See Seminar 12, "Adding Sound to Enhance a Site," for more information on the individual sound compression format settings.
Audio Event: MP3, 16 Kbps, Mono	Click the Set button to access the Sound Settings dialog box for the movie. You can globally set a compression format for all event sounds in your movie through this dialog box. Any event sound that you did not individually set with a compression format will use this global setting. See Seminar 12 for more information on the individual sound compression format settings.

Flash Setting	Description
Override Sound Settings	When selected, overrides all individually set sound settings you might have set during the movie development. See Seminar 12. This setting is useful if you need to make several versions of a Flash movie—for example, one for Web and one for CD-ROM. You can override and increase the sound quality for all sounds used in the movie for the CD-ROM through this option.

Tip

The Flash tab can be quickly accessed through the Property Inspector. If you select the movie by clicking anywhere in the work area, the Property Inspector displays information on the Flash movie. Click the Flash Player 6 button to display the Flash tab of the Publish Settings dialog box.

The HTML Tab

The HTML tab enables you to customize the HMTL settings of the HTML-generated page (see Figure 16.3).

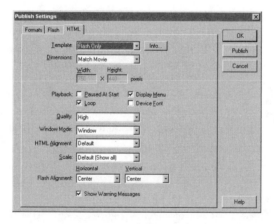

Figure 16.3   The HMTL publish settings customize the OBJECT and EMBED HMTL tags.

As you know, the SWF file must be embedded inside an HTML page for a browser to view it. To embed an SWF file inside an HTML document, you must use the OBJECT and EMBED HTML commands. These commands instruct the appropriate browser—Netscape or Microsoft Internet Explorer—to display the Flash file. When you publish the file, Flash generates the needed HTML page with all the coding required for viewing the site on all the popular browsers. Table 16.3 covers the HMTL tab publish settings.

Tip

You can create your HTML template to be used for displaying your Flash SWF file. If you place this template inside the Flash MX directory in the **First Run/Html** folder, the template is accessible in the Template option pop-up menu.

Table 16.3   HTML Tab Publish Settings

HTML Setting	Description
Template	Pop-up menu displaying a list of HTML templates designed with the required code for displaying the SWF file. Through this setting, you check the version of the Flash Player that the end-user has installed on his system. If you click the Info button to the right of this option, a description of the HMTL template is displayed (see Figure 16.4). You'll find all HTML templates in the **First Run/Html** folder in the Flash MX directory.
Dimensions	Sets the WIDTH and HEIGHT attributes of the OBJECT or EMBED tags, specifying the dimensions for displaying the SWF file in the HTML document. Click the Dimensions pop-up menu and choose a menu choice. Then, click in the Width and Height boxes to set the value. The Percent menu choice allows the Flash movie to size to a percentage of the end-user's browser. Therefore, it's always visible in the correct proportion for viewing in a browser window of any size.
Playback	**Paused At Start:** Stops the movie from playing upon loading. The end-user must click a button in the movie or choose Play from the Display menu that is accessible by (Control-clicking)[right-clicking] the SWF object displayed in the browser to play the movie.
	Loop: Loops an SWF file to the beginning of the movie when the last frame of the movie is reached. This option is on by default. If you use a **stop** action in the movie, this option is obsolete.

HTML Setting	Description
	Display Menu: Enables the Display menu to appear when the SWF file is (Control-clicked)[right-clicked] in a browser. The Display menu is a shortcut menu with a list of menu choices for controlling the SWF file playback in a browser window.
	Device Font: This is a Windows-only setting that enables an anti-aliased font to be used for all static text in the movie that has the Font attribute of Devise Font applied. This setting works well with smaller text in a movie because it makes the text easier to read. It also can reduce the movie file size.
Quality	**Low:** When this is selected, the Flash Player gives preference to playback speed over appearance. Anti-aliasing is not used with this setting.
	Auto Low: When this is selected, the Flash Player first gives preference to playback speed but will improve appearance when it can. The Flash Player checks the user's machine processor to see whether it can handle more, and then turns on anti-aliasing.
	Auto High: When this is selected, the Flash Player emphasizes appearance and playback speed equally at first, but will forfeit appearance for playback speed if the end-user's processor cannot handle both. Anti-aliasing is turned on at first, but if the playback speed drops below the determined frame rate, anti-aliasing is turned off. This will improve the playback speed.
	High: When this is selected, the Flash Player gives preference to appearance over playback speed. Anti-aliasing is always turned on, but if the movie does not contain animation, any bitmap image used in the movie is smoothed. If the movie does include animation, bitmap images are not smoothed. This is the default setting for Flash.
	Best: When this is selected, the Flash Player always provides the best quality, ignoring playback speed entirely. All displays are anti-aliased, and all bitmaps are smoothed.
Window Mode	This option is a Windows platform–only feature. It allows you to take advantage of the transparency, absolute positioning, and layering capabilities available in Internet Explorer 4.0 or above.

continues

Table 16.3   Continued

HTML Setting	Description
HTML Alignment	Sets the ALIGN attribute for the OBJECT, EMBED, and IMG tags in the HTML code. You designate the position for the SWF in the browser window through either Default, Left, Right, Top, or Bottom.
	Default: Centers the SWF in the browser window. Affected edges are cropped if the browser window is smaller than the movie.
	Left: Aligns the SWF along the left edge of the browser window. If necessary, the top, bottom, and right sides of the movie window are cropped.
	Right: Aligns the SWF along the right edge of the browser window. If necessary, the top, bottom, and left sides of the movie window are cropped.
	Top: Aligns the SWF along the top edge of the browser window. If necessary, the bottom, right, and left sides of the movie window are cropped.
	Bottom: Aligns the movie along the bottom edge of the browser window. If necessary, the top, right, and left sides of the movie window are cropped.
Scale	Determines how the movie is placed in the boundaries you specify in the Width and Height fields of the Dimensions option. If Percent was selected in the Dimensions option, this setting does not apply to the movie.
	Default (Show all): Displays the entire movie in the specified dimensions that you set in the Dimensions option. There is no distortion with this option.
	No Border: Scales the movie to fit the dimensions set in the Dimensions option. No distortion occurs to the movie, but it can be cropped to fit the dimensions.
	Exact Fit: Distorts a movie as it fits the movie into the dimensions set in the Dimension option.
	No Scale: Prevents the movie from scaling if the browser window is resized.

HTML Setting	Description
Flash Alignment	Sets the SALIGN parameter of the OBJECT and EMBED HTML tags. It determines how the Flash movie is placed in the movie window contained within your browser window.
Show Warning Messages	Select this option if you want to see warning messages for errors in the HTML code.

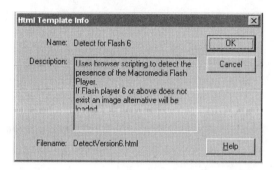

Figure 16.4   The name of the template used is displayed at the bottom of this dialog box.

When you publish the movie, the settings you selected for the HMTL code generates the OBJECT and EMBED tags with the appropriate attribute. OBJECT is the HTML tag that displays a Flash movie in Microsoft Internet Explorer, and EMBED is the HTML tag that displays a Flash movie in Netscape.

> **Warning**
>
> If you position an object half on the Stage and half in the work area, when you publish your movie, the object will appear on the Stage only if you set your Scale option in the HTML tab to Exact Fit. If you do not use Exact Fit and you allow scaling, any objects positioned off the Stage in the work area might be visible when viewing the published movie.

Accessing Tabs for Other Graphics Formats

When you select any of the graphics format options on the Formats tab of the Publish Settings dialog box—GIF Image, JPEG Image, PNG Image—a new tab is accessible in the Publish Settings dialog box. You can customize the settings for the individual graphics format that you have selected. For example, if you wanted to create a GIF file of the first frame of the Flash movie that has interlace applied to it, you would choose the GIF tab and select the Interlace option (see Figure 16.5).

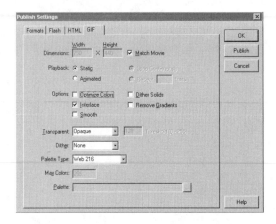

Figure 16.5   Interlacing a GIF image causes an image to display gradually as the image loads.

A complete discussion of each of these graphics formats is outside the scope of this book. However, you can find complete descriptions of all the graphics options for each of the graphic tabs in the Help file for Flash MX. Choose Help, Using Flash and go to the Publishing link to find the descriptions.

The QuickTime Tab

QuickTime 4 and later added a new media track that enables Flash MX movies to be part of the QuickTime movie. Therefore, you can import a QuickTime movie into Flash MX and add layers above or below the layer that holds the imported movie. You use the layers to create any additional content you want for more functionality and animation. Then, you must export or publish the movie back to QuickTime format.

If you have selected the QuickTime (.mov) format on the Format tab of the Publish Settings dialog box, the QuickTime tab appears. This tab provides custom settings for exporting the FLA movie into QuickTime format (see Figure 16.6).

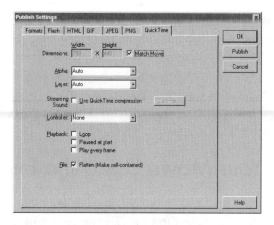

Figure 16.6   The Publish Settings dialog box creates movies in QuickTime 4 format by copying the QuickTime movie onto a separate QuickTime track.

Projector Files (Mac and PC)

Through the Macintosh Project or Windows Project options in the Format tab of the Publish Settings dialog box, you can generate a projector file of the movie. The projector file has all the functionality of a Flash SWF file but can be displayed in the projector of the selected operating system. This enables anyone to view a Flash movie because both the Macintosh and the Windows Projectors are part of the operating system.

> **Note**
>
> In addition, some FSCommands are available that can be used when creating and using a projector file. If you purchase a third-party tool such as SWF Studio, you get an even larger set of FSCommands.

Understanding the Publish Process

After you have designated your publish settings, you can either publish the movie by clicking the Publish button in the Publish Settings dialog box or save the settings to the Flash FLA movie by clicking OK to close the dialog box. With the settings saved, any time you publish the movie, Flash uses the saved settings to generate the appropriate documents.

When Flash publishes a movie, it combines all layers of the FLA file into one layer for the published movie. Guide and motion guide layers are not included in the published movie. Flash also applies compression to sound and bitmap images based on the settings you select in the Publish Settings dialog box. If you compare the file size for the FLA Flash movie to the SWF Flash Player file, you will see a dramatic decrease in file size.

Exporting Your Movie Using the Export Command

When you become more proficient in your Flash development, you might find the Export command of Flash MX quicker to use for exporting your movie to various formats. There are two export commands under the File menu: the Export Movie or the Export Image commands. When activated, both of these commands display an Export dialog box that enables you to choose just one format for exporting your movie (see Figure 16.7).

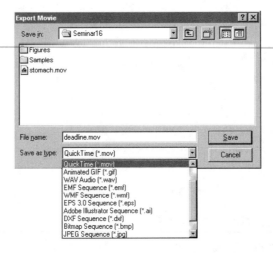

Figure 16.7   The Export Movie command offers many different file formats for exporting the Flash FLA file.

Based on the file type that you choose to export the Flash FLA movie, another dialog box displays, enabling you to set the custom settings for the movie in that file format (see Figure 16.8).

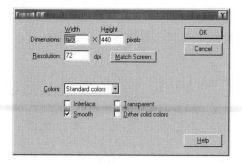

Figure 16.8   Use these animated GIF settings to export the FLA movie to a GIF format.

Tip
It's always wise to have a relationship with an ISP. Knowing what their hosting capabilities are and who to contact with questions is beneficial for any type of Web development.

Testing the Published Movie

Finally, you should always test your Flash movie on the many different platforms and browsers in which it will be viewed. For Web delivery of a Flash movie, you'll want to check the movie in the current versions of the popular browsers as well as on older versions of the browsers. Because a variety of computers are available today, you also should test the movie on different computer systems, such as Macintosh or PC-based machines. Test, test, and test some more, before you post your Web site on the Internet. This ensures your visitors a pleasant and engaging experience.

Publishing the Site for Internet Access

The Honeycomb movie is complete. You have all the activity movies created and functioning. Buzzy Bee is communicating the appropriate information and all buttons are working. The login captures the end-user's name, and everything is complete on the development side. Now you need to prepare the movie for publishing. This requires setting your publish settings to generate an SWF file of the movie and creating the HTML page required for viewing the file in a browser. You will also generate a GIF image to be used as an alternative image in case the end-user does not have the required Flash Player plug-in. This workshop will guide you through the publishing process.

Setting the Formats Tab Options

To begin the publish processing, you first want to set the publish settings for the movie. You want the movie to be viewed on many different platforms and through all the browsers, and you know that your target audience will have a range of computers from new to very old, as well as a variety of Internet connections. Therefore, you will set your publish settings to ensure that all users can access the site.

First, you must set the Formats tab settings. To set your Formats tab settings, follow these steps:

1. Open the `Honeycomb.fla` file you created in Seminar 13, "Enhancing the Site Interface and Interactivity," or access or open the `16Honeycomb.fla` movie in the `Seminar16/Samples/` directory and save this file as `Honeycomb.fla` in the directory with your other Honeycomb site files.

2. Open the Publish Settings dialog box by choosing File, Publish Settings. This displays the Publish Settings dialog box with the Formats tab active.

3. Because you are delivering The Honeycomb site over the Internet, you must generate an SWF file of the movie along with the HTML page. Leave these two default settings selected.

4. You also will want a GIF image that you will use as an alternative image if the end-user does not have the Flash Player 6 plug-in. Click the GIF Image (.gif) option; notice that this displays a new tab, the GIF tab. Your Formats tab in the Publish Settings dialog box should resemble Figure 16.9.

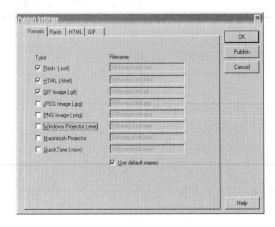

Figure 16.9   Leave the Use Default Names option selected because you want to keep your filename for all generated files consistent with the honeycomb.fla filename.

Setting the Flash Tab Options

After you've selected the formats for generating different files for The Honeycomb site, you need to set the Flash tab settings that customize features of the actual Flash SWF file. To set the Flash tab settings, follow these steps:

1. Click the Flash tab to access the Flash movie settings; now, you will customize the actual SWF file. Because you have used Flash MX actions and features, you need to keep the Version option set to Flash Player 6.

2. Leave the Load Order option set to the default option of Bottom Up. Because you used a preloader for the movie, this option does not apply. You use this option for sites that do not have a preloader to help alleviate streaming issues that might occur as the movie loads in.

3. In the Options section of the Flash tab, turn on the Generate Size Report option because this will generate a concise report on the movie performance frame by frame. This is a useful feature for analyzing the site.

4. Select the Protect from Import option to disable others from importing The Honeycomb SWF file into a new Flash FLA file.

5. Select the Omit Trace Actions option so that the compressed SWF file will be smaller in size.

6. Select Compress Movie to create the smallest sized SWF file as possible. This feature is a Flash MX feature and causes The Honeycomb SWF file to be viewable only on Flash Player 6.

7. Leave the Password box blank.

8. Set the JPEG Quality setting to 80. This will cause the `hexagon.gif` file that you used in the movie to be compressed to 80% of its original file size.

9. You have one event sound, the buzzing noise, in The Honeycomb site. Because it's not very complex, it could be reduced in quality and file size. Click the Set button to the right of the Audio Event: MP3, 16 Kbps, Mono option. This displays the Sound Settings dialog box. Keep the compression set to MP3 but set the Bit Rate to 8Kbps. Leave the Quality setting set to Fast (see Figure 16.10). Click OK to close the Sound Settings dialog box.

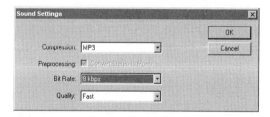

Figure 16.10   The Quality setting of Fast is recommend for Web delivery.

10. Do not click the Override Sound Settings option because you want to leave intact any individual sound settings you created for the movie. The Flash tab should resemble Figure 16.11.

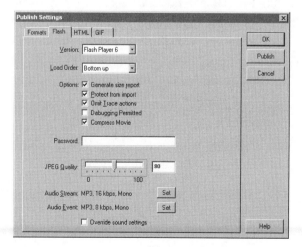

Figure 16.11   By setting the Version to Flash Player 6, all the new Flash MX functionality that you used in the movie is preserved in the SWF file.

Setting the HMTL Tab Options

Next, you want to set the HMTL settings for the movie. These are the settings that apply to the generated HTML page. Because you have used images that display in the work area before they move onto the Stage, you will need to use an exact fit so that all that displays is the movie objects on the Stage. To configure the HTML tab settings, follow these steps:

1. Click the HTML tab. For the Template option, click the pop-up menu and choose the Detect for Flash 6 menu choice. Because you need to publish this movie for Flash Player 6, setting up an HTML page that checks for this is good. If the end-user does not have the Flash Player 6 version, an alternative image is loaded into the HTML page. You selected the GIF Image option in the Formats tab. By default, Flash will use the format of the graphics image you select as the image that it calls in the HTML code for the alternative image.

2. For the Dimensions option, choose Percent from the pop-up menu. Then, set both the Width and Height boxes to 100. This causes the Flash SWF to automatically scale to fit within the boundaries of any size browser window. Again, you are seeing the beauty of Flash being a vector-based application. Everything, including text, scales to be proportioned to the size that the browser window determines.

3. Deselect the Playback Loop option and select the Display Menu option. The Display Menu option enables the Display menu to display when the end-user (Control-clicks)[right-clicks] the SWF file in the browser window.

4. Set the Quality option to Auto High. This setting assumes that the end-user's system is powerful enough to display the movie with anti-aliasing turned on. If there is not enough power, Flash automatically turns anti-aliasing off and focuses on playback of the site.

5. Because you are delivering this site to many end-users with many different browsers, leave the Window Mode option set to the default of Window.

6. Leave the HTML Alignment option set to Default.

7. Set the Scale option to Exact Fit.

8. Under Flash Alignment, set the Horizontal and Vertical options to Center. This centers the SWF file in the HTML document.

9. Click the Show Warning Messages option to turn this on. The HTML tab should resemble Figure 16.12.

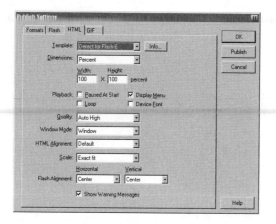

Figure 16.12 When the Show Warning Messages option is active, a warning message displays if there are any conflicts with the HTML OBJECT and EMBED commands.

Setting the GIF Tab Options

Now in the GIF tab of the Publish Settings dialog box, you will customize the generated GIF file. To set these settings, follow these steps:

1. Click the GIF tab to access the GIF settings for the generated GIF file of the site.

2. Under Dimensions, keep the Match Movie default setting selected.

3. Under Playback, keep the default setting of Static selected.

4. Under Options, select the Optimize Colors, Interlace, and Smooth options.

5. Keep the rest of the settings at the default settings in the GIF tab (see Figure 16.13).

6. Click OK to close the Publish Settings dialog box, saving the movie settings.

7. Save the Honeycomb.fla movie.

Tip

You can create animated GIFs using the GIF Image (.gif) option. This is useful when you are creating banner ads and need to have two versions of the movie, one that is an SWF and another that is an animated GIF.

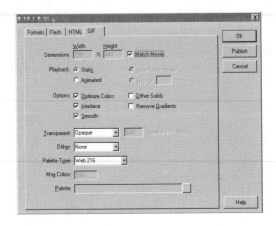

Figure 16.13   Your GIF tab should resemble this figure.

Warning

If you click the Publish button in the Publish Settings dialog—bypassing the OK button—the movie publishes with the new settings but does not save those settings for the Flash FLA movie. You must reset these settings if you want to use them again for another publishing of the movie.

Publishing The Honeycomb Movie

With the publish settings set, now you can publish your movie, generating the SWF file, HTML file, and GIF file. To do this, follow these steps:

1. Before you publish your movie, be sure you have the `honeycomb.fla` file in the directory where you want all the generated files to be held.

2. Check that you have SWF files for all the Activity movies. These SWF files are loaded into The Honeycomb movie when the activity buttons are clicked. If you do not have these files in this directory, move them or create them by testing the FLA version of the movie and moving them to this directory.

3. To publish The Honeycomb movie, choose File, Publish. The Publishing dialog box displays, showing the progression of the publishing process.

4. To check the files that have been generated, go to the operating system level for your computer and explore or browse to the folder holding your honeycomb files. You will see all the new documents that Flash generated (see Figure 16.14).

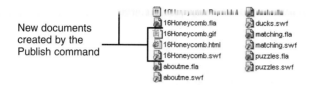

New documents created by the Publish command

Figure 16.14 Flash generates all files as indicated in the Formats tab in the same directory as the FLA file.

Testing Published Movie Files in a Browser

To view The Honeycomb site, you need to have the Flash Player 6 plug-in installed in your browser of choice. When you install Macromedia Flash MX, the Flash Player 6 can also be installed for updating your browsers. The Flash Player 6 installation is part of the Flash MX CD-ROM. You can also get a copy of Flash Player 6 at Macromedia's Web site at www.macromedia.com/software/flashplayer/ for downloading and installing it. Now test your movie in your browser by following these steps:

1. Open your browser of choice. In the browser, choose File, Open and navigate to the directory that holds all the files for The Honeycomb site. Locate and open the honeycomb.html document.

2. The Flash SWF file loads into the browser window and begins to play. Work through the site by logging in, and then click all the Activity buttons and try the activities.

3. Resize the browser window and notice that it scales to fit within the new browser window dimensions.

That's it—that's all it takes to publish the movie. Now you should test the movie on the various platforms and browsers.

The final step for Internet viewing is to post to a server the HTML file and all other SWF files used in The Honeycomb Web site. You will need to talk with your ISP for this process.

> **Tip**
>
> If you test your movie in a browser that does not have the Flash Player 6 plug-in, the browser will display the **honeycomb.gif** file. This file was generated when you published the movie. If you open it, you will see that it contains nothing, just an orange, 750x440 rectangle. This is because Flash generates the first keyframe of the movie, and in the **honeycomb.fla** file, this is a blank Stage. But you can develop this GIF file further to display a message stating where the visitor can go to get the plug-in. To see an example of a GIF file with this information, open the **honeycomb.gif** file located on the **Seminar16/ Samples/** directory of the CD-ROM that accompanies this book.

Understanding the Size Report for the Movie

You generated a size report when you published this movie. Let's look now at the report by following these steps:

1. The `honeycomb_Report.txt` file is a simple text file that can be opened in any text editor. Open your text editor, such as NotePad for Windows or Simple Text for Macintosh.

2. Open the `honeycomb_Report.txt` file in the text editor and examine the report. Notice that it provides the following information:

   • First, it provides a breakdown of the frame bytes for every frame in the movie. The `honeycomb.fla` file was composed of 100 frames, and 100 frames are listed one after another in the report.

   • Next, the report displays the shape bytes and text bytes for Scene 1 of the movie. The Honeycomb is composed of only one scene, so this is the entire text and all the shape bytes used in the movie.

   • The report then gives a breakdown of all the symbols used in the movie and the amount of symbol bytes and text bytes used in each symbol.

   • The bitmap compression provides information on how much compression was applied to any embedded bitmaps in the movie. This would be the `hexagon.gif` bitmap image.

   • The report then provides information on the compression that was applied to both types of sounds in Flash: event and streaming sounds.

   • The last bit of information this report provides is information on any embedded fonts used in the movie. Notice that this is about 20KB worth of additional file size because the Arial font is embedded throughout the movie in the various input and dynamic text fields.

As this report shows, your movie is not really very large in file size due to the use of symbols and instances for most of the objects in the movie, as well as the use of the `loadMovie` action to load in other SWF files. Although the movie plays as if it were all one movie, all the activity movies are their own SWF files. Pretty darn cool! Flash is a viable and exciting solution for Web development.

Seminar Summary

The final process for Flash Web development is publishing the Flash FLA movie into the format you need for your audience playback. This could be HMTL or a stand-alone projector file. Just as other versions of Flash made use of publishing, Flash MX also has the powerful publishing feature! Through the Publish Settings dialog box, you can set the various formats for your movie to be exported as well as customize many of the settings for these formats. The workshop stepped you through the publish process for The Honeycomb site. You'll find that this process basically stays the same for most of your Flash movies. You might tweak a setting here or there, but if you're developing for Web delivery, you will count on Flash to create the HTML page and the SWF file for display in a browser.

Remember to always test your movie on various platforms and computers. Not everyone has the latest and greatest machines and software, and the only way you can plan for this is to test your site.

Book Summary

Well, that's it for this book—I hope you enjoyed it and have learned much. A lot of information, techniques, and skills have been covered since you first cracked this book open. To summarize this book, let's review some of the important areas and features of Flash development that were covered:

- You've learned many of the drawing tools of Flash MX. You can find more information on those that were not covered by pressing F1 to access the Flash Help file .

- You've learned how to set up your Flash movie with dimensions, background color, and frame per second rates. You've used many of the design aides, such as guides, pixel snapping, grids, and rulers.

- You've learned how to create text blocks and fields. You used static, dynamic, and input text fields throughout the workshop portion of this book.

- You've created symbols and used instances of these symbols throughout the workshop portion of this book. As expressed in Seminar 4, "Using Symbols in a Movie," it's your challenge as a Flash developer to use your symbols and instances wisely throughout a movie's development.

- Importing graphics and other file types was covered. Throughout the book, you imported graphics, sound, and video clips.

- Animation was covered, both shape and motion tweening, as well as frame-by-frame animation. You also learned how to use ActionScript to create animation. All animation features are powerful for helping to communicate your movie's message!

- You've learned how to use buttons, movie clips, and Timelines to cause interactivity on the Stage. The workshop portion of the book provided many forms of hands-on practice with different functionality that can be created through these features of Flash.

- Flash MX's new feature of components was explored, and you used some of the Flash UI components to create different areas of the workshop project.

- Adding sound and video clips to a movie was also covered. You learned how to configure and compress your sound and video clip files in both the discussion and workshop sections of this book.

- ActionScript was covered for many different types of functionality, from simple `gotoAndPlay` actions to very complex `if` and `else` statements. You created preloader functionality for The Honeycomb site in the workshop portion of this book. You also created four activities for the workshops: a Matching activity, About Me activity, the In Quest of Ducks activity, and the Slider Puzzle activity. All these activities required various ActionScript-generated functionality covering many areas of ActionScript and Flash development.

I hope that you are seeing how deep Flash MX is in both Web development and application development. Many topics haven't been covered, but this book is a good start to getting you on the road to successful Flash development. I wish you good luck in your Flash endeavors and, as with anything, practice, practice, practice. As you get better, you'll find that you are limited only by your imagination when developing in Flash!

Appendix A

Setting Up Macromedia Flash

In this appendix

- Installing Macromedia Flash MX 568

- Installing the Macromedia Flash Player 6   568

Installing Macromedia Flash MX

Getting new software can be thrilling. It makes you smile because you're excited to use the product, so you dig in and learn the features and functionality. But major disappointment occurs when you realize you don't have a computer with enough processing power or RAM to handle the application. To help avoid this disappointment, Table A.1 lists the system requirements for authoring a movie in Flash MX.

Table A.1   System Requirements

Windows	Macintosh
200MHz Intel Pentium processor or equivalent processor	Power Macintosh
Windows 98 SE, Windows Me, NT 4, 2000, or Windows XP	Mac OS 9.1 or later or Mac OS X version 10.1 or later
64MB of RAM (128MB recommended) (128MB recommended)	64MB RAM free application memory
85MB of available disk space	85MB of available disk space
16-bit color monitor capable of 1024×768 resolution	16-bit color monitor capable of 1024×768 resolution
CD-ROM drive	CD-ROM drive

Installing the Macromedia Flash Player 6

After you start developing movies in Flash MX, viewing your movie in a browser requires updating the Flash Player for that browser. This file ships with the Flash software and can also be downloaded from Macromedia's Web site at www.macromedia.com/downloads/. At the end of the Flash MX installation process, Flash asks whether you want to install the Flash Player 6 and locates the browsers you have installed on your system. Follow the prompts to update your browsers with the Flash Player 6.

If you need to download the Flash Player 6 from the Macromedia Web site, follow these steps:

1. Go to the URL www.macromedia.com/downloads/, and click the Macromedia Flash Player 6 link. This opens the download page for the Flash Player 6.

2. Click the Install Now button.

3. Follow the prompts and, when asked, choose the browser that you want to update with the Macromedia Flash Player 6 plug-in.

4. When you reach the end of the installation process, you can install additional browsers. Click the Install button to proceed with installing another browser with the Flash Player 6 plug-in.

Note

Although Macromedia has renamed the latest release of Flash to Flash MX, the Player file is called Flash 6 Player.

Appendix B

What's on the CD-ROM

The accompanying CD-ROM is packed with all sorts of exercise files to help you work with this book and with Flash MX. The following sections contain detailed descriptions of the CD's contents.

For more information about the use of this CD, please review the `ReadMe.txt` file in the root directory. This file includes important disclaimer information, as well as information about installation, system requirements, troubleshooting, and technical support.

Toohnioal Support Ioouoo

If you have difficulties with this CD, you can access our Web site at
http://www.newriders.com.

System Requirements

This CD-ROM was configured for use on systems running Windows 98 SE, Windows Me, Windows NT 4, Windows 2000, or Windows XP Macintosh. Your machine will need to meet the system requirements in Table B.1 for this CD to operate properly.

Table B.1   System Requirements

Windows	Macintosh
200MHz Intel Pentium processor	Power Macintosh or equivalent processor
Windows 98 SE, Windows Me, Windows NT 4, Windows 2000, or Windows XP	Mac OS 9.1 or later or Mac OS X version 10.1 or later
64MB of RAM (128MB recommended)	64MB RAM free application memory (128MB recommended)
50MB of available disk space	50MB of available disk space
16-bit color monitor capable of 1024×768 resolution	16-bit color monitor capable of 1024×768 resolution
CD-ROM drive	CD-ROM drive

Loading the CD Files

To load the files from the CD, insert the disc into your CD-ROM drive. If AutoPlay is enabled on your machine, the CD-ROM setup program starts automatically the first time you insert the disc. You can copy the files to your hard drive or use them right off the disc. If you choose to save a file that you are accessing from the CD-ROM, you will need to select a location on your hard drive for saving the file.

NOTE: This CD-ROM uses long and mixed-case filenames, requiring the use of a protected mode CD-ROM driver.

Exercise Files

This CD contains all the files you'll need to complete the exercises in *The Flash MX Project*. These files can be found in the root directory's folder. All files are located in a `Samples` directory that is nested inside a `Seminar` directory that coincides with the name of the seminar in the book. For example, if Seminar 4 calls for `honeycomb3.fla`, you will find this file in the `Seminar04/Samples/` directory.

> **Note**
>
> If you are using a Macintosh, you might need to open the exercise and seminar files by selecting the All Files for the View option of the Open dialog box. Most of this book was created using Flash MX on the PC platform, and although these files can be opened on a Macintosh without any loss of Flash movie functionality, they are not always visible in the Open dialog box unless you use the All Files for the View option.

Read This Before Opening the Software

By opening the CD package, you agree to be bound by the following agreement:

You may not copy or redistribute the entire CD-ROM as a whole. Copying and redistribution of individual software programs on the CD-ROM is governed by terms set by individual copyright holders.

The Flash MX FLA files, Flash MX SWF files, graphics files, code, images, actions, and The Honeycomb Web site from the author are copyrighted by the publisher and the author.

This software is sold as is, without warranty of any kind, either expressed or implied, including but not limited to the implied warranties of merchantability and fitness for a particular purpose. Neither the publisher nor its dealers or distributors assumes any liability for any alleged or actual damages arising from the use of this program. (Some states do not allow for the exclusion of implied warranties, so the exclusion might not apply to you.)

Index

N

O

VISIT OUR WEB SITE

WWW.NEWRIDERS.COM

On our web site, you'll find information about our other books, authors, tables of contents, and book errata. You will also find information about book registration and how to purchase our books, both domestically and internationally.

EMAIL US

Contact us at: **nrfeedback@newriders.com**

- If you have comments or questions about this book
- To report errors that you have found in this book
- If you have a book proposal to submit or are interested in writing for New Riders
- If you are an expert in a computer topic or technology and are interested in being a technical editor who reviews manuscripts for technical accuracy

Contact us at: **nreducation@newriders.com**

- If you are an instructor from an educational institution who wants to preview New Riders books for classroom use. Email should include your name, title, school, department, address, phone number, office days/hours, text in use, and enrollment, along with your request for desk/examination copies and/or additional information.

Contact us at: **nrmedia@newriders.com**

- If you are a member of the media who is interested in reviewing copies of New Riders books. Send your name, mailing address, and email address, along with the name of the publication or web site you work for.

BULK PURCHASES/CORPORATE SALES

The publisher offers discounts on this book when ordered in quantity for bulk purchases and special sales. For sales within the U.S., please contact: Corporate and Government Sales (800) 382-3419 or **corpsales@pearsontechgroup.com**. Outside of the U.S., please contact: International Sales (317) 581-3793 or **international@pearsontechgroup.com**.

WRITE TO US

New Riders Publishing
201 W. 103rd St.
Indianapolis, IN 46290-1097

CALL/FAX US

Toll-free (800) 571-5840
If outside U.S. (317) 581-3500
Ask for New Riders
FAX: (317) 581-4663

New Riders

VOICES THAT MATTER

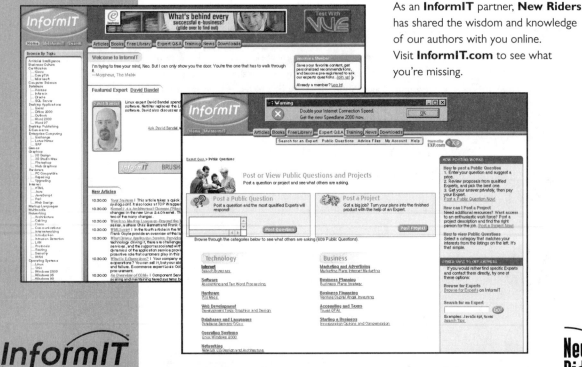

Publishing
the Voices
that Matter

OUR AUTHORS

PRESS ROOM

| web development | design | photoshop | new media | 3-D | server technologies |

EDUCATORS

ABOUT US

CONTACT US

You already know that New Riders brings you the **Voices That Matter**.

But what does that mean? It means that New Riders brings you the

Voices that challenge your assumptions, take your talents to the next

level, or simply help you better understand the complex technical world

we're all navigating.

Visit **www.newriders.com** to find:

▸ **10% discount** and **free shipping** on all book purchases

▸ Never before published chapters

▸ Sample chapters and excerpts

▸ Author bios and interviews

▸ Contests and enter-to-wins

▸ Up-to-date industry event information

▸ Book reviews

▸ Special offers from our friends and partners

▸ Info on how to join our User Group program

▸ Ways to have your Voice heard

New
Riders

WWW.NEWRIDERS.COM